Journey of Song

African Expressive Cultures
Patrick McNaughton, editor

Associate editors
Catherine M. Cole
Barbara G. Hoffman
Eileen Julien
Kassim Koné
D. A. Masolo
Elisha Renne
Zoë Strother

Journey of Song

PUBLIC LIFE AND MORALITY IN CAMEROON

Clare A. Ignatowski

INDIANA UNIVERSITY PRESS
Bloomington and Indianapolis

This book is a publication of
Indiana University Press
601 North Morton Street
Bloomington, IN 47404-3797 USA

http://iupress.indiana.edu

Telephone orders 800-842-6796
Fax orders 812-855-7931
Orders by e-mail iuporder@indiana.edu

Portions of chapter 9 previously appeared in *Cultural Anthropology: The Journal of the Society for Cultural Anthropology* 19(2), published by the American Anthropological Association and the University of California Press.

© 2006 by Clare A. Ignatowski

All rights reserved

No part of this book may be reproduced or utilized in any form or by any means, electronic or mechanical, including photocopying and recording, or by any information storage and retrieval system, without permission in writing from the publisher. The Association of American University Presses' Resolution on Permissions constitutes the only exception to this prohibition.

The paper used in this publication meets the minimum requirements of American National Standard for Information Sciences—Permanence of Paper for Printed Library Materials, ANSI Z39.48-1984.

Manufactured in the United States of America

Library of Congress Cataloging-in-Publication Data

Ignatowski, Clare A.
　Journey of song : public life and morality in Cameroon / Clare A. Ignatowski.
　　p. cm. — (African expressive cultures)
　Includes bibliographical references and index.
　ISBN 0-253-34646-0 (cloth : alk. paper) — ISBN 0-253-21794-6 (pbk. : alk. paper)
　　1. Tupuri (African people)—Cameroon—Social life and customs.　2. Cameroon—Social conditions—1960–　I. Title.　II. Series.
HN819.A8I385 2006
305.896'361—dc22
　　　　　　　　　　　　　　　　　　　　2005022441

1 2 3 4 5 11 10 09 08 07 06

To my parents, Elizabeth Kinzie and Albert Ignatowski, whose sensibilities as an artist and a scientist shaped my world.

> The point is not that culture is a "complex" "thing" but rather that it cannot be gotten "right" . . . It is not an end, or a blueprint for thinking or acting, but a constant beginning again—a search, an argument, an unfinished longing.
>
> KATHLEEN STEWART, *A Space on the Side of the Road*

lainso Fele welcomed me at the Club Kwoïssa in Yaounde. Kenso's enthusiasm for learning about the spiritual practices of his grandmothers became an important avenue of inquiry for me as well. Taïwe Felix Mouhamad helped me understand the perspectives of young men who were caught in Cameroon's economic crisis.

I also thank *gurna* song composers—Sogole, Teodandi, Noumnamo, Wore, Ringwa, and Houyang—for trusting me enough to share their art and politics. The *gurna* members at the Mogom camp were especially open to and tolerant of my entering their world.

Not all my support was from Tupuri people. Jim and Marilyn Erickson selflessly shared their knowledge of Tupuri language and ways of thinking over iced drinks before electricity came to town. Posted in Doukoula, teacher Alain Boaye provided me with important "outsider" perspectives on Tupuriland. The Anglophone community in Maroua nurtured me in important ways, especially the late Marie Foncham and Joseph Ngonga. My life with them, and others, would fill a second book.

Of course I had a great deal of support in the United States as well. Inspirational in her quiet passion for Africa and African Studies, Sandra Barnes has been a rock-solid source of wisdom for me over the years. At the University of Pennsylvania I appreciate the support and encouragement of Roger Abrahams, Fred Erickson, Kathy Hall, Catherine Lacey, John Lucy, Julia Paley, Peggy Sanday, and Greg Urban, each of whom offered unique perspectives on my work. I have also benefited from the insights of those who offered suggestions as this research unfolded, including Karin Barber, Dickson Eyoh, Eric Gable, Dorothy Holland, Tanya Luhrmann, Achille Mbembe, Flagg Miller, Steve Parish, and the anonymous reviewer for the Indiana University Press. I benefited greatly from the "Words and Voices" symposium on orality in Africa in 1997, co-organized by David William Cohen, Stephen Miescher, and Luise White. Deb Augsburger, Kristin Cahn von Seelen, Cati Coe, Jane Cowley, Kathryn Geurts, Wendi Haugh, Catherine Newling, Elisa von Joeden-Forgey, and Kristina Wirtz shared pointed critiques, tactics, hope, and laughter that supported my work during its "unwashed" moments.

This study stands on the foundational research of Suzanne Ruelland of the Université de Paris. Her years of meticulous work on the Tupuri language was a constant reference for me, and her dedication to Tupuri studies was inspiring. She generously commented on the entire manuscript, though remaining errors are mine. Joanny Guillard kindly granted permission to reprint photographs from his pioneering work, *Golonpoui*.

I am grateful to scholars and teachers who earlier in my education shared their love for poetry and ritual: Peter Balakian, John Ross Carter, George Hudson, Marilyn Thie, and Betsy Voss.

Dee Mortensen at Indiana University Press has been a patient supporter of *Journey of Song,* and I am deeply appreciative of her efforts to shepherd this work to press. Kate Babbitt copyedited skillfully and humorously.

Lee Cassanelli and Paul Kaiser at the African Studies Center at the University of Pennsylvania have provided important support to me over the last several years of this project. I thank Elisabeth Kvitashvili for allowing me the time to write at a critical moment in this book's life.

I have benefited too from funding from diverse sources, including the Social Science Research Council, the Wenner-Gren Foundation, the Institute for International Education's Fulbright Scholarship, the Sigma Xi Scientific Research So-

ACKNOWLEDGMENTS

Raa du (Tupuri): to call out names to confer fame and appreciation

If thanks could be read as a story, then mine would begin with Maïcomshuki, my stalwart neighbor in Tupuriland who laughed uproariously whenever I pronounced her name. Without speaking a word of French (and me, in 1985, speaking only a word of Tupuri), she reached out and showed me how worthwhile it would be to engage with her and the Tupuri people. Later, I would meet Wasdi Blandine, Dassinwa Rose, and Tergal Pauline, all of whom showed me friendship and the joys and challenges of life in Doukoula. However, guidance in understanding Tupuri culture came from Toukrou Antoine, who, as a lycée student, became my Tupuri language tutor and, twelve years later, my intellectual sounding board. His poetic sensibility combined with his passion for history has made a significant mark on my understanding of Tupuri verbal art and sociopolitical organization. Toukrou proofread much of the *gurna* song transcription in this study, though remaining inaccuracies are my own.

This study would not have been possible without the integrity and diligence of my research assistants, Dourwé Paul and Hedjakga Jean-Pierre Awé. Dourwe had a remarkable knack for ferreting out and delighting in the controversial angle of every phenomenon. Like the yin of yang, Awé exhibited tenacious concentration and stick-to-itiveness in transcribing interviews and in assisting me to translate *gurna* song, even during his days of fasting. It was the indefatigable Hounkao Emilienne who sent me Dourwé and Awé and who became a friend and collaborator in women's development projects. Maïgama Josephine was equally dynamic and invaluable to my learning. Her untimely death in childbirth was a tragedy to all who knew her. By sharing with me his lycée *gurna* songs and unique commentary on what it was to be a composer, Dangmoworé lent a great deal to this study. To this day I am saddened by his premature death.

I had numerous other mentors in my effort to understand Tupuri culture. Kidmo Mbraogue enabled me to conduct interviews with elders in Douaya and shared his subversive love of the dance. Kléda Samuel provided insights into the song tradition which he has studied alongside his duties as a Catholic seminarian. Domga Makouly and Kaoga Rigobert, both Tupuri radio disk jockeys, offered me their perspectives as cultural activists. In Lara village, Farsia enabled me to make contact with the composer of Dawa and transcribed his compositions. Baï-

NINE Multipartyism and Nostalgia for the Unified Past: Discourses of Democracy in *Gurna* Politics 177

TEN Conclusion 197

NOTES 203
BIBLIOGRAPHY 213
INDEX 221

Contents

ACKNOWLEDGMENTS ix
NOTE ON ORTHOGRAPHY AND SONG NOTATION xiii
MAPS xv

ONE Introduction 1

TWO Maïtené's Modern Life:
Song as Negotiation of Public Morality 24

THREE "Better than Family, Better than Girls":
The Tupuri *Gurna* Society 41

FOUR Defying the Modern:
Play of Identities in *Gurna* Dance Exhortation
(*Bɔ'ge Fɔgɛ*) 75

FIVE "Telephone of the Dance":
Circulation of *Gurna* Song Discourse 93

SIX "Rise Up, Gather Like Storm Clouds":
Poetics of *Gurna* Song (*Siŋ Gurna*) 109

SEVEN "I Become Your Boy":
Power, Legitimacy and Magic in Song
Composition 142

EIGHT Staging Conflict through Insult:
Competing Systems of Justice 159

ciety, and the Department of Anthropology at the University of Pennsylvania. The Spencer Foundation for Research Related to Education and the University of Pennsylvania Dissertation Fellowship provided generous support for writing. A National Academy of Education/Spencer Foundation Postdoctoral Fellowship enabled me to flesh out the wider implications of my research, as did a Science and Diplomacy Fellowship from the American Association for the Advancement of Science in Washington, D.C. I am grateful to all of these institutions for their professional and financial support.

In making the transition from Cameroon to the United States, from one life to another, the patience and confidence of my husband, Eric Tchadi, has been vital. His care for our dear son, Bilalay Victor Tchadi, gave me the opportunity to publish this research. My sister Marie Zuzack visited me twice in Cameroon. Finally, my heartfelt appreciation goes to my parents, Albert Ignatowski and Elizabeth Kinzie. Their loving support, as well as the education they lavished upon me over the years, are among the invisible roots that enabled this book to come to fruition.

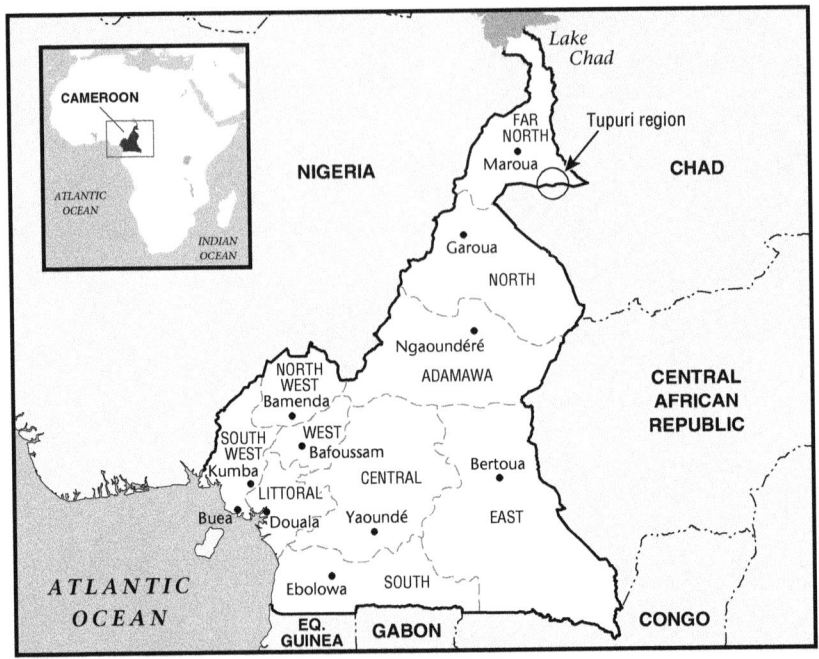

Map 1. The Tupuri region in the Far North Province of Cameroon

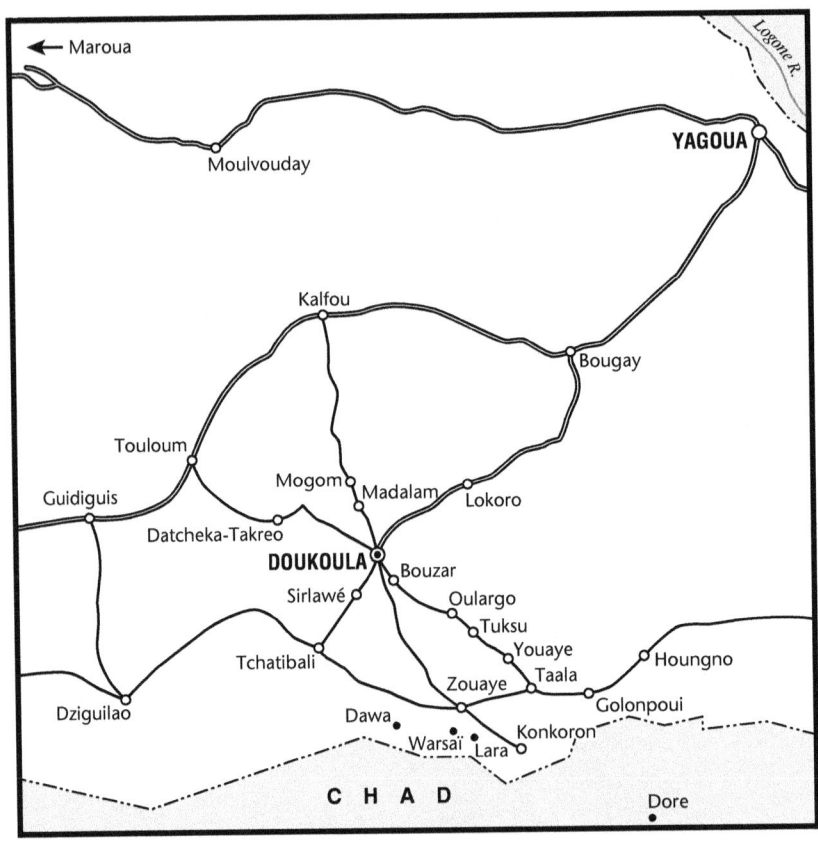

Map 2. Detail of the Tupuri region (Cameroon)

NOTE ON ORTHOGRAPHY AND SONG NOTATION

I have used the orthography provided in Suzanne Ruelland's *Dictionnaire Tupuri-Françis-Anglais* with minor alterations.

Consonants: b, ɓ, c [English "ch"], d, ɗ, f, g, h, j, k, l, m, mb, n, nd, ny, ŋ, ŋg, p, r, s, t, w, y, and '.

Vowels: a, ã, e, ɛ, ẽ, i, ĩ, o, ɔ, õ, u, and ũ

Ruelland notes four tones in Tupuri: high, mid-high, mid-low, and low. For ease in reading, I will not note tone, though I have noted where a word's meaning is ambiguous without it. For the names of people, places, and associations in Tupuri, I retain the conventional French-language phonetics. For example, Club Kwoïssa is the proper noun for the Yaounde-based dance troupe; however, the dance for which it was named is denoted as "*kuwaysa.*"

For notation of *gurna* song, I use the attribution of the village of the senior composer, followed by the seasonal year of the song and the verse number. For example, (Z., 97/98, v. 22) designates verse 22 of the *gurna* song from Zouaye, composed by Doumnano and Djingue for the *gurna* season October 1997 to June 1998.

I have designated songs by village of composition because this is conventional in Tupuriland (e.g., "*siŋ Tuksu*" refers to the song from Tuksu village). Also, composition was collaborative, so a single composer name would not suffice. All locations are in Cameroon, unless otherwise designated: Tuksu (T.), Dawa, Chad (D.), Zouaye (Z.), Lycée de Doukoula (L.), Konkoron (K.), Yaoundé (Y.), and Maroua (M.). Composer names for each location are noted in the bibliography.

For *waywa* and *lɛɛlɛ* song (denoted as "w" and "l," respectively), the numerical designation (for example, w, 12) refers to the sequence in my collected song corpus. Composition dates, authorship, and provenance for these genres are difficult to pinpoint because composers prefer to remain anonymous, especially for the *waywa*.

Journey of Song

ONE

Introduction

COMPETING MORAL ORDERS AND THE *GURNA*

This study arises from experiences of discontinuity. In 1985, as an agricultural trainer in the Far North Province of Cameroon, I spent my weekends attending spectacular death celebration dances, accompanied by high school (lycée) students. We would pick our way to the dance across expansive sorghum fields, crackly dry after the harvest. Soon we would be enveloped by hundreds of spectators crowding around a massive pulsating ring of dancers. Beige dust would rise up from the hundreds of shuffling feet, lightening the dancers' dark-brown bodies, powdering their eyelashes and brows. The dancers' torsos were cocked diagonally so they appeared to work the earth, each pumping the air with a long stick clenched, parallel, in the right hand. The young women wore jet-black bras and brightly striped dish towels wound tightly around their hips. The men, some older and pot-bellied from ritual fattening, wore white shorts and fiber cords festooned across their mud-smeared chests. Drummers in the center of this mass of rotating dancers would pound out a low, relentless rhythm that held the entire scene in suspension. This was the *gurna* dance, the ancestral dance of the Tupuri people, the way the Tupuri released the spirit of the deceased to the world of the ancestors and commemorated the value of a human life well lived.

My sense of discontinuity and the roots of this inquiry began when I tried to look at the *gurna* dance through the eyes of the eighteen-year-old lycée students who were my companions. As some of the few French-speakers in the small town of Doukoula, they were my first refuge in a new place and my guides to the large public dances that marked the Tupuri calendar. Versed in French philosophy and literature and aspiring to become civil servants in the Cameroonian government, they attended lycée without books, computers, or electricity. Twice a day they streamed in front of my house, walking long distances on empty stomachs between their homes and the lycée, which had been constructed out of town in a once-haunted no-man's-land called Horniwa. The students' powder-blue uniforms cut sharp lines against the earth-brown landscape around them. Before dusk, they paced the bush, their eyes buried in handwritten notebooks in an effort to memorize their teachers' dictations verbatim. The national exams would determine whether they would become tenured civil servants—prestigious salaried office workers—or whether they would revert to farming like their parents: hot days, hoe in hand, hectares of sorghum, peanuts, and cotton to till.

With these stakes in mind, I began to wonder how my companions, the lycée students, viewed the *gurna* dances we attended together. Although all were quick to admit that the *gurna* was an important symbol of Tupuri ethnic identity, did they still see this ancestral institution—with its dance society, bush camps, elaborate song tradition, and demanding moral code—to be of value in their lives? Was the network of cross-clan solidarity and prestige promised by the *gurna* as important to them as it had been for their parents? If so, how would they reform the time-consuming ritual practices in light of their responsibilities as students and salaried workers? How would they interpret the dire warnings of the "modernizing" Christian churches against such "animist" traditions? These questions seemed especially pertinent as young people began to be forced back to the village as a result of Cameroon's economic crisis, which began in 1986. Students felt these macrolevel socioeconomic changes more dramatically by the early 1990s, when government scholarships and civil service recruitment were eliminated. Disillusioned and bitter, Cameroonian youth had been moving back from unemployment in the cities to pursuing agricultural work on their families' farms.[1] Upon their reintegration home, how would they "re-vision" the ancestral traditions of their villages?

However, when I returned to Tupuriland in 1996 and again in 1997, I discovered, as many have before me, that my research questions seemed to dissolve before my eyes. I had asked How did youth reproduce and revise tradition in light of their school experience? But the category of "youth" proved to be too large and unwieldy. There were many kinds of youth, and therefore the question Which youth? constantly reset the question. Furthermore, the more I discovered about the *gurna* society, the more complex and all-encompassing it appeared to be; to comprehend the poetic and sociopolitics of the *gurna* songs was a task in and of itself. Eventually I began to ask larger questions about how competing moral orders were negotiated in a community and how public performances were implicated in this process. These foundational questions seemed vital to understanding how rural traditions such as the *gurna* would fare in the "chaotically pluralistic" conditions of "the post-colony" (Mbembe 2001, 102).

Social scientists have sought to analyze the complexity of the contemporary world in terms of modernity and postmodernity. They have noted the increase in the global traffic of media productions (through television, film, popular music, and the Internet) and in the movement of people across space (Appadurai 1996; Gupta and Ferguson 1992; Hannerz 1992; Harvey 1989). To this I would add the influence of colonial and neocolonial institutions such as schools, the military, and the modern nation-state, through which elites establish value systems that may differ radically from those already present on the ground. One result of these changes is an increasing coexistence of multiple moral orders and value systems within a single locale. The question then arises how these alternative moral orders and value systems are negotiated in societies, both individually and collectively. To put it in terms of my own narrative, How does the student view the *gurna* dancer? What is the dance to him/her? And, reciprocally, how is he/she represented in the dance? Ultimately, does the coexistence of different sets of interests (those of the student and those of the *gurna* dancer) shift the value or possible meanings of the dance?

To address questions about communal moral order, anthropologists have classically taken the avenue of public representations. From studies such as Clifford Geertz's Balinese cockfight (1973) and Victor Turner's examination of polysemous ritual performance (1967), we learn that culture is fundamentally public and that moral orders are constructed through the enactment and manipulation of symbols. However, current research has greatly enlarged this view by emphasizing the contested and fractured nature of culture. Even public representations that appear cohesive and "natural" are in fact momentary products of sometimes-hidden cultural politics—debate, struggle, calibration, and recalibration of moral value across multiple constituencies or stakeholders.

I bring a sensitivity to this contested nature of public morality to my study of a cultural form whose ostensible function is to project an image of unity and solidarity to local communities. The *gurna* is a dance society practiced by the Tupuri people of northern Cameroon (Central Africa) and understood by them as "ancestral."[2] In this study, I ask how Tupuri people construct and debate moral orders through the mediation of public representations offered by the *gurna*, especially that of song. Among the Tupuri, as for many ethnic groups in northern Cameroon, song[3] in the context of dance was (and continues to be) a site of public censure, retribution, and debate. The ritual space of the dance and the poetic license afforded by song work together to create an arena where conceptions of strength, power, foolishness, and naughtiness are broadcast to the public. It is here that competing moral orders are dynamically reworked and renegotiated, as individuals "speak" to one another in the coded language of the dance.

In order to account for the richness of song in Tupuriland, I have come to understand the notion of moral order as having twin kernels: morality and value.[4] Morality involves configurations of right versus wrong and is intimately connected to systems of social control designed to ensure that individuals adhere to what is "right." Value, which involves notions of usefulness and desirability, is determined by ranking objects along an established hierarchy. As this study shows, public evaluations of morality and value are part of legitimizing discourses through which local actors attempt to solidify their social positions.

These value systems and moral orders are not, of course, free floating but arise from specific local institutions whose members have a stake in their perpetuation. For this reason my research focuses on dance and song in the context of the institution of the *gurna* society. I also consider the *gurna*'s articulation to state-sponsored institutions in Tupuriland: schools, the civil service, and the judicial system. Multifaceted and multifunctional within Tupuri society, the *gurna* defies simple categorization or a single definition. As a dance association, the *gurna* requires its members to spend their days in a camp on the edge of the village during the nine-month dry season. There, men and young women adhere to a strict moral code, engage in body fattening, and learn the songs and dances they will perform at public death celebrations. Since men must contribute lactating cattle to the society, the *gurna* indexes an indigenous system of wealth, prestige, and social status. Although the *gurna* is not a youth initiation rite per se, it has been the main avenue for young men and women to learn local history, to enter into sanctioned sexual relations, and to find marriage partners. A site where life-long friendships are forged, the society provides an important social network for its members. Outside of Tupuriland, the *gurna*—with its distinctive costuming and circle dance—has become a symbol of ethnic identity for Tupuri in multi-ethnic settings in Cameroon, such as schools and urban neighborhoods (see figure 1).

The *gurna* and its vibrant song tradition is the focal point of this study not simply because it is a salient cultural practice visible to an outsider but because it is a consciously circumscribed site for the inculcation of moral value and the attribution of prestige in Tupuri society. That is, the Tupuri recognize the *gurna* as a repository of communally held moral values and as a guardian of an ideal of Tupuri personhood. However, in spite of the communal nature of the *gurna* enterprise, Tupuri people also understand dance and song—of which *gurna* is a dominant, but not the only, type—as an important arena for mediating conflict and calibrating personal and collective reputation. Although it is highly public and egalitarian, the *gurna* remains a vital site for the reinscription of certain sanctioned differences in society: between married and unmarried women, successful and unsuccessful men, and locally-oriented versus cosmopolitan individuals. Villages play out status differences in their ability to organize for the *gurna* dance by attracting many dancers and spectators and offering generous quantities of sorghum beer.

But why would a dance society be important in today's world—a world guided by international markets, governance by nation-states, and increasingly sophisticated telecommunications technology? To put it simply, people mediate and experience these global forces through their local cultural systems. It is through their familiar rooted institutions that new meanings and values are hammered out: the new integrated into the old. It has become a truism in the popular media to state that Africa is experiencing rapid change and to offer images of modern-traditional hybridity that are at times superficial—chiefs in traditional regalia sporting designer wristwatches and the like. What is more difficult to unravel is the complexity of change processes underlying even apparently stock ethnographic subjects, such as cattle-human relations (Hutchinson 1996), witchcraft (Geschiere 1997), and song (Vail and White 1991). In these, African peoples are seen to be sorting out apparently conflicting sets of moral orders—initiations and schools, bridewealth and global markets—in ways that work for them, given the constraints in which they find themselves. In examining the negotiation of moral order through an ostensibly "traditional" dance and song system, I seek to understand how communally held values are challenged, defended, reinscribed, and sometimes forgotten—how change is wrestled out on the terrain of the familiar.

PUBLICITY AND CHANGING VALUE(S)

This book investigates Tupuri dance-song as a social space where public opinion can be shaped. How does the dance-song arena enable changing moral standards and conceptions of value (prestige and worth) to be staged and negotiated publicly? How do communities recalibrate notions of morality and value in light of new opportunities and risks associated with modernity? To answer these questions I use two concepts that warrant explanation: the public sphere and modernity.

Jürgen Habermas's (1962/1989) study of *Öffentlichkeit,* translated as "publicity" or "public sphere," described in historical-sociological terms the rise of the bourgeois public sphere in Europe in the eighteenth and early nineteenth centuries. His public sphere was a zone of informal association between the public at large and the government where public opinion was hammered out among citizens, ultimately to guide public opinion. Habermas suggested that at the heart of democratic societies is the ability of private citizens to create consensus through rational-critical debate. As influential as this notion has been, it has also been critiqued and refined to reflect the reality that marginalized social groups were (and continue to be) excluded from the dominant public sphere and that they create their own competing discourses and alternative (or counter) public spheres (Fraser 1992, 1997; Public Culture 1994).

In this book, I do not intend to compare Tupuri song, dance, and associational life to Habermas's description of the bourgeois public sphere. The Tupuri world of song is markedly dissimilar to the bourgeois public sphere that Habermas described: it does not involve transparent rational-critical debate, depend on a literate citizenship, and support governmental authority. However, Tupuri song does constitute an informal institutional realm in which a community collectively airs public matters and a lively discursive world has a central place, albeit through the aesthetic turns of satire, metaphor, irony, and indirect speech. Where I use the term "public sphere," my intention is not to index the specific characteristics of Habermas's idealized public sphere but rather to call upon some of the underlying tensions, themes, and terms that Habermas proposed. My use of the concept is intended to help us think beyond individual song texts to the institutional power that the entire performance matrix holds in Tupuri society. By performance matrix, I mean the situation of song discourse within dance and the associational practices and politics underlying it as well as the participation of the wider audience in creating, interpreting, and responding to this discourse. The advantages of this broader view of Tupuri performance enables us to begin to discern how it interacts institutionally with other forms of justice, socialization, prestige-making, and standard-setting that operate in contemporary Cameroonian society (such as those in schools and courts and through urban migration, civil service employment, etc.).

In his specificity about the historical and cultural context of the bourgeois public sphere, Habermas left open the door for examining other types of public spheres that naturally function in quite different ways in other times and places (see for example Graham 1993).[5] What the more generic term "public sphere" offers, however, is ways to capture the associational underpinnings of public discourse, ways that speech communities create institutional power, and the possibility that speech practices of citizens may craft an informal governance. Habermas's work also draws attention to the power and meaningfulness of "publicness," or publicity, in a society and the interplay between the public and the private realms. His analysis challenges anthropologists to specify the cultural and political construct of publicity in societies. Finally, in his concern for the ways that, in his view, the bourgeois public sphere was eroded by mass market–based advertising and the social welfare state, it is clear that his concept of public sphere includes the undergirding socioeconomic foundations that support it and (and this is important) that it can change or be transformed when new conditions emerge.

Tupuri song in general and *gurna* discourse in particular involve the movement of stories and information from the private realm of individuals, households, and village communities to a wider Tupuri public where people of many clans, villages, and, in urban areas, regions of Tupuriland came together. Welded to individual prestige-building, song and dance in Tupuriland provide a communal arena for attempting to persuade, inculcate, and debate sets of moral values. It also is an arena where public justice is achieved outside the formal court system. The aesthetic conventions of the song and dance are intimately tied to the politics of its performance, including the comprehensions and incomprehension of audiences. Without endorsing all dimensions of Habermas's argument, such as his view of the modern degradation of rational political discourse, the term "public sphere" enables me to denote the multiple levels important to my analysis: associational life (or civil society), a historically constituted discursive genre, the moral imperative of communal governance, and the public dimension of a social space where opinions can be shaped.

In his discussion of the disintegration of the public sphere, Habermas was grappling with the effects of modernization and modernity, although he did not use these terms. In my experience in Cameroon, people from all walks of life cited *le modernisme* as an explanation for change, especially in relation to shifts in cultural practice or in the relative power of indigenous institutions vis-à-vis those associated with the nation-state or Christianity. For this reason, two ethnographies that take on the subtleties of cultural change in the face of modernity were invaluable to me: Peter Geschiere's *The Modernity of Witchcraft* (1997) and Sharon Hutchinson's *Nuer Dilemmas* (1996). Geschiere describes the persistence of witchcraft in contemporary Cameroon as a moral economy through which Cameroonians seek to make sense of the huge accumulation of power by the elite. They employ witchcraft discourse, namely accusation, to keep the power of the wealthy in check. So-called modern forms and uses of witchcraft interpenetrate with those associated with local village life.

Hutchinson is concerned with how the Nuer have dealt with the enormous changes their society has faced under British colonialism and after decades of civil war. She approaches the problem by examining how the Nuer have adjusted their moral universe—their rites, courtship practices, judicial system, and political participation—to accommodate changes over which they had little control (such as the influx of arms and the commodification of cattle wealth). She notes that changes in the moral code (for example, the definition of incest) are tentatively tried out by pragmatic individuals and are contested among various social groups who have a stake in them. Both Geschiere and Hutchinson understand moral value as publicly constructed through communitarian cultural practice, though unlike functionalist models, these processes are far from transparent but rather are ambiguous, invisible, and contested. Methodologically, both focus on local discourses, or metacommentaries, about change in cultural practice and the moral assumptions they index.

The deconstruction of the dialectic of modernity and tradition has become increasingly important in anthropology. Still, this literature is troubled by the paradoxical emptiness and richness of the term "modernity." On the one hand, modernity is the lively expression of Western empirical rationalism, political liberalism, and specific forms of the capitalist production that radically revised older notions of time and space (Harvey 1989). On the other hand, ethnographers working in non-Western societies have found a range of historically constituted meanings and uses of the term "modernity" that may at times refer back to Western meanings but are by no means limited to them (Comaroff and Comaroff 1993; Ferguson 1999; Ivy 1995; Miller 1994; Rofel 1999). These "alternative" or "vernacular modernities" point to a definition of modernity that is relational, a modernity whose meanings are dependent on their discursive context.

The relational dynamic of tradition and modernity is never politically neutral but is rather inflected with West/Other power dynamics (for example, Ong 1999). Marking off the "modern" constructs its opposite, "tradition"—a binary that triggers assumptions about space, time, movement, and value. Tradition would be local, backward leaning, static, and culturally particular, while modernity becomes that which is global, future reaching, progressive, and totalizing. As anthropologists have blurred this binary, they have explored its ironies and shown how the meaning of modernity can differ across localities. For example, the construct of "tradition" is seen to be generated by modernist subjectivities and projects, often by the nation-state seeking to solidify its authority (Handler 1988). In her study of contemporary Japan, Marilyn Ivy (1995) sees "traditional" as a modernist register or trope containing anxiety over cultural loss, transmission, and stability. In China, modernity becomes an equally powerful imaginary or cultural construct through which the state promulgates its future-oriented policies against those of older discredited generations (Rofel 1999). James Ferguson (1999) has studied how the "myth of modernization" in Zambia becomes a persistent foil against which people evaluate their everyday lives. The twin terms of modernity and tradition have become an important way of talking about and evaluating shifts in value and morality that have come with global change. In this study, I refer to modernity and tradition sparingly and in the emic terms suggested by my informants and Tupuri discourse. Tupuri song is replete with references to modernity whose meanings are more subtle than the clunky term "modernity." An underlying theme of this book is the ways that modern Tupuri lifestyles and identities interpenetrate and shape older Tupuri moral orders.

SONG AS PRODUCTION OF MORAL VALUE

My approach to song and dance as a particular site for the production of moral value involves two broad levels. First, Tupuri song is understood as a communicative system or public sphere endowed with certain powers within the society. Those with voices in this system—most obviously *gurna* members—maintain their dominance through its perpetuation. In this mode, "song" is not merely episodic or sporadic but becomes rather "the song," an expression of and constituent element of institutional power. The second level of my framework concerns the range of social functions performed within the domain of the songs themselves. I found that five or so functions, crossing various song genres, were most vital. Through song, performers punished individuals for wrongdoing, staged interpersonal conflict through insult, conferred prestige to one another, engaged in social commentary, and—in the case of *gurna* song—promoted the dance and *gurna* society itself. *Gurna* song was especially eclectic, multifunctional; all of these "tasks" were performed many times over within a single song.

Tupuri song involves the production of a social space, a public arena where the collective work of the society is carried out. As Bauman and Briggs note, this arena is not only located in the performance itself but "is tied to a number of speech events that precede and succeed it (past performances, readings of texts, negotiations, rehearsals, gossip, reports, critiques, challenges, subsequent performances, and the like)" (1990, 60). At the time of my research, the *gurna* song system involved a funneling of information from individuals in villages to composers, dissemination and learning of the song, and a bedrock of gossip and everyday discourse in which song messages were digested and commented upon.

If, as Bauman and Briggs state, "performance . . . provides a frame that invites critical reflection on communicative processes," then there are a number of vital elements that enable song to create a ritual space (60). First, its performance involves the privileging of certain voices: for *gurna* song, these voices are the *gurna* members who intone the songs produced annually by specialized composers. In the case of *lɛɛlɛ* song, women follow the lead of women composers who have won their trust. Second, these voices are given a certain license to speak in ways not permitted in everyday society. This license is poetic; what is articulated within it is not necessarily to be taken literally or transparently. Both song and dance are prone to aesthetic sleights of hand, such as irony, parody, reversals, and elisions, which may entirely invert or obscure their meanings. For this reason, I argue that there is no simple one-to-one correspondence between the personal identity of a performer and his or her performance persona. If one considers Western theater, this point seems obvious, although it is all too often forgotten when African performance in putatively "traditional" contexts is considered.

There are a variety of reasons why Tupuri people attended the huge death celebration dances performed by the *gurna* society, ranging from prosaic recreation to the classical notion of *communitas*. I am particularly interested in the power of the dance and song to moralize, punish, and discipline the populace. Two forces seemed to come together in a powerful alchemy. An insatiable public appetite for scandal is fed by a poetic license invested with the right to censure in song. Public knowledge of the song as a site where scandal will be broadcast, creates, not surprisingly, an eager audience. This is hardly an obscure point to those who observe popular culture media in U.S. society—tabloids, talk shows, entertainment magazines, and so forth. In Tupuri song, this enactment, even celebration of humiliation is strongly linked to public control of morality. Performers can reveal compromising information about individuals and insult them in fantastic ways because people widely accept song as a sanctioned site of social discipline and pedantry. Song is invested with the right to expose the shameful or embarrassing behavior of individuals and broadcast it throughout the region wherever dance is staged.

However, this social control was far from dour. Like tabloids in American society, Tupuri songs recounting outrageous things people did are entertaining, even fascinating. However, this mechanism of social control is not one sided; it works both sides of the proverbial carrot and stick. In addition to insult and satire, *gurna* song is replete with praise and greetings conferring prestige to individuals and their networks. Men and young women are encouraged to join the *gurna* society and the broader public to admire its power. The song itself provides a conventional repertoire in which actors attempt to shape public opinion about the *gurna* society and morality more generally.

As an interloper in Tupuri society, I was particularly sensitive to the moments when the song veered into social commentary, performing a metacultural function (Urban 2001). Through stylized exhortations (*bɔ'ge fɔgɛ*), insult (*darge*), and social commentary in Tupuri performances, performers invoke wider debates about the future trajectory of Tupuri society. As Hutchinson shows in her 1996 study of the Nuer, the power of ethnography may be in its exploration of the moral dilemmas facing a people. How do people collectively, though differentially, interrogate the dilemmas that changing socioeconomic conditions put before them? Less concerned with charting culture as a specific code, convention, or logic, anthropologists have recently "concentrated more and more on how conflicts of interest, perspective, and power among various age, gender, wealth, and status groups are continuously being renegotiated and worked out 'on the ground' " (Hutchinson 1996, 28). My goal in this study is not simply to describe Tupuri dance and song genre but to convey a sense of the value systems and models of personhood promoted by the *gurna* and to plumb the deeper dilemmas the Tupuri saw before them.

During my stay in Tupuriland, I heard many Tupuri people debate and wonder aloud about the moral-economic dilemmas they faced as a people. Should girls be permitted to experiment with "modern lifestyles"? What is the value of schooling when the state has failed to provide employment as it once did? Is farming still valuable? Why are so many turning to alcohol? What forms of social solidarity, networks of belonging, are truly valuable, reliable? Will Christianity entirely rework the Tupuri moral landscape, as it claims it will? These dilemmas give rise to new moral positions that are collectively worked out though song and dance, though they are rarely consistent or universally consented to across the entire society. In song lyrics and dance gesture, I found local actors weighing in on these wider debates about changes in Tupuri society. In this sense, social commentary—the attempts to produce "strongholds" of social value—are part and parcel of the situated politics of the song. That is, if individuals use the song to destroy their enemies and promote their allies, it is often in ways that make statements about what should constitute respectable behavior.

Finally, apart from the intricacy of interpersonal politics, Tupuri song is also about itself—its own vitality as a mode of discourse. By extension, performers use song to promote its institutional base—the *gurna* dance association. Repetition of a discursive form often involves a reinscription of its social value. By the very use of the song, the value of Tupuri song is reinforced as a public sphere that has not been antiquated by newer media (such as radio) or by governmental institutions seeking to insert themselves into local power relations. Passing over the official powers of law and order, individuals still turn to the song to bring public complaint against a neighbor. And in spite of the new forms of prestige conferred by schools, such as literacy, schooled identities, and salaried livelihoods, song is still mobilized, year after year, to confer special forms of prestige available only to great dancers. How and why do dance and song create a moral universe that still continues to fascinate the Tupuri?

POLITICS AND POETICS OF VERBAL ARTS IN AFRICA

Indebted to a rich and varied literature on the "politics and poetics" of verbal arts (Briggs and Bauman 1990) in Africa and elsewhere, this study draws on some fundamental observations about how performance "works." The best studies examine discursive genres in their fullest sense—in terms of their poetic dimensions and in terms of who performs it and when, where, and why.[6] The power of verbal art—be it poetry, song, or political oratory—is seen to be intimately connected to the social actions for which it is deployed, which in turn shape it aesthetically. From the bottom of a social hierarchy, performers may use their artistry to challenge structural inequality, resist a political regime, or remember values otherwise occluded by the dominant discourse. In these cases, verbal art is often coded, indirect, or articulated in subterranean fashions. On the other hand, from the top of a social hierarchy, performers may help to legitimate the authority of political regimes or consolidate the prestige of elites. Laterally or in egalitarian contexts, performers mobilize verbal arts to maintain peaceful relations where there is potential for conflict or to enable multiple political actors to come to consensus. In all cases, the aesthetic contours of the discursive form are not epiphenomenal but are informed by the social actions for which they are used. At one moment or another, Tupuri song discourse can be seen to be put to use in nearly all of these plays of power.

This study draws on the field of African verbal arts which Ruth Finnegan first launched as a systematic study in 1970; five dynamics are foundational to my project. First, verbal art can create special moral worlds and subjectivities over and against the broader society. Second, it tends to operate within a zone of freedom or poetic license. Third and fourth, oral genres in Africa are often utilized in two ways: in conflict resolution, broadly defined, and in the crafting of new identities, sometimes as new versions of the old. And finally, while many scholars recognize the multimodality of most African performance—the interconnection among music, word, bodily movement (dance, gesture), and visual arts (costuming, masquerade)—few succeed in analyzing all these elements together. This book represents an effort to step in this direction.

In Tupuriland, dance and song are, I suggest, resources where lifeworlds, with their attendant moral value systems, are created. This view is not new. In Lila Abu-Lughod's study of Egyptian Bedouin oral poetry and Karin Barber's study of Yoruba praise-singing, oral performance activates a special subjectivity that enables individuals to connect to forces invisible in everyday society to enhance hidden dimensions of the self. For the Bedouin, poetry allows expression of emotion that has no other outlet in that society. Abu-Lughod argues that this "poetry of sentiment and self be viewed as their corrective to an obsession with morality and an overzealous adherence to the ideology of honor" (1986, 259). While Tupuri song is not concerned with human intimacy and interior subjectivity of individuals, its performers evoke the special lifeworld of the *gurna* that is equated with moral and social well-being.

Sharing with Abu-Lughod an interest in text as "a thread leading into the inner aspects of a society's imaginative life," Barber (1991, 2) focuses on *oriki,* a praise-song genre performed by Yoruba women. In *oriki,* she finds that "literary texts function like nodal points in the flow of speech," acting as "enduring landmarks in the field of speech" (2). According to Barber, the attribution of *oriki* in public performance is a vehicle for Big Men to acquire prestige, implicating the past in the process (4). While *gurna* song gestures only to a generalized ancestral past, it is, like *oriki,* an important tool for consolidating personal and collective power through evocative presentation of oral poetry.

The poetic license vested in Tupuri song is critical to its vitality, as it is to much of African verbal art. Leroy Vail and Landeg White show how a range of poetic genres across South Central Africa are linked by a poetic license that frees the performer to express opinions that could otherwise breech other social conventions (1991, 43). In this way, verbal arts have become a site of resistance against colonialism by safeguarding a repository of repressed historical memory which could be mobilized in performance (Apter 1998; Hofmeyr 1993; Vail and White 1991; White 2000). As we shall see, poetic license afforded by the *gurna* song has allowed song composers to challenge traditional rulers.

The performance of verbal art is a common modality for managing conflict within society and seeking consensus in African communities. Tupuri song is not a political discourse for those with authority to govern; rather, it is an avenue for the venting of grievances between individuals and villages and for correcting transgressions of social norms. This role for a performance of "wounding words"—be it insult, lampoon, or satire—is widespread in Africa, though recent descriptions examine genres that died out after the colonial area. For example, Tanure Ojaide (2001) describes *udje* dance songs in Eastern Nigeria that involved a "war of songs" through theatrical exchange of abuse. Like Tupuri song, individuals were satirized by name in *udje*. Daniel Avorgbedor (2001) describes *halɔ*, a sociomusical drama in Anlo-Ewe–speaking Ghana that involved a call and response of insult accompanied by drumming and aggressive gesture. *Halɔ* was officially proscribed in 1962, while *gurna* song continues to be robust today.

Still another line of study in verbal arts has been the role of popular song in constructing new ethnic or cosmopolitan identities, particularly in urban areas in Africa. This strand has an early predecessor in L. Clyde Mitchell, whose 1956 study of the *kalela* dance in the urban Copperbelt (modern Zimbabwe) examined how ethnic categories continued to be reproduced by urban migrants and expressed in the licensed satire of song. In Veit Erlmann's 1996 study of South African *isicathamiya*, David Coplan's 1994 study of Basotho migrant song (*sefela*), and Christopher Waterman's study of urban Yoruba *juju* music (1988), verbal art in popular music becomes a creative space for constructing new identities and subjectivities forged from the collective experience of rural-urban migration and proletarianization. Waterman emphasizes the role of urban musicians as cultural brokers whose ability to negotiate diverse cultural styles across social boundaries produced new musical genres evoking a modern African elite identity (Waterman 1988, 232). In this view, popular arts provide both social space and expressive tools for negotiating broad social change, a perspective that is especially relevant in my study of the permutations of the *gurna* society that Tupuri students and urban dwellers have created beyond the village. For these self-described "moderns," participation in *gurna* clubs involves self-conscious efforts to generate continuity of elements of Tupuri culture.

Finally, African performance is multimodal—it is compelling precisely because it involves a seamless weaving together of verbal, kinesthetic, and visual expression. While no analysis can do everything, this book seeks to consider the interacting and layering effect of costuming, song lyric, improvisational dance gesture, and underlying moral codes and social organization that give the *gurna* its full meaning(s). This analysis will draw connections between the rhetorical level of song and the sociopolitics of its composition, dissemination, and interpretation by audiences and between the meanings of the song and the visual and kinesthetic dimensions of the dance within which it is nested. My purpose is to attempt to convey as fully as possible how Tupuri dance-song is experienced sensually and how it is lived in society, interwoven with everyday moral challenges and opportunities.

ENCOUNTERS WITH THE TUPURI PEOPLE

The Peace Corps assigned me to Cameroon in 1985—randomly, I am sure, as large government bureaucracies tend to do. My assignment material was blunt: I would be posted in an agricultural training center "far from the distractions of city life" and I should expect "extreme heat and dust." Both were accurate. What was not mentioned in the orientation materials were the political-economic conditions that made development work extremely challenging—gross mismanagement by the Cameroon government.[7] The civil service was characterized by corruption and complacent inertia at all levels. The authoritarian regime of President Paul Biya held firmly onto power through clever political maneuvering buttressed by widespread patronage and strategic use of the security forces.[8] In a remotely located Young Farmer Training Center where I was assigned to train the Cameroonian staff in adult pedagogy, few felt motivated to do much training and the center was continuously embroiled in battles with the farmer-trainees over the provision of meat and the work schedule. I responded to this moribund work situation by designing my own pedagogical projects with international NGOs (such as Save the Children and CARE) and by learning to drink sorghum beer (*yii*) in town, attending *gurna* dances, and ferreting out the most animated weekly markets in the region. It was this second set of activities that brought me into contact with the Tupuri people so that I began to appreciate their intelligence, energy, and warmth. Stoic and grim to outsiders, the Tupuri break into smiles and joking when they relax among themselves around a jug of *yii*. It was in this way that I also realized the poverty of a development mindset in which all activities are divided neatly into two imaginary camps: "good" for economic development and "bad" for economic development. What I needed were the tools of ethnographic research which would enable me, nine years later, to penetrate the surface of Tupuri society—to grasp their values, preoccupations, and modes of communication and to truly engage Tupuri people in discussion of issues and dilemmas facing them as individuals and as a people.

Like other animist groups of northern Cameroon, the Tupuri are a product of numerous migrations and amalgamations of ethnic groups who took the Adamawa-Ubangi language of Tupuri (Pontie 1972/1984, 208). Numbering 300,000–400,000 (Ruelland 1999, 1), Tupuri-speakers today span both sides of the Cameroonian-Chadian border (see map 2). My research area was in the southern *bec de canard* region[9] of the Far North Province, Cameroon, particularly the *arrondissement* of Kar Hay in the *départment* of Mayo Danay. Every time I moved between the Fulbe-dominated provincial capital, Maroua, I was struck by how fully the Tupuri occupied their alluvial floodplain region. One of the most densely populated regions of Cameroon, Tupuriland is dotted with open-air family compounds composed of round mud houses, granaries, and dung-covered corrals for their highly valued cattle (see figure 2). With the exception of Mount Dore just across the border in Chad, the abode of the Tupuri spiritual leader (*waŋ-Dore*), this land is extremely flat. During the agricultural season of July through December, one can see far across the expansive emerald fields of cane-like sorghum and snowy cotton. This region fascinates agricultural agronomists for its moisture-retaining clay soils that enable an indigenous dry-season sorghum to produce grain with virtually no rainfall. After the harvest and the cooler, dusty harmattan season (December–January), regions that are farmed are reduced to the sharp stubble of dried sorghum stalks, feasted upon by herded cattle. In the bush areas, low-lying shrubbery remains green throughout the hot season (March through May). Temperatures easily reach above 100 degrees Fahrenheit, which the new rains of June only make humid.

Though it lacked the dramatic "moonscape" of the Mandara mountains so attractive to tourists on the western side of the Far North Province, the Doukoula region where I made my home as a Peace Corps volunteer (1985–1987) and as an ethnographer (1997–1999) was quietly magnificent. When I walked on the narrow paths between villages, I charted my way by the towering trees that dotted the landscape singularly and majestically like ships on the sea. In the rainy season, brilliant white egrets rose over the vibrant green fields edged by seasonal ponds. Tupuriland was inundated each rainy season, rendering it inaccessible for four months of the year. Historians blamed this seasonal flooding for the failure of the Fulbe jihadists to subdue the "pagan" Tupuri during their nineteenth-century conquest of northern Cameroon. Their cavalries apparently got stuck in the mud. But the Tupuri proudly take credit for successfully repelling the Fulbe, pointing to their simple but effective throwing sticks (*garaw*).

Unlike the Far North ethnic mosaic of seventy-five ethnic groups, rural Tupuriland appears largely homogenous, with the exception of central Doukoula, which is controlled by Fulbe merchants and artisans. However, within the Tupuri ethnic group, there are some sixty clans, many revealing traits of other incorporated ethnicities.[10] Little is known of the Tupuri before the seventeenth century, though it is thought that they were dislodged by the Laka and Péve chiefdoms of Chad and migrated north of the Mayo Kebbi to Dore. Dore has been the spiritual center of the Tupuri for at least twelve generations (approximately 250 years), and most contemporary clans trace their lineage to the Dore (Garine 1981, 180).[11] Tupuriland sputters out north of Doukoula, edging into the multiethnic Fulbe-Massa-Tupuri towns of Guidiguis and Yagoua. Other ethnic groups tend to see the Tupuri as insular and resistant to interacting with outsiders. Both in and outside their homeland, Tupuri people maintain their language and vehemently resist Islamization, which has strongly marked the rest of the Far North. In the rural areas, French is rarely spoken. However, some Tupuri have converted to Christianity; first to Catholicism (after missions were established in the early 1950s) and more recently choosing from an array of mainstream Protestant and evangelical churches.

The mass of Tupuri in the rural homeland are subsistence farmers of sorghum, peanuts, and cowpeas. Men derive cash from small-scale cotton farming, which they invest in cattle. Women acquire cash through home beer-brewing and small-animal husbandry (goats, sheep, and pigs). Although Tupuri in the rural regions continue to suffer from lack of modern infrastructure (as of 1999, there were few paved roads, no telephone lines, and poor government services), it is no longer possible to speak of the Tupuri monolithically as "isolated." Tupuri men were recruited by the French colonial administration[12] and then the Ahidjo regime[13] for careers in the military. When these veterans returned to their villages after retirement—hence the root of the common *quartier* name Quinze Ans (Fifteen Years)—they brought with them new wealth as well as cultural practices from southern Cameroon. These new practices ranged from using cement gravestones to an interest in Western-style schooling. But more recently there has been a continuous emigration from rural Tupuriland, as the land is exhausted from intensive cotton cash-cropping (introduced to farmers by the French beginning in the 1950s). With the population expanding beyond the capacity of the soil fertility and the current level of agricultural technology, there is seasonal malnutrition every year. Children play in the summer months with distended bellies and reed-like arms. Erratic rains virtually ensure periodic famine.[14] In the 1990s, Tupuriland received American food aid every year for seven years. During my sojourn the international development agency Action Against Hunger was conducting research on children's weight gain in attempt to understand whether food aid—after it was sifted through the corruption of officials—actually reached the needy population. To stem wide-scale famine, the government has collaborated with SODECOTON, the parastatal cotton company, to resettle Tupuri people in less-populated regions of the North Province (Touboro). Additionally, Tupuri people have migrated on their own initiative to cities throughout Francophone Cameroon

(Yagoua, Maroua, Garoua, Yaoundé, and Douala), and agro-industrial plantations in the south (Mbandjok). Tupuri people are represented in the highest ranks of the Cameroon government and are known for their high representation in the military and in the Ministry of Animal Husbandry.

My experience of the material poverty of Tupuriland—what my neighbors called *la misère*—was a continuous backdrop to my research. Although I was relieved to return to Tupuriland freed from the mantle of international development (and the imperative to "do something"), I was plagued by chagrin at the thought of conducting research on song and dance amid famine. The rains of the summer of 1996 were poor. By the time I was ready to plunge into my research in the fall of 1997, the rural population was clinging to life, waiting for the September harvest. Because the roads were flooded, food aid distributors failed to deliver bags of soybean-corn meal (called "*usa*" in Tupuri, after the USA label on the sacks). The aid did not arrive until *after* the 1997 harvest of a bumper crop. Although I could contribute nothing to the alleviation of the famine, I pursued community development efforts as a second strand to my research.

Women's development projects did not relate topically to my research on *gurna* song, but these efforts deepened my relationships with several dynamic community organizers who in turn put me in touch with informants and assistants who became vital to the success of my study. While my research does nothing to alleviate the hard lives that Tupuri face in rural areas, I believe that my goal of deeply understanding the indigenous value systems and communicative modes developed by the Tupuri contributes to understanding why development projects imposed by outsiders often do not work as they were intended. I came to realize that while Tupuri people, like all Cameroonians, could participate in formal education, business, and the goals of national development, there are cross-cutting values and forms of social organization that do not neatly map onto these imperatives. And it is these cultural resources, such as the *gurna,* that many Tupuri people return to or vilify when the modern sector forsakes them.

EXPLORING TUPURI PERFORMANCE GENRE

Earlier I described how my interest in Tupuri *gurna* dance and song evolved from a broader interest in understanding how youth were revisioning their ethnic traditions in the face of national economic crisis. I found that by studying the *gurna* intensively in the villages around Doukoula, Kar Hay, I was in a better position to recognize iterations of the *gurna* outside the rural context, in cities and schools. Throughout this study, I use the term "rural Tupuriland" to designate regions that have been majority Tupuri for several centuries (Mayo Kebbi, Chad, and Mayo Danay, Cameroon), as opposed to regions where Tupuris have recently migrated in large numbers (along with many other ethnic groups), such as the Far North provincial capital, Maroua; the national capital, Yaoundé; and organized resettlements in Touboro. It was only through in-depth study of the cultural practices of the *gurna* in rural Tupuriland that I could recognize innovations, revisions, and ellipses of this tradition. For example, in the capital Yaounde, Club Kwoïssa has emerged as a folkloric dance troupe based on the *gurna.* Instead of holding cattle in common as is practiced in the village *gurna,* club members pool their wealth as monthly dues, similar to rotating credit associations common in southern Cameroon. In another case, Gurna Club members in the Lycée de Doukoula substitute powdered milk for fresh cow's milk, since they couldn't afford the cattle that are the basis of the *gurna* camp in the village.

I conducted most of my research in the densely Tupuri region south of the small town of Doukoula, where I was based. When I returned to Doukoula in 1996 and then 1997, many of my Tupuri friends and colleagues from my Peace Corps days in the mid-1980s welcomed me warmly. (One was so surprised to see me again that she said that when she saw me walking in the market, she thought I was a ghost!) I picked up my Tupuri-language learning where I had left off. Even among new friends and informants, the fact that I had lived among them before and could remember conditions of the previous decade helped me develop the trust essential to ethnographic research. My strategy of maintaining a second house in the provincial capital for writing up fieldnotes and taking a break from village life had the inadvertent advantage of keeping my Doukoula friends from growing tired of me. In the provincial capital, Maroua, I conducted research with the Tupuri émigré community there, including their neighborhood cultural associations that showcased the *gurna,* their social gatherings in beer parlors (*ŋgel-yii*), and the Gurna Club in the provincial teacher-training center (ENIEG, École Normale des Instituteurs de l'Enseignement Général).

Taking a "vacuum-cleaner" approach to fieldwork, I talked to anyone and everyone (in Tupuri or French), from six-year-old children to the town *sous-préfet,* elderly blind grandmothers to university-bound high school students, French priests who had spent most of their lives in Doukoula to southern Beti civil servants who couldn't wait for a transfer out. I found that asking the same provocative questions of many people—especially about the *gurna*—enabled me to gauge the range of opinions and emotions for this rich symbol. (I found that certain questions garnered the greatest reactions: Is the *gurna* increasing or decreasing? Will it die out one day?) As I began to focus on *gurna* practices, including its song tradition, I depended more heavily on the *gurna* members themselves and their specialist song composers. I spent many hours observing activities in *gurna* bush camps and in intensive interviews with song composers in which they explicated their lyrics and described the processes involved in song composition. Elderly men and women who had lived in a radically different colonial world were invaluable in helping me imagine the meanings and realities of Tupuri life in the past. Their memories of sexual initiation, courtship, marriage, village warfare, the social organization of dance, and the advent of changes such as cloth clothing and cotton farming were especially enlightening. I gained access to these elders through their children and grandchildren who were my friends or research assistants. Their sense of wonder about what they had never thought to ask their elders took their roles far beyond that of interpreters toward fellow interlocutors and researchers.

I delved too into topics that are not directly reported in this study but are critical to my understanding of Tupuri modes of thought and practice. From Mbulna, a diviner catering to Tupuri émigré of Maroua, I experienced the practice of divination (*halge*) and the unseen powers of spirits (*sōore*). My research assistant, Dourwe, was raised in a family which was the first in his village to convert to Catholicism, but he had a genius (along the lines of Nigerian writer Ben Okri) for describing the world of soul-devouring witches and roving spirits existing in an invisible double world of the living. When I had gained their trust, my closest friends described to me the nuances of *saŋgu* (*gri-gri,* French; magical herbs) as well as their efforts to discard them for Christian beliefs and practices.

Many of my conversations with young adults centered on the dilemmas they face in navigating the diminished horizons of opportunity in 1990s Cameroon. Young people were acutely aware of generational differences between themselves and their elders. Due to falling export commodity prices beginning in 1986 and large-scale governmental mismanagement and corruption, Cameroon had been gripped by an economic depression that even thirteen years later was showing few signs of amelioration. By the mid-1990s, the government had eliminated higher-education scholarships, ended civil service recruitment for school graduates, and drastically cut civil servant salaries. Teachers had been especially hard hit and embittered by the reluctance of the government to cut salaries of the military, whose loyalty was needed to buttress the unpopular government. The result was a dramatic decline, even near-collapse, of the education system that was once one of the best in Central Africa. The axiomatic connection between schooling and jobs and ultimately national economic development—the promise of modern education—was seriously questioned. Those who had pursued the French lycée curriculum knew that they were likely to farm cotton or repair bicycles for a living once they left school. My discussions with youth revealed a cognitive dissonance in which they were respectful of village-based orders such as the *gurna* but preoccupied with the difficulties of forging a livelihood in an unrelenting economic depression.

These struggles are frequently referred to in the *gurna* songs composed by students for their Gurna Club at the Lycée de Doukoula. By contrast, composers of the village-based *gurna* song, whose main audience is farmers, refer to these broader political-economic woes less frequently and more obliquely. For these reasons, as I amassed a corpus of Tupuri song, I was careful to collect from as many different contexts and genres as possible. Although I took the highly salient *gurna* as my research focus, I worked from the assumption that multiple song genres thrived across the society. Performers speak to one another across genres, borrowing ideas and forms, building from and commenting on prior messages. In Tupuriland, as elsewhere, specific social groups (women, youth, men, Christians, etc.) are known to practice, and thus control, different song genres. As a result, a song is thought of as expressing the perspectives of its social group. "If you want to know what women think, listen to their *lɛɛlɛ* songs," I was told.

The three major song genres collected, translated, and interpreted for this study are the *gurna, waywa,* and *lɛɛlɛ*.[15] *Gurna* song (*siŋ gurna*), each song some 350 lines in length, is produced by specialized composers and is widely disseminated and mastered by *gurna* society members for performance at village death celebrations. (Various subtypes of *gurna* song will be described later.) *Waywa* songs, of which I collected eighteen, are spirited short ditties composed anonymously by youth to be performed during the rainy-season dances while the *gurna* society was off for the season (see figure 3). *Waywa* songs lampoon foolish behavior or social transgressions by actual individuals in the village. The third song genre, *lɛɛlɛ,* is composed and sung by married women at wakes, funerals, and drinking parties. *Lɛɛlɛ* were either bawdy or piquantly critical of women's lot vis-à-vis men. *Gurna* and *waywa* songs are accompanied by drum percussion and are intended to animate large public dances held in open dance sites (*laale*). Usually accompanied by a single drummer or none at all, *lɛɛlɛ* are performed more intimately in a family compound where women were gathered.

A fourth major song genre that was popular in Tupuriland during my stay was the *didilna* (or *dilna;* Massa borrow), a harp-based griot performance presented by small "orchestras" of three or four musicians (see figure 4). *Didilna* is the Tupuri version of the griot musical style that is widespread in West Africa and well studied among the Mande and Hausa. *Didilna* performers appear without fail at any social occasion where elites relax around sorghum beer and sponsored *didilna* praise song with cash gifts. I listened to and tape-recorded *didilna* but chose not to include it in my study because it differed quite strikingly from *gurna, waywa,* and *lɛɛlɛ*. It was improvisational, independent from dance, and was oriented toward catering to elites, none of which applied to the other forms.

I do not want to imply that there are only four song or dance genres in Tupuriland. In fact, there have been many historically and some remain, though they are in the process of dying out, such as *jõo ka'araŋ* (dance for the festival [*few ka'araŋ*] in April), *dãa* (flute music from the Kéra of Chad), *maga* (short satirical songs performed for death celebrations before the *gurna* was introduced to Tupuriland), and *jõo-piri* (the Hausa/Fulani–borrowed courtly praise song with bugle and drum accompaniment). Also, Christian churches (Catholic, Lutheran, and Pentecostal) have produced a prolific number of Christian hymns in the Tupuri language. This genre, *siŋ-Baa* (lit. "songs of God"), is beyond the scope of the present study. And to be thorough, it is important to note that residents of Tupuriland are part of the audience for Cameroonian and West African popular music, disseminated by radio and cassette tape. Cameroonian *makossa,* Congolese *soucous,* and even American country and western (e.g., Dolly Parton) was often heard blaring from Doukoula bars, though they were rare in the surrounding villages.

I sought *gurna* song (*siŋ gurna*) from both rural and urban areas, from village contexts as well as modern institutions such as schools. The more copious and elaborate *siŋ gurna* are those produced for *gurna* societies in villages in rural Tupuriland. Members of the *gurna* camps (*jak-kawre*) who were literate generously shared the song transcriptions they had written up in the camps to help members learn the song. In some cases, where the song had not been transcribed or the transcription was lost, individuals transcribed it for me from a tape or their own memory. In Cameroon in the 1990s, as opposed to Chad, which had its own composers, *gurna* song was composed by specially recognized composers located in three villages. Noumnamo and Djingue of Zouaye village were the most popular composers at the time of my sojourn. Sogole of the village Tuksu was considered a controversial "upstart" composer. In 1997–1999, he had a loose collaborative relationship with a composer called Dayle, who lived in Youaye. The third nexus of song composition, located in Dawa, Chad (just over the Chad-Cameroon border), involved a collaborative pair of composers. Teodandi wrote for Cameroon and frequently visited the market in Warsaï, Cameroon, to keep up his contacts. His partner in Chad was Dabla (Dapsala). The songs I endeavored to collect were those for the 1997/1998 and 1998/1999 *gurna* seasons from all three compositional nodes (Zouaye, Tuksu, and Dawa). To round out the village-context *siŋ gurna,* my corpus also includes one song (1998/1999) composed by a sixteen-year-old youth (from Konkoron village) for the children's *gurna,* the *gurna-fiiri.*

I also collected *siŋ gurna* from settings outside villages, specifically schools and urban cultural associations. Dangmoworé, an eighteen-year-old student at the Lycée de Doukoula, worked with me to transcribe, translate, and explicate four years of *gurna* songs that he composed for the Gurna Club at the lycée (1995–1999). Ringwa, another student-composer, was studying at the ENIEG in Maroua. He produced a song (1998/1999) that had double use—for the Tupuri students at the ENIEG and the Tupuri cultural association in the provincial capital, Maroua. Finally, I collected *siŋ gurna* produced by a composer in the Cameroon capital of Yaoundé for use by a Tupuri cultural heritage association/dance troupe called Club Kwoïssa. These urban and institutional versions are derivative of the rural forms: that is, composers from rural Tupuriland brought the genre and the art of composition to the urban areas where they migrated as students and salaried workers. Still, the split is not simply urban versus rural but institutional versus village as well. Even in rural Tupuriland itself, *gurna* songs are composed in the school context; for example, in the Lycée de Doukoula, which is "miles" away from village *jak-kawre* in social, though not in geographical, terms.

The process of collecting, transcribing, translating, and explicating Tupuri song was an enthralling intellectual journey for me; the songs continually provided me with new windows into Tupuri culture (practice, meanings, and symbols), aspects that hitherto had been hidden from me. Learning how widespread—and limited—competency in song was in Tupuri society was part of the process. (This is explored in detail in chapter 5.) The research project made my experience of Tupuri song different from that of many Tupuri people. This truth hit home to me when *gurna* members, eyeing my notebook and tape recorder, asked me whether after my work I would be able to sing the songs. I had to admit not. Instead, my knowledge of song would involve understanding how they worked sociologically and how they related to happenings in the villages and in the politics of the *gurna*. I also sought to understand—in a conscious way—the principles of the song's performative power, why people returned again and again to the dance and song. Some of these insights were gained from discussions with the small class of *siŋ gurna* composers who composed beyond the villages, in *gurna* clubs in lycées and professional schools. These student-composers were ideal informants because not only were they able to translate Tupuri concepts into French but they were able, due to their formal educational background, to reflect systematically and metacognitively on their composition practice and song poetic conventions.

My research was not limited to textual study; I attended and videotaped many death celebration *gurna* dances, rainy-season *waywa* dances, and others, such as the women's *lɛɛlɛ* dance at funerals and state-sponsored dances that were organized as part of official ceremonies and celebrations. Through videotaping, I could ask my assistants to review the event afterward and comment on the organization of the dance as well as dance movements and impromptu heckling by dancers and audience members. Overall, my fieldwork methodology conformed to the season, networks, and priorities of the *gurna* genre I studied.

SOCIOPOLITICAL ORGANIZATION IN TUPURILAND

In the following chapters, I show how Tupuri song and dance performs cultural-political work; that is, how Tupuri people use them as vehicles to comment on individual behavior, provoke intervillage rivalry, recalibrate personal prestige, chastise the behavior of social subgroups (such as students, unmarried girls, polygynous men, married women), and promote communal unity and a sense of belonging. But even as one grasps the multifunctional nature of dance and song, one might ask *why* the Tupuri found, and continue to find, it necessary to perform these social tasks through verbal and dance performance. In an effort to respond to this difficult question, researchers have typically pointed to the advantages of indirection in performance arts for resolving conflict without face-to-face humiliation or violence (Labov 1972, 168; Pierson 1993/1999). While this psychosociological dynamic is certainly true, I consider as well the broader sociopolitical context within which Tupuri verbal and performance arts emerged. Tupuri social organization is especially relevant given the elaborate collectivity of the *gurna* as a village-based regional network of men. Tupuri dance and song performed (and, to a lesser extent, continues to perform) functions that might, in other societies, be carried out by a centralized chieftaincy or, in contemporary times, by the administration of the nation-state. In short, the flexible, egalitarian political organization of the Tupuri depends on the cultural politics of dance to achieve a certain social cohesion and channel struggles for dominance.

Today there are three overlapping systems of authority: the modern governmental administration, the system of traditional chiefs, and the older Tupuri institution of earth priesthood. Before the arrival of German colonialists in the 1880s and then the French, who routed the Germans after World War I, Tupuri society was organized as an acephalous segmentary lineage system. This equalitarian political organization achieved social cohesion not through the rule of chiefs but rather through affiliation of kinship (by patrilineal lineage and clan) and by residency. The Tupuri were (and continue to be) identified by approximately sixty clans (*kawre*),[16] divided into the moieties (supraclans) of Dore and Gwa. Each clan was founded by a putative ancestor (*moobe*), who established his lineage in a new region. Clan affinity determines marriage—the Tupuri are strongly exogamous—and land tenure is marked through the timing and specific ritual practices of the annual tutelary sacrifice. The incorporation of neighboring ethnic groups (such as the Massa and Moundang) into the Tupuri is evident in certain clan names (Barre and Mbarhaï, respectively). Patrilocal and patrilineal, Tupuri families are based in nuclear family compounds (*tiŋ*) consisting of a male head (*panbe*) and his wives (*wãayre*) and children (*weere*). The eldest male son is expected to live nearby and inherit the rights and responsibilities of maintaining the lineage. Today villages are usually not entirely composed of members of a single clan. Where several clans are present, they must each have an earth priest (*waŋ-siri*) who serves the sacred forest (*jak-siri*) where the souls of the deceased ancestors reside.

Although there was no political chieftaincy in Tupuri society during the precolonial era, the ritual power of the *waŋ-siri* was considerable. He regulated the village through his performance of propitiary rites to *baa* (supreme deity) and the ancestors and by determining the timing of agricultural tasks, such as seeding and harvesting. He even called "weekend" days of rest. Conflicts that eluded the powers of family patriarchs were resolved at the *waŋ-siri*'s compound, and he presided over villagewide ceremonies of atonement. Each village *waŋ-siri* was accountable to the high priest recognized by all Tupuri, the *waŋ-kulu* or *waŋ-Dore* who resided (and continues to reside) in a mystical state, nude and in isolation, at Mount Dore, Chad. This hierarchy was symbolized by his power to periodically collect taxes (*kal-kaw*) in the form of goats, which were forcibly seized by his officials as they passed through Tupuri villages in Cameroon and Chad. The power of the *waŋ-kulu* was also represented during the annual sacrifice (*few kage*) of the Dore clans. Each village *waŋ-siri* was required to wait for the drum signal from Chad that the sacrifice had been successfully conducted there before he could conduct his own. In turn, on the village level, each family head waited for the signal of the *waŋ-siri* before he could perform his. Therefore, clans and lineages across the Tupuri region were loosely brought together under the ritual regulation of the *waŋ-siri* institution.

In this context in which there was no administering state, dance had an important role to play in bringing together villages and in enabling men and women to find (exogamous) marriage partners. Like contemporary sports teams, dance provided a contained, stylized arena for villages to play out their competition for dominance. Elders with whom I spoke emphasized that since people in the past did not know the contemporary systems of weekly markets, schooling, and public transportation, they would have been isolated in their villages if not for the dances. Associated with death celebrations (*yii-huuli*), festivals (such as *few kage*), and seasonal recreation (such as the rainy-season *waywa*), these massive dances brought people together across vast distances over which they would travel by foot, sometimes for several days. It is also in this precolonial context that the *gurna* society diffused to the Tupuri from the east. As discussed in chapter 3, the *gurna* provided an egalitarian social organization that cut across clan but retained the notion of an affinal collectivity. In the *gurna* complex (its camps, dance performance, and regional dissemination of song), the Tupuri created a village-based form of social organization that matched their broader political structure of flexible egalitarianism.

In contemporary times, Tupuri dance may be less urgent, due in part to shifts toward a more rigid, centralized political order brought by the Cameroon nation-state. Throughout much of Africa, including Cameroon, European colonialism was carried out through the imposition of a hierarchy of "traditional" chieftaincies, some created anew where there were none. In Tupuriland, when colonial powers "pacified" the region, they recognized the famous Tupuri war chief, Djonga, as the *lamido*[17] of Doukoula (*canton* of Kar Hay), even though this title was foreign to Tupuri sociopolitical organization.[18] A hierarchical system of traditional chiefs was created in Tupuriland (as elsewhere) to carry out the colonial projects of taxation, forced labor (*courbé*, French), and justice.[19] This system supplanted much of the power of the indigenous *waŋ-siri*. Today in Tupuri villages, there are two offices: the traditional chief (*lamido/lawan/djaro*, Fulfulde; *waaŋ-wuu*, Tupuri[20]) and the earth priest (*waŋ-siri*), of which only the first is legally conferred by the national government. Occasionally these are both held by the same person, but usually the *waaŋ-wuu* deals with administration, directly under the *lamido* of the *canton,* while the *waŋ-siri,* the most senior clan member, is responsible for purely ritual functions. Traditional chiefs throughout Francophone Cameroon, including the *lamido* of Doukoula, have been closely aligned to the national government and the ruling party since Independence.[21]

Upon this dual political system a third layer was superimposed—the administration of the modern nation-state. The French prefecture system of unitary republican rule (*commandement*) was continued in Cameroon after colonialism ended. Local (municipal) government was recently created in the late 1990s and is extremely weak. The current Cameroon government, under Paul Biya, is heavily dependent on the national security forces (military, gendarmes, and police) to ensure its power. With this new political order came the modern ideologies of citizenship and nationalism. Although geographically far from the capital of Yaoundé, the Tupuri men began to participate in the new nation-state, first as military recruits favored by the first president, Ahidjo, and then as students in the public school system which led to civil servant positions. Of course the population in the Tupuri homeland was affected by taxation and national law and decrees, such as the requirement to grow cotton and President Ahidjo's demand that all "naked" tribesmen wear clothes. In 1975, the Tupuri youth initiation (*gɔɔni*) was banned by governmental action.[22]

These changes in the political construction of personhood and in social organization have affected the meaning of indigenous Tupuri dance and song—though in complex ways. Although *gurna* dance still primarily appears during death celebrations, there has been a folklorization of this genre (as well as others) for use in state functions. As the *gurna* is inserted into state ceremonies as "entertainment," the Tupuri are symbolically represented as an ethnic group incorporated into the all-powerful Cameroon nation-state. At a more fundamental level, the opportunities that young people have to pursue formal education and salaried work threaten the future of the *gurna* as a viable association in the village. However, there is also evidence that new forms of the *gurna* are being created in school contexts as extracurricular clubs and in urban neighborhoods as cultural heritage associations.

OVERVIEW OF THE STUDY

Although the heart of the study focuses on the social action of *gurna* song in Tupuri society (chapters 5 through 9), I felt it necessary to preface this with broader discussions of how song and dance operate in Tupuri society, especially as public spaces for the moral regulation of the community. Therefore, chapters 2 through 4 do not focus on the *gurna* song per se but instead on other song genres (*waywa* and *lɛɛlɛ*), *gurna* dance gesture and discourse (*bɔ'ge fɔgɛ*), and the institutional base of the *gurna* society itself.

Chapter 2 illustrates how song and dance function as a site of public debate, censure, and retribution in Tupuri society. In the *waywa* songs examined, young men attempt to shore up power they feel they have lost vis-à-vis young women due to changing courtship practices. These songs also point to contemporary debate over girls' rights to delay marriage and select their own marriage partners as well as boys' difficulty in paying bridewealth during Cameroon's period of economic decline. However, the songs do more than simply mirror these tensions; they are created by individuals to sway public opinion and redress particular wrongdoings. This case study of Maïtené also explores how songs emerge from gender-based genres and become instruments in a gender politics of morality.

In chapter 3, my point of departure is the observation that institutions undergird public discourse, through which they promote certain values in society. Here, I describe the ethos, practices, and functions of the *gurna* in Tupuri society; that is, the institutional context within which *gurna* song was produced. Involving an imbrication of power across many social domains, the *gurna* is a multifaceted institution in which Tupuri men collectively wield their influence in key dimensions of social life: funerary celebration, socialization of youth, courtship, policing of behavior, and intravillage relations. The chapter also explores the plasticity of the *gurna* as it is transported to modern institutions and urban settings. Furthermore, instability in the meaning, value, and function of the *gurna* in Tupuri society across different factions (married women, *évolués* [educated people], Christians) destabilizes claims about the efficacy of the song as a mechanism of social control.

Chapter 4 builds on this description of the *gurna* society in order to explore the contradictory relationships among collective identities, performance, and the production of value in the wider society. A playful improvisational dance movement (*bɔ'ge fɔgɛ*) is analyzed as a symbolic inversion of the social hierarchy and a mouthpiece for the revalorization of the local networks and value system represented by the *gurna*. Although the dance discourse strategically utilizes modern/traditional and local/national dichotomies, analysis of the performance reveals a more complex commentary among the Tupuri: that the ineffectiveness of the nation-state warrants a reappraisal of the value of indigenous institutions.

Next, I focus on the *gurna* song, moving from the song as a communicative system and poetic genre to its role in the cultural politics of prestige and dominance among Tupuri men and villages. Chapter 5 describes the channels of communication through which the annual *gurna* song (*siŋ gurna*) is produced, disseminated, inculcated, and then performed for the larger community. Through the medium of the song, there is a circular flow of information about village happenings that moves between the *gurna* song composer and individuals in his client villages. The song system offers opportunities for both solidarity-building and rivalry as *gurna* members across large distances select and master one of several annual *gurna* songs offered by competing composers.

While chapter 5 takes a sociological view of the pathways and systems of socialization underlying the *gurna* song, chapter 6 provides a more detailed view of the song lyrics themselves, including key conventions and metaphors. Five rhetorical forms constituting the poetics of *gurna* song are described: a) praise/greeting; b) metacommentary on the dance; c) insult; d) recounting of shameful acts; and e) social commentary. However, the coherence of this typology is deceiving, because in practice, the text of the song assumes multiple audiences and takes on different meanings depending on the context of its use. The song has one set of meanings in the dance performance context, another as a text shared among *gurna* members, and another as it circulates as gossip in the villages.

Chapter 7 draws attention to the social construction of the song composer. This chapter discusses how the composer enhances his ritual power and legitimacy as a composer. Three areas are considered: a) transmission of the social role of composer through localized "dynasties"; b) strategic construction and erasure of the composer's persona in the song text itself; and c) the use of magical herbs in the composition process. These are best viewed as fields in which contests for legitimacy are waged. Furthermore, the status of composer as one vested with poetic license has recently been threatened by the expansion of national security and judicial systems where plaintiffs might charge the composer with libel. This shift in the relative status of the Tupuri *gurna* song institution vis-à-vis newer institutions is explored further in the next chapter.

Chapter 8 focuses on insult. It shows how conflicts between individuals and competition among the song composers are dramatically staged through insult in the annual *gurna* song. We see how verbal abuse in song is tied to systems of justice, both local and national. Although this articulation is not new—insult was upon occasion tied to witchcraft accusation—the growing hegemony of the national justice system has had a dampening effect on the use of verbal abuse in Tupuri song, particularly in cities.

Chapter 9 focuses on the cultural politics of the song. It lays out several ways in which dissemination of and affiliation through the song are considered political processes in local Tupuri terms. It examines how the politics of the *gurna* are reified in language borrowed from the national discourse on democracy, which is in turn reinterpreted to comment on local changes in cultural practice and the moral standards for politics. This borrowing of a lexicon from the national level is one way that local practitioners of an ostensibly "traditional" ("ancestral") institution revitalize their practice and build connections to the wider world while still maintaining the primacy of their own vision.

Finally, in the conclusion, I reflect on why Tupuri song, dance, and the *gurna* society continue in spite of modernist predictions that such ethnically based cultural practices would die out in favor of national forms. I consider what these practices offer the Tupuri people, including a familiar safety net in times of trouble and a license to air information and moral commentary in a publicly acceptable fashion. Whether the *gurna* can in the future move beyond its parochialism to become a more outwardly oriented cultural-political movement in Cameroon remains to be seen.

TWO

Maïtené's Modern Life

Song as Negotiation of Public Morality

Fascinated by the scandal surrounding a particular young woman, Maïtené, I asked my research assistant, Dourwé, to write down the background of the case in a small notebook I gave him.[1] A native of Maïtené's village, he eagerly agreed and wrote:

> Maïtené was a girl who remained for a long time at her parents' house. She made meatballs for sale, wore pants, and joined the opposition political party. She refused every suitor who came to ask for her hand in marriage. She joined the upstart Protestant church and was confirmed. She conceived a child out of wedlock, aborted it and, to the villagers' horror, threw the fetus in a well. The church decided to expel her.
>
> Later Maïtené became pregnant again, though this time with a teacher in training. Delighted to have snagged a *petit fonctionnaire* [junior civil servant], she went to his village[,] where he promptly abandoned her to his mother and left for the South. Maïtené gave birth to a baby boy and lives in uncertain terms with her mother-in-law, with her brideprice still unpaid.

MAÏTENÉ IS SUNG

In 1996, songs about the modern life of Maïtené rippled throughout Tupuriland in the rainy-season *waywa*. The *waywa,* or dance of the youth, was known throughout Tupuriland for its trenchantly satirical songs and flamboyant costuming (see figures 5–7). Organized at the level of the village by youth, usually under the protection of an elder, the *waywa* has become a massive event during the harvest season. As the land begins to dry and the sorghum heads are cut from their towering stalks, hundreds of dancers and thousands of spectators gather not only for the dance itself but for a day of socializing and large quantities of sorghum beer. It is in the context of these *waywa* dances, as well as the smaller ones in the villages, that I first heard the story of Maïtené.

Emerging from local gossip in the village of Mogom, the persona of Maïtené was objectified in songs composed for the *waywa* dances. Sung tirelessly by the colorfully costumed dancers as they trotted around the dance circle, the Maïtené songs presented the follies of the girl who refused to get married. So popular were these dances that even Maïtené herself attended them. Her baby slung on her back, tied tight with a cloth, she listened to "her song" and took a couple of turns around the circle, dancing stick in hand. But was the romp really so lighthearted? Why did these songs become so popular in Tupuriland? Was there a collective hunger that they tapped into?

When I discussed this question with individuals, some of their enthusiastic reaction was sheer admiration for how thoroughly Maïtené was *chasonnée*, that is, made into a song and "published" throughout the region. But, beyond that, their reactions were also a unanimous recognition of certain tensions in Tupuri society that are aired by the song. The Maïtené songs tapped into and reflect an important recent trend in Tupuri society: young women's reluctance, if not refusal, to marry. However, in watching the phenomenon of Maïtené, it seemed to me that the song encapsulated ambiguity in contemporary Tupuri society about the changing status of young women and expressed insecurities that young men feel vis-à-vis marriage during a period of economic depression in Cameroon.

Most broadly, this chapter is about how social control is exercised through song and dance in Tupuri society. More specifically, it is a case study of a debate on the appropriateness of modernity for girls. Recent anthropological literature has sought to break down the unitary term modernity that is centered in the West in favor of understanding multiple modernities that are locally constructed and historically situated (Abu-Lughod 1998; Comaroff and Comaroff 1993; Ivy 1995; Rofel 1999). Local discourses about modernity often seek to regulate the right to "be modern." Who deserves the privilege of "being modern" and who does not? Who is competent to "pull it off" and who will botch it? Who is abusing their status and freedom as a modern person and who is suffering these abuses? In Tupuriland, these are hotly contested questions because, among many reasons, they are closely tethered to the construction of gender. Should girls be permitted to "be modern"? If so, are the privileges and status conventionally afforded to boys thereby reduced? Will modernity in young women transform the conventional markers of the feminine in—according to local views—dangerous or perverted ways? For these reasons, although this study focuses on performance marked as "traditional,"[2] it speaks to the broader field of cultural studies in which public representations of women as licentious or untrustworthy ("bad girls") are mobilized in the media when these women challenge existing gender norms (Fraser 1997; Miller 1998; Sanday 1996).

In Tupuriland, song and oral poetry are highly public; they are discursive spaces where the dirty laundry of specific individuals is hung out and ridiculed, thereby producing an allegory. These cases become negative models, or anti-models (Miller 1998); they publicly delineate the boundaries of appropriate behavior by providing models or images of their transgression. However, unlike commercial media representations of "bad girls" in industrialized countries, songs in Tupuriland are intimately connected to ordinary actions and gossip occurring every day in Tupuri villages. They emerge from a wellspring of village-level micropolitics and discourse about appropriate and inappropriate behavior. As a result, song performance is a site where social norms and values—such as the relationship between gender and the privilege of "being modern"—are reinscribed, questioned, and debated. In this chapter, I examine how these questions are posed and responded to by different sectors of Tupuri society in the context of their song.

The category of "song" is rarely approached as such in Tupuriland. Instead, song is understood in terms of genre, each one associated with a social category of which it is thought to be expressive (such as women, youth, the *gurna*, elders, etc.). This chapter draws on song material from two genres: the *waywa* and the *lɛɛlɛ*. The *waywa*, the rainy-season performance genre associated with youth, involves short songs composed anonymously by young men. The composer's anonymity is preserved by first launching the song in a village other than his own. These songs expose the foolish or shameful behavior of individuals by name—behavior such as bestiality, greed, wastefulness, theft, and incest. The poetic license that enables youth to compose these songs arises from children's rights to perforate public space by incessantly chanting insulting, satirical refrains about any adult who they feel has wronged them.[3] Considered to be light, playful ditties, certain *waywa* nonetheless are extremely popular and often circulate for years, marking the generations. Although many young women dance the *waywa*, *waywa* song composition is dominated by young men.

In contrast, the *lɛɛlɛ* is the performance domain of woman, usually married women. Sung wherever women were among themselves, drinking, celebrating or mourning, the *lɛɛlɛ* range from bawdy songs about the pleasures of sex to trenchant critiques of husbands' treatment of their wives. *Lɛɛlɛ* are understood by men to be expressions of the real, lived experiences of women that in everyday life tended to be unvocalized. Commentaries on Maïtené, judgments about her lifestyle, emerged in both the *waywa* and *lɛɛlɛ* genres. Maïtené was first "sung" in the context of the *waywa*, but women answered back through their *lɛɛlɛ*. This chapter will explore this intertextual volley, as well as some of the references from other songs in each genre that are critical to understanding how discourse regulating modernity emerged from established discursive conventions in Tupuri song.

BECOMING A LIVING ALLEGORY: SONG AS HUMILIATION AND FAME

When I first heard the song of Maïtené, it was difficult for me to understand why it was so fiercely popular in Tupuriland. To me the lyrics seemed if not cryptic then fairly banal. What was it about the song that captured the public imagination such that the mere mention of Maïtené's name brought forward spontaneous laughter? It was only after the lyrics were painstakingly explained to me and even later when I began to grasp more fully what it meant to be a girl in Tupuri society that I began to understand. However, the first thing that had struck me about the Maïtené phenomenon was the power of public humiliation.

Several genres of Tupuri song are unabashedly didactic, aspiring to extend social control over what is seen as unruly behavior in the eyes of the composers—and by hegemonic extension, the community at large. *Waywa* songs are expressly intended to ridicule shameful behavior (*sōore*), indiscretions, and foolish actions in order, ostensibly, to discourage others from conducting themselves in such a way. However, as much as the songs moralized, they are far from somber lectures. Rather, they are gleeful romps in which the follies of actual individuals are broadcast and delighted over in the context of the dance. The public humiliation of the offending individual is savored by the spectators; part of its fun is in the incessant repetition of the lyrics by the dancers as they move around the dance ring. In an effort to feed the public's appetite for scandal and insult, new *waywa* songs are anonymously composed each year and older popular ones are trotted out again year after year until they fade with the rise of a new generation.

The first song about Maïtené to come out was this one:

Maïtené diŋ may jar Mogom ba ba.
Boo boutique ɓan ɓay yaw-la?
Pir le' ti pɔŋ ɓan ɓay Mogom.
Tene ndo maŋ mbɛgɛ lɛ ma caa nay pir no.
Tɛɛ kawre ɓɔɔŋ ba wɔɔ liŋ sɔ yaw-la?
Ndo jɔŋ diŋ kanda may karway maa ni Tene.
Yee kulot maa jɔŋ kanda.
Wur laa mbɛ wɛ Maïtené ndo hay ni war ga lay.
May po mbɛ liŋ caw kɔdɛ.
Ndi da' may po maa nen Ahidjo liŋ bɔɔŋ caw ga. (w, 1)

Maïtené is a girl from Mogom from way back.
Has she set up shop near you?
A horse fell on the dike at Mogom.
Tené, you took up a knife to cut the horse meat.
All the girls of your generation, are they still at their parents' house?
You only make meatballs, girl.
You sleep with men in order to buy trousers for selling your meatballs.
We know it, Maïtené, you will never be married.
What girl is this who stays at her parents' house?
I never saw a girl from the time of the former president Ahidjo still at home.

The year after this song, *waywa* dancers repeated these new lyrics, deepening their insult of Maïtené:

Maïtené boo tol takla.
Maïtené maŋ ti parti MDR.
Ga sɛ ko cōore parti takla.
Maïtené, may sɛ de bak bii mo no!
Kōo bargiŋ ni man mbɛ sɛ jɔŋ yɔɔ mbɛ laay so.
Wur laa mbe wɛ Kaossiri Sirandi
kaŋ Tene gɔ wer man day. (w, 2)

Maïtené built a concrete house this year.
Maïtené chose the MDR Party.
She thought this party was tasty this year.
Maïtené, what a crazy girl!
She made love in her mother's kitchen and committed incest too.
We heard that Kaossiri Sirandi [her father]
offered Tené in marriage for only one cow.

One afternoon at a *waywa* dance, while we were being jostled among the crowd of spectators, my research assistant tapped my arm and pointed with his eyes out onto the sea of dancers, saying in his usual indirect way, "There's a certain somebody."

"Who?"

"Maïtené."

I don't know what I was expecting from the girl who committed incest, served up horse meat, and chose the wrong political party, but Maïtené turned out to be, at least in appearance, very ordinary. Dressed in a green *pagne*, she shuffled around the dance circle, surrounded by her friends. Seeing her dancing among the other young women, I couldn't help but ask myself what it felt like to be a living allegory. Does her simple appearance at the dance where dancers were singing "her song" belie a wellspring of shame within her? Or is there something in this for her as well—fame, notoriety?

It took me a year to finally get an interview with Maïtené. It was not that she had refused, but the politics of her stigma seemed so delicate that I could not just rush to her village and ask to talk to her. The problem was how to conduct an interview with someone whom the community had censured as useless and who, as a young woman, was understood to be without voice to begin with. My research assistant made several abortive attempts to see her. His first try brought out anxious villagers thinking he was there on bicycle to announce a death. On the second try, they assumed that he was there to conduct a community development meeting. No one could imagine that Maïtené could be wanted for discussion with a *je-wuu* ("European" person). It was only on the third try that he was able to furtively meet Maïtené and arrange for her to visit my house in town on her trip to the weekly market to grind sorghum at the electric mill. The risk of her being silenced by the strangeness of my concrete house with wooden furniture was outweighed, in my mind, by the certainty that she would be silenced and later made the object of more gossip if I were to attempt to interview her in her own compound. I wanted very much to understand the secrets of her feelings about being "sung."

But I was disappointed with my interview with Maïtené; it felt like an inquisition or a cross-examination. Girls in Tupuri society, and women to a large degree, are understood to be without voice, which means that they have little say in official business or even domestic decision-making. Even though I sincerely wanted to learn about how Maïtené felt about her representation in the song, her embarrassment or stoicism or perhaps the strangeness of my concern (in her eyes) made our conversation strained. A naiveté that fieldworkers have to unlearn again and again is the notion that our own interest in a subject doesn't immediately change the existing power structures that regulate discourse on that subject.

Although I was far from the center of American media during my fieldwork in Cameroon, some of the media craze of the Clinton sex scandal must have permeated my consciousness as I reflected on the publicity of the *waywa* and its effect on Maïtené. In *The New York Times Magazine*, journalist Frank Rich (2000) describes the American genre of mediathon—"a relentless hybrid of media circus, soap opera and tabloid journalism." In Rich's interview with Monica Lewinsky about her experience as both witness and subject of the media circus, she described how violated she felt when qualities were attributed to her media persona that had no relation to her "real" person. She described reacting to and attempting to counteract the media projection of herself by dressing better and fixing her hair. Maïtené found herself in a similar position as both the object and observer of herself as "media" persona.

Sorting out Maïtené's reaction to having been sung is complex, in part because in Tupuri society, stoicism is highly valued. There tends to be a large gap between one's feelings in the heart and how one presents oneself. As expected, when pressed, Maïtené denied having been embarrassed by the songs. "Even if they sing the song ten times, that doesn't bother me!" However, listening between the lines of her effort to present herself as cool and in control, I heard a combination of anger and resignation. Others said that Maïtené must surely have reveled in her instant fame, though her notoriety must have felt uncomfortable because she made some fundamental changes in her life. She decided to marry and have a child. She quit the opposition political party and joined the dominant party, of which her husband was a member. She returned to the more mainstream Catholicism, leaving the more strident Lutheran church. At one level, the social control exerted by the songs and the gossip surrounding them had their effect; they made an allegory of Maïtené and likely shaped her behavior. However, a functionalist, social-control interpretation is not the whole story because it obscures the lines of tensions arising from recent changes in Tupuri society.

"THE GIRL FROM WAY BACK": THE NEGATIVE VALENCE OF GIRLS' MODERNITY

If the song of Maïtené resounded with rural Tupuriland, it was because the details of the lyrics were emblematic of a controversial new social identity, the "modern girl." Depending on context and the speaker's situated social position, there are many variations on the meaning of the modern in Tupuri society. For example, students tend to self-identify as modern because they are educated in what were originally defined as Western modes of knowledge and in European languages.[4] Evangelical Christians tend to locate their modernity in their disbelief in "pagan" Tupuri tenets, such as the existence of spirits, propitiation rites involving animal sacrifice, and divination. The term "modernized" is also widely used in a less ideological manner to refer to any practice that has been culled from the past and brought into contemporary life, even if, ironically, the practice occurred in the register of "traditional." For instance, I heard the *waywa* dance referred to as the *kuwaysa modernisé,* the *kuwaysa* being a dance performance genre of the previous generation. So, even though the *waywa* is "traditional" (in local parlance), it is modernized—a modernized *kuwaysa*—by its very nature of being current, being with us today. Although the various meanings of modernity in Tupuriland could be treated in much more detail, for the purposes of this chapter, I allow the Maïtené songs themselves to set the agenda.

If the Maïtené controversy is viewed as a referendum on the rights of girls to be modern, then the litmus of this modernity is located squarely in girls' refusal to marry. "Maïtené is a girl from way back," mocks the *waywa* song (w, 1: line 1). But in addition to marriage refusal, which seems to trigger a whole set of "naughty" behaviors or transgressions, the songs are riddled with other telling details that define the parameters of girls' modernity: economic independence, political participation, sexual promiscuity, and freedom from ethnically based taboo. The Maïtené persona partook of all these freedoms in the song, where they are deliberately charged with a valence of disrepute, even perversion.

In the recent past and in more rural locations, girls married at puberty, after menarche. Parents selected a marriage partner from their network of contacts or from the suitors who presented themselves. The agency afforded to the girl to choose her own partner depended on the severity of her parents and other factors, such as whether the suitor was capable of paying the large brideprice. Today, however, this tradition is under serious contestation; young people, including girls, want to select their own marriage partners without regard to ability to pay the brideprice. In any event, according to tradition, there was no socially legitimate reason why a girl should not be married by the age of 18, and girls often married as young as 12. That a girl might exert her will to refuse marriage was unthinkable. To eschew marriage to "save oneself" for a better lot in life or to sift through all the available men until one suited her tastes was simply not acceptable to the older generation.

Maïtené—the real-life young woman as opposed to the song persona—was highly aware that her actions elicited disgust from the older generation. She described herself in their eyes:

> There are some people who think that this girl should marry that one. There are people who when they see you like that [unmarried and living at home], they are shocked by you. They don't want to see you like that.

The song's criticism of Maïtené's choice to be home with her parents "since the era of Ahidjo" was not simply personal; it was a travesty against the community. (Amadou Ahidjo was the former president of Cameroon who left office in 1982.) The song also mentioned that all the members of her generation had long since married, tarring Maïtené with another transgression: the failure to follow along smoothly with the life-cycle passages of her age set.

Her small-business enterprise was also ridiculed. "Has she set up shop near you?" (line 2), the song asked, referring to Maïtené's petty trade in meatballs and, more generally, to the new phenomenon of girls having their own small businesses and, potentially, some income independent of their parents. When Maïtené sold meatballs she went to the market, either the large weekly market in Doukoula or one of the tiny bush markets outside the town, with a covered metal dish filled with tiny meatballs. She sold them one by one for 50 francs CFA (or approximately 10 cents) each. As innocuous as these activities sound, according to Tupuri tradition, there was no time that a girl or woman was considered to be economically independent. Girls passed from dependency in their parents' house to dependency in their husbands' house. If a woman was widowed and not very old, then she was inherited by her husband's brother or by an elder son of one of her co-wives. If she was quite old and chose not to be inherited, she would be cared for by her oldest son and would often, even in decrepitude, travel long distances to be near him. The general principle was that girls and woman were not to be ever considered capable of economic independence apart from their families.

So when Maïtené was accused of setting up shop, she was accused of transgressing the norm of female dependence. In discussions with me, Maïtené responded to this line in the song:

> They just say that because when I was at the house, I made every effort to find some means for dressing myself and for buying clothes. So for this reason, people said that I didn't want to get married, because I did that. This is why they composed the song.

One of the most visible and important duties of a husband is to dress his wife. Therefore, by definition, for a girl to earn money to dress herself—to aspire to economic independence in this way—meant that she challenged the institution of marriage. If women did conduct petty trade, raise small livestock for profit, and cultivate their own fields, it was *within* the institution of marriage and they were assumed to personally own little property. Until recently, there was little possibility for unmarried girls to earn, save, and spend their own money.

Additionally, "setting up shop" or "building a *boutique*" connotes a convergence of wealth, modernity, and sexual promiscuity. This is evident in other songs, such as a *lɛɛlɛ* song (#4): "Young men build shops to pick up prostitutes." ("*We jōore no./ Boo we boutique maa ndal gawlare no.*") The second Maïtené song continued in this vein: "Maïtené built a concrete house this year." ("*Maïtené boo tol taklai.*")[5] To build a concrete structure, to create a business, connotes prostitution.

For each image of wealth and modernity attributed to Maïtené in the songs, the next image demonstrated how she bungled her efforts to be modern. "Maïtené chose the MDR Party. / She thought this party was tasty [*de cōore*] this year" (w, 3: line 3). The use of the adjective "*de cōore*," connoting "delicious" or "sweet," suggested that her choice of political party was based frivolously on fashion or taste. The MDR (Mouvement pour la Defense de la République) was an opposition political party created during the political liberalization of the early 1990s; it had a strong Tupuri base. The MDR was later discredited when its leader was co-opted by the government and then passed over for reappointment. Dourwé, Maïtené's village "brother," reported to me that she was often seen at the *waywa* dances sporting her free MDR T-shirt so that everyone would assume she was a party faithful. When the MDR lost its popularity, Maïtené looked foolish.

In addition to discrediting Maïtené's economic and political independence, the song maligned her morality. Maïtené was accused of "taking up a knife to cut the horse meat [for her meatball business]." Tupuris have few food taboos except for the eating of horse meat. Horses are prestige items, associated originally with the nineteenth-century Fulani jihad when great cavalries swept over northern Cameroon and enslaved most of the indigenous ethnic groups. More prosaically, in 1996, everyone was familiar with an accident that occurred in Mogom in which a horse being led along the road was broadsided by a cotton truck. As Maïtené claimed and Dourwé corroborated, she wasn't even in Mogom when the horse was killed. But Doumsia, the song composer, had cleverly selected a well-known truth and built a believable lie upon it, all the better to malign Maïtené. The implication is that Maïtené, a boorish modern girl, transgressed even the most fundamental Tupuri taboos in her effort to turn a profit.

In the next lines she is accused of having sex in her mother's kitchen and even worse, committing incest; it was no wonder that her father "offered Tené in marriage for one cow." Although brideprice fluctuates over time, since at least the 1950s, Tupuri people have cited ten cows as the usual brideprice for marrying a Tupuri woman. The song goes to great lengths to show that Maïtené had habitually transgressed traditions Tupuri people hold dear. As a result, regardless of her modernity, she was reduced to being almost worthless on the marriage market. According to the song, modernity was something that Maïtené, and by extension all such unmarried older girls, couldn't quite manage. The implication was that girls were not capable of "being modern"—running their own commercial activities, choosing to be politically active, or selecting their own sexual partners. If they were permitted to do such, so the song went, they would just use their newfound freedoms to behave in a sexually immoral fashion.

In this masculine view, girls' aspirations toward modernity are portrayed as pretentious; they became possessed by *karway,* uncontrolled sexual desire. A feminist analysis might suggest that these songs publicly construct a licentious sexualization of women in order to control them just at the moment when they appear to be making individual economic gains. However, this argument is too simplistic because sexual ribaldry is a stock convention of the *waywa* genre—

images of bestiality and incest are commonplace—for *both* male and female persona. In an analysis that accounts for this, I examine how modernity was harnessed to notions of sexual prostitution, noting that these were the terms of the discourse about modern life, in both male- and female-dominated song. However, first we will peel back another layer of Maïtené's story.

DOUMSIA'S VENDETTA: MEN'S ECONOMIC INSECURITY AND CHANGES IN COURTSHIP

The songs maligning Maïtené did not arise spontaneously out of a broad consensus about the proper place of girls in society. Rather, there were specific micropolitics of revenge in Mogom village that gave rise to the composition of the Maïtené song, although these were much less widely known than the song itself. This was how the story was described by Dourwé, who had followed Maïtené's hardships:

> Maïtené is a girl who stayed a long time at her parent's house. She had traveled to the provincial capital of Maroua to look for a better life, but she didn't succeed in finding it. So, she came back to the village of Mogom and then went to her aunt's house at Dgiba where she continued her business of selling meat patties (*kanda*).
>
> There, a guy named Doumsia saw her and found her comfortable in his eyes, that is to say, he fell in love with her. He wanted to marry her. He went to Maïtené's father to negotiate the marriage and her parents agreed. But Maïtené herself did not accept the marriage.
>
> One day, Maïtené was selling *kanda* at the market of Guibert and Doumsia came up to her. But Maïtené wouldn't speak to him. He insulted her and she insulted him back. Then Doumsia started to hit her, and Maïtené's *kanda* spilled all over the ground. Furious, she went to complain to the chief of Daiba. The chief called for Doumsia in order to try the case. It came out that Doumsia had knocked over the *kanda* because Maïtené had refused his offer of marriage. Doumsia told her that he was doing her a favor by marrying her, to save her from the shame of having stayed single so long at her parent's house. She refused. "Why? Does she think she is more beautiful than all the other girls?" he said. In the end, the chief forced Doumsia to pay for the *kanda* he spilled.
>
> Later, to get revenge on her publicly, Doumsia composed a *waywa* song on Maïtené. And it was he himself who led the song. He climbed a tree and beat the large wooden *waywa* drums so that he could be sure Maïtené could see him. On that day Maïtené was wearing her *culotte* [trousers, French borrow].

The dancers picked up the lyrics and chanted them over and over again. Several hours later, while she was in her parents' compound pounding sorghum, Maïtené's friends came to tell her that there was a song being sung about her. At the root of the Maïtené controversy was the sting experienced by a snubbed suitor.

In Tupuri society, courtship of a girl has always been considered dangerous for the suitor. There is always the possibility of rejection, so practices and discursive forms have developed for courtship to protect what we would call the ego of the man. *Jak-jõo* (lit. "language-dance") was a form of indirect speech traditionally used between the suitor and the girl's mother during courtship visits. Simple words were expressed metaphorically, such "the dog's mat" for "earth." Women were thought to excel in this linguistic wordplay. They showcased their skills in their lɛɛlɛ songs in which sexual euphemisms abound. For example, "*soole,*" literally "hernia," denoted lust. "*Kal,*" from the French term "*caler*" (to block), became "penis." Although courtship visits involved conversation primarily between the prospective mother-in-law and the suitor, the girl and the suitor had a moment to speak directly when he was escorted back to the road.

Today, it is recognized that courtship practices are changing. People point to the influence of the weekly markets and schools which have provided new contexts, other than the dance and the parental compound, in which young men and women can interact. In the past, the dance (*dak-jõo*) was a major site for men and women to see one another and set up liaisons, although under the strict surveillance of the *gurna* society, which regulated interactions at the onset of courtship. In order for a man to speak to a girl (*ndalge may*), he would first have to get permission from the "chief of the girls" (*waŋ-mayre*), who monitored the activities of girls associated with the *gurna* camp. Now, in school, church, and the market, men and women interact directly with one another without these intermediaries. The use of *jak-jõo* is disappearing, and, as one middle-aged adult noted to me, a girl is likely to say to a boy who tries to talk to her "*Fouts le camp!*" ("Beat it!") As young women find a greater freedom in their speech through the influence of schooling and the church, men are becoming vulnerable in new ways. For this reason, the relatively few Tupuri girls who go far in school are widely thought by men to be "spoiled." There is a vibrant discourse about the ways that educated girls have been "ruined."

Cameroon's post-1986 economic crisis has had differential effects on men and women: an increased vulnerability for men and new vocality and independence for women. For young males, the crisis has meant sharply reduced chances for education and employment, which since the early 1990s they have been groomed to expect. Young men are having trouble affording marriage, both in terms of actually paying the brideprice and in terms of being economically independent so that they can be perceived as credible suitors. This economic situation has made men more anxious about their chances in the courtship process than they were in the past.

In contrast, young women have seen their horizons broadening in recent years. In the past, there was never an expectation that they would go to school beyond primary level or that they would have salaried jobs. Now the world is opening up for girls. More and more they are acquiring the ability and courage to speak in the community, to make life decisions independently of their parents, and to engage in petty trade and manage their own money.

Overall, this is a volatile situation in which just at the moment that men feel most vulnerable to girls and their families, the girls themselves are gaining power. In the 1990s, more and more girls were asserting this power in ways that directly affected men. They were refusing to marry young, and they insisted on choosing their own marriage partners according to their own criteria, which may have differed substantially from those of their parents. As one young woman pointed out to me, with a resentful tone, "Parents will 'sell you' for a high brideprice when it's not in your interests to marry the man they choose." More and more, young women were eschewing polygynous marriage. They were refusing to stay with husbands who mistreat them—even if it meant leaving their children. They were becoming more discriminating in marriage, more likely to leave aside the increased social status that came with marriage.

It is this vein of discontent and instability in contemporary Tupuri society that the Maïtené songs tapped into. The songs expressed the point of view of frustrated young men who resent the increased autonomy of young woman. It is not surprising that songs lampooning a girl who refused to marry would appear in the context of the *waywa* dance, since the dance itself is a site for the public display of masculinity. In the past, girls could be forcibly seized into marriage at the dance in a dramatic move called *maŋge-may* (lit. "catch a girl"). The *maŋge-may* could occur at any dance, though it was conventional at the massive *waywa* dances of the *few kage* (annual harvest festival). A girl would be captured and dragged forcibly by a suitor's friends to his compound. Sometimes the suitor had paid some of the cash deposit (*sulay-bii*) that is the first stage of marriage negotiation but feared the competition of other suitors, so he publicly took the girl away. Today the *maŋge-may* exists in the context of dance largely as a gesture of mutual engagement; few women are forcibly seized into marriage in this way. Still, in the view of young men, the bold statement of virility represented by the *maŋge-may* is an extension of the display of youthful vigor in the dance itself. The dance provides a license of legitimacy for extraordinary powers, especially male power.

THE AMBIGUITY OF NONMARRIAGE

Another reason the Maïtené persona was so popular and fascinating to many in Tupuri society is that it tapped into an ambiguity that had arisen around gender. Talk about the recent trend of women's nonmarriage is different depending on to whom one is speaking. Young women tend to say that they do indeed want to marry but cannot find a man to marry. At the same time, young men tend to say that women today, especially those who have gone to school, are spoiled—they don't want to marry but would rather just sleep around. Part of what is unsaid in this cross-gender combat is that today, men are less capable of paying the brideprice required to marry a Tupuri woman and to support them materially. Even more deeply buried is the fact that in the current climate of economic decline, girls' lack of access to the modern sector (education, salaried employment, capital for business) has left them unable or less willing to marry men without means. In other words, just as men have learned through the social contract of modern education to expect office work and a middle-class salary if they attend school, so women too have aspirations of upward mobility. However, for women, these aspirations generally must be achieved through marriage because their access to civil service employment is limited.

These shifts in how women view marriage has resulted in the emergence of a new social category that defies conventional Tupuri definitions of gender. The major Tupuri categories for females are unmarried girl (*may*), married woman (*wãay*), and a woman who has been widowed, separated, or divorced (*gawlaŋ* or *muswaŋ*; see figure 8). How does one categorize a woman who has never married and still lives with her parents but is no longer young? In the recent European past, this woman was an "old maid," someone to be stigmatized and pitied. However, in contrast to the popular image of "old maid," "the girl from way back," as

Maïtené was called in her song, is seen as a threat, as a person aspiring to modernity in a way that disrupts the social order.

Young women who seem to be bypassing marriage are perceived as a threat to the order of patrilineage; that is, the expectation that each person be affiliated with a patriline (*wɛrɛ*) that in effect owns their labor and the products of their labor. Girls (*mayre*) are affiliated with their father's patriline. In this strongly patrilocal society, a newly married woman (*may-waare*, lit. "woman-stranger") is integrated into her husband's patriline, clan, and village gradually and purposefully. Women who become severed from their husband's patriline either through divorce or his death are herded back within; after the death of a married man, his wives are inherited by his brothers. However, if the widow is old, she is given the choice to move to her brother-in-law's compound or to remain where she is, under the protection of her eldest son. In the case of divorce, all children except infants remain with the husband. In short, in the present as in the past, Tupuri society makes every effort to prevent both women and men from living as atomic individuals outside the protection of a patriline.

In the past, a woman who was not securely attached to a patriline was a *gawlaŋ*, meaning that she was divorced or widowed. However, today, the category of *gawlaŋ* has been expanded to include the new category of prostitute. It is interesting that in the *waywa* songs, Maïtené is called a "crazy girl" (*may sɛ de bak bii*) and a "nymphomaniac" (*may karway*), but not *gawlaŋ*. Women warned in their *lɛɛlɛ* song that Maïtené should avoid becoming a prostitute. As long as Maïtené had never been married and still lived with her parents, she was not yet *gawlaŋ*. Or at least her status as *gawlaŋ* was contested. Although unmarried, she had ceased to be a girl because she was the age of a woman. So within this social universe, a girl such as Maïtené defied all the major social categories for women— *may*, *wãay*, and *gawlaŋ*. In the eyes of the community, Maïtené represented a person who was not properly gendered and was therefore unstable, untrustworthy.

NO FACILE FEMINISM: MARRIED WOMEN DIAGNOSE MAÏTENÉ

The Maïtené persona also appears in two songs emerging from the performance genre controlled by older women, the *lɛɛlɛ*. When women are among women, drinking *'argi* (distilled alcohol) or *yii* (brewed sorghum beer) at a funeral or party, they sing about life from a distinctively female point of view. They ridicule men who bollix up the delicate balance of power in polygynous marriages. They point out the foolishness of women not properly brought up and co-wives who fight. They reprimand fathers who demand too much brideprice and thereby impoverish their own daughters in their husbands' houses. Tupuri men understand the *lɛɛlɛ* to be a place where women reveal their secrets, expose what they are thinking and feeling in ways they cannot in everyday life.

Responding to the young men's *waywa* songs, women composed this *lɛɛlɛ* song while Maïtené was still seen to be refusing marriage. The lyrics were short, but they were repeated over and over again:

> Maïtené, ndi day da war ma jɔŋ jɔŋre ga, Maïtené.
>
> Maïtené, I don't want to marry just to find a lot of work, Maïtené. (1, #3)

Imagining that women's song discourse would be feminist in a way familiar to me, I walked around for a year misinterpreting it. Originally, I assumed that the women were backing up Maïtené's refusal to marry by pointing out that marriage brings a great deal of work to women. No one could argue that Tupuri women living in rural villages do a tremendous amount of hard physical work from dawn to dusk: fetching water from 100-foot-deep wells sometimes a mile away, farming with handhoes, caring for children, cooking and processing food, gathering firewood, brewing sorghum beer for income, and so forth (see figure 9). However, regardless of these realities, this *lɛɛlɛ* song in fact mocked younger women who refused to marry. It taunted Maïtené with the implication that she was lazy, refusing to rise up to the duties of married women.

In a second *lɛɛlɛ* song, composed after Maïtené was married to a schoolteacher in training, the women took a cautionary tone. It is here that Maïtené was explicitly said to be suffering from *dulnya*. Recognizing its unstable meaning, I have chosen to translate *dulnya* as "modern life." Occurring frequently in Tupuri song, *dulnya,* an Arabic loan word, most often means "life"; however, in the context of *gurna* song, it can mean the *gurna* song or lifestyle. Its connotations as "life" vary, as does the English term: a) individual lifespan; b) generational lifespan; and c) the indeterminate, inscrutable aspect of life, as in "That's life!" As in line 3 below, *dulnya* can also mean a lifestyle or mode of living—here, Maïtené's lifestyle. And, finally, *dulnya* as "modern life" connotes a life shot through with complexities or troubles that overwhelm a person, as in line 2.

> *Maïtené yaa sa' mbo hɛn war ɓɔa jɔŋ nen mo. (1)*
> *Maïtené hay wer war yee ga dulnya raw ne. (2)*
> *Dulnya ma ni Tené ndi ko n ge da pa. (3)*
> *Hiyaya! Daïrou mo caw ba su mbay baa. (4)*
> *Baa Tene raw de mba jɔŋ bordel Kalfou. (5) (1, 24)*

> Maïtené, cling to your husband, because they will trick you. (1)
> Maïtené didn't stay with her husband, since modern life overwhelmed her. (2)
> The life of Maïtené, I want to see it. (3)
> Hiyaya! Daïrou is over there. (4)
> He takes Maïtené away to be a prostitute in Kalfou. (5)

The song cautions Maïtené not to be tricked into a life of sexual promiscuity but to cling to her husband. The "modern life" that threatens to overwhelm Maïtené is a life of prostitution into which her former boyfriend, Daïrou, would lead her—"He takes Maïtené away to be a prostitute[6] in Kalfou." While part of the song appears to be an admonition or a prediction, the women also sing with biting sarcasm "the modern life of Maïtené—I want to see it." Skeptical of promises of freedom, the *lɛɛlɛ* singers seem to counsel Maïtené that in spite of a world of changes, women are still more powerful when married and settled in a patrilineage. They see promises of new freedoms as a trick to degrade women and strip them of the few protections they have within marriage.

It would be easy to conclude from this that older women are the reactionary, status-quo-oriented forces in society. However, it is important to understand their admonitions in the context of the poverty and oppression under which young women live. More than anything, this song captures how older women are evaluating the promises of the modernity for the next generation of women. Clearly lacking was any mention of Maïtené making it on her own in the world. Without access to schooling, capital, or employment, women are unprepared to do much outside of marriage except engage in prostitution. This bleak picture is the "modernity" of which the women sang.

MODERNITY AS PROSTITUTION

The sexualization of Maïtené in song—that she was filled with wayward lust (*karway*) or was on the verge of prostitution—should be thought of in a light of a broader discourse about social change in Tupuri society. In public discourse, modernity is often equated with prostitution. Girls are thought to pay for their freedom from patriarchal authority in the household through prostitution. Even the few Tupuri girls who reach lycée are subject to being understood as prostituting themselves to their male teachers (especially those from southern Cameroon) in exchange for high grades. Amid this robust discourse about prostitution, it is not surprising that married women tended to be critical of prostitution. A husband's purchase of sexual favors drains money from the household and dilutes his attention to his wives. In this *lɛɛlɛ*, women feared contracting AIDS from their husbands' infidelities:

> *Gawlaare no, SIDA na ti la ɓaŋ hun-la?*
> *SIDA na ti Tchatibali karway de war meege.*
> *Sug ɓi mo laa nduu SIDA wa.* (1, 17)

> Prostitutes, where is AIDS now?
> AIDS came to Tchatibali, my husband's sexual desire overflows.
> I don't want to hear that the AIDS has come here.

Tchatibali is a village where the only industry in Tupuriland is situated: a factory where locally grown cotton is de-seeded. When it was built, many prostitutes (*gawlaare*) were drawn there to provide sexual services for the salaried workers. The song composer, who lived over the border in Chad, feared that the free women would return, bringing AIDS with them.

Another song that was extremely popular during my fieldwork warned women to behave themselves by calling upon their husbands to whip lascivious women (*bordelle*) soundly:

> *Wɛrpeere no, caa berin se naaren nday da ga ɓuy.*
> *Wāayn raw mo wɛ liŋ bordel na,*
> *Ndo gaw gɔ tee wɔ gɔ faale tiŋ ni nday ɓan sɔ.* (1, 13)

> Men, cut a switch to use on women you don't like.
> If a woman disobeys you, acting like a prostitute,
> You'd better kill her quick and bury her behind the house of her lover.

Like many of the *lɛɛlɛ*, the tone of this song is playful, so it is not clear whether women are expressing a mock collusion with their husbands to whip wives who were promiscuous or whether they intend to reprimand frivolous women, as in this *lɛɛlɛ*:

> *Maïdaï de hāa.*
> *'A tuf sāare ne jar se de den gormo wa.*
> *Maïdaï da ndo jɔŋre mo na guigic se ɓe guigic se ɓe*
> *do may jar Kalgam no no.*

Hiyaya Paul baa mo caw ba se bay ba?
Maŋ million hā n gɔ ne may jar Kalgam no. (1, 8)

Maïdaï is wicked.
She slobbers all over people, drunk on gin.
Maïdaï wants her work to be strutting and swaying around
    in front of the people of Kalgam.
Isn't it Paul that you see over there?
Took millions of francs and gave it to the girl who's for all the people of
    Kalgam.

Here Maïdaï was a drunken, prurient woman; a more explicit translation of one line of the song would be "a girl 'owned' by all the revelers of Kalgam village." Her poor husband, Paul, paid a high brideprice for Maïdaï and got a wife who spent all her time drinking liquor (*'arki*). When people tell her do some work at the house, she refuses, shrugging her shoulders and strutting around to the various bars ("*guigic se ɓe guigic se ɓe*"). Maïdaï flaunts the high brideprice which married women claim mark their respectability. By acting like a *gawlaŋ*, free woman, she denigrates men's material commitment to marriage that women hope will protect them from abuse from their husbands.

However, in spite of the fact that women often chide each other for behaving like prostitutes, and young men certainly have a discourse of such claims (such as Maïtené's case), there are also *lɛɛlɛ* in which the female composers turn the tables on the stereotype of female licentiousness. In the following *lɛɛlɛ*, women point out that it is not just women who were "loose" nowadays, but men too:

Wɛrpeere no, tum de lumo lundi 'a gawlaare ɓuy.
Pan sɛ n hay le ti lumo Maroua caa kelew nay,
Nduu liŋ wāayn ɓe ga gawlaŋ ɓɔ no.
Hiyaya man yaŋ gawlaŋ caw ndaŋ yaw.
Ndi laa jak bii su ga man ɓɔ diŋ gawlaŋ mbal mbale. (1, 18)

Men, on Monday market day everyone is a prostitute.
One man bought a kilo of meat at the Maroua market to eat,
Came home and called his wife a prostitute.
Hiyaya! Your mother is a whore up 'til now.
I heard yesterday that your mother is really a whore.

This *lɛɛlɛ* expresses the popular belief that the frenetic commercialism of the market day compromises everyone: "Men, on Monday market day everyone is a prostitute." In claiming this universality of moral degradation, women counter men's implications that only women are prostitutes. Men prostitute themselves in the way they spend their money outside the house. They go to the market and buy meat for themselves and then come home to complain that the family meal is not good. The implication here is that rather than staying home to cook, the wife has been out on the town, behaving like a prostitute (*gawlaŋ*). The wife resents this suspicion on the part of her husband, his waste of the family savings on expensive market meat for himself adding insult to injury. She retorts, "Your mother is a prostitute!"

For both men and women, sexual misconduct—in the idiom of prostitution (*gawlaŋ*)—was a key term of the debate in which conceptions of modernity were implicated. To be modern was strongly associated in these songs with being sexually promiscuous, though of course not all allegations of sexual misconduct were leveled at individuals claiming a "modern" identity. Far from being victimized by this discourse of female lascivious, women appropriated the terms of the debate and leveled allegations of "prostitution" at men, their mothers, and even their fellow co-wives. In their lɛɛlɛ, women spoke back to men in the public arena of song.

TRUTH, LIES, AND THE HEGEMONY OF SONG

In this final section, we explore more generally how value was constructed in Tupuri song. The composition of a *waywa* song is artful in its mixture of truth and lies. Key incidents or truths about a person's life are selected and reified and then embellished with falsehoods that touch upon widely accepted taboos in Tupuri society, such as incest, bestiality, or the practice of witchcraft. However, for dancers and spectators of the dance, to distinguish between what is truth and what is a lie in the song is beside the point. Rather, the purpose is for listeners to delight in the song, taking note of its sting. They know full well that the details of the lyrics may very well be lies, perhaps lies concocted to settle a personal score. However, as with a witchcraft accusation, the maligned person is always and unquestionably in the wrong. In this sphere of public accusation and spectacle, there is no question of various "sides" to the incident or the notion the allegation might be unfounded. By the very fact of the song's having come out, the accused is guilty of wrongdoing. Whether or not Maïtené actually cut meat from the dead horse or had sex in her mother's kitchen (and she said she did not), spectators assumed that she had failed to handle her personal affairs correctly. Otherwise, why would she be in the position of being sung? This circularity—recognition of culpability indexed by the song itself—brings us back to the much more complex question of the efficacy of song as social control. Can song and dance actually produce social constraints on a large scale?

During my interview with Maïtené, she intimated that she had made changes in her life such as her marriage not just because she was the butt of the *waywa* and *lɛɛlɛ* songs but because of everyday gossip as well. In her own words, "It's better to get married because when you are at the house and you refuse to get married, everyone is angry at you. Everyone says anything against you, when it's not like that."

Maïtené's dilemma raises the question of the relationships among discourse, social construction of moral order, and individual practice. The structural-functionalist paradigm of anthropology emphasizes a more or less direct causal relationship between ritual and social organization, arguing that social relations are constituted through the enactment of a shared, consensual view of the "normal" encoded in ritual practice. Sometimes this enactment involves a temporary reversal of the normal, though to the same effect. However, in spite of Maïtené's apparent capitulation to social pressure, to take this view would mean underestimating the power the women's *lɛɛlɛ* songs have in qualifying Maïtené's vilification. Rather than merely objectifying her as a naughty modern girl, they point out the potentially protective aspects of the married status and the dangers of modernity for girls when and if it was nothing more than prostitution. While "being sung" certainly had an effect on Maïtené, and possibly on other young women aspiring "to be modern," the dialogic context in which song is "broadcast" ensured that this social control was neither airtight nor uncontested.

The power of the Tupuri song tradition persists because of its conventionalized strategy for moving private affairs into the public limelight for censure and commentary. As Nancy Fraser has shown in her analysis of the Anita Hill–Clarence Thomas hearings of 1991, the line drawn between publicity and privacy is politically wrought, inflected by assumptions about gender, and encoded in the very institutions that sponsor discourse in the public sphere (Fraser 1997). Although hearings in the U.S. Senate and the song in rural Tupuriland are strikingly different discursive settings, her argument about the power of making the private public is nonetheless applicable. The power of song to regulate public morality in Tupuri life has a hegemonic status, in the Gramscian sense. Song is a widely accepted way for individual private lives to be represented publicly as allegory.

However, given this hegemonic status, the power of song is qualified in two ways. First, it is a resource accessible to all, even those who have less authority such as women and youth: In their *lɛɛlɛ* song, women provided a different perspective on Maïtené's case than the masculinist *waywa*. Second, song can be occluded entirely. Self-described "moderns" have evaded the power of the song by eschewing it entirely. Evangelical Christians argue, often extremely fervently, that "traditional" (here, ancestral, non-Christian) dance is satanic. They see (non-Christian) dance as a slippery slope to greater sins, such as animal sacrifice. Furthermore, they argue that the song that accompanied dance, such as the *waywa*, is inherently divisive to society. In its place, they advocate the notion of Christian fellowship, although they retain the right to make moral judgment, albeit in Christian terms. Ironically, those who eschew song and dance as "divisive" often use the highly divisive categories of "saved" Christian versus "damned" pagan to buttress their evaluations.

Moral orders are represented within specific song genres and negotiated among them, even across those who claim to reject the public sphere of traditional song altogether. Scandal amplified by song has the effect of promoting certain sets of values while discrediting a targeted individual in an entertaining fashion. Although songs about Maïtené did not have the force of a judicial decision, they might have been even more powerful operating as they did in the slippery realm of public opinion.

THREE

"Better than Family, Better than Girls"

The Tupuri Gurna *Society*

I have always found the *gurna* dance magnificent. Approaching the dance ring, I would move with the other spectators streaming along the village paths, pulled by the magnetism of the booming drums in the distance. Their throbbing would strike me deep in the chest; I never failed to feel my heart leap at the communal excitement. At the height of the dry season, a cloud of tawny dust would hang overhead, kicked up by the hundreds of dancers' shuffling feet. Children would dangle on the branches of the few majestic trees to get a bird's-eye view. The pounding mass of dancers would circle the dance site tirelessly, the thunder of the drums, the dancers' low bellow of the song together producing a hypnotic effect.

If I had not experienced this *gurna* dance in rural Tupuriland, I would probably have overlooked the lightly assembled dancers of the Club Kwoïssa in Yaoundé. There in Cameroon's capital, a two-day journey to the south, Tupuri civil servants, security guards, and students gathered on Saturday afternoons to reproduce a version of the impressive ritual of their homeland. In the walled compound of the Club Kwoïssa, they constructed a representation of ethnic heritage to showcase to other Cameroonians during state ceremonies.

Similarly, if I had not seen *gurna* in the village, how would I had have known what university students were suggesting when they described the Club Djak Kao at the University of Yaoundé? Club Djak Kao was derived from the *jak-kawre*, the *gurna* society camps that dot the Tupuri region and provide the foundation of the *gurna* dance association. On the edge of their villages, members of the *gurna* would lounge languidly near their collective cattle corral, imbibing milky porridge, laughing together, and sharing the words of the *gurna* song. For Tupuri students in the competitive and individualist Francophone school system, the *jak-kaw* was a metonym of male solidarity (*barge*) and peace (*jam*) that they re-created in new ways through their club.

The Club Kwoïssa and the Club Djak Kao are two examples of the movement of cultural forms from a rural homeland to an urban setting, specifically to ethnicized self-help associations. Since the work introduced by the Manchester School (Gluckman 1963; Mitchell 1956), anthropologists have struggled to explain the relationship between the urban and rural in Africa, particularly the existence of "tribal" markers in modern urban contexts. According to Geschiere and Gugler (1998, 315), current discussion of urban-rural dynamics in Africa is framed neither as "either . . . or" nor as evaluations about whether rural connections have been "maintained or broken." Instead, the connection is "resilient, highly variable, with dynamics of its own, and not just dependent on personal choice" (ibid.). They and other analysts assert that political liberalization in Cameroon during the early 1990s has resulted in a greater importance for local, ethnically based forms of political organization (309). They go as far as to suggest that "democratisation seems to evoke an obsession with 'autochthony,' origin and belonging" (319). These "obsessions" have been mediated through cultural forms, such as homeland burials, elite associations, and chiefly titles. While I would note that the power of these "obsessions" varies by ethnic group and region, they do seem to serve to demarcate insiders and outsiders and shape the distribution of rights and resources.

Recent scholarship on Cameroon traces the relationship of national-level politics to ethnically defined bases, with attention given to the cultural forms that act as vehicles or markers of these political dynamics. For example, Geschiere shows how witchcraft operates as a "precarious balance between 'leveling' and 'accumulative' tendencies" in the modern Cameroonian political-economy and its attendant moral order (1997, 16). In this study, I am similarly interested in the movement of cultural forms across social levels. Here, the *gurna* is presented not as an archaic throwback or a remaining survival of precolonial times but as a rural, ethnically based form of social organization that has proved resilient and meaningful enough to be mobilized in extremely diverse settings, such as schools and urban neighborhoods. In my analysis, I eschew the notion that emergence of the *gurna* idiom in urban or modern institutional settings represents an unconscious enactment of a "traditional" mentality. Rather, Tupuri actors have strategically drawn upon and recreated the *gurna* outside of the Tupuri homeland in an effort to resolve new challenges they face in their émigré context.

These urban iterations of the *gurna* society are important, though the logic of fieldwork led me first to the *gurna* institution in rural Tupuriland. Although I do not intend to revive a notion of "village purity," I do find that the meaning structures of the *gurna* are firmly grounded in particular sets of practices operating most elaborately in the village, such as the establishment of camps, body fattening, and competitive song. This chapter describes how the *gurna* operates in rural Tupuriland—its ethos, practices, and functions in the broader Tupuri society. From there, it will then be possible to glimpse how Tupuri actors have transported the *gurna* to other settings, telescoping its practices and reshaping its functions.

The circulation of *gurna* song (*siŋ gurna*), the main thrust of this book, both arises from and is constituted by the institutional fabric of the *gurna* society. Institutions undergird oral discourses and the production of value in society. To understand how power is constituted in Tupuri society, it is vital to understand how *gurna* discourse—including but not limited to song—circulates within institutional structures, promoting in turn the legitimacy of its own discourse.

In writing about the Tupuri *gurna,* I seek to focus on its dynamism at three levels: its multifunctionality, its mutability, and its fluidity as a node of value created by competing social actors. By multifunctionality, I mean that the *gurna* defies simple categorization because it performs multiple functions within both homeland and émigré Tupuri society. Here I examine four aspects: the production of male solidarity, socialization of youth, courtship, and the spectacle of funerary dance. Its mutability refers to the many ways Tupuri people have uprooted the *gurna* from its rural home and brought it into new contexts such as urban cultural associations, state functions, and educational institutions. Responding to new social needs, practitioners have, in the process, pruned certain aspects of the ritual complex to fit new contexts. Finally, I seek to understand the *gurna* as it is represented in a fluid arena in which both insiders and outsiders compete to define the dominant terms of value in the society. That is, what is the value of membership in the *gurna* society today? What is the value of mastery of the *gurna* dance, discourse, and reputation? What are these relative to other competing value systems, such as Western-style schooling, civil service work, and Christian fellowship?

Origins of the *Gurna*

When asked why a certain cultural practice is maintained, anthropologists are commonly told, "Because our ancestors did it like that." So I wasn't surprised when Tupuri people said the same of the *gurna*. Nor was I surprised when they confidently proclaimed that "To be Tupuri is to do the *gurna*" and that "As long as there are Tupuri on the earth, there will be the *gurna*." What was surprising was that in the same breath, *gurna* members readily admitted that the *gurna* had been borrowed from the Massa, the neighboring ethnic group to the northeast.[1] It seemed paradoxical that the *gurna* could be trumpeted as quintessentially Tupuri yet also flagrantly borrowed from another ethnic group. But in these conversations about the origins of the *gurna*, this paradox was deftly resolved as "The Massa invented the *gurna*, but it was the Tupuri who perfected it."

As I discovered, the Tupuri relish the elaborations, such as the lengthy song genre (*siŋ gurna*), that buoy the dance and spur spirited competition among song composers. There is also the development of the *jak-kaw*, whose moral code and internal hierarchy was so distinct that analysts have called the *gurna* "a state within a state" (Seignobos 1995, 12) or a "counter-hegemony" (*contre-pouvoir*; Ruelland 1988, 16).[2] The foundation of these *gurna* camps is the symbolic act of collective herding, as each *gurna* member is required to bring a cow to his camp. In contrast to the intimacy of the *gurna* camps, the society also provides the public spectacle of dance at death celebrations. There, hundreds of *gurna* members gather to commemorate the deceased in a collective dance as expansive and energetic as resources allow.

Although Tupuri claim to have perfected the *gurna*, the Massa version, *guruna*, according to Dumas-Champion (1983), was elaborate as well, though in different ways. The Massa *guruna* involved four phases divided by the annual cycle, each varying in degree of proximity to the *farana* (base community) and purpose. In contrast to the Tupuri *gurna*, whose members primarily identify as dancers, Dumas-Champion locates the primary identity of the *guruna* in wrestling. Ritual wrestling was a metaphor for the competition of men for marriageable young women (10), and the collective herding of cattle in the *guruna* articulated to matrimonial exchange of cattle as bridewealth (122). Among the Massa, the *guru-fatna* phase (March through May), involved collective herding in a bush camp, much like the Tupuri *gurna*. However, the Massa organized strictly by agnatic kinship, while the Tupuri organized more loosely, across patrilines. Furthermore, the Massa *guruna* involved a phase of individual body fattening at the compound of a friend or relative (*guru-walla*) and a phase of gathering for collective fishing (*guru-sarana*; 120–152). The Tupuri practice neither of these phases in their *gurna*. The Massa *guruna* was organized around segmentary war alliances, while the Tupuri *gurna* is mobilized for the spectacle of large collective dance as part of funerary rites. Dumas-Champion does not report the song as significant for the Massa *guruna*. For the Tupuri, the *gurna* song is highly elaborated, both as a poetic form and as a social system of communication and affiliation.

Although the Tupuri made significant modifications to the Massa *guruna*, they retained many of the essential principles: the value of collective herding, the glorification of the milk-giving cow, and the fattening of the body for public display, especially for courtship. The Tupuri *gurna* is inflected with many aspects of Massa culture, and these are seen as prestigious. For example, Tupuri *gurna* members take on Massa sobriquets, and Massa phrases pepper Tupuri *gurna* song, though wordplay in French and Fulfulde is equally popular today.

I found that Tupuri *gurna* are proud of identifying "survivals" of Massa culture in their practice. However, they have their own explanations for the raison d'être of their *gurna*. Elders report that before the *gurna*, the Tupuri danced a song genre called the *maga* for funerals. It consisted of a circle dance performed to short, repetitive lyrics (much like the *waywa* of today). Gradually the *maga* gave way to the *gurna*, though even today sometimes *maga* is performed in the beginning of the *gurna* season if not enough dancers have mastered the new *gurna* song. Elders also point out that the *gurna* dance has its roots in the circumambulation of the compound of the deceased by mourners during a funeral. Even today, when a member of the family of the deceased arrives at a funeral, he is expected to make three swift jogs around the compound of the deceased before going to the gravesite. As for the value placed on commensal milk drinking, Noumnamo, a senior *gurna* song composer, pointed out that prior to the *gurna*, groups of friends might gather under a tree to share milk before heading off to a funeral. He stressed that this was the practice during the funerary rites (*huuli*), not the subsequent death celebration (*yii-huuli*), during which the *gurna* perform today.

Local discourses about the origin of the *gurna* also include an appreciation of the power of the *gurna* and the death celebration dances to bring together large numbers of people who would never have come into contact with each other otherwise. Elders in particular made this observation, recalling a time before the arrival of large weekly markets, public transportation, and schools—all of which regularly bring masses of Tupuri people together today (see figures 10 and 11). However, it is certainly not the case that the *gurna* was borrowed to fill a performance vacuum in Tupuriland. Rather, there were myriad song and dance forms, including the *maga-jaw* and the *jõo-ka'araŋ*, some of which have become archaic. Elders understand the *gurna* genre as having "muscled out" other dance forms because it was thought to be more aesthetically exciting. As they put it, each new generation chooses what is pleasing to them and allows the rest to pass from memory.

Elders also talked with levity about the practical dimensions of their performance practice. For example, several informants noted that in contrast to the markets of the recent past, the intense commercial activity of contemporary marketplaces has made the context of the death celebration more suitable for dance. "If the *gurna* were there [at the market], drinking milk, filled with joy, someone could leap out and be crushed by a truck! So for this reason, they stopped dancing in the marketplace." The Tupuri see themselves as active practitioners of the *gurna,* while the Massa, in their view, no longer practiced their *"gurna."*

FUNCTIONS AND FACETS

Friendship, Prestige, and Masculine Networks

"Friendship is better than family, better than a lover." (*"Barge daŋ kaw daŋ may ma naw."*)[3] This conventional phrase in *gurna* songs praises the solidarity created among men by the bond of the *gurna* society. Solidarity appears as well in names *gurna* members give to their cattle, such as Maïsewoïnla (lit. "surpasses the woman"). As an institution, the *gurna* expresses an ideal of male solidarity that cuts across clan identity. Tupuri society is structured by clan (*wɛrɛ*), which is significant for the purposes of marriage (i.e., maintaining exogamy), new year sacrifices, and land distribution. Villages in Tupuriland are usually composed of several clans; however, when the men of the village form a *gurna* society through the establishment of a *jak-kaw,* men of all clans came together in a bond of fictive fraternity.

Male friendship begins in childhood and develops in the context of herding. Any Tupuri male who grew up in the village can remember long hours herding his parents' goats, sheep, and cattle in the bush under the hot sun (see figure 12). As elementary schooling has increased, fewer boys spend their childhood years herding. Instead, they express the intensity of childhood friendship as having been *sur le banc ensemble* (on the school bench together). Still, many boys pass through an age when they herd before they are permitted to attend school. While herding, they pass their time together in the bush making slingshots, hunting birds, roasting their catches over tiny campfires, and ravishing peanut fields. Men might never discuss these childhood activities, but nonetheless they were formative of male consciousness. The solidarity that develops among the *gurna* members as they rest in their camps outside the village is reminiscent of this bonding among youth in the bush. In fact, the term for dancer (*we-jõo*) means "youth-dancer."

Beyond individual consciousness, the *gurna* functions as a metaphor for and the practice of solidarity at multiple levels—in the village as well as at the national level in terms of an ethnic symbol of the Tupuri people. The *gurna* dance and the practice of the camp evoke a romantic pastoralism even within a rural setting. The *gurna* represents "the good life," which is encoded in the term *"dulnya"*: a world in which there is overabundant food, peace among men, and overflowing joy expressed by the *gurna* in dance and song. It enacts a miniature "society within the society" that serves as an ideal model for the larger community.

The beginning of the Tupuri year is harvest time, October, when the sorghum ripens and farmers cut its heavy beaded heads from their stalks. At this time, the men of each village establish their own *gurna* society, which is linked informally to other village *gurna* societies. For the region surrounding Doukoula where the *few kage* (Festival of the Cock) was celebrated for the new year,[4] the organization of the *gurna* season begins at the huge *maylay* dance during these celebrations. Then, in each village, the *gurna* society installs itself with the permission of the village chiefs (*waŋ-wuu* and *waŋ-siri*) in a *jak-kaw* at the edge of the village. The term *"jak-kaw"* (lit. "mouth-family") evokes the fictive parentage of the *gurna.*

(figure 13 shows typical elements of a *gurna* camp: tethers for attaching cattle at night, drums, a raised shelf, and a shady tree under which the members rest.) The members elect a *gurna*-chief (*waŋ-gurna*). He is responsible for sacrificing a chicken for the health of the camp and for planting the *jak-jiŋ*, the fetish resembling a stake in the ground, to protect the camp. In this sense, the *gurna jak-kaw* mirrors a family household, where the patriarch plants a *jak-jiŋ* to protect his household and monitor his wives' behavior.

In addition to planting the *jak-jiŋ*, the camp is formed by the act of each male *gurna* member's bringing a lactating cow and her calf from home. Those who have none borrow from a friend. The cattle are tethered to sticks planted in neat rows within the camp and they remain part of the camp throughout the entire *gurna* season. Expressing a kinship or symbiosis with their animals, the *gurna* share this space with the cattle. They often mark off the entire camp by encircling it with a straw fence. Over the nine-month dry season when there is little agricultural work, the *gurna* members spend many hours there. They lounge under the shade of the tree and share camaraderie, meals, and milk drinking. They discuss village affairs among themselves and learn the annual *gurna* song they will perform at the death celebration dances.

Gurna membership is egalitarian (for men). A man cannot have a reputation for theft or causing conflict, but otherwise, all men over the age of 16 are admitted—with cow. During my stays in Tupuriland, I spent quite a bit of time considering whether the *gurna* should be understood primarily as a men's society. The scarce research literature on the *gurna* (Guillard 1965, 140–141) makes no mention of the participation of women. Admittedly, older women's roles in the *gurna* appear to be marginal. Married women, as well as youth, are forbidden from entering the *gurna* camp. Men always explained to me that women had to take care of the children and the house instead. Women's names do not appear in the *gurna* songs, except as the subjects of shameful acts that are recounted in the songs, as the objects of suitor's intentions, or as the mothers of great dancers. However, unmarried young women (*mayre*, pl.) *do* join the *gurna*, and the male *gurna* members insisted upon their importance in discussions with me. One senior *gurna* member explained: "When girls come to the *gurna*, it's for completing the group of *gurna*, not for sleeping with men. You can't just have men [in the *gurna*]; you must have girls too."

There is also the tradition of having a newlywed woman (*may-waare*) participate in the *gurna* for a year or so before she begins childbearing as a way of welcoming her to the village.[5] The requirements for participation of girls in the *gurna* society are not as onerous as for men. They perform on equal terms with the men during the death celebration dances, executing the same dance steps. But due to their age and gender, girls are not expected to contribute cattle to the society. Although they drink milk and spend time at the camp during the day, they do not spend the night there, and I did not observe them performing work tasks.

As with many ostensibly masculine performances and rituals in Africa, the supportive role of women is considered fundamental. This sense is encoded in the name one *gurna* gave his cow at the *jak-kaw* of Mogom, "Waïwãné," which meant "the wife ordered it." He explained that his wife had asked him to go join the *gurna*. Whether or not this was true, this is a sentiment that I heard often from men when I asked them what their wives thought of their membership in the *gurna*. They suggested that the women encouraged them to join, contrary to my (unvocalized) assumptions that the women would be disdainful of the *gurna*, would feel excluded. The *gurna* felt that the women were proud of their membership. They were aware that their participation rested on the support of their wives, because it was the women who would have to agree to prepare extra meals for the men to bring to the camp. If a wife refused this additional work, her husband would have a difficult time joining.

In Tupuriland, there is usually one camp per village. However, if the village is very spread out or if there has been a conflict in the *gurna* group, there might be more than one camp, each in a different quarter of the village. The *gurna* choose the site based on its proximity to a water source, either a hand-dug or modern well, so that the cattle can be easily watered. The site is usually on the edge of the village, out of sight of most of the family compounds.

Although the camps appear to be stable, they are in fact in a continuous state of flux. When I took surveys of the camps, I found that a village's camp might not have run that year or the year before or it might have started up but closed down halfway into the season. There were several reasons for this. First, a camp might not run if a member had died or one of the leaders, such as the *waŋ-gurna*, had lost a close (adult) family member. In these cases, the members were considered to be in mourning; the joyfulness of the dance, even though it occurred for death celebrations, was inappropriate. Camps also closed down abruptly during the dance season if such a death occurred. Also, the camp would not run if too many of the members were experiencing famine that year. Although *gurna* are careful to avoid saying that they waste food, it is recognized that one needs plenty of sorghum to participate in the *gurna*. Members told me that the greatest threat to the future of the *gurna* was not Christianity or modern attitudes but rather the lack of sorghum, which is ever more acute as soil fertility declines and the population grows.

In addition to time spent in the camp and the performance of *gurna* song and dance, the *gurna* identity is also constructed through naming. Each *gurna* takes a sobriquet that usually mirrors his physical appearance or personality. Most were in Massa, again indicative of the prestige status of the Massa language within the *gurna* world. For example, Tchagalna ("giraffe," Massa) is given to tall *gurna*, Derguelé to one who is robust and stocky, and Wedingué to the joker. These sobriquets are used among *gurna* and appear in praise and greetings in the *gurna* songs. The names members give the cattle they bring to the *gurna* are also significant. They are often in Massa and illustrate the close relationship between the *gurna* and their cows. Names of cows are often handed down from father to son or the name encodes the fact that the cow itself was handed down from the father and therefore was not borrowed for the use in the *gurna*. Such names include Louwaïna Baba (lit. "cow [Massa] of my father") and Senga ("the sacrifice cow of my father").[6] Just as names are used to indicate initiation status through specialized suffixes and thus bind all initiated men, *gurna* sobriquets both reflect and constitute the bonds among *gurna* members.

Aside from a sense of solidarity with other men and the prestige that comes with *gurna* membership, why did men join the *gurna*? Richard Laga, a young Tupuri *évolué* (age 25), described *gurna* participation in terms of forgetting one's individual worries and developing an interest in the realm of village affairs:

> When you're in the *gurna*, you have a better idea of what's happening in the village. He who does the *gurna* is often stimulated to dance, to play games.

In contrast, the other who isn't in the *gurna*, he is interested in his personal life, in the life of his family. . . .

They say that at certain times, the *gurna* forgets almost everything. When you're in the *gurna*, you dance, you drink [milk], you forget almost everything. . . . In contrast, the one who is "there," who doesn't go to the *gurna*, who stays in the house, the little problems of life bother him. . . . He is involved in his personal problems: what's going to happen in the future, what he will do for his children. The *gurna* thinks that he's already provided grain for his children, so that's enough.

According to Laga, *gurna* membership involves a pulling away from the domestic compound (*tiŋ*) and one's immediate family (*kaw*) and reattaching oneself to a broader community through the *gurna*. Because of the discussion that goes on in the *jak-kaw* and its role in socialization of youth, the *gurna* takes as its subjective realm all the concerns of the village. (This subjectivity seems to contrast with Dumas-Champion's characterization of the Massa *guruna* as a manifestation of the collective interest of agnatic kin groups in protecting its collateral wealth, its cattle.) In my discussions with members, the value of the *gurna* as both a symbol of and a vehicle for producing satisfaction arose frequently. I often heard phrases such as: "When there is grain, when there is milk, then we dance. There is peace [*jam*]." By contrast, the *faŋdi* (non-*gurna*, Massa borrow word), or "those who stay home," were thought to be embroiled in their personal problems and tended to be "out of the loop" of village-level news. There was also the urge to join the *gurna* even when there wasn't enough sorghum because the very act of performing the *gurna* produced the subjective experience of prosperity and ease that Laga called "forgetting."

However, young people, such as Laga, often note the contrast between the interests of the *gurna* and those of educated youth. The discursive world of the *gurna* is understood to powerfully constitute their world. Oriented to the issues of the village, the *gurna* ignores information about the world outside, some of which could have been critical to youth (either members or nonmembers) who aspire to succeed in the modern sector. Laga explained:

In the *gurna*, they talk about what is happening in the activities of the village. They talk little of what is happening outside the village; they aren't interested. If there is, for example, a change of leadership in a country, they say that it's not their problem. In contrast, the youth who have a good level of education, they are more interested in what happens outside of Tupuriland. . . . For example, if there is a military recruitment, he [the *gurna*] will say it's not their problem. But the youth who are there, they're interested.

Although there is no technical reason why youth with so-called modern aspirations (salaried work and/or Christian faith) could not also join the *gurna*, they tend to eschew membership because it involves immersion in a world they are trying to escape; that is, the world of village-level affairs. Instead, young people such as Richard Laga tend to try to move to the city or, if they remain in Tupuriland, to immerse themselves in Christian churches and networks of "Christian fellowship." Everyone seemed to agree that the *gurna* was a world unto itself, a place where you "could blow into your flute, and everything is fine." However, Tupuri *évolué* tend to feel restless with this collective sense of satisfaction, having been primed by the school system to demand other forms of prestige and ease.

Socialization, Discipline, and Retreat

The solidarity of the *gurna* network is built through diverse socialization processes: systems of moral discipline, internal rank and order, and sexual initiation within the *gurna* society. As a form of retreat or *cure de lait* (French), the *gurna* also develops the body through ritual fattening. Finally, the learning of the annual *gurna* song was a third major area of socialization.

The *gurna* can be understood as a bush school; that is, a site of learning, moral instruction, and socialization apart from and predating Western-style schools in the region. However, the *gurna* is not the Tupuri youth initiation per se. The Tupuri initiation ritual, *gɔɔni*, was borrowed from the Massa and was held every nine or so years in Chad until 1975, when it was outlawed for Cameroonians. Nonetheless, the *gurna* built on the age-sets created by this initiation and played a vital educative role, complementary to the *gɔɔni*. Socialization in the *gurna* revolves around a code of moral behavior and development of the body and voice for song and dance performance. More informally, the *gurna* also socializes men and women into the affairs of village society and history through daily talk and sharing of news.

The *gurna* of which I have spoken so far involves the participation of adults: age 16 and older for men and age 13 until marriage for women. It is correctly termed *gurna-day*, or *gurna* of the cow. Playing off the central metaphor of the cow for the *gurna*, a separate grouping exists for children aged 6 to 15: the *gurna-fiiri*, or *gurna* of the goats. Although the children do not actually bring goats to their camp, they reproduce all the major elements of the adult *gurna* in miniature, practicing them alongside the adults. Their camp, a smaller enclosure near the *gurna-day* camp, is entirely initiated and run by boys with the support of the men. *Gurna-fiiri* compose their own *gurna* song, have their own drums, and wear dance costumes that mimic those of the adults. (See figure 14; note how some of the *gurna-fiiri* performing at a death celebration have smeared numbers in clay on their backs like those on the backs of the shirts of soccer players.) One *gurna-fiiri* composer, Houyang of Konkoron village, emphasized in his song of 1998/1999 the importance of the boys separating from their mothers and coming out to join the *gurna*.

Ndi da' wel po suwah war caw na ga yuri kig se we kiŋ lay,
Wo-sɛ hay men mo gɔ jɛŋ man ɓɔ je'e la? (K., 98/99, v. 10)

I found a certain boy crying that a carp was stuck in his throat,
Who told you to go near your mother?

At death celebration dances, the *gurna-fiiri* form their own dance ring near the adults, reproducing the major organizing principles of the *gurna* dance (such as the song leader, the accompaniment of drums, and circumambulatory dancing).

If there is a conflict of interest between the *gurna* and the Western-style schools, it is particularly felt at the level of the *gurna-fiiri*. Elementary school attendance has replaced the *gurna-fiiri* for the majority of boys. However, in 1992, when elementary school teachers went on strike during the democratization movement, adults in Doukoula sought to revive the *gurna-fiiri* for their children.

When boys approach young adulthood, at approximately age 16, they make the transition from the *gurna-fiiri* to the *gurna-day*. Within the *gurna-day*, boys undergo sexual initiation, termed *nage-may* (lit. "to spend the night with a girl").

Older *gurna* members plan for the younger to undergo the *nage-may* by arranging for him to spend the night with a woman. In the past, this would have been a young woman who was eligible to be sent out (ɓɔ'*ge may ti naw*) by her parents in exchange for a gift of goats. By the late 1990s, prostitutes were sought, since parents were eschewing the ɓɔ'*ge may ti naw* ritual for their daughters. In the morning, the *gurna* announces the *nage-may* to the village by beating drums and challenging the young man to a wrestling match (*gumu*) to test his strength after his having "worked" all night. From this day hence, the young man wears red kaolin (*guway*) in round patches on his torso and upper arms during the dance to indicate his maturity. His rank vis-à-vis all the other *gurna* is determined from the date of his *nage-may*. For the purposes of age status, seniority is determined from the *nage-may*, not the birth date. Men undergoing their *nage-may* are not necessarily virgins, but these prior sexual experiences do not count because they have not been formally announced to the village. Today, young men who pursue school rather than the *gurna* tend to avoid the *nage-may*, discounting its importance.

Although the *gurna* is equated with the expression of joy and the good life, it is not seen as carnivalesque in the sense of involving reckless abandon to desire. Rather, the *gurna* presupposes strict moral discipline. Upon entering the society, members agree to adhere to certain rules. The two most important are to maintain peaceful relations with all the other members and to avoid alcohol consumption. A high premium is placed on harmony in the camp, so aggressive behavior, such as fighting, theft, and the practice of witchcraft, is punished by expelling the offending *gurna* member from the camp. When this happens, the camp beats the drums to announce the expulsion to the entire village, although such cases are rare.

Alcohol is forbidden, not only because intoxication can lead to quarreling but because it is seen as counterproductive to the fattened body sought by *gurna* through their milk drinking. As I will discuss in chapter 4, alcohol and milk are posited as oppositional. In the course of my fieldwork, I observed that the *gurna* did drink sorghum beer (*yii*), though never in the camp, and attended the local markets together to drink. Even if the *gurna* could not reverse the tide of alcohol consumption that was gripping Tupuri society, it nonetheless acted as a voice against excessive drinking.

Although the spirit of the *gurna* is strongly egalitarian, discipline is maintained in the camps through both formal and informal forms of hierarchy. Informally, younger members, as ranked by their *nage-may*, are expected to obey orders from their elders. Work is assigned according to age; the least desirable jobs go to the younger or to *gurna* who are being punished for an infraction of the rules. For example, the youngest haul water from the wells for the cattle, herd, and carry the drums to the dances. Middle-aged *gurna* do such tasks as hand-mixing the sorghum porridge. The elders relax, most often on mats in the shade. Discipline and work allocation by age-grades is of course the norm in most African societies, and the *gurna* serves as a microcosm of gerontocratic social organization.

More formally, each camp elects leaders: the *gurna* chief (*waŋ-gurna*), assistant chief (*gɔɔ-waŋ*), secretary (*secrètaire*, French, or *je yerge*, Tupuri), counselor (*conseiller*), and chief of girls (*wan-mayre*). These officers manage the work and resources of the camp, resolve conflicts, mete out punishments, and supervise the behavior of the members. In general, though, the camps are self-monitoring and democratic; the standards are maintained consensually by all the members.

When there are infractions, the offending *gurna* is required to compensate the group by paying a chicken. Through these fees, plus the collection of dried-sorghum couscous remains (*furum-hɔɔlɛ*), which are sold, the camp maintains a small fund. At the end of the season (June), they use this kitty to feast.

In addition to the maintenance of order and harmony within the camps, the *gurna* pursue another form of discipline that undergirds the prestige of the society: body fattening. One of the major raisons d'être of the *gurna* is its role as a restorative retreat. Taking place after the harvest of foodstuffs (sorghum, corn, cowpeas, and peanuts), the *gurna* is an opportunity to restore the body after the hard work and annual famine of the agricultural season, from June through September. Each year, the previous year's food supply is depleted just at the moment when people need to eat more in order to exert themselves to plant anew. Due to the low-fat diet and extremely strenuous farm work, keeping weight on the body is a constant concern for rural Tupuri. The *gurna* is designed in part to address this seasonal nutritional pendulum by providing a season and a context for intentionally replenishing the body weight.[7]

This value on the fattened body—a swelling belly and full buttocks—is celebrated in the *gurna* dance as an aesthetic ideal. The large, fattened body "presents well" for the dance. To this end, the *gurna* eat as much as possible in the camp, meals of leaf sauce and sorghum couscous[8] and a special milky porridge that they mix themselves from additional couscous, water, and milk from the camp's herd (see figure 15)—hence the importance of cattle for the *gurna* as a source of milk. Milk, which is never consumed in the village, takes on a ritual value among the *gurna*. *Gurna* songs, cattle names, praises, and exhortations are replete with references to milk drinkers (*gurna*) and cattle that produce copious milk.

Courtship

Much dance around the world is related to courtship. In the *gurna* society, both aesthetic and moral aspects of courtship are important. Participation in the *gurna* dance is considered a critical life phase for girls: through the dance, young women present themselves to the community as eligible for marriage. Through a pleasing display of the body—rhythmic dance steps, stamina, a cool nonchalant attitude, and the ability to follow the male lead dancers—girls establish themselves as desirable for marriage. The relative "nudity" (as it is known locally) of the dance costume makes this bodily display even more compelling. In the 1980s and 1990s, girls wore short, tightly wrapped loincloths while men sported white shorts and a variety of body decorations. Although both men and women are equally interested in their personal self-displays during the dance, it was widely assumed that they had different intentions. Girls are assumed to be most interested in attracting suitors who will attempt to contact them after the dance. Although men too seek the admiration of women and ultimately marriage partners, they are also preening to establish their reputations as superior dancers among the other *gurna*.

In many dance genres, such as Western popular dance, women and men dance together as an expression of their romantic intentions for one another. The *gurna* is not so direct. To an outsider, the *gurna* dance may appear as a free-for-all, but, in fact, men and women take care within the mass of dancers to dance only with their camps. That is, they move forward single file in a line formed by members of their camp, organized from tallest to shortest, alternating male and female. Flirtations occur during the dance, such as when a girl follows a male dancer who peels off from the main dance line. However, the courtship aspect of the dance is often not played out directly between dancers but between the dancers and the spectators. While the *communitas* generated by the dance involves the kinesthetic experience of dancing together, Tupuri people tend to describe the dance, especially its courtship aspects, in terms of visual display and admiration. Men are expected to view young women at the dance and devise plans to talk later. Women form opinions about suitors based in part on their dancing skill.

The *gurna* society plays a major role in regulating courtship, particularly in mediating speech between men and women. However, this role has been weakened with the rise of weekly markets and schools where young men and women have free and unfettered access to one another. Still, male access to the girls who joined the *gurna*—and I found between three and six per camp—is mediated by the *waŋ-mayre*, the "chief of girls." If a potential suitor wants to speak to a girl (*ndalge-may*), he is required to get permission first from the *waŋ-mayre*, who is also responsible to monitor the girls' return to their family compounds after the death celebration dances. By the time the dance has ended and the copious sorghum beer brewed for the celebration has been drunk, the sun has begun to set. Still, hundreds of visitors linger. These evening hours are considered to be awash in lascivious behavior. Although Tupuri society places no particular moral value on female virginity (except recently among some Christians), girls are closely supervised within the *gurna* society because their parents want to control their sexual liaisons.

In addition to presenting themselves publicly in the dance as eligible for marriage, girls are encouraged to join the *gurna* in order to benefit from the socialization that occurs in the camp itself, particularly learning to talk correctly to men. Although the girls I observed in the camps were very quiet, as was considered fitting for them, their exposure to men outside their immediate household doubtlessly reduces their shyness. It is not forbidden for girls to marry men within their own *gurna* camp, but they tend to marry outside; their fellow members are seen as brothers.

Dance and the Spectacle of the Death Celebration

The most salient raison d'être of the *gurna* society is to provide an outlet for the love of dance in individuals and a magnificent spectacle of dance to commemorate the deceased. I have taken care to join these two functions—love of dance and mortuary practice—because in Tupuriland they are accepted as coterminous. After the necessary mourning, the occasion of a death is seen as an opportunity to get up and dance, to display one's body, dancing ability, and vitality (see figure 16).

When a death occurs in Tupuriland, mourning and burial take place over a three- to five-day period at the compound of the deceased. (Both death and the funerary rituals are termed *huuli*.) Usually hundreds of visitors attend, traveling long distances on foot and sleeping on mats each night in the deceased's compound. Lamenting, giving gifts, serving sorghum beer, and the burial itself occur at this time. The *gurna* do not appear. If there is dance, it is on a small scale and is not presented as a spectacle. Women spontaneously break out of their ritual mourning to gather for their *lɛɛlɛ*, the bawdy song performed in a dance circle.

Dance is seen as an expressive extension of mourning, even though the topical nature of the songs is anything but funereal. (Many of the *lɛɛlɛ* concern adulterous relationships and sexual pleasure.) If the deceased was initiated, older men chase the uninitiated away and dance the *maga-jaw* on the grave, using the secret initiation language, *jak-gɔɔni*. Dance and mourning often occur directly on top of the grave with the mourners rolling over the freshly mounded soil.

In contrast to grief of the *huuli*, the *yii-huuli* is festive and joyful, occurring months or even years after the death. Organized by the family of the deceased once the considerable financial requirement has been amassed, the *yii-huuli* commemorates the life of the deceased, provided that he or she died in old age. The death of children is never marked by a *yii-huuli*, as such a death is considered tragic. In the broadest view, the *yii-huuli* is the occasion that sends the deceased's soul out of the land of the living. Until this point in time—which is marked by the ritual pulling down of the deceased's house—the soul is understood to be still present in the family compound. It might even require daily food and could potentially cause mischief. The *yii-huuli* serves to release this soul to join the souls of the other ancestors in the sacred wood (*jak-siri*) at the edge of the village.

The dance of the *gurna* society provides the focal spectacle of the *yii-huuli*. Its enormity and vigor is a display of the community's respect for the deceased as well as the "loud noise" necessary to chase the deceased's soul away. Even though the *gurna* dance is performed ostensibly for the death celebration, the Tupuri with whom I spoke did not link the *gurna* to the mystical aspects of death, such as ritual purification, propitiation, or danger. Rather, people preferred to conceive of the *gurna* dance as reflective of a simple love of the dance, a human vitality that was associated with youthfulness, no matter what the age of the dancer.[9] There is a widespread appreciation that many people feel a passion or have a taste for the dance that must be expressed. This sentiment was explained to me by a longtime friend, a middle-aged Tupuri woman who was a devout Catholic and successful trader. She admitted to being personally uninterested in the dance. However, when she saw my line of research, she exclaimed, knowingly, "Yes, the Tupuri love the dance so much!" Suddenly enthusiastic, she went on to describe how her sister went to every dance, delighting in wearing a live chameleon around her wrist. (A chameleon was an attention-grabbing adornment, since many believed them to be magical and dangerous.) Dance is popularly conceived as the vital center of Tupuri society, expressed through the youthful enthusiasm of those who love the dance.

One renowned *gurna* song composer explained that the love of the *gurna* dance surpasses mortuary obligations: "It's not death that has maintained the *gurna*. Instead it's the desire to dance. In the past, one danced during the market, even without death." I was told that the *gurna* could be heard chanting "May an old woman die!" ("*Da ga wãay kulu mo huu!*") They egged on death so they might dance and show off their prowess. The awesome, unforgettable spectacle of the *gurna* dance seemed to throw out a life-affirming challenge to death.

How are the *gurna* mobilized for the *yii-huuli*? Planning a death celebration is a complex affair involving the entire family. There are meetings among the sons and uncles of the deceased to coordinate the various elements: the date of the event; gravesite sacrifices; gift-giving, including a class of gifts from the sons and sons-in-law to the brothers of the deceased (called *faray*); and the provision of food and drink to the guests and the *gurna* dancers. In cases where elites and officials are to be invited, a tent and chairs have to be provided as well as appropriate liquors. In rural areas, the entire village is involved in receiving visitors. Attendance is open to the public, but key members of the extended family are expected to attend and thus must be fêted properly. Easily 400 20-gallon jugs (*daŋ*) of *yii* are brewed by the village women for the event. As I was told even by a teetotaling Pentecostal, "The distribution of *yii* is not haphazard." Each guest receives a *daŋ* whose size is in proportion to his/her status and in recognition of gifts given (either in cash or goats).

The *gurna* dancers are summoned to the *yii-huuli* in advance. The night before, a call is put out by talking drum, traveling dozens of miles, village to village. On the morning of the death celebration, the *gurna* gather at their camps; they don their costumes, eat together, and warm up to the song and dance with the drummers (see figure 17). Then they move together as a camp toward the village hosting the death celebration, stopping to visit friendly camps along the way. Many travel by bicycle; at the dance site, bicycles are lined up by the dozens, one against another, like dominoes.

At the compound of the deceased, the host family provides a cow as a gift to the mass of *gurna* who have assembled for the dance. In the past, a ritual slaughter of the cow, called *pawge-day* (lit. "hack-to-pieces cow"), was intended to display the machismo of the *gurna*. The cow was given alive to the *gurna*, who butchered it still standing, blood flowing everywhere. By the late 1990s, the gift of the cow was still made, but the *pawgue-day* was abolished as too dangerous and *"sauvage."* Some pointed to this change as proof that the *gurna* had been modernized.

In mid-afternoon, when the sun is slightly less hot, the *gurna* dance begins. A large area on the edge of the village is demarcated with a thin string to restrain the spectators from crowding in on the dance circle. The dance begins with groups of *gurna* from the various villages shuffling in formation around a large ring (*maŋge jōo*) to the beat of wooden drums. Gradually, the other dancers join in and the dance ring becomes a thick pulsating mass created by dozens of strings of dancers following one another single file. Each camp dances in line formation ("arranged," *cirgi*), alternating men and women. As the mass of dancers moves around the ring, individual or small groups of dancers play off against this backdrop. For example, while doing the *laage ɓurgi* ("throwing up dust") movement, a dancer might peel off from the dance line and shuffle counterclockwise back to a friend behind him. He might stomp his foot in front of his friend, who will then accompany him back to his place in line before returning to his original place. In the *ɓɔ'ge fɔgɛ* movement (to be discussed in detail in the next chapter), a dancer will suddenly burst out of line to confront the crowd of spectators with an insulting challenge meant to amuse.

In the wide view, the dance is organized in concentric circles (see diagram 1). The center of the dance ring is always clear of dancers, like the eye of a storm. The song leader (*entonneur*, French; no Tupuri term) is positioned at one end of this center. He paces the *gurna* song and sets the pitch and rhythm by bellowing out a low moan between each of the verses. The dancers sing the verses in unison, taking a momentary breath during these breaks provided by the song leader. The effect of the song during the dance is of a low drone; individual lyrics are very difficult to comprehend. The song leader's role is "to hold up the song," to prevent it from collapsing into chaos. He is surrounded by a small ring of a ten or so dancers who transmit his pacing to the larger circle of dancers moving around them. This inner ring is called the *man-kɔm*, which literally means "senior wife," denoting one who directs the household. The drummers form another small ring within the clear center (see figure 18). The *gurna* drum is a massive wooden drum carved from a tree trunk, suspended from the neck and supported by the drummer's bent knee. At any given moment, there are five or six drummers. Drumming is an extremely strenuous activity. The drummers are physically powerful; sweat pours from faces as they play. Many spectators swear that the drummers use *saŋgu* (magical herbs) to sustain themselves. The drummers, song leader, and members of the *man-kɔm* are specialists in the song, but they are not professional; they are *gurna* from the various villages participating in the dance. Periodically, they switch off with those from other villages. To me, the switchover seemed nearly seamless, but I was told that conflicts occasionally occurred during this trading off. The entire mass of dancers is encircled by a thick ring of spectators who stand and gawk for hours in the sun.

Costuming is a vital element of the dance, an opportunity to display personal creativity within certain constraints. Both male and female dancers carry wooden throwing sticks (*garawre*; sing. *garaw*) in the right hand, held upright to counterbalance the forward diagonal tilt of the body. Tupuri people often identify the three-foot-long *garaw* as their traditional war weapon. Although the *gurna* is not understood as a warrior dance per se, its imagery—the use of the *garaw* and the movement of dancers in formations by villages—is metonymic of the vitality and collective unity associated with war. To counterbalance the *garaw* in the right hand, each dancer carries an object of their choice in the left hand for balance. The dancer's choice of item, such as a calabash, an old briefcase, a boom box, and so forth, is a way of showcasing coolness and creativity. Once a friend who attended a dance with me joined in on the dancing, nonchalantly usurping my videocamera bag for his left hand.

According to Tupuri aesthetic categories, *gurna* dancers, and in fact all dancers, rightfully perform "nude." To wear body decoration and certain costumes, as dancers did during my sojourn, does not preclude this "nudity." Although the category of nudity might have been stable over time, the actual forms of body decoration and costuming have changed as prevailing conventions about bodily propriety have shifted with historical conditions. In Tupuriland it was commonly said that "our ancestors were naked." However, prior to the 1970s, women, including female dancers, wore pubic aprons (*cache-sexe*, French; *sukway*, Tupuri). (Figure 19 shows female dancers circa 1956, and figure 11 shows women in the market during the same era.) The contrast between the dance costumes and everyday dress was much less stark then than it is today. Male dancers wore goatskin loincloths (*faage*, Tupuri), plant-fiber ornaments, and occasionally shorts (see figure 20). In the 1970s, cloth clothing was forcibly introduced by the Muslim Fulbe-dominated Ahidjo regime; women were fined if they came to market without blouses. In addition, Christian missions and wider exposure to the outside world probably influenced the shift to cloth clothing. In the 1980s and 1990s, *gurna* dancers wore costumes that simulated nudity. Men wore white shorts, kneesocks, shoes, and hats of their choice. Their chests were festooned with woven plant-fiber ornaments (*togo*) and were smeared with white clay (*puuli*). Women wore loincloths fashioned from striped dishtowels, over which they tied a beaded pubic apron that rested on the buttocks. They wore black brassieres, kneesocks, and plastic shoes. For both men and women, the *gurna* costume was called "*torse nu*" (French, "nude torso") and was the main element of proper presentation for the dance.

56 Journey of Song

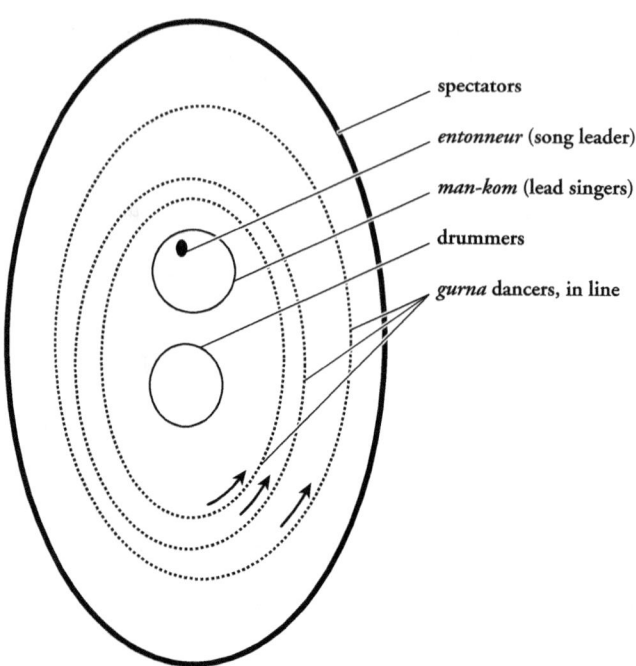

Diagram 1. Schematic diagram of the *gurna* dance

Although not as flamboyant as the youthful *waywa* dancers, the *gurna* frequently invent serendipitous forms of body decoration, pieced together in bricolage fashion. I observed male dancers wearing military berets (with their insignias removed), strange bird beaks dangling from their hips, and hand-drawn pornographic images attached to their hats. Once I saw girls ingeniously using long wooden brushes obtained from the cotton-gin factory as their *garawre*. Status objects such as watches (working or not) and sunglasses are popular as well. *Gurna* dancers design their costumes in their camps and see them as an avenue for expressing individual cleverness, within the boundaries of convention.

All that has been touched on in this section—from the sound of the music and song to the dance steps and the costuming—represents the sensory and social experience that constitute the allure of the *gurna* dance. When Tupuri people speak of their passion for the dance, they refer to the excitement of being a participant in a spectacle. With the successful spectacle, there is the possibility for dancers to garner prestige, fame, and reputation.

DISCOURSES

Christian Critique of the *Gurna*

The meaning of the *gurna* cannot be captured by an objectivist study of its practices. Multiple meanings of the same cultural form are produced by the diverse factions of Tupuri society through their commentary, both discursive and practice based. The significance of the *gurna* in Tupuri society is renegotiated continuously. For the success of each death celebration, the *gurna* rely on the goodwill of spectators who choose to come out to witness the spectacle. And each family sponsoring a celebration acknowledges the power of the *gurna* through their gift of a cow to the dancers. Many of these "commentaries," especially those that are practice based, are unconscious. That is, inclusion of the *gurna* in funerary practice is viewed as commonsense or taken for granted. However, other commentaries are highly self-conscious and strategic. When evangelists preach against what they see as the satanic practices of the *gurna,* they cast doubt on its continuing importance in a gradually Christianizing society.

In 1997, I returned to Tupuriland to attempt to "overhear" a community's discourse about the *gurna* in all its diversity. To overhear is ideal, but anthropologists speed up that process through elicitation of certain topics. It was very easy to elicit conversation about the *gurna;* Tupuri people were almost always emotive about it. They would compliment me on studying a subject widely seen as central to Tupuri society. However, perhaps due to this central symbolic role, the *gurna* is also taken for granted. Its hegemonic status means that community discourse about it is not particularly vehement or even contestatory. Still, I found the *gurna* to be a prism through which many other metacultural commentaries (Urban 2001) on Tupuri society pass. These commentaries include critiques by Catholic missionaries and, more recently, by evangelical Protestants against many aspects of the *gurna*: animal sacrifice, dance, nudity, and body fattening, which they call food "wastage." There is also a subtle marginalization of the *gurna* by Tupuri elites and a subterranean critique by married women in the *lɛɛlɛ.* And finally, local intellectuals express nostalgia for what they see as lost or weakening elements of the institution—its educative role and power to keep political authorities in check.

Christian churches in Doukoula varied enormously, ranging from the well-equipped French Catholic church established in 1952 to the American Lutherans who came in the 1980s to the mushrooming Pentecostal movement of the 1990s. (Although no statistics are available for the number of Christian Tupuri, one clergyman estimated in the late 1980s that it might be 10 to 15 percent, though the proportion would be higher in small towns such as Doukoula. The proportion is almost certainly higher now.) Each of these churches approaches its mission in a unique fashion, taking different stances—and different stances over time—toward indigenous animist Tupuri beliefs and practices. However, it is possible to describe the range of arguments that Christians, both expatriate and Tupuri, have made about the *gurna.* These critiques cluster into two strands, one using Christian morality as a point of reference and the other using the ideal of modernist development.

Moral critique centers on animal sacrifice. Christians across the board take offense at the *jak-jiŋ* (proprietary fetish) that establishes the *jak-kaw* and is the object of sacrifice to activate its powers, claiming that the death of Jesus Christ obliterates the need for humans to sacrifice animals. Also, Christians believe that putting one's faith in magic (the *jak-jiŋ*) is a form of worshipping false gods, which is prohibited by the Ten Commandments. Pentecostalists, though not Catholics, forbid their adherents to attend dances (*gurna* or otherwise) because they feel that dances distract people from God, pulling them into lasciviousness and drink. One priest told me that the major problem of the *gurna* for Catholics was that after the *gurna* dance men and women sought illicit sexual liaisons. This is ironic in light of the fact that it is the *gurna* that is responsible for monitoring the behavior of girls in their camps and closely regulating even the speech of male suitors.

The other pole of critique concerns economic development of the region. The flashpoint was what Christians term "waste," though *gurna* themselves understand this as prosperity. The sharing of meals and milk-laced porridge by *gurna* in the camp is directed toward body fattening so that the dancers can "present well" at the dance. Christians tend to see the excessive consumption of food by a small group of men as leading to famine for all, especially women and children. They also deplore the brewing of *yii*. Even though *gurna* practices mitigate against beer drinking, massive quantities of beer are produced for the death celebrations at which the *gurna* perform and draw spectators. Some priests called the hours of leisure time *gurna* spend in the camp "laziness" that is counterproductive to the economic development of the society. However, every time I visited the camps, I saw *gurna* members doing small work tasks there, such as making rope, ironing clothes, mending shoes, and tending the calves. It is not clear what the men would be doing with their time outside the *gurna,* because the *gurna* season mostly coincides with the dead season for agriculture. Furthermore, the *gurna* gather in the camp in the late morning or afternoon, after the household and farming chores are completed. In spite of Christian critiques of the *gurna,* many *gurna* members are Christian and see no contradiction in their participation in both traditions.

Some Tupuri Christians who are not *gurna* members have succeeded in detaching the *gurna* performance from the *yii-huuli.* Once I attended a death celebration by a prominent Catholic for his daughters who had died in adulthood. After a memorial service in the church, he hosted the town at his family compound with the full range of drink from whiskey to Coke to local sorghum beer. There was much excited greeting and conversation, as there would be at any *yii-huuli*; however, the *gurna* were not invited to perform. The dance component was entirely absent. However, at Christian funerals, the *gurna* song and dance was often replaced by a growing repertoire of Tupuri Christian song (*siŋ jak-Baa*). In this particular case, the host was a wealthy businessman who had made it big in the south, the leader of a devout Catholic family, so there was nothing untoward about the type of *yii-huuli* he organized. However, it is widely known that even if one is Christian, the funerary rites that one organizes for one's parents should be according to the *parents'*—not one's own—religious affiliation. A devout Christian might find himself organizing a *yii-huuli* replete with propitiary animal sacrifice and the *gurna* dance performance for his animist parent, even if he himself eschews these "traditional" practices. The bedrock gerontocratic orientation of the society is not questioned, even if Christian options are becoming increasingly popular for individuals fashioning their own lives.

Women's Critique of *Gurna*

In addition to critique and modification of the *gurna* brought by Christians, there were other forms of critique outside of Christian institutions. Earlier, I described that even though the *gurna* was doubtlessly a masculinist practice, it was nonetheless ostensibly supported and, some would say, encouraged by women. Young women, particularly those out of school, participate in small numbers. However, do married women ever complain about an organization that excludes them and takes an extra portion of the family's food resources? Although I never heard women spontaneously complain about the *gurna,* they did express themselves through the *lɛɛlɛ*, a genre produced and performed by women when they drink together during parties, funerals, and death celebrations. In some of their *lɛɛlɛ*, knowing full well that men were overhearing them, women criticized the power men invested in their *gurna*.

For example, this *lɛɛlɛ* excoriates fathers who make life hard on their daughters by exacting more and more bridewealth from their daughters' husbands. This song is from the point of view of the daughter's mother, whose voice is rarely considered in the negotiation and disbursement of bridewealth.

>Ndi wii Teosou fɛr Maïwalia ne war ɓɛ.
>Kɔŋnɛ laɓ ne.
>Ndɔ bo yonyon caw ga ndo gẽe ga.
>Ndɔ baa mbɛ day ti gurna.
>Hɔɔlɛ ma regen fãy bay dage wa sɔ. (1, 7)

>I ask Teosou to return Maïwalia to her husband.
>She's dying of hunger.
>You're crazy not to farm.
>You grab a cow to take to the *gurna*.
>And there's no more food to eat.

There is not enough food each year in the family of Teosou, a patriarch. His daughter, Maïwalia, has been married out, but her husband is slow in giving the cattle for her brideprice. So Teosou decides to repossess his daughter; that is, take her from her husband's compound. At her father's compound, since there is not enough food, Maïwalia is hungry and loses weight. Her mother thinks it is a disgrace to take the woman from her husband's home, where she would have eaten well, and make her live in her father's compound, where there is famine. To make matters worse, Teosou decides to participate in the *gurna* this year, which ties up a cow and requires extra food.

In this *lɛɛlɛ*, women refer to the unequal distribution of power in the family. Men manifest their control of both material resources and people by their management of cattle through the institutions of bridewealth and the *gurna*. In this view, the *gurna* is a public manifestation of the right of men to manage the wealth of the family, which consists largely of cattle (*hɔrɔgɛ*), and develop networks of solidarity among themselves. Women are outside the decision-making process, though the mother-in-law receives goats (*faage-fiiri*) as part of her daughter's bridewealth.

Such asymmetry of power by gender, encoded in the circulation of cattle, has been well documented by Africanist anthropologists (Evans-Pritchard 1940). Hutchinson (1996) and Comaroff (1985) have explored contemporary shifts in bridewealth practices, such as commodification of cattle. Despite the recent changes in Tupuri marriage practices, especially the greater likelihood that girls will refuse marriage and the decreasing ability of men to provide bridewealth, cattle in Tupuriland are still tied to the acquisition of wives and continue to be a significant symbol in the village *gurna*. There have been few changes in the requirement that a cow be provided to the camp in order to join the *gurna*. However, where the *gurna* has been transported to urban and institutional settings, collective herding of cattle has been entirely excised from the society in favor of cash contributions to the club treasury. These shifts, discussed below, took place as the *gurna* was transferred from the realm of a local elite to that of a national elite in a folkloric register.

GURNA OUTSIDE THE VILLAGE
Making the *Gurna* Elite

In their observations of Africans moving from rural homelands to urban areas to pursue salaried employment, anthropologists (particularly in Southern Africa) have tended to understand cultural expression as processes of "detribalization" and "retribalization."[10] In spite of the complexity of urbanization and ethnicity, a dichotomy between urban and rural identities often reemerges with a tacit association of the urban with the West and the rural with so-called traditional Africa. In an attempt to move out of such binaries, analysts have developed reconceptualizations that avoid this essentialism, such as the study of popular culture (Barber 1987, 1997) and cosmopolitanism (Ferguson 1999). Consideration of factors such as reruralization and media technology has brought more attention to the reciprocal feedback of cultural practice across urban and rural contexts. In my own research, I found that the *gurna* did not have just rural and urban versions; a larger process of "modernization"—or, to use the term I prefer, "making elite"— was at play both inside and outside Tupuriland.

Tupuriland is overwhelmingly rural, though today significant Tupuri enclaves exist in several cities outside of Tupuriland. The *gurna* described so far in this chapter pertains to its practice in Tupuri villages, where the rural context and subsistence agriculture have shaped every element of the society, from its valuation of cattle to its emphasis on long hours spent in the bush camp and even the disciplinary thrust of the *gurna* song genre. However, even *within* rural Tupuriland, there are several spin-offs of this village *gurna*, as I call it, efforts on the part of Tupuri people and the Cameroonian nation-state to negotiate one another. This negotiation involves an attempt on the part of the *commandement*, the centralized governmental structure of the state, to incorporate local cultural distinctiveness into its rituals of legitimacy (Barnes 1996). Its purpose is to make palatable its political authority over the region by co-opting local prestige institutions such as the *gurna*. On the other side, Tupuri people have collectively introduced their own versions of the *gurna* into modern state-run institutions such as schools and universities. In doing so, they have established a space for coded critique of these same institutions and a safe place for the practice of Tupuri brotherhood. This is inevitably tied up with a growing consciousness of ethnicity—the practice of ethnic solidarity as an enclave within a broader multiethnic community (that is, any Cameroonian city where Tupuris have migrated).

In this section, I briefly outline three zones where the *gurna* has been reconfigured by the elite in a process of folklorization. In the first, *gurna* in the Doukoula *canton* are commissioned to perform during state ceremonies. These celebrations are designed to legitimize the *commandement* structure. In the second, the *gurna* has been reconfigured by students as an extracurricular club, the Gurna Club, in the Doukoula lycée, where Tupuri students were the majority (Ignatowski 2004b). Finally, in the cities of Maroua and Yaoundé, far from the Tupuri homeland, Tupuri migrants have created urban cultural associations that showcase *gurna* dance for a broader audience. These members are equally concerned with transmitting Tupuri cultural heritage to youth who have grown up outside the homeland. These three iterations of the *gurna* idiom in new contexts point to a certain transportability and plasticity in the form as well as some degree of syncretism in the new sites.[11]

In Doukoula, the *chef-lieu* of the Kar Hay *arrondissement,* the *gurna* was recruited by the local, though centrally appointed, government to provide entertainment for state ceremonies. These included the federally mandated holidays of May 20th (Unification Day)[12] and the Festival of Youth/Fête de Jeunesse (February 11) as well as regularly occurring events, such as the installation of the new *sous-préfet* (district officer) and administrative visits (*tournées*) by governmental officials (see figure 21). For these events, the administration in Doukoula collaborated with local government (the mayor and the traditional chiefs) to put on a state ceremony with all the pomp and circumstance that a small town could muster. These events would take place at the stadium, a small concrete raised dais facing a yawning dusty arena, punctuated by a towering flagpole. Protocol was fiercely maintained by an appointed chief of protocol. Inevitably, these events would include parades by the schoolchildren of the region, clad in simple uniforms and organized by grade cohort, a highly choreographed *arrivée* of dignities by car and jeep, a lineup and greeting of local elites, and speech-making. The masses of citizen-spectators would line the arena, standing and straining to catch a glimpse of the proceedings.

The *gurna* would be called by the administration to provide opening and closing entertainment to these state ceremonies. After the citizens had assembled at the arena and before the state dignitaries arrived, the *gurna* would beat their drums to announce the opening of the entertainment. They would move en masse from the sidelines into the center of the arena, where they would perform the *gurna* dance for twenty minutes or so or until the chief of protocol made the sign to exit. After the ceremonies were completed—usually about two hours—the *gurna* would tie up the performance with another short dance. When the entire event was concluded, the dignitaries and elite would be invited for *un cocktail* at the residence of the *sous-préfet.* The chief of the *gurna* assemblage would receive "*une enveloppe*" containing a cash payment from the administration. It was the *gurna* camps in the immediate region of Doukoula that had contact with the administration and would receive invitations to dance at these state functions.

The second domain where the *gurna* made inroads into the modern state was in public high schools (*lycée*) and training institutions, such as ENIEG in Maroua. Schools with significant Tupuri student populations—both inside and outside rural Tupuriland—have had *gurna* clubs since at least the 1970s. In the lycée of Doukoula, the Gurna Club was a branch of the Theater Club and was treated administratively as an official extracurricular activity. However, it was created through the initiative of the lycée students, who saw the club as a space where they could express their cultural heritage, even though—or perhaps because— their attendance at the lycée precluded their participation in the village *gurna.* However, the institutional structure of the lycée and the daily exigencies in the lives of the students constrained the Gurna Club considerably. Even through the students elected a leadership board reflective of those of the village camps (*waŋ-gurna, waŋ-gɔɔ, waŋ-mayre,* etc.), the members had only one event at which to perform the *gurna* dance: the *soirée* (evening variety show) of the National Youth Day celebrations. At this time, the *lycéen-gurna* members, mostly male, donned their *gurna* costumes and presented a short 30-minute version of the *gurna* dance on stage in front of an audience of school administrators, teachers, town officials, and the wider public. They sang the *gurna* song composed by a *lycéen*-composer, a lycée student who hailed from the "dynasty" of *gurna* composers who composed for the village *gurna* system. Much shorter than the village *gurna* song, the lycée song was packed with both praise and critique of school employees, commentary on correct sexual behavior, exhortations to maintain the *gurna* tradition, and skepticism about the national education system.

Although the lycée Gurna Club did not perform at village death celebrations with the other *gurna*, students still valued the club as a site where they could express dissident or insubordinate views of the school faculty and represent the power of the *gurna* in the context of the school. They made an effort to pursue as many of the *gurna* practices as possible, such as drinking milk, fashioning leather *faage* for their costumes, and gathering to learn the songs. However, they also modified these practices. While in the village camps, the chief of girls (*waŋmayre*) was male, in the Doukoula Gurna Club, a female student was chosen to coordinate the few female members. The *lycéen* did not succeed in maintaining a camp because of the time constraints they were under as students. Although the Gurna Club depended on the initiative of the students themselves, they tended to transfer their expectations for the paternalistic role of the nation-state to the club. For example, Dangmoworé, a *lycéen-gurna* song composer from 1995 to 1999, expected the school administration to provide a small budget in order to conduct the ritual animal sacrifice to open the club. He also aspired to buy powdered milk for body fattening, since the student members did not own cattle. Some years the administration provided the equivalent of two dollars for these needs, but usually the students complained bitterly about the lack of administrative support.

The third area to which the village *gurna* system was transported is Tupuri urban cultural associations. These voluntary associations seek to valorize Tupuri identity and provide a mechanism for the maintenance of Tupuri solidarity in the multiethnic contexts of Cameroonian cities (such as Maroua, Garoua, and Yaoundé). Members of these associations always spoke to me about the importance of exposing their children who had grown up outside of Tupuriland to the fundamental aspects of Tupuri culture, which they defined primarily as the Tupuri language and dance. These urban associations take on a variety of organizational forms. For example, in the Far North provincial capital of Maroua, during the time of my fieldwork, the local Tupuri community created a cultural holiday by overlaying the Tupuri harvest celebration (*few kage*), with its Maaserew dance, onto the international January 1 holiday. So on New Year's Day, the Tupuri of the Maroua region united to dance the Maaserew in *gurna* style, even though no formal *gurna* institution was in place. Many of the dancers had been *gurna* in their villages before migrating to Maroua. A composer from the Maroua teacher-training college, Ringwa, had composed a short *gurna* song which he and others had attempted to disseminate to the dancers.

Ringwa and other Tupuri cultural leaders, such as the disc jockey of the Tupuri-language radio station, complained about the difficulty of organizing cultural events in the city. First, there is the problem of coordinating Tupuri in the different quarters of the city where they tend to reside in enclaves. These Tupuri quarters (such as Pont Vert, Pitoaré, and Paalar in Maroua) tend to function as competitive villages did in rural areas but without the mechanisms to coordinate them. In 1998, there was, for example, a great deal of misunderstanding and one-upmanship which made the celebration of the Maaserew New Year extremely difficult. The two dominant quarters could not agree in whose quarter the dance should be held, with other quarters weighing in on either side. Second, without the network of village-based *gurna* camps, the learning of the annual *gurna* song and socialization in the dance in the city is difficult. The song has to be learned in the local beer parlors (*ŋgel-yii*) without the benefit of the discipline imposed by the village-level *gurna* camps.

At the other end of the spectrum of these urban cultural associations, a highly organized dance troupe and cultural club, Club Kwoïssa, was established in the national capital of Yaoundé by a high-ranking Tupuri functionary (see figure 22). The club is composed of a variety of Tupuri men and women, some of whom are well educated and others who are unskilled salaried workers (usually security guards) in Yaoundé. Some had been *gurna* members in their villages in far-away Tupuriland, while others had spent their entire lives outside Tupuriland and self-consciously wanted to reconnect with their ethnic heritage. The club had an elaborate system of by-laws, leadership positions, and internal fund-raising mechanisms typical of voluntary associations throughout Cameroon. They were officially registered with the state, though not created by it. Because its leader was an official in the Ministry of Animal Husbandry and a skilled drummer, Club Kwoïssa is well positioned to be commissioned by the government to provide cultural entertainment at various state functions; it even travels abroad to do so. They have their own *gurna* song composed by a composer in Yaoundé; he uses the conventional song forms but draws his content from the Tupuri émigré community in Yaoundé. The club performs a reasonable version of the *gurna* dance in costumes that are modernized versions of the ancestral standard. Rather than wearing the white shorts that are de rigueur for contemporary rural *gurna*, club members had fashioned facsimiles of ancestral *faage* from burlap sacks while they waited for their order for "real" *faage* to be produced. They practice the dance on Sunday afternoons, drink sorghum beer together, and conduct monthly business meetings, though they maintain no *gurna* camp.

In the late 1990s, the vast majority of villages in rural Tupuriland had a *gurna* camp, even if the membership was less than a dozen men. At a fundamental level, the *gurna* appears to be threatened by forces of modernization. Children immerse themselves in school rather than the *gurna-fiiri*. Young people seek salaried work in cities or try out petty commerce rather than spend time with fellow farmers in the *jak-kaw*. Some Christians, regardless of occupation, turn away from ancestral traditions in a sincere effort to feel more Christian or to network more effectively with other Christians. However, if we take a less literal definition of the *gurna*—seeing it as a paradigm, symbol, or idiom—then it is evident that the *gurna* is not disappearing but is gradually being reconfigured in response to changing conditions. Although many village practitioners involve themselves in the *gurna* without the slightest interest in how outsiders see them,[13] to an increasing number of students, intellectuals, and civil servants, the *gurna* appears "ethnic" or "folkloric"; that is, representative of the uniqueness of the Tupuri people in the multiethnic Cameroon nation. To them, the *gurna* is a highly resonant symbol that represents the Tupuri at their best: unafraid, healthy, and unified. The values the *gurna* claim—bodily vigor, power in numbers, solidarity across clans, moral rectitude, and wealth in animals—are still meaningful for contemporary Tupuri of all classes. However, in demarcating these core values of Tupuri personhood, I do not mean to suggest that they find expression only in the *gurna* or that newer values or forms of prestige (such as formal education and military and civil careers) are not also embraced by Tupuri people. Rather, these values are touchstones that can be strategically recalled and enacted in the newer contexts of urban life, schools, and citizenship in the Cameroon nation.

FIGURE 1. *Gurna* dancers and spectators, 1998.

FIGURE 2. Tupuri family compound in village of Ndourndour just outside Doukoula. A raised granary is to the left of the house. A cross on the roof indicates that the family is Christian.

FIGURE 3. Young man dances the *waywa* in sunglasses and necktie. His costume includes a plastic sandal attached to his hips. Sirlawe, 1997.

FIGURE 4. *Didilna* orchestra, praise singers for community events. Doukoula.

FIGURE 5. *Waywa* dancers in proper dance posture, 1998.

FIGURE 6. Dust rises up from the *waywa* dance (*Maylay* festival) in the distance. Lara, November 1998.

FIGURE 7. *Waywa* dance. Lara, November 1998.

FIGURE 8. Tupuri girls (*mayre*) in the small town of Doukoula, July 1996.

FIGURE 9. Women at work in a family compound. In background, research assistant receives a gift of sorghum from his mother. Madalam, October 1998.

FIGURE 10. Weekly market (*lumo*) brings people together in Doukoula. Sorghum beer is sold in clay jars (center). September 1998.

FIGURE 11. Market in Datcheka, ca. 1957. Note that most women wore lip disks, a practice that is now obsolete, even though older women continued to wear them throughout the 1980s and 1990s. Photo: Joanny Guillard.

FIGURE 12. Boys responsible for herding their family's goats and sheep line up for a photo in front of brightly painted map of Cameroon at the Lycée de Doukoula. July 1996.

FIGURE 13. *Gurna* camp (*jak-kaw*) with cattle tethers. *Gurna* relax under the tree in the center of the camp. Mogom, January 1998.

FIGURE 14. Children *gurna* (*gurna-fiiri*) perform at death celebration. Bouzar, 1998.

FIGURE 15. In their camp, *gurna* add milk to sorghum meal to mix porridge for body fattening. Tuksu, February 1998.

FIGURE 16. *Gurna* dance at a death celebration (*yii-huuli*) in Baolang, February 1998.

FOUR

Defying the Modern

Play of Identities in Gurna *Dance Exhortation*
*(*Ɓɔ'ge Fɔgɛ*)*

A hefty dancer in white shorts with a broad chest smeared with white clay peeled off from the dance line and loped up to the crowd. Stopping abruptly a few feet from the inner layer of spectators, he jerked his body, straight-legged, into a menacing stance. His arms were frozen and he gazed, as if unimpressed, over the crowd, displaying his nonchalant coolness in the heat of the dance. Suddenly he exhorted, "*Hay yo man-day no! Tõo dik yaŋ ne wel po ɓil 'ansɔ!*" ("Hey ho, my cow! Watch out, you boys, or your urine will be blocked!") In a flash, he turned around and loped back, shuffling straight-legged, swinging effortlessly back to the place in the dance line from which he had emerged. Without missing a beat, he melted into the mass of dancers making their way around the ring. This was a *ɓɔ'ge fɔgɛ*, an improvised dance movement that occurs spontaneously during Tupuri dances. It is the focus of this chapter because it provides an avenue for exploring the relationships between performance, identity, and the production of value in Tupuri society.

In 1985 when I first attended Tupuri dances—both the lighthearted rainy-season dances (*waywa*) and the *gurna* dances organized for death celebrations—I habitually cowered behind the first line of spectators, apprehensive of the imposing dancers. In 1997 when I returned to Tupuriland with camcorder in hand and the project of filming and analyzing the dance, I was forced to confront the vague fear that lay behind my fascination with it. It was not that my filming was prohibited, since these dances were public functions open to all.[1] However, the camera and doubtlessly my outsider presence seemed to attract the menace of the dancers. Sometimes they would come up to me with a heavy stamp of the feet and stare me down. Other times they would call out something in Tupuri, usually a demand for money. Under the pressure to either learn quickly or give up my project, it dawned on me that the fear the dancers generated in the course of the dance, their intimidation of the spectators and their demands for gifts and recognition, were all part of the imaginary constructed by the dance. From then on, as I filmed, I was able to play subtly with the dancers. In spite of their menacing stances, I learned to congratulate them, display my own apprehension, and give them their due as the spectacle they were.

No longer fearing for my safety, I began to realize that the dancers were creating a unique discursive space through their performances of the ɓɔ'ge fɔgɛ, as unpredictable as these were. The ɓɔ'ge fɔgɛ, which means "to throw out a challenge," was an improvisational dance movement with antecedents in the performance aspects of wrestling. It was usually performed by a single male dancer who detached himself from the mass of dancers or by a segment of a line of dancers who are affiliated by village. Sometimes the movement was silent, the dancer creating drama through his deadpan performance of a blasé gesture like cigarette smoking. Or he might throw out an exhortation to the crowd before turning on his heel and dancing back to his place in the dance line. (Figure 23 shows a pair of dancers performing a ɓɔ'ge fɔgɛ.) These exhortations, although spontaneous, were drawn from a repertoire of conventional formulas, images, and sentiments associated with the values of the *gurna* society. With a humorous and playful tone, they extolled the vigor of *gurna* dancers and praised the members' cows, the symbolic foundation of the *gurna* camp. They also denigrated non-members (*faŋdi*). However, what was most interesting to me about the ɓɔ'ge fɔgɛ was their oblique assertions about Tupuri experiences of modernity. In my analysis, I saw them calling into question the value of the national modernization project for the Tupuri person by valorizing its opposite: the *gurna* society and lifeworld and the dignity of farming. They especially denigrated students and schooling and the effeteness assumed to characterize those who did not take up the hoe. These critiques, although evanescent, were important because they tied into broader dilemmas facing contemporary Tupuri society, such as alcoholism, the decline in soil fertility, and the devaluation of education. In fact, the dance context ritually gave the dancer the opportunity to discipline, chastise, and insult in ways that would be unacceptable in everyday society. Through the dance, systemic fault lines in the society were made visible.

This chapter focuses on the verbal art of the ɓɔ'ge fɔgɛ in order to illuminate the modality of dance as a site for critique of modern identities in the Tupuri lifeworld. To examine this, I explore three levels of interpretation. At the first level, the dance exhibits certain identities and categories that structure the broader society. The most fundamental of these is the distinction between *gurna* members and nonmembers (*faŋdi*). However, this conventional dialectical dichotomy is not static. Recently, through their ɓɔ'ge fɔgɛ, dancers have extended or modernized the *gurna*/*faŋdi* opposition to comment on newer class-based distinctions, such as that between the farmer and the civil servant or student.

Second, like many carnivalesque performances, the dance provides a space for ritual inversion. Some analysts have emphasized the homeostatic function of such rituals of inversion—that they allow a venting of jealousy over inequality or powerlessness without actually overthrowing the political-economic order (Gluckman 1963). I examine not the establishment of political regimes but the calibration of competing sets of moral value. The ritual inversion of the ɓɔ'ge fɔgɛ posited older, village-based valuations of health, socialization, and livelihood against newer, "modern" forms that were oriented to the Cameroon nation as a whole.

Finally, to counter the notion that the dance creates a simple dichotomy between modernity and tradition or local and national, I will comment on the indeterminate flexible relationship between social categories, dance performance, and identity. In this view, dancers may repudiate social categories to which they themselves belong outside of the dance. The dance permits a disassociation of personal identity and performance identity, so that social categories (i.e., the *gurna,* the civil servant, the student) can be represented, commented upon in words and gesture. The *bɔ'ge fɔgɛ* form was mobilized by dancers in different dance contexts. For example, on National Youth Day, students, often the butt of village-based *bɔ'ge fɔgɛ*, performed *gurna* identities as members of the lycée Gurna Club and used the form to critique their superiors, the school administrators.

Overall, my approach is to provide a fine-grained analysis of a specific dance movement and its attendant discursive patterns in order to shed light on cultural contestation occurring in the broader Tupuri society. However, this is impossible without reference to the larger field of political-economic conditions in Cameroon. Due to falling prices of export commodities beginning in 1986 and large-scale governmental mismanagement, Cameroon had been gripped by an economic depression for eleven years at the time of my research. This decline, which was as much moral as economic, was simply called *la crise* (the crisis). For two years running, Cameroon was internationally humiliated, cited as the most corrupt country in the world by the watchdog agency Transparency International (1998, 1999).[2] On the domestic front, the national government failed to offer civil service employment for school graduates and cut teachers' salaries in half. The result was a dramatic decline in the quality of the education system and a severing of the taken-for-granted connection between schooling and civil service jobs. It is this critical questioning of the value of education that lies behind the *bɔ'ge fɔgɛ*.

DYNAMICS OF SPACE, POWER, AND DISCIPLINE IN THE DANCE

Although most dance performance involves a distinction between dancer and spectator, it is the particular construction of that distinction that is important. In Tupuri dance,[3] the dancer is not a mere entertainer and the spectator is not merely a passive consumer or connoisseur. The relationship between spectators and dancers was playfully adversarial. "Stand back! You with your swollen head like that!"[4] a dancer exclaimed as he swung dangerously close to the mass of spectators. "Swollen head" referred insultingly to hair on the spectators' heads: The *gurna* shave their heads, which is metonymic of mourning practices[5] (see figure 24). The *bɔ'ge fɔgɛ* exaggerated the underlying dynamics of Tupuri dance—the playful antagonism between the dancers and the spectators and the right of the dancer to discipline the spectator.

A typical dance begins in the late afternoon when the heat of the day has diminished. Throughout the afternoon, the spectators are pulled by their fascination into the pulsating vortex of the dance. They encroach bit by bit onto the dance space, crowding forward eagerly to see who is dancing and how. "Brush your *guway* against them," shouts one dancer to another as they veer sideways to shear back part of the crowd. To the *gurna* dancer, the red kaolin is a proud emblem of sexual prowess, and is something that dirties or repels the spectators, since they have no right to wear it.

As the dancers move around the circle, they suddenly advance on the crowd. The spectators—children and adults, male and female—fall backward onto themselves, giving way in mock panic to the dancers. At the last moment the dancers swing around the circle, enveloping the new space stolen back from the spectators. As one *gurna* song proclaims: "We are going to provoke you with our dance.

When Guirling resounds loudly, if the spectators [faŋdi] don't flee, they'll be crushed to death."[6] Part of the play of the dance is this dynamic interaction.

The sweating energy of the dancers along with the throbbing of the drum in the center of the ring together create the centripetal momentum of the dance. The new evangelical churches in Tupuriland have forbidden their faithful to attend these dances, warning that they could be sucked into the dance and the ways of Satan. Although the churches give a distinctly evangelical spin to the meaning of the dance, their warnings seem to recognize the hypnotic power of the dance to pull the spectator in. Against the powerful backdrop of the dance, the ɓɔ'ge fɔgɛ is a foregrounding movement. Dancers perform it over and against the *gurna* or *waywa* song that is sung by the mass of dancers behind them. By necessity, their movements are brief and sharply delineated. They demand an excellent sense of rhythm because after lurching forward toward the crowd to perform his ɓɔ'ge fɔgɛ, the dancer must then reintegrate back into his line of dancers without missing a beat. Although on the surface these moves appear to expel the spectators from the dance, they are, in fact, intended to do the opposite. By ridiculing the *faŋdi* (nonmembers) and promoting the power of the *gurna*, the ɓɔ'ge fɔgɛ performers seek to entice new members to join.

Here is how one dancer, Taïwé, reflected on the spontaneity of the ɓɔ'ge fɔgɛ and the technique of pulling everyone into the dance through the persuasion of mockery. I had asked him whether he ever planned his ɓɔ'ge fɔgɛ in advance:

> No, they are completely spontaneous. When you feel content, you just express yourself, give your opinion.... You see your friend in the audience and you want to motivate him to dance, to egg him on. You make up the ɓɔ'ge fɔgɛ on the spot. It will be directed toward everyone in the vicinity, but you want your friend especially to be struck.

In addition to being a site of discipline, the dance is a collective expression of unity and numerousness, not according to a romantic image of *communitas* in the eye of the anthropologist but according to explicit ideologies voiced by Tupuris in everyday discourse and in song lyrics. Even though the gesture, discourse, and categorical distinctions drawn by the ɓɔ'ge fɔgɛ appear contentious, rude, even menacing, the dance has its own logic of seduction; it seeks to create a hegemonic power to speak for the community.

In the dance, the imaginary of the heroic person is created—a performance persona central to Tupuri ethnic identity. The dancer, *we-jõo* (pl. *weere-jõore*), is understood in terms of youthful vigor. *Weere-jõore*, literally "youth-dance," denotes *gurna* dancers of all ages. Unlike the association of youthfulness with immaturity in the West, these dancers are thought to display superhuman (though not supernatural) qualities. Explicitly linking contemporary Tupuri with their ancestors, in part through their costuming, *gurna* dancers fit a discourse I heard frequently about the extraordinary powers of human beings before the colonial age, such as their extreme longevity and resistance to disease. The *weere-jõore* exhibit great stamina and power unlimited by gender. Both male and female dancers are admired for their energy; they move tirelessly around the dance circle for hours in the blazing heat. Furthermore, in the framed context of the dance, dancers gain the right to discipline the audience and, by extension, the people at large. The dancers' disciplinary role is expressed in admonitions and cajoling in *gurna* and *waywa* songs and by taunt and mockery in the ɓɔ'ge fɔgɛ.

The taunt or challenge of the ɓɔ'ge fɔgɛ may have its roots in wrestling (*gumu*). Wrestling and dance were closely associated in Tupuri society; wrestling perhaps arose as a spectator sport in order to enliven the dance.[7] At the onset of a match, a wrestler would present himself to the audience. Striding into the wrestling ring, he would hurl provocations to his opponent and boast of his own strength and courage in an effort to intimidate his opponent and gain the upper hand in the match. This performance of self-promotion and taunting moved from the arena of wrestling to that of dance, where it has been infused with new meanings.

Tupuri dance involves a social cleavage between dancer and spectator for another reason: Wrestling and dance are both sites where youth are encouraged to express their vivacious energy. Young men exhibit their attainment of manhood by performing acts of bravado. In the context of the dance, these range from performing the *ɓɔ'ge fɔgɛ* to frenetic drumming to executing the *maŋge may*, the capture of a girl for marriage. Although they are not expected to distinguish themselves through such acts of daring, young women, often as young as 13 or 14, perform their vitality by keeping up with the often much older and larger male dancers, no matter how loud, dusty, and animated the dance becomes.

COURAGE AND THE AESTHETIC OF THE FATTENED BODY

"*Hay yo*, my cow! You don't join the *gurna* and you're skinny like a cow that eats plastic. Watch out, a big wind is going to blow you away!"[8] a dancer calls out to the crowd, facing them in his ramrod stance. This *ɓɔ'ge fɔgɛ* is evocative because it brings together two key symbols operative in the *gurna* aesthetic world: the cow and the size of the body. As I will describe in the next section, the cow has come to stand for the human body and, more broadly, an evaluation of health. Recent literature on the body as an analytic field has explored how "social categories are literally inscribed on and into the body, which with prescriptions about body fluids, cosmetics . . . and ornamentation, acts as a signifier of local social and moral worlds" (Lock 1993, 135). As a signifier in northern Cameroon ethnic identity politics, the body has a bearing on the self-presentation of the dancer in the *ɓɔ'ge fɔgɛ*.

The development of a large, corpulent body is widely admired by Tupuri people. They judge a strong, tall body with a round belly as a sign of health and wellness, and they tend to see themselves as physically robust, in contrast to their historical adversaries, the Muslim Fulbe. Admiring slenderness, Fulbe men and women draped themselves in long flowing robes designed to cover the body entirely. The Tupuri *gurna* is organized around gorging and body fattening, while Islam emphasizes periods of fasting (Ramadan). There are other important historical reasons for the construction of Tupuri ethnic identity through the body. Ethnic identity construction involves a recognition by others of a certain characteristic made salient by historical exigencies and an internalization of that representation by the group itself. For at least the past 150 years, Tupuri identity has involved the image of warriorness, but a warriorness that was defensive rather than imperialist. This warrior quality was strongly localized in the body, perhaps building on local body development practices, such as dance and *gurna* body fattening, that predate Tupuri contact with the Fulbe.

Although the Fulbe Islamic jihad of the early nineteenth century was successful to varying degrees in subduing the mosaic of mostly animist ethnic groups of the Far North, the Tupuri especially were noted for their ability to repel the

Fulbe cavalries.⁹ Their reputation as courageous warriors was further enhanced in the colonial era when mostly Tupuri and neighboring Massa and Mundang were recruited into the Free French Army and then redeployed in the 1950s against the Bamiléké and Bassa anticolonial guerila movement in the south. Northerners were preferred for these military recruitments because it was assumed that they would be loyal, since their homelands were out of reach of the insurgent UPC[10] stronghold in the south. The Fulbe were disinclined to join the colonial military except as officers, since their power had been directly supplanted by the colonial administration. Upon their return to Tupuriland, these veterans had far-reaching influence on both the material and symbolic economies of their villages. This disproportionate recruitment of the Tupuri, Massa, and Mundang into the military continued after Independence under the first president Amadou Ahidjo, a Fulbe. He, in fact, packed his elite Republican Guard with animist northerners; he distrusted his fellow Fulbe and believed non-Muslim northerners to be "faithful, loyal men, of great bravery and courage, born of people of a warrior tradition who know how to do battle" (Schilder 1994, 250). Tupuri were thrown into the spotlight in 1984 when an attempted military coup was uncovered and Tupuri officers were found to be on both sides.

In addition to this historical identity as warriors, the Tupuri today have a national reputation as hard workers, especially in projects requiring physical labor, and for being responsive to discipline. In addition to their overrepresentation in the military, police, and gendarmes, Tupuri men have flocked to Yaoundé to take jobs as security guards. In rural Tupuriland, people explained to me that large strong bodies are assumed to be necessary for the intense hand farming they do. And, of course, these bodies were also seen as suitable for the display and self-presentation required by the dance. In fact, the reason given for body adornment involving smearing the body with white clay (*puuli*) or sorghum flour or spattering it with milk was to show off the girth of the body. Exploiting the dramatic contrast between dark-brown skin and the ghostly white powder smeared over it, the dancers did appear larger. Like an optical illusion, the body covered with *puuli* seemed to expand.

The body aesthetics of the *gurna* and, by extension, the Tupuri people, are expressed variously: through the dancer's body adornment, in the dance movement itself, and in the words of the *bɔ'ge fɔgɛ*. At the climax of the *bɔ'ge fɔgɛ* movement, the dancer stands completely still, frozen for several seconds before the audience, with his arms and legs spread wide. This stance is intended to set the body off so that it appears large and intimidating. By stopping the body's movement entirely, the dancer calls the spectators' attention to just the body itself; they can admire it momentarily, undistracted by dance motion. After several seconds of self-presentation, the dancer returns to the mass of dancers. For such a movement to succeed, dancers must possess not only a properly conditioned body but also a pride in the body. For this reason, many told me that they do not have the courage to dance the *gurna*.

COW AND SELF

Hey ho, I've a cow that gives milk. Come here and I'll give you some. You seem very unhappy![11]

If health and wellness were located for the *gurna* in the strong body, this body was nourished by the cow. The relationship between the *gurna* member and his cow was fundamental and multileveled. First, one of the few conditions for men to join the *gurna* society was the ability to bring a lactating cow to the *gurna jak-kaw*. Usually encircled by a sorghum-stalk fence, the camp encompassed a corral where the *gurna*'s cows and their nursing calves were tethered to stakes. The camp was bathed in the odor of cow manure and its attendant flies; the ground was soft with manure. Among the tasks allocated to the *gurna* members were herding the cows during the daytime, fetching water from the well for the herd, and caring for the calves too young to pasture. (This involved periodically squirting water from one's mouth directly into the calf's mouth as it is pried open with the fingers.) Some *gurna* slept at the camp each night in order to guard the herd from theft. To join a camp was to experience a closeness, even a unity, with the cattle.

Second, *gurna* bonded with their cattle through drinking milk, one of the underlying purposes for the formation of the *gurna* camp. By consuming cow's milk, the *gurna* were able to develop fattened bodies, especially the distended belly. Each day in the *gurna* camp the members mixed sorghum couscous with water and milk to produce a porridge that was shared among members. Girls affiliated with the *gurna* camp arrived in the afternoon to chat and drink the milky porridge from large calabashes. Even though women were uniformly responsible for food preparation in the society at large, in the camp it was only the male *gurna* who mixed the sorghum porridge. For this reason, consumption of milk in the camps should be understood as having ritual importance.

Many ethnographies of pastoralist peoples have shown that where cattle are at the material base of the society, they are often symbolized such that conceptualizations of personhood are expressed as identification with cows (Evans-Pritchard 1956; Hutchinson 1996). Cattle among "so-called 'cattle complex' people . . . appear simultaneously to personify individuated identities, values, and ties, and to act as generalized icons of the social structure qua structure" (Comaroff 1985, 72). In Tupuri society, patrilineage is bound with the transfer of cattle through bridewealth practices. The *gurna* society elaborate on this economy of cattle by ritualizing their possession as a symbol of masculinity. Most ɓɔ'ge fɔgɛ formulaically begin with a salute to the dancer's cow, generically: "*Hay yo manday!*" ("Hey ho, my cow!") or by name: "If I'm fat, it's thanks to my milk cow called Tchabroudi."[12] The spectators (*faɳdi*) are pitied because they lack milk and are therefore unable to develop an attractive body. "Stand back, poor man who doesn't have even a single milk cow."

In addition to valorizing the *gurna* society as an institution, the dancers use the ɓɔ'ge fɔgɛ to create an image of masculinity that circulates more widely in the society. The cow is often a metaphor for these masculine qualities. "My Bufda! My Bufda! The cow that eats from the mortar! The cow that eats from the mortar!"[13] Bufda, a common name given to cows meaning "yellow" (*bufibufi*), was a cow that was not content with eating sorghum stalks in the field like the other cows. Strong and intimidating, she could come up to the mortar where women are pounding the sorghum to help herself. This ɓɔ'ge fɔgɛ suggested that like Bufda, the *gurna* was dominant, taking only the best to eat.

Who was the ideal person promoted in the ɓɔ'ge fɔgɛ? The *gurna* represents himself as someone who has mastered the difficulties of life. He has expertly farmed his fields so that he has the wealth to contribute a cow and join his peers at the *gurna* camp. They meet daily at the camp on the edge of the village to spend time luxuriating in male companionship, the passage of time, and the drinking of milk. Unlike the *faɲdi* who remains in the village, the *gurna* has much to eat and enjoys camaraderie and the sensations of being sated. With their enlarged bellies, they "present well" for the dance. In contrast, according to *gurna* ideology, the *faɲdi* live miserable, parsimonious lives and have shriveled skinny bodies unsuitable for the dance.

These oppositions are often expressed through the dichotomy of fatness versus emaciation. Fatness, associated with wealth and physical and moral well-being, is expressly cultivated by the *gurna*. The *gurna*'s milk drinking is a metonym for the entire *gurna* complex: participation in the bush camps, mobilization of the *gurna* network, body-fattening practices, and adherence to the system of *gurna* law or moral standards. The tone or character of *gurna* masculinity is expressed as praise for the *gurna*'s corpulence, stamina in the dance, and nonchalance about hygiene that more effete city dwellers (or "the modern person") might fear, such as unsterilized milk, proximity to the cows, heat and dust at the dance site, and so forth.

BƆ'GE FƆGƐ AS SOCIAL CRITIQUE

The dance is not only a spectacle but also a discursive space in which dancers both point to and comment on debates alive in Tupuri society. In their roles as *were-jõore* (dancers), they are permitted to mock and discipline the spectators in ways not permitted in daily life. Although these exhortations are momentary, they occur in the special channel of communication that is ritualized and set apart from everyday life. My concern is not to reify one particular discursive pattern but to show how it taps into broader concerns in Tupuri social life and expressed sentiments that are unspeakable in other contexts.

Within the *bɔ'ge fɔgɛ* that I witnessed in the context of dances or that informants told me about, I discerned references to three dilemmas that most Tupuri people would see as critical to their survival. The first area concerns the role of alcohol in Tupuri society. In contrast to the minimal consumption of alcohol before 1970, contemporary Tupuri society, both urban and rural, is seized by high rates of alcoholism. Within this social problem is a more subtle questioning of the meaning of health. What is a healthy body? What is needed socially in order to produce it?

The second area of social critique concerned the proper livelihood of the Tupuri person. Many researchers have commented on the rerauralization of Africa in light of diminished opportunities for urban employment and education as World Bank/International Monetary Fund structural adjustment policies were implemented during the 1990s (Gubry et al. 1996). Farming has long been a forte of the Tupuri people. However, after nearly four decades of cotton farming and increasing population pressure, Tupuri complain of annual famine, even during years when rains are favorable. Caught between the rock of diminishing agricultural yields and the hard place of the vagaries of the modern economy, young Tupuris are asking themselves where they fit in. For some young men, farming is no longer a lifelong endeavor. Instead, through cotton cash-cropping over the summer, it is a way to earn school tuition in order to escape from farming altogether. Relations between such youth and their peers who remained in the village are inevitably tinged with jealousy, which finds its way into the ɓɔ'ge fɔgɛ.

Finally, a third dilemma is What should Tupuri people make of the recent modern experiment with schooling? How should schooling be valued in society? Young people see tuition rates rising beyond what their families can pay. At the same time, their older brothers who went to school in the 1980s are unable to find employment. It was self-evident that the old contract between the state and the people had been annulled—the contract in which an educated individual would automatically be rewarded with salaried civil service work. With this changed national scene, many Tupuris who remained in the villages wonder not only whether school is economically worth its investment but also whether it is worth the changes it exacts on the person, a separation from the moral structures of the village. It is just such a commentary that dancers of the ɓɔ'ge fɔgɛ make within the rhetoric of the dance.

Each of these three dilemmas are pressure points within the society, places of doubt and confusion. In the context of the dance, they are indexed elliptically through such metaphors as "drinking milk" (participating in the *gurna*), "buying pens" (affording school), and "bending over" (farming). Most important, the dance provides the social space for ritual inversion. Like many other dance rituals across Africa, the ɓɔ'ge fɔgɛ temporarily inverts the conventional social order in which salaried workers have a higher social status than farmers. Through the dancers' taunts, the prestige of the educated elite is called into question, challenged by the evocation of (what are seen as) indigenous Tupuri values that run counter to modern identities. In this inverted worldview, suddenly the *sous-préfet* is poor and the dancer fabulously wealthy—thanks to his cow. And the highly educated student is hapless while the farmer is content and well fed. Attendant notions of poverty and wealth, weakness and health are redefined or reverted back to their putatively "traditional" meanings. While no one would imagine that in actual life an individual cannot be *both* Tupuri and modern—in fact, some of the dancers themselves are civil servants—for the purposes of the dance, discourse that reifies and dichotomizes Tupuri identity is reveled in.

ANTINOMY OF MILK AND ALCOHOL

Many ɓɔ'ge fɔgɛ play with an opposition between milk and alcohol: "Take the liquor—that's what your blood is made up of now. As for me, I have my milk here."[14] In these exhortations, the dancer mocks the spectators who, thinking themselves modern, spend their money on alcohol. Three kinds of alcohol were available: local sorghum beer (*yii*); distilled liquor (*'argi*), produced by village women as a way of earning cash; and commercial bottled beer, sold in bars in Doukoula. (Bottled beer is prohibitively expensive for all but salaried civil servants.) In criticizing alcohol consumption, the performer runs counter to the overwhelming popularity of drink in Tupuri society. He takes on a key symbol of contemporary life, positing the value of its opposite: the milk-drinking *gurna*.

Abstinence from alcohol in favor of milk drinking is a rule of the *gurna* society—at least in the camp itself. In the village, *gurna* are as likely to enjoy a jug (*daŋ*) of *yii* as any other man; however, they are forbidden from drinking in the camp and discouraged from drinking excessively. In addition to fomenting disharmony among members, alcohol is thought to prevent the *gurna* from gaining weight. "It's liquor that makes you skinny, isn't it so?"[15] a dancer taunted. The rotund body of the *gurna* is thought to be diametrically opposed to the emaciated alcoholic who drinks liquor all day.

Another dimension of this opposition is in the way that wealth is imaged. "Come have some milk. You have none for yourselves," a dancer baits the spectators. In defining wealth in terms of milk, the *gurna* society calls attention to two key dimensions of its moral order: collectivism and cattle as cultural capital (Bourdieu 1972/1989, 184). While sorghum beer is given freely and shared liberally among attendees at funerals and festivals, by the 1980s, there was an increasing trend in Tupuri society for individuals to purchase beer with cash to drink exclusively with a small group of friends. This drinking occurs in a special section of the large weekly market (*lumo-yii*), in small bush markets, and in compounds of women who specialized in brewing (see figure 25). Many find this shift in alcohol consumption practice—from ritual to commercial, collective to selective—alarming. They point to the increase in *l'individualisme* ushered in by *le modernisme*. It is interesting that they do not tend to blame shortage of cash on the economic crisis but rather on an ideological shift toward self-centeredness.

Through the *ɓɔ'ge fɔgɛ,* the *gurna* society calls attention to its value of collective solidarity represented by its commensality with milk. Milk was never bought or sold in Tupuriland. Milk obtained from the cows of the *gurna* camp is immediately consumed in the camp; members pass calabashes of milky porridge among themselves. Furthermore, it is the collective herding of the cattle that provides this milk. The *gurna* bind themselves to one another in brotherhood through their cattle, an arrangement that stands apart from and predates commodification of cattle. An image of this collectivity, and the sense of well-being it claimed to generate, is expressed in this *ɓɔ'ge fɔgɛ*: "Go back home with your economic crisis. Take some milk. When you drink that, money isn't anything."[16] The performer draws a concise contrast between the value system of money— with its unpleasant underside, the economic crisis—and the value system of the *gurna* society, its collective solidarity symbolized by milk drinking. This discourse plays with two competing paradigms of health and wellness, one putatively modern and connected to the nation-state and the other putatively ancestral and local.

However, competition between two seemingly diametrically opposed systems does not in itself explain why a discourse might arise about it. The answer might be found in anxiety about the consequences of excessive alcohol consumption in Tupuri society more broadly. By all accounts, there has been a phenomenal rise in alcohol consumption in Tupuriland, in both rural and urban areas. The weekly market in Doukoula has become practically synonymous with mass drunkenness. *Gurna* are hardly immune to the pressures to drink regardless of their membership in the society. *Waŋre-gurna* (*gurna* chiefs) often call for stricter adherence to the rule of abstinence. Some even suggested to me that young people today choose to join the *gurna* society in a conscious effort to reduce their alcohol consumption.

Some more critically inclined observers, such as a Tupuri sociologist (Koulandi 1999), noted that the poverty of women was an important piece in this dilemma. Brewing beer and distilling liquor were the only way most women could access the cash they needed to pay for necessities such as health care and school tuition for their children. In many households in Doukoula, wives brew *yii* to sell to their own husbands and his friends. Men use the cash they earn from cotton farming—assisted by their wives' labor—to purchase the drink. Women are in the ironic position of working once again to access the benefits of their own labor.

A final aspect of the dilemma of alcohol in Tupuriland is the linkage between beer brewing and famine. Consumption of sorghum in the form of beer means that there is simply not enough grain available during the annual "hungry season," June to September. When I mentioned this problem, I was told that women were forbidden to use the family grain reserves for commercial beer brewing. It was true that women purchased sorghum at the market for their brewing, but this simply shifted the problem of supply from the family to the wider market. In an attempt to prevent famine in the late 1990s, the Doukoula mayor issued a prohibition against beer brewing during the Christmas holiday.

Although *ɓɔ'ge fɔgɛ* do not in and of themselves offer a solution to alcoholism and the corrosiveness of the alcohol economy, they nevertheless interrupt the near-obsession with sorghum drinking that has recently gained predominance in Tupuri society. Both beer and milk commensality operate as symbols of well-being and sociability in Tupuriland, though each is associated with systems of social networking. The *ɓɔ'ge fɔgɛ* promote the *gurna* as an alternative form of solidarity to the more casual friendships that develop around drinking sorghum beer in beer parlors. The *gurna* provides a model of bodily health and sociability associated with the ancestors and the putative harmony of the village.

REVALORIZATION OF FARMING

In addition to promoting specific forms of solidarity and health, the *ɓɔ'ge fɔgɛ* also provide a discursive space where *gurna* valorize themselves as superior farmers. They criticize the spectators for being lazy, for refusing to pick up the hoe. "You people who refuse to bend over, take these peanuts!"[17] exclaims one dancer, thrusting a whole peanut plant at the spectators. He chastised them for being dependent on the foreign food aid that had come for seven years straight. "You fatten yourselves on USA food aid, but us, we fatten ourselves on milk."[18] The *gurna*, in this view, is not only a dancer and a member of the *gurna* society but also a man capable of feeding himself and his family through the power of his labor on the land. When the dancers valorize themselves as farmers, they contrast themselves with civil servants who as salaried workers purchase their food in the market. The colonial heritage of education in Africa means that education was and continues to be conceived almost exclusively as a gateway into the civil service. For this reason, dancers discursively treat students and civil servants as a single category. Students are merely future civil servants, and both are unable to produce their own food.

Given this context, the larger question was about the proper livelihood of a Tupuri person. There are several layers underneath this question. The first involves Tupuri ethnic identity in contrast to that of the Fulbe. The classic West African ethnographic formulation has focused on the symbiotic relationship between the pastoralists, the Fulbe, and animist sedentary farmers such as the Tupuri. However, this portrayal is simplistic. In fact, in Cameroon, the relationship has been exploitative. Fulbe merchants from both inside and outside Tupuriland buy large quantities of sorghum from farmers during the harvest months when the price is low. Then, at the end of the season, when grain becomes scarce and the new harvest has not come in yet, the price climbs high and farmers are forced to buy back grain at inflated prices. During the famine of 1998, unscrupulous merchants sold sorghum originally purchased at 8,000 CFA per sack for 50,000 CFA on credit (see figure 26). Farming families bonded together to purchase sacks at these exorbitant prices to avoid starvation.

It is hardly surprising that in this economic context, Tupuri and Fulbe generally have a different valuation of the occupation of farming. Both Tupuri men and women put a great deal of energy into their farming and genuinely take pride in their agricultural labor. As I walked on footpaths through acres of farmland of sorghum, peanuts, and cotton, I frequently heard Tupuri people congratulating and encouraging one another in their work. On any given day during the planting season, the entire village was emptied for the fields. Although most farming is conducted by the nuclear or extended family, collective farming (tɔrla) is common. The host reimburses the helpers with huge jugs of sorghum beer brought directly into the field. Even urban Tupuri women often go to great lengths to rent or purchase land on the edge of the city so they can farm. Students make an effort to return to the village in the summer to farm cotton so they could pay their tuition. Fulbe farm as well, though they prefer commerce and skilled trades, such as leatherworking and tailoring. They do not tend to valorize farming as a worthwhile livelihood in itself. Their ideal is to hire laborers from animist ethnic groups to cultivate their land at low wages. In the past, in regions outside Tupuriland where Fulbe were in larger number, non-Fulbe slaves were used to farm plantations.

Valorization of farming is reflected in the *gurna* institution. When asked about the *gurna*'s purpose, Tupuri people often make the connection between developing the body, strengthening and nourishing it, and farming well. The *gurna* is conceived of as a nine-month retreat to rebuild the body after the strenuous agricultural season (July to October). After the labors of the season, the body is thought to be depleted and in need of replenishment for the next growing season. *Gurna* camps disband in June just as the first drops of rain started to fall.

But why do the *gurna* need to valorize farming in their dance? As I have suggested, one reason might be the maintenance of their ethnic identity in contrast to Fulbe ethnicity and a revalorization of it in light of Fulbe economic exploitation. However, this is a static explanation. Other factors make the question of livelihood more pressing. It would not be an exaggeration to state that there was and continues to be a silent crisis in farming for the Tupuri. There is no longer enough land to support the increasing population, and the existing land has become increasingly infertile after years of cotton cultivation. Many families are finding it difficult to grow enough food to last until the next harvest. "Every year there is famine" is a constant refrain. Through government-sponsored resettlement programs, Tupuri villagers are emigrating in large numbers from the Mayo Danay to regions in the southern reaches of the northern provinces where there is greater rainfall and more land. Furthermore, the introduction of fees for schooling, health care, and veterinary supplies, which were mandated by the IMF's structural adjustment programs, and increasing transportation costs created a greater need for cash. Although recent years have seen wildly fluctuating seasonal prices for sorghum, the Tupuri customarily have not used sorghum as a source of cash income. Farming of cotton, the cash crop introduced by the French in the 1960s, does not provide enough revenue to meet the needs of the vast majority of families.

In light of the growing realization of the rising inadequacy of sorghum farming, why would dancers boast of their prowess as farmers? The following performance was by a single dancer who came up to the crowd to throw out his ɓɔ'ge fɔgɛ three times:

> "You planted one quarter [of a hectare]. Instead of farming, you didn't farm. I'll buy a cow. My hoe here! I'll buy three cows! If the famine strikes me, I'll sell two. Your hairy heads are the sacred forest, like that for no reason. Take a look at this!"[19] he exclaimed, brandishing his hand hoe.
>
> Later, he stepped forward and exhorted, "Instead of farming, he didn't farm, saying that grain [food aid] will be distributed. You will starve to death this year."[20]
>
> He added, hoe in hand, "I always buy two hoes. This one is already finished. I'll buy another one. You waste your time blaming the floods there. This year's fish are even better than milk."[21]

This dancer was performing his customary role as disciplinarian of the people. In this case, the people, cast as faŋdi with their "bushy heads," were chastised for their laziness and dependence on food aid. During the agricultural season of which he spoke, huge rains had flooded the fields. As a flexible survivor, he had fished in these floods and found the fish better than the gurna's milk. More than just disciplining the people, the dancer provided an imaginary of the people as survivors. He set himself up as a model of the person who could rise above the hardship of famine and flooding.

Elsewhere in the dance, there is a symbolic defiance of death and a sublimation of hardship. At the end of the dance at a death celebration, it is not unusual to see several gurna leap up on the freshly whitewashed tombstone of the deceased, dancing with great vigor while the wave of hundreds of dancers move around them toward the homestead of the deceased. (In figure 27, a gurna dances on top of a horse with bravado while the rest of the dancers move forward in unison behind him.) Other ɓɔ'ge fɔgɛ express fascination for physical endurance and stoicism about pain. "No rain all year! No rain all year! The real dancers show up! The real dancers show up!"[22] A year in which there was no rain—and therefore famine and hardship—is viewed as an opportunity for dancers to test their mettle. The implication is that many men and young women would show up to participate in the gurna during a year of abundant rain and crops, but only the hard-core "real" gurna would show up during a difficult year. Dancers' love for the dance is thought to be so powerful as to be undaunted by physical hardship in the village.

On one level, the dance provides a context where the people are disciplined to be better farmers and where farming is valorized as a legitimate livelihood for the Tupuri people, amid many difficulties. But, at a deeper level, the dance recreates and plays back to the people a psychology of forbearance of suffering. If survival is as much a psychospiritual process as a physical one, then it is not surprising that the dance with its power to ignite the imagination is a critical site for engendering the survival of the people.

CRITIQUE OF SCHOOLING: DISCOURSES OF LOSS AND SEPARATION

In the ɓɔ'ge fɔgɛ "Hey ho my cow! Watch out you boys, or your urine will be blocked!" the dancer entertains the spectators by poking fun at schooling. Urine was threatened to be blocked by the tightness of Western-style belts, a symbol of the clothing and, by extension, lifestyles of elite students and civil servants. By wearing belts, elite educated men distance themselves from farmers, who wear old loose trousers to work their fields. Dancers sport body adornments (*togo*), woven fiber knots which are tied loosely around the hips so their fringes sway with the movements of the dancing body. This hip decoration contrasts with the smooth, tight belt which seems to symbolize the excessive discipline of modern life in state-run institutions.

In his *gurna* song composed for the lycée of Doukoula, Dangmoworé, student and *gurna* song composer (see figure 28), sang too of the ridiculousness of belts:

We jōo mba diŋ ma ra bɔlgi na fɛr gɔ,
Sa' yo mbɛ deŋ ndɔ tigir po galay ma jōore. (L., 97/98, v. 2)

In the past, the youth were made for the dance,
Now, they tuck their shirts in their belts, though not frogs, youth.

The fact that Dangmo himself was in the final years of lycée when he composed this song didn't prevent him from pointing out the gulf between youth of the past and youth today. Youth of the past were "made for" the dance: Their primary mode of socialization was the dance. When they reflected on the past, Tupuri people spoke of an intimate association of the dance with youth and youthfulness. One was a youth (*we*) if one danced, regardless of age; a dancer was termed *we-jōo*. And conversely, to be a youth meant to be a dancer. Dangmo's comment on the existence of belts was his way of saying that youth no longer dance—that this intimate connection between the dance and youth had been severed. Students cinch themselves with their belts in the same way that a hunter of frogs ties a string around the abdomen of a frog he has caught. To a Tupuri audience, this brings a vivid image of dead frogs dangling from a rope when a hunter returns from the bush. The metaphor in the song is a pathetic image of the moribund student cinched by school and modernity. It is ironic that after Dangmo had helped me by transcribing and translating his Gurna Club songs, I asked him what I could give him as a gift. Without a moment's thought, he requested *une ceinture*. When I gave him money for the belt, he was overjoyed and came to our next session wearing a new brown belt with his lycée uniform.

In Dangmo's creativity, it is possible to see the flexible relationship between identity and oral discourse and between consciousness and social structure. Like bourgeois intellectuals who use Marxist theory to critique social structure that privileges the bourgeoisie, Dangmo could be fully engaged as a student yet still create the intellectual space to parody that identity. The vitality of the oral tradition in which he was steeped—his father was a *gurna* composer—provided him with a discursive space and the aesthetic tools to make such moves.

The current disillusionment that many youth felt (and continue to feel) toward education in post-crisis Cameroon is just one of many reactions the Tupuri have had toward the option of Western schooling in their region. In contrast to southern Cameroon, where British Baptist missionaries established schools as early as 1844, colonialists established schools in northern Cameroon much later. One reason was that the German, and later the French, stereotyped the north as inhabited with Muslims who had their own traditions of Koranic literacy and schooling. Until quite late, out of deference to Fulbe Muslim hegemony, the colonial government made the north out of bounds for Christian evangelism and education, even though non-Fulbe groups make up some three-quarters of the northern population (Kofele-Kale 1986, 55). More than any other northern ethnic group, the Tupuri vehemently resisted Islamization, and they continue to do so. The first Western-style schools were not established in Tupuriland until the 1950s, by Roman Catholic missionaries. Highly skeptical of schooling, the first generation of villagers exposed to it did not easily agree to send their children there. However, over the past fifty years, these initial reservations have given way to the opposite reaction: a strong enthusiasm for Western-style education. Today, although it is significantly lower than for southern Cameroonians, Tupuri school attendance was perceived to be among the highest of the seventy-five ethnic groups of the Far North Province.[23] In Tupuri villages, schools overflow with students at all levels (see figure 29). In spite of their poverty, and tired of waiting for the bankrupt government, parents pool their resources to build their own schools. In spite of the downsizing of the civil service and the imposition of tuition fees, there was still strong support for schooling during my stay in Tupuriland, especially for boys, during the late 1990s.

However, since the onset of *la crise* in Cameroon, this valuation of education exists side by side with a vibrant discourse of loss. This sense of loss is expressed in many different registers: sardonic bitterness, passionate nostalgia for pre-crisis life, and gloomy prophecies for the future, to name just a few. Schooling has become a major discursive trope for these commentaries on modernity. Themes appearing in some of the *ɓɔ'ge fɔgɛ* that I collected include despair over the lost utility of school, weakness associated with the new modern identities, and echoes of the perspectives of the unschooled.

One *ɓɔ'ge fɔgɛ* heard at a death celebration in 1996 encapsulated the sense of being stuck in the middle of two systems, a feeling that many people aspiring to the middle class expressed even after the *crise* had endured nearly fifteen years. "You have diplomas that are worthless. Instead of joining the *gurna*, you refuse, so you are unhappy like this."[24] Here, a dichotomy is drawn between schooling and membership in *gurna* society. "Diplomas" is the gloss for *"wuu de derewal,"* literally "elites with paper."[25] This *ɓɔ'ge fɔgɛ* comments not only on the apparent incompatibility between schooling and *gurna* but on the post-*crise* psychology of elites. Because they are schooled, they are said to be changed, to have become rigid and resistant to joining the *gurna.* They are seen to be afraid of slipping back into village-oriented identities. The *ɓɔ'ge fɔgɛ* performer points out that not only have *"wuu de derewal"* made the mistake of putting their eggs in the basket of schooling and the state but when the national situation changed, their continued rejection of local solidarities such as the *gurna* further isolated them and made them "unhappy." In this discourse, the post-*crise* modern person is imagined as a miserable person who, in spite of his education and diplomas, can neither gain state-sponsored prestige nor bear to revert back to village-sponsored prestige available through *gurna* membership.

This image of being modern yet lost is expressed in this *ɓɔ'ge fɔgɛ*: "You, you're lost like that for nothing. Get away from me with your 'i'!"[26] This statement draws on a subjectivity associated with parents or elders who have not been to school. Dourwé, the first member of his family to attend school, explained: "Our parents in the village have no idea what goes on in the school. But they hear the children repeating in loud voices the letters of the alphabet, especially clearly enunciated letters like 'o' and 'i.' " This sense of exclusion that elders may have felt when schools were first established in Tupuriland is now appropriated to refer to a newer exclusion that has emerged from post-*crise* frustration. "Get away from me with your 'i'!" The dancer repudiates modern institutions such as school and the civil service that seemed no longer to hold out the promises that they once did. And with this repudiation comes a revalorization of the ancestors (*moobe*) and (what were understood as) ancestral ways of life. "You students, get away from me! My grandfather didn't know things like that."²⁷ Through dance, performers dichotomize the world of schools and of ancestors.

These *bɔ'ge fɔgɛ* appeared at *yii-huuli* as well as *waywa*. However, dancers also hurl *bɔ'ge fɔgɛ* during *gurna* dances that are performed as part of state-sponsored events. Shifting to a folkloric register, one such dance was performed for National Youth Day. Throughout Cameroon, on February 11, the administration in every city and town leads Youth Day celebrations to showcase school students and to exhibit the power of the youthful sector of the population. There are parades in which school students march in their uniforms in formation in front of a raised dais of government and political elites. In Doukoula, each grade level stops in the stadium arena and performs a song-and-dance composition they have practiced under the tutelage of their primary school teachers. These are line dances, similar to the drill teams of African-American girls in the United States and the South African dance presented in such musicals as *Sarafina*. Those who have attended Youth Day celebrations in other regions notice that in Tupuriland, the dance component is particularly elaborate. Even the teachers dance alongside the students and compete with one another to show off the greatest energy.

For Youth Day in Doukoula one year, the lycée students presented a more sophisticated program in the evening, called *la soirée*. This was a variety show with a wide range of presentations: comedy, Makossa song and dance,²⁸ and a performance by the Gurna Club of a short version of the *gurna* dance on stage. Their *bɔ'ge fɔgɛ* were directed toward the administrative elites who were invited to the *soirée* and were prominently seated in front on more comfortable, if rickety, chairs, holding mimeographed programs for the evening. Due to the system of ethnic patronage, administrators of the government *commandement* are usually southern Cameroonians, often from the same ethnic group as President Paul Biya. Therefore, the *sous-préfet* of Kar Hay did not speak Tupuri (or any northern language). However, the *proviseur* (headmaster) of the Doukoula lycée for the past twelve years had been a Tupuri. The rest of the audience reflected the population of Doukoula: mostly Tupuri, with some Fulbe and members of other ethnic groups who had come to Doukoula to work. The ethnicity of the audience was significant because the lycée's Youth Day soirée was one of the few school-sanctioned functions in which Tupuri rather than French was permitted. The non-comprehension of Tupuri by the majority of teachers and high officials gave the members of the Gurna Club freedom to express themselves in song and dance that they had not been afforded in the regular school context. They took advantage of the deafness of their non-Tupuri teachers to their local discourse.

The *bɔ'ge fɔgɛ* of the *lycéens* during the Youth Day soirée resembled those performed in village dance contexts. However, rather than being directed at students in general, many were directed toward the specific elites in attendance: the *sous-préfet* and headmaster. They asserted the themes of school rejection and the superiority of the dance and the *gurna* complex. "What's best is the dance. Certain people say that it's school. Mr. Principal, I don't want any more of your school."²⁹ They proclaimed the satisfactoriness of local systems of wealth and wellness, symbolized by milk, in the face of poverty that students faced in their bid to become modern. "You students, you don't have money to buy pens. Take one here. As for us, we drink our milk. Ya! Ya!"[30] Or, "Mr. Sous-Préfet, I only eat dried fish and drink my milk with red sorghum couscous—and look how fat I am! You eat all kinds of meat and still you're skinny. Come and drink milk."[31] Again, there was an inversion of power: The students were those facing poverty, while the *gurna* (read peasants) were those with plenty.

The discourse of bodily strength and the repudiation of effeteness frequently comes up around the newer social distinctions that are changing Tupuri society. When I asked about men who attended school and who then decided to join the *gurna*, I was told stories about how those who were *évolué*, or modern, weren't tough enough to join the *gurna*. Somehow modern school-based knowledge had eroded their toughness. For example, in school, students learn that diseases, such as the tuberculosis that was endemic in the area, can be transmitted in milk. A modern person therefore knows that one should boil fresh milk before drinking it. But in the *gurna* camp, drinking milk is a highly symbolic act. In the eyes of the *gurna*, to boil the milk before imbibing flies in the face of the *gurna*'s self-image of toughness; in short, it would be effete. Students performing the *bɔ'ge fɔgɛ* picked up on this discourse and directed it to their superiors, the school administrators: "Since you don't have a cow, come take some milk each one in turn. Grains of sand in the milk won't hurt you, Mr. Principal,"[32] they taunted.

The *bɔ'ge fɔgɛ* is clearly a dichotomizing discourse: *gurna* against *faŋdi*, students, and civil servants, fatness against thinness, local wealth against modern poverty, and so forth. However, this discourse is not an essentializing one—that is, the *gurna* role can be taken on by those who appear to be the ones who are excluded, such as students. It should be noted, however, that these were not just any students; these students had joined the high school Gurna Club and had taken the pains to learn the student-composed lycée *gurna* song and perform in *gurna* costume (see Ignatowski 2004b). With this cultural flexibility came a bicultural subjectivity that was expressed by a lycéen-*gurna* in his *bɔ'ge fɔgɛ* "You say that one cannot follow two hares at the same time. Look at me: *gurna* dancer while still a student. You're just lazy!"[33] With this, the *lycéen-gurna* added to *bɔ'ge fɔgɛ* discourse the possibility of biculturalism or an identity containing within it multiple selves. It is interesting that this assertion was expressed with typical *bɔ'ge fɔgɛ* attitude—with the accusation of laziness on the part of the *faŋdi-lycéens*. For these students, the *gurna* idiom proved to be a playful, labile resource for remembering indigenous forms of socialization.

INTERPRETING THE CRITIQUE OF THE *BƆ'GE FƆGƐ*

The performance of the *bɔ'ge fɔgɛ* promoted the prestige of the *gurna* institution, including the *gurna* dancer's livelihood as farmer and specific forms of male solidarity, discipline, and bodily health encoded by the *gurna*. But given the playfulness and humor of the performance register, how are we to interpret the implications of this critical discourse? How was it articulated to broader opinion-making about the value of modernity, especially education, in Tupuri society? Did the dancers truly believe that the *gurna* institution was a viable alternative to schooling? Did the dancers actually promote farming as the best form of livelihood? At stake in these questions is the problem of reading or interpreting specialized ritual discourse in a performance frame—where play, parody, and irony may obscure meanings—in terms of their broader historical context. To read the *bɔ'ge fɔgɛ* literally would mean ignoring not only its humorous wink but also the wider public opinion or common sense to which it appears diametrically opposed. In spite of the dancers' mockery of schooled identities, education was still overwhelmingly valued regardless of the fact that it did not ensure employment as it once did. What then are we to make of such a paradox? Why does antischool discourse occur in the most public spectacles of the society, especially one that emphasizes social unity?

One approach to this problem highlights the internal discourse of the *gurna* itself. In this view, antimodernity discourse has more to do with the revalorization of the indigenous practice of the *gurna* than anything else. This anxiety about the future of the *gurna* comes in the face of its erosion by many factors which local people tend to conceptually bundle as modernity (*le modernisme*). These include school attendance by youth, loss of leisure time, and conversion to Christianity, all of which tend to occlude *gurna* membership. Schooling not only takes up much of the time of young people, it occupies their minds in such a way that it crowds out the priorities and preoccupations of the *gurna* lifeworld. As described in chapter 3, Christian beliefs collide with some *gurna* practices, such as propitiary rites to establish the camps. Although there might have been widespread enthusiasm for schooling and Christianity, the *gurna* mobilize an antimodernity discourse in attempt to shore up their own prestige. In such a view, there is a clash between different levels of value in Tupuri society—between the *gurna* and Western-style education—that is given expression in the ritual frame of the dance.

However, a second approach to interpreting the *bɔ'ge fɔgɛ* tilts the prism slightly; it does not highlight the local cultural politics of the *gurna* but sees the discourse as a commentary on national conditions. In this view, the *bɔ'ge fɔgɛ* does not so much reject modern means of accumulation as much as it exposes the insecurity of the state, the precariousness of the modern sector. Dancers caution against relying on the school and state while at the same time they revalorize the *gurna* society—its networks and moral order—as an enduring indigenous resource for Tupuri people.

While the contradictions between the modern order of national institutions and the local order of Tupuri forms of socialization have not been resolved—for example, schooling directly interferes with *gurna* membership—the *bɔ'ge fɔgɛ* seems to signal that men will be judged according to specific Tupuri values whether or not they attempt the trajectory of education, employment, and migration to the south. These values—the solidarity of masculine networks, collective management of resources, the aesthetics of the fattened body, and the dignity of farming—are enacted in the *gurna* dance. However, the dancers of the *bɔ'ge fɔgɛ* do not call simplistically for a return to tradition. Rather, they actively reach out to mediate the failures of the nation-state, to provide a safety net to those stranded by the modern system who have left the protective order of the local networks.

This case, which involves a single genre of dance and oral discourse, does not, of course, represent all the ways that Tupuri people are negotiating change. However, it does show how communities—or factions of communities—use ritually framed performance to enact strategies for coping locally with larger economic problems that encompass the nation. Promoting specific sets of values, these strategies or models circulate well beyond the immediate performance site. They shape the larger economy of value in the society and become part of the cultural repertoire of identity construction—in this case, of a prestigious Tupuri personhood.

> *Wii Walne Jõoday kaŋ me téléphone.*
> Ask Walne Jõoday to accompany me to the telephone.
>
> *Foga Blaowe téléphone day day.*
> Foga Blaowe, the telephone of the cow, arrives.
>
> *Ndi ma' télégramme wɔ su wɔ Houla.*
> I sent a telegram yesterday to Houla.

FIVE

"Telephone of the Dance"

Circulation of Gurna *Song Discourse*

DISCOURSE AND SOCIETY

Even where they lack telephone lines, reliable mail service, and paved roads, *gurna* members are proud of their society's communication network. Composers of *gurna* song (*siŋ gurna*) routinely draw upon images of modern technology— "telephone," "telegram," "mail," "car"—as metaphors for the communicative and institutional power of the *gurna* dance society. In their lyrics, *"téléphone,"*[1] *"télégramme,"* and *"courrier"* (lit. "courier" or "messenger") refer to individuals or entire *gurna* camps considered to be dynamic. Because of their great enthusiasm for the dance, these *gurna* are, metaphorically speaking, veritable relay stations, transmitting the song to camps far away. These "telephones" acted as expeditors of the composer's words, just as modern technology quickly transmits messages. Or, in a region where most people walk or bicycle, a dancer was *"mooda-jõo"* (lit. "vehicle-dance"); he propelled the *gurna* forward with his enthusiasm, as a car transports people. I call attention to these poetic uses of images of modernity to make the point that *gurna* members are highly conscious of their society as a social network within which vital communication flows. They metaphorically signal the efficacy of the *gurna* song system, that it has the power to connect members over great distances. Karin Barber says such instances of "metatextual insights," moments when texts "turn around and throw into relief their own discursive operations" (1999, 46).

This local perception of the *gurna* song as a form of communicative circuit relates to broader theoretical questions about the relationship between discourse and social organization. How does the circulation of texts constitute social relations and contribute to the creation of collectivities? In *Metaphysical Community,* Greg Urban explains the problem in terms of two distinct dimensions:

> On the one hand, social organization is the objective field in which, through which, and by which discourse circulates. It is the medium ... for the physical movement of discourse across space and time by means of replication. On the other hand, social organization is the interpretation of the social world through discourse. It is the meaningful apprehension of individuals as members of

groups ... part of the broader intelligibility by which sense perceptions are interpreted. (1996, 25–26)

Barber wrestles with this same interconnection between discourse and society in her masterful study of *oriki* praise-singing:

Because *oriki* are crucial in making the relationships, human and spiritual, that constitute the Yoruba world, they reveal connections and hidden faces in society that would not otherwise be accessible. By attending to what people say themselves, through the concentrated and oblique refractions of *oriki*—and through what they say about *oriki*—we learn how people constitute their society. Texts like this can lead into the heart of a community's own conception of itself: without which, any description of social structure or process will remain purely external. (Barber 1991, 2)

In Urban's view, social organization is the medium through which discourse moves; however, it possesses a specific shape molded in turn by its own discourse. Barber's observations point as well to this constitutive power of discourse; that through *oriki*, Yoruba people create social relationships that make up their world and that through this specialized genre and discourse about it, outsiders can find a window into Yoruba self-conceptions.

I approach the song (*siŋ gurna*)—some might call it oral poetry—associated with the Tupuri *gurna* society in a similar fashion. The *gurna* society is a social institution, a network of fictive kinship that is both constituted by its song tradition and acts as a vehicle for it. While a number of *gurna* practices may be thought of as the glue holding the association together across a large geographic region, the verbal production of the *siŋ gurna* is among the most salient. While the circulation of song discourse is not a unique purpose for the *gurna*, it is vital to it because it enables other social dynamics to occur, such as the recalibration of the personal prestige of dancers and broadcasting of village news. In the dance performance itself, song is foundational since it underlays the drum rhythm that in turn structures the entire collective dance movement.

In this chapter, I describe *gurna* song as a communicative system. Of special concern is its role in constituting the *gurna* society and a broader public sphere based in song. I describe the circulation of *gurna* song discourse—the specific communication channels through which song is produced by composers, disseminated to the *gurna* camps, learned by members, and finally performed to the broader public. The patterns of this communication channel are important because they mirror key aspects of Tupuri social organization and habitual ways that the collective work of Tupuri society are conducted: how prestige is conferred, conflict is resolved, individuals are censured, and moral constraints are negotiated and reinscribed.

One such pattern in Tupuri society, reflected in many facets of the *gurna* society, is the creative tension between solidarity and contestation. Bringing together men of various patrilineages into individual camps, the *gurna* produces social cohesion across clans. However, without rupturing this cohesion, the very structure of the *gurna* also fosters competition among dancers and villages. True to much African performance, the *gurna*, an emblem of solidarity and friendship, also provides an arena where conflict is publicly staged through performance of vitriolic words.[2] The potential for both friendship and contentiousness is embedded in *gurna* practice. The contentious aspect of this public arena is produced by key aspects of the communication channel. First, the song production process is open to community input and thrives on the reporting of conflict for its aesthetic valuation. Second, there is competition among song composers for the loyalty of *gurna* camps, which produces a lively politics of affiliation. On the other hand, the solidarity-producing aspect of the *siŋ gurna* public arena is buttressed by the sharing and learning of the *gurna* song each year by hundreds of *gurna* members. In this view, the song—both as text and performance—is an artifact and tool of community-building.

The success of *gurna* song as a communication channel depends on the successful socialization of performers into the song. This process, in turn, produces those with insider knowledge. As a result, in this chapter I am concerned not only with providing an overview of *gurna* song as a communicative system but also with the processes of documenting, learning, and comprehending the song. At both sociological and poetic levels, the *gurna* song is rife with distinctions between those who know and those who do not, between what is intended to be known and what is to be obscured. I learned not to assume uniform comprehension of the song across all dimensions of Tupuri society. In order to understand the efficacy (or even the effect) of the public sphere created by *siŋ gurna*, we must consider the patterns of insider/outsider access to *gurna* song knowledge. For this reason, I have provided four sections on socialization and competency, beginning with my own processes of transliteration and translation. The next sections show how the song was learned by hundreds of *gurna* dancers, including consideration of changes brought on by the new technologies of tape-recording and literacy. Further changes in song learning associated with urbanization are considered in the final section. Here, as social organization has shifted away from the *gurna* society in cities, Tupuri people have begun to practice the *gurna* in a piecemeal fashion, deemphasizing competency in the verbal art form. If the public sphere produced by *gurna* song structures the dissemination of information and provides a space for social commentary, then these changes are potentially transformative for Tupuri society.

FROM STORIES TO SONG

After the annual harvest festival in November, as the male villagers are organizing the *jak-kaw*, the renowned *gurna* song composers (*jar kaŋ siŋ*) release their compositions for the year. The song is anticipated eagerly by the *gurna*. They send emissaries toting tape recorders to acquire the song and bring it back to the camp, where the members will spend the next two months mastering it. Often, the opening verses of the song refer to the anticipation surrounding the seasonal appearance of the song, conventionally referred to as "thing" (*mo,* or *mon lɛ*): "*Mon lɛ wɛ ndumgi pa sɔ maa jōore no.*" ("The song is starting to resound again, dancers"; T., 97/98, v. 1.)

The shared experience of the *siŋ gurna* is one of the factors that binds the individual members together as a collectivity. But why is the song important to the *gurna* members? How does *siŋ gurna* constitute their society? The experience of *gurna* members with the song begins with the decision of the camp to affiliate with a particular composer whose song they will acquire, learn, and perform at all the death celebrations throughout the season (November through June). Each composer produces one major new song each year. As a group, the *gurna* members practice the song they have selected every afternoon in the camp until they had mastered it. They will collectively experience shame or glory if the name of one of their members appears in the song lyrics that year.

At the spectacular *gurna* dance, a focal point of Tupuri death celebrations (*yii-huuli*), *gurna* camps perform the song publicly with other camps in the region. The song paces the dance, so their mastery of the song affects their dance competence.[3] Camps dance in large rings together with other camps that have adopted the same composer's song. In the region where I conducted research, three composers were active during the late 1990s.[4] It is through their affiliation with particular composers that many camps in a region are brought together as well as embroiled in rivalry. Because of these large dance rings, it was easy to discern how *gurna* camps have affiliated with specific composers and which of these composers was the most popular that year. Although *gurna* usually told me that they affiliated with a composer because they found his song pleasing, in fact, there are often a host of strategic or political reasons for their choice.

In contrast to the Western model of the individual composer-artist composing in solitude, the composition of *siŋ gurna* is fundamentally collaborative. *Gurna* members and villagers provide fodder for the song each year.[5] However, in the end, it is the composer who is responsible for formulating the song's lyrics, choosing what is included and excluded, albeit with advice from his counselors. A two-way circulation of information flows between the villages and the composer. The composer has what he called his "secret agents"[6] in many of the villages in the region. As residents of these villages, these agents or contacts funnel information about controversies, interpersonal conflicts, and bad behavior of villagers back to the composer for possible inclusion in his annual song. Additionally, individuals in the village can, on their own initiative, transmit information they want included in the song back to the composer through the secret agent. Or they might visit the composer in person. The composer amasses this information, culls it, verifies it, and then composes a 70-verse song from it. He "packages" the information according to specific aesthetic conventions, such as ellipsis and ritualized insult. The song is then disseminated back out to the villages through the *gurna* camps; thus information is "played back" to the villagers in the form of song at the *yii-huuli*. *Gurna* members and composers describe this public sphere as a newspaper of sorts. Speaking to me in French, they sometimes used the term *"publier"* ("to publish") to describe how information is released and publicized in the song. It is taken for granted in Tupuriland that the song is a public forum to air happenings in the region.

Villagers bring various kinds of information to the composer in the hope that he will include it in his song. Sometimes these stories (*wãare*) involve a bitter conflict between two individuals in which one wants to publicize the deplorable actions of the other. If the composer includes this information, the malevolent actions will be revealed for all to hear and the individual will be further maligned in a string of graphic, though conventional, insults. At other times, in an effort to enhance their reputation, *gurna* come to the composer in hopes of having their own names or the name of their *gurna* camp (denoted by village) appear in the song. This is a form of public recognition that many crave.

There is some sensitivity among composers about how they received such visits and solicitations from the villagers. According to convention, the composer is not supposed to receive money in exchange for putting names or information in the song. However, it is widely known that composers accept all kinds of gifts, usually sorghum beer and meat, from dancers in the course of these meetings.

Sometimes "an envelope" containing cash comes to a composer from a particular camp. But composers describe a more fluid relationship between patronage gifts and the final product, the song. Composer Noumnamo explained that if someone gives him money in the course of a visit, he might wait a few years before publicly recognizing his "friend" (*bar*) by inserting his name in the song. Composers exercise the power of discretion in selecting when and which information will be released in the song.

Praise-naming is a widespread characteristic of African expressive culture.[7] However, there are fundamental differences between praise in *gurna* song and praise in other West African verbal art. In the Tupuri *gurna*, the relationship between gifts and inclusion of names in the song is suppressed; there is no discourse of such monetary exchanges in the song itself. This is in stark contrast to Yoruba and Wolof praise-singing, in which the patron's ability to pay for florid praise is ostentatiously part and parcel of the performance itself (Barber 1991; Irvine 1989). "[T]he praise-song costs.... It is one of the unavoidable, large expenses a Wolof notable must incur on his way to attaining political position and maintaining any claim to rank; and moreover, it is a sign of his ability to pay. During a performance a griot may even display the money he receives, so that all may see and admire the person being praised as a potential patron" (Irvine 1989, 261). In Tupuri *gurna*, there are no pleas from the composer-narrator for material support, and the relationship between the composer and his praisees is obscured rather than highlighted. By way of contrast, in the Tupuri *didilna*, a genre of praise-singing for elites similar to the West African griot tradition, performers weave demands for gifts and drink directly into the words as they improvise. Patrons of the *didilna* accrue prestige through their praise words.[8] Even though such discourse does not exist in the *siŋ gurna*, composers depend on cash gifts from those who seek access to the song.

When the composer is ready to release the annual *gurna* song, the song becomes public in two steps. First, at the beginning of the new *gurna* season, the composer releases the song to the *gurna* camps, hoping they will chose to adopt his song over those of competing composers. The second level of dissemination occurs when the song has been adopted and mastered by the *gurna* and they perform it to an audience of hundreds, sometimes thousands, at death celebration dances. However, the song also has informal routes of dissemination. Gossip circulates in the villages about the scandalous verses in the song well before it is actually performed. Soon after the composer releases the song to the *gurna* camps, the wider public will have caught wind of the most damaging insults contained in the song.

Up to this point, I have described the song system in rural Tupuriland. However, the *gurna* idiom has been transported to schools, universities, and urban associations for Tupuri cultural revival outside the homeland. As I observed these clubs in various locations in Cameroon, I discovered that the aesthetic principles of *siŋ gurna* are among the few elements of the *gurna* institution that is transportable to cities where Tupuri people have migrated. The song tradition is a foundational element of the *gurna* that can be practiced in the city, whereas other particularities of *gurna* practice in rural areas, such as ritual fattening or collective herding of cattle, cannot. Urban cultural associations (such as Club Kwoïssa in Yaoundé) use the song production to bond and discipline the Tupuri community in multiethnic settings, even where other elements of the *gurna* have been dropped as impractical in the urban setting.

DISCOVERING INSIDER/OUTSIDER KNOWLEDGE

Ndi maŋ avion ndi wo Amerique ɗa.
Claire wãayn yaŋ tum mbɛ ti jɔŋre 6ɛ no?
Goodbye 6ɔ lay Baa kay mo. (L., 98/99, v. 8)

I take a plane; I go to America.
Madame Clare, are you still in your research?
Good-bye, God will help you.

When I first began translating *gurna* song, I thought the process would be fairly straightforward, limited only by my Tupuri language competency. I did not imagine that my own learning process would be a baptism by fire, that to crack the songs I would have to undergo a long process of trial and error, enlisting many people from different levels of Tupuri society for help. However, what I gained from my circuitous route was not just comprehension of song lyrics but an understanding of how the song operated as discourse in the wider Tupuri society; that is, who knew what about *gurna* song and why. Over time, I began to see the song not as a question of mere translation but as one of perceiving a graduated or cascading system of knowledge. As a process that took me to many different people for assistance, the path of my research moved from outsider to insider and then back. That route enabled me to be skeptical when song composers assumed perfect transmission of their songs to the public.

My first efforts to translate a song came when I began to visit a *gurna jakkaw* near Doukoula, where I lived (see figure 30). Sitting on the dung-soft ground on woven straw mats with the *gurna* members under the tree that shaded the camp, I challenged them: "Teach me the song!" One literate *gurna* pulled out a handwritten Tupuri transcription of the song in a slender school notebook, dirtied by numerous handling of its pages. Under his surveillance, I painstakingly copied the first several verses of the song into my notebook. He explained that he had learned to write Tupuri at the Catholic mission where he had been a member of the church's farmer organization network. But when it came to translating these verses into French, Francophone though he was, he could not seem to find the words to express them. After an hour of collaboration, we were finally able to translate one three-line verse. Pleased to have finally begun my apprenticeship, I nevertheless realized—after learning that the songs numbered seventy or so verses—that I couldn't expect to decode *gurna* song in this fashion. My Tupuri was not strong enough for me to comprehend the lyrics directly, and the *gurna* members did not master French well enough to explain the song's meanings. The conclusion I mistakenly came to was that my problem would be solved by taking my Tupuri song transliterations to Tupuri-speakers who spoke excellent French.

Naturally, I turned to a Tupuri friend with whom I had a vibrant intellectual relationship. Maïgama Josephine was a brilliant 35-year-old woman who had had the rare privilege of completing lycée and attending college in the capital. Dynamic and critically minded, she was involved in establishing a women's development organization with other elite women in Maroua at the time I met her. Busy as she was, raising her two children and managing a household of dependent relatives, she nevertheless immediately responded to my request for help. However, when we sat down together in her house to look at my song transliterations, it quickly became obvious that translation would be anything but easy. I watched as she supplied the French translation for each Tupuri word—*mot-à-mot,* she insisted. But in the end, the phrases did not make sense. Finally she threw up her hands in despair, saying that she couldn't make head nor tail of this Tupuri. As she apologized profusely for not being able to help, I reassured her that she *had* helped, and as I took my leave I asked myself "What kind of Tupuri is this?"

As I moved along the twisting alleys through the neighborhood back to my house, I realized that *gurna* songs, even though public, were in fact artifacts from a subcultural world that excluded all but its members. I had naively thought that any Tupuri-speaker could help me without taking into account the specialized knowledge and competencies that were part and parcel of the *gurna* world. In fact, as close as she was to me intellectually and socially, Maïgama was probably the last person who would be competent to translate *gurna* song. Highly educated, a daughter in a devout Catholic family, she had not been exposed to the song as a *may* (girl) who, just after puberty, might have joined the *gurna* to announce her marriage eligibility. Eschewing the *gurna* camp during her adolescence, Maïgama was busy studying for her lycée exams, which she passed with spectacular scores.

My next line of attack was to try the "cultural brokers": Tupuri men who had been part of the *gurna* milieu but who also had since had wider life experiences. I reasoned that their biculturalism might bridge the gaps in my comprehension. Kaïno was an irrepressible jokester whose intellectual genius took him to Bamako in the 1980s on a government scholarship to earn a Ph.D. in veterinary science. When I met him, he was back in Doukoula, his native region, dragging around, unemployed, drinking too much. He had been ostracized by the ruling political party which also controlled the government because he had dared to join the opposition party. A Tupuri political ally had given him a temporary opportunity by asking him to manage the Doukoula bakery.

One afternoon, I found Kaïno relaxing in the bar in Doukoula with a 50-year-old man in a red cap and long robes typical of Muslims, though clearly he was Tupuri. Lemmo had been a gendarme for twenty-eight years and had retired to Doukoula. I learned that neither man had actually been a member of the *gurna* society because their studies and careers had taken them far from Tupuriland. However, when I pulled out my tattered transliteration of the *gurna* song and laid it on the old metal café table sticky with beer, they leapt into the project of translating and explaining it to me. What the men lacked in precision, they made up for in élan. They exuberantly explained the meaning of the lyrics to me, approximating the actual words.

For example, Lemmo explained that in the context of the *gurna*, the word *sir* meant not so much "land" or "earth" as "sector" in the sense of a region of political control. *Sir* referred to the composer's ability to retain popularity with *gurna* camps. However, his translation of the lyrics was imprecise. For example, he translated "*Gariyame ndi fɛr mbi ti ŋgel po nda paa*" as "If the *gurna* is a huge pond, then I am a hippopotamus. I leave the pond to go somewhere else." Later, I discovered that a better translation was "Gariyame, I'm leaving to go elsewhere." But Lemmo's translation is understandable if one is working with the transcribed rather than the performed version of the song. He had taken the term "Manbrao" from the line before and translated it as "pond of the *gurna*." In fact, Manbrao is the proper name for the pond near the song composer's own camp. In that line, the composer greets and encourages his dancers ("*weere* Manbrao"). Working from the notion of "the *gurna* as a pond," Lemmo then translated Gariyame literally as "hippopotamus" rather than recognizing it as the proper name of a particular *gurna* member. Many *gurna* sobriquets are Massa words for animals denoting physical largeness (hippo, giraffe, etc.). Lemmo explained that the composer was boasting that he was so magnificent (like a hippo) that he would leave all the other *gurna* in the pond behind him. In subsequent conversations with the song composer himself, I learned that in this line, he was simply referring to his need to keep moving to disseminate his song: "I'm leaving to go elsewhere."

Even though Lemmo's translation was imperfect, there were patterns to his errors (for example, translating proper nouns literally), and he also got the main gist of the composer's meanings, such as elaborate forms of self-promotion. From this, I realized that Kaïno and Lemmo, even though they had never been *gurna* themselves, were nonetheless versed in the prevailing metaphors, concerns, and structures of feelings associated with the *gurna* society. They had a feel for the composer's need to promote himself above all others and for meanings that denoted the field of charged power relations that characterize the *gurna*. I attributed part of this knowledge to their status as highly successful men, even though their success occurred outside the *gurna* in the university and military, respectively. However, because they were not participants in the actual *gurna* network, Kaïno and Lemmo lacked knowledge of the highly specific stories, actors, and events to which the annual song referred. This insight led me to realize that the songs were not ultimately translatable in a generic fashion (either literally or figuratively). Instead, I needed to be privy to the specific stories, enmities, and alliances that were behind the song, that in effect motivated it. And there was no one to give me this kind of knowledge except for the composer himself. This realization launched my series of interviews with *gurna* song composers.

Unwittingly, I began not with the entrenched dynasty of composers but with an upstart composer who was challenging their dominance. Sogole, the composer of the *gurna* song I had been struggling to translate, was a middle-aged man, slender, with kind eyes. He tended to be taciturn, though when he spoke, he did so forcefully and succinctly, often parrying my questions with another question. My interviews with Sogole (as well as with other composers) were seldom private; he was always surrounded and assisted by his advisors (*courriers*) and members of his village's *gurna* camp. We worked from an initial translation that my research assistant, Awé, and I had produced after hours of work that often felt like deciphering word games (see figure 31). In these interviews, I asked the composer about what he thought were the most "delicious" (*de cōore*) parts of his song, the meaning of intriguing metaphors, the stories behind the names appearing in the song, and any consequences he experienced as a result of his song.

In tracing the song back to the composer and soliciting his assistance, did I find the source of the song's meaning? Was the composer the ultimate authority? Many of my questions were answered: The composer explicated the song, verse by verse, zeroing in on lines I found particularly problematic or intriguing. When I asked about various specific verses and about songs from previous years, the composer called forth one of his *courriers* to sing the words to us all. He used the *courrier* like a tape recorder, a human repository of past songs. In addition to explaining metaphors, insults, and greeting, Sogole revealed to me how the song interfaced with his ongoing conflict with a competing composer that had resulted in his going to jail. However, in spite of all this information on the song, the complexities of translation did not cease with my contact with the composers. Two difficulties remained: The first fell into the domain of the politics of knowledge; the second was what I came to call a fragmentation of knowledge.

The politics of knowledge can be boiled down to a single question: Who was I that Sogole could reveal his composition secrets to me? Highly conscious of being *je-wuu* (a Westerner) in a region where the only "Europeans" were a handful of Christian missionaries, I imagined that the composer would limit information he would reveal to me out of mistrust of missionaries, since they were generally not supportive of the *gurna* tradition and its "pagan" rites. When this did not appear to be a factor, I imagined then that the composer would distrust the fact that I moved among all composers, even his archrivals. In fact, the composer took an aggressive stance toward his rivals and wasn't at all concerned that I would foment conflict with my questions—conflict was his bread and butter! Later I learned where his sensitivities lay.

In the course of one of his visits to my house on market day, Sogole pulled away from his entourage and explained his real concern in hushed and deliberate voice. At the end of each of my visits, I had given a modest cash gift to the composer and one to the *jak-kaw*. Apparently, after my departure, a robust gossip mill had begun the rumor that in fact the composer might be receiving a much larger sum of money from me and that he was jealously hiding it from his network of *courriers*. He reassured me that I was his *bar* (friend) and that this was his problem to deal with. Confused by the conversation (which was couched in much more indirect terms), I later suspected that this was his way of telling me that he wouldn't mind receiving larger cash gifts. What was most interesting to me was that in spite of the reputation Tupuri have for being closed and secretive to outsiders, there seemed to be no taboo against my asking for and obtaining insider knowledge about the song, including details about individuals who had come to the composer to ask him to right wrongs or exact revenge in the song. Once launched by the composer, the song was considered highly public and accessible to all, even those like myself who needed the finer points spelled out. Once again the rub was over allocation of material resources.

Because the song was composed by a single person, I expected that the composer would be able to tell me all the background behind all his lyrics. To my surprise, I discovered that because the song functions as a sort of community bulletin board, the composer's knowledge can at times be partial. He might not know exactly what conflict existed between two neighbors when one came to him for insult. Ideally the composer's "secret agents" in the village were supposed to confirm all stories before they were included in the song. Nonetheless, the composer was at times in the position of composing with shreds of intelligence given to him by others, whose roots he might not fully understand.

In a parallel fashion, the interlocutors of the songs (both the *gurna* and the wider public) heard references to people and stories in the lyrics about which they had no knowledge. Of course, because the song covered a wide geographical area, different listeners would have different levels of insider knowledge about people referred to in the song, depending on where they lived and their own social networks. Also, non-Tupuri-speakers overheard the songs. Civil servants from all over Cameroon who had been posted in schools and government offices in Tupuriland occasionally attended *gurna* dances out of curiosity and for lack of other leisure-time distractions. One schoolteacher from the south told me when I asked that "these songs are about the heroic exploits of the Tupuri people." Of course, he came to such a conclusion by noticing the powerful, warriorlike quality of the dance accompanying the song. He was not privy to the meanings of the lyrics. It is ironic that the students in the lycée where he taught had included his name in the lycée Youth Day *gurna* song in the context of an accusation of theft of their

Theater Club funds. Later the student composer told me that he had been confronted by the teacher, who had heard that his name was in the song even though he did not speak Tupuri. The student composer kept silent, maintaining the insider knowledge of the song.

I understand this fragmentation of knowledge—that no one knows everything, that all knowledge is situated—to be an inevitable part of the wide-ranging communicative system of the *gurna*. The partial, incomplete quality of knowledge (by the composer, by the *gurna* members, and by the wider audience) does not seem to undermine the essential cohesion of the system. However, as a "scientific" researcher, I sought an omniscient view that Donna Haraway calls "god-trick" (1991, 191): attempting the highly artificial task of understanding all verses of the song equally and to the greatest depth possible. While I never attained my "perfect" translation—there was always a verse to puzzle over, a metaphor to decode, a story to reveal—I nevertheless was able to see not just the competency of various community members but their areas of incompetence or incomprehension.

Some *gurna* camps had "mislearned" the song in minor ways—they inserted one word or name for another. But these vagaries in the transmission of the song were amazingly rare. It is more interesting to note the difference in interpretation listeners constructed from the same line. For example, Ringwa, an urban composer, composed the following lines:

Madeleine bay wāyn wa Djouboyang,
Nday ɓɔ' Tapsou ti sɛŋ daa Guenede,
Madeleine gēe ma jɔŋ wāre sōore.
Maŋ war ɓɛ coo yaw la.
Sɛn mo caw say ɓɛ baa jobo ga. (M., 98/99, v. 28)

Madeleine isn't a woman, Djouboyang, (1)
You put Tapsou up to that, Guenédé. (2)
Madeleine grew up doing shameful things. (3)
Could that change now that she's married? (4)
No one will have any use for her. (5)

Dulnya coo sɔ bɔɔ raw jag wer piri gɔ.
Sir naa coo sɔ wejōore.
<u>Naare jɔŋ wɔɔ bay facture pa.</u> (M., 98/99, v. 29)

Modern life has changed and overwhelmed men. (6)
Our land has changed, dancers. (7)
<u>Women are without receipts.</u> (8)

I asked several people for their interpretation of line 8: "Women are without receipts." Danwe, a young man living in Doukoula, was having enormous trouble paying the brideprice of five cows to his wife's father. After he obtained a salaried job with a modest income in the provincial capital, his father-in-law decided to call in his debt, threatening to take him to court for nonpayment of the brideprice. Not surprisingly, Danwe's interpretation of the line from Ringwa's song centered around his anxiety about brideprice. He said, "In these days of the economic crisis, men are not able to afford to pay brideprice when they marry. So now women are without 'receipts'; we have to marry them just like that." But Ringwa told me of his intended meaning: that women are behaving badly in the "modern times" (*dulnya,* line 6). The song recounts how Tapsou is forced to commit suicide with malaria medicine because his wife, Guenédé, dominated him (line 2). The composer described his metaphor of "women without receipts" as a way of saying that women today do not engender confidence, they are illicit, without papers (of the sort that gendarmes demand at the country's numerous road checkpoints). Even though the composer and one listener had two different interpretations of the metaphor—metaphors are, of course, purposely open to multiple interpretations—it is interesting to note that both men understood problems with "modernity" to be located for men around their dealings with women, that the state of women was a marker for the larger health of the society. Again, multiple interpretations were not inconsistent with an overall coherence in the *gurna* song discourse.

My experience of working with *gurna* song (in transcription, translation, and explication) revealed to me that the song was highly dependent on prior knowledge of village news and social relations to be comprehensible. Also, it contained an entire specialized vocabulary of conventional metaphors and syntax that made it obscure to all but *gurna* insiders. But regardless of various levels of comprehension of listeners, the song nevertheless operated as a cohesive public sphere, especially when one considers the circulation of gossip and commentary on the song that occurs outside the performance domain.

LEARNING SONG IN THE VILLAGE

Bar ɓi Klo tum diŋ antenne-jõo. (L., 98/99, v. 15)
My friend, Klo, is always an antenna for the dance.

As should be clear now, the *gurna* song system does not rely on a few expert performers but is a democratic practice involving mass participation of members. This system, however, poses its own challenges. How is it that hundreds of dancers, spread across dozens of villages, can learn a new song of seventy or more verses each year? What are the contexts and pedagogies for this socialization into the song? What changes occur over time?

In the beginning of the *gurna* season, when the new songs come out, village *gurna* camps send one or two members to the compound of the composer with whom the camp has chosen to affiliate that year. These envoys of the song have a reputation for memorizing well or they bring a tape recorder. In the evening, the composer and his *courriers* sing the new song very clearly in a form that I came to call its "pedagogical form" while the envoys from the camps record it. During the critical opening weeks of the *gurna* season (November and December), the composers also appear in public to present their song. They make visits to camps and appear in public places such as the weekly markets to sing the entire song several times for tape-recording by *gurna* members. Their objective is to encourage as many *gurna* camps as possible to adopt and master the song. Cassette tapes of the pedagogical form of the song are sold each year in a small shop in Doukoula (copied one by one rather than mass produced).

The pedagogical form of the song is a very clear, deliberately enunciated version. A *courrier* with a particularly strong, clear voice sings in duet with an "*entonneur*" ("song leader," French)[9] in an antiphony or call-and-response pattern, a fundamental element of African performance (Thompson 1999 [1966], 80). The *courrier* sings the verse and then the *entonneur* punctuates it with a whistle for several seconds before he moves to the next verse. In the context of the actual dance, this break in the verses is supplied by a low, bellowing moan of the *entonneur*, who is positioned in the heart of the dance ring. The *gurna* dancers chant the verses in unison. In the special pedagogical form of the song, these breaks are made even clearer by the *entonneur*'s whistling through a *siili*, a goat-horn whistle. The sound was purposely crisp and clean so that *gurna* could learn the patterns of entrance and exit in the song correctly—an African aesthetic principle that Robert Farris Thompson calls "killing" or "cutting" the song (1974, 18). Specialists in *siŋ gurna* explained to me that this break between the verses is necessary for the singing dancers to catch their breath. The verses are sung in a single burst except for slight (comma-length) pauses, so such a break was necessary. These specialists also note that the *entonneur* "holds up" the song and paces it with his bellowing.

Although the antiphony appears in both the pedagogical and live forms of the song, the former sounds quite different from the ultimate performance of the song at death celebration dances. Even for Tupuri-speakers, it is extremely difficult to make out the words of the song at the *yii-huuli*. The hundreds of singers blur the song by singing at slightly different rates and by mumbling or intentionally moaning through sections when they are not sure of the words. Tremendous drumming and spectator noise at the dance adds to the din. As the result, the pedagogical form of the song and practice in the camps are important for effective learning of the song. When the song is performed in public, its power lies not in a transparent communication of lyrics but in an overall effect of strength and unity in the dance, supported by the song rhythm.

CHANGES IN SONG LEARNING: TAPE RECORDERS AND LITERACY

In Tupuriland I was frequently told stories of how the people of the past had prodigious powers: They surmounted hardships that we use modern technology to overcome. It was said that the ancestors lived to be much older, up to 125 or 150 years, and that today we need modern medicine while they did not. As part of this discourse, I was told that in the past, before schooling existed in Tupuriland, remarkable individuals would crop up in society, people with fabulous memories. They only needed to hear the entire *gurna* song three or four times to commit it to memory. These were the individuals who would work as *courriers* with the composers. Now, with the rise of tape-recording and literacy, these memorizers were said to have entirely disappeared from society—they are no longer born.

In the late 1990s, *gurna* members used tape-recorded versions of the song as a pedagogical tool as well as another technology: literacy. The introduction of literacy to the song-learning process is recent because Western-style schools have existed in Tupuriland only since the 1950s. The Catholic missionaries who established these schools were critical of indigenous institutions such as the *gurna*, so the use of literacy in service of the *gurna* song was an unintended consequence of missionary instruction. Even now that school-based literacy is more widespread, the dissemination of the *gurna* song has remained largely oral-aural. Most village composers today, who are generally of the generation that predates mass education, are not literate. Dissemination of the annual song from the composer to the *gurna* is entirely oral, either through memorization or tape-recording. Literacy comes into the process at the level of the camp as a technique for assisting fellow members to learn the song.

I found that there are usually one or two *gurna* who are literate within each camp. They transcribe the song in small school notebooks. One of their challenges is a lack of familiarity with written Tupuri, since indigenous languages are not taught in Cameroonian schools. Christians are exposed to written Tupuri through Catholic hymns (*siŋ jak-Baa*) or the Lutheran Tupuri Bible (Wāare ma de Cōore), and a few *gurna* members may have studied Tupuri literacy informally at one of the missions. The song transcriptions in the *gurna* camps use improvised transliterations with erratic spelling and punctuation. But form is not a concern—only the efficient learning of the song for performance. After the members have mastered it, the transcription is tossed aside. Contrary to theoretical literature on literacy that emphasizes the documentary power of literacy and the cognitive transformations it is thought to effect (Goody 1977; Ong 1982), the production of a written archive of the song is not valued among the *gurna*. As each year passes, old songs simply pass into oblivion. Any juicy scandals or clever turns of phrase are remembered informally over beer and male camaraderie.

However, some *gurna* report that the introduction of literacy to the *gurna* song, even in this limited form, is having disruptive effects on the traditional power relations between the generations. Ndarwe, himself a literate farmer and sometime *gurna*, speculated that the younger *gurna* who have attended school and are now learning the song through transcriptions are undermining the power of the elders. As described in chapter 3, the *gurna* is age-graded; each member is ranked within the camp according to the years since his *nage may* (sexual initiation).[10] The "natural" order is that elders who had been *gurna* for many years will be more competent in learning the song. But Ndarwe speculated that although some nonliterate *gurna* are impressed by writing, the fact that younger *gurna* learn the song more quickly through the aid of transcriptions undermines elders' prestige. Ndarwe explained this disruption in terms of the connection between dance competency and knowledge of the song: "When a line of dancers went forward in the dance to execute a *bɔ'ge fɔgɛ* [a challenge], how would it look if a senior dancer did not know the song's rhythm? That would be shameful."

These shifts in song competency and socialization tie into a wider discourse I often heard about the effects of schooling. What happens when a person who has gone off to school returns to the *gurna* camp in the village? As a result of attending school, an *évolué* ("civilized person") tends to possess new subjectivities, habits, and status that separate him from the mass of *gurna*. Literacy is just one of these urbane qualities; shame about "nudity" (the required *gurna* dance costume) and discomfort with the *gurna*'s rustic behaviors of sitting on the ground and drinking unpasteurized milk are some others. This discourse is by now familiar: schooling, urban living, and salaried work tend to change a person permanently, to disassociate or alienate him from his natal roots.

However, Tupuri understandings of literacy cannot be boiled down to such a simple formula. The *gurna* as a local practice is not always seen as isolated from state institutions and modern technologies such as literacy; it is interpenetrated with them. For example, consider the metaphor "*konkur*" in recent *gurna* songs; it functions as an elliptical metacultural commentary on the state and the *gurna* genre. "*Konkur*" ("*concours,*" French) means literally "competition" or "tournament," although in Cameroon's French-based administrative system, it refers to the national civil service exams that determine the fate of all students. For admission to professional training programs or recruitment for civil service positions, graduates are required to pass these difficult *concours*. And because Cameroon's private sector is limited, the *concours* take on extraordinary significance. The elimination of these state-sponsored exams as a part of the downsizing of the civil service during the 1990s is widely understood to have economically undermined an entire generation of young Cameroonians.

In the Tupuri dance context, however, the meaning of this culturally potent term was subtly reshaped. Among the *gurna*, *konkur* refers to the composer's "publication" of praises of *gurna* members in the song. The "posting" of names in song is parallel to the posting of exam results. "*Ndi hã ɗu konkur yaŋ gɔ.*" ("I will publish the names of the competition"; D., 98/99, v. 23). Or "*Konkur kɔl ti wãre jõo.*" ("The exams have become the lyrics"; T., 98/99, v. 2). One composer, Sogole, explained that here *konkur* has two meanings. First, during the period when the national exams were cancelled due to *la crise*, the "exams" were "with the dance." That is, the prestige-making that the modern education system used to confer on individuals had shifted back to the village level to the arena of dance. When one failed, the other stepped in. Although there is no escaping the duality of a state-sponsored "modernity" and a local "tradition," I understand this relationship as one of interpenetration of two systems of prestige and one in which the local poaches on the meanings of the national. While no one would deny the importance of schooling for social mobility among the Tupuri, there did appear to be a revitalization of the prestige systems of local cultural practice with the decline of the state.

Sogole went on to point out to me that his second meaning for *konkur* was that the song has become written, whereas before it was entirely oral. As all meaning is situationally constituted, I suspect that Sogole's observations of changes in the song system from oral to literate may have been influenced by our immediate research context. *Gurna* members, composers, and other Tupuri-speakers seemed to be fascinated by my extreme reliance on written forms of the songs during my research; I always worked with a transcribed version of the song in order to translate it and solicit explications of its meanings (although I collected tape-recorded versions as well). In short, *my* song-learning was highly literate—to some, bewilderingly so. (Whenever I fell ill, my friends were quick to blame my "reading too much.") As theorizers of postmodern ethnographic practice have pointed out (Clifford and Marcus 1986; Marcus and Fischer 1986), one cannot eliminate the influence of the effects of the research itself on the continuing reconstitution of cultural practice. My use of word-processed versions of the song in the *gurna* camps probably tended to throw weight to the literate faction of *gurna* members. They probably noticed that in spite of the challenges of the Tupuri language, I as an outsider was competent in manipulating the songs in ways that insiders were not (and vice versa). For example, using my transcriptions, I could move easily back and forth between verses. Perhaps this literacy gave a new possibility to the *gurna* song: a potential for the song to be picked up and comprehended by a non-Tupuri. Through transcription and translation of the song, the ways of the *gurna*, though never secret, have become more transparent to outsiders.

LEARNING SONG IN THE CITY

In spite of minor shifts brought by literacy and recording technology, socialization into the *gurna* song seems to be relatively stable in rural villages I visited. Larger changes were evident in cities where Tupuri people had migrated. Those interested in perpetuating the *gurna* were faced with the difficult task of translating a pastoral institution to an urban setting. In Maroua, the provincial capital of the Far North, I spoke with Tupuri cultural leaders, including song composers, Tupuri-language radio disc jockeys, leaders of Tupuri cultural associations, and émigré students and intellectuals. They discussed a porousness between the village and the city that, through the movement of migrants, allows for some degree of cultural competence in the *gurna* to be maintained. That is, when men who were *gurna* members in the village migrate to the city, they bring their dancing and singing competencies and cultural knowledge. However, barriers to a vibrant *gurna* practice remained, and these are a source of constant irritation for these self-defined cultural leaders.

For example, in Maroua, it was impossible to maintain the *jak-kawre* that were foundational to the rural practice of the *gurna*. In the countryside, *gurna* spend many hours together in camps in quiet isolation from the village. Although materially spartan, there is the luxury of time and conviviality in these camps. The environment is conducive to a relaxed apprenticeship in the annual *gurna* song. In contrast, *gurna* dancers in the city tend to use the beer parlors (*ŋgel-yii*)[11] as their site of learning. These parlors are simple patios nestled in residential Tupuri neighborhoods where women make money by brewing large quantities of sorghum beer throughout the week for sale. The mostly male clientele sits informally on wooden logs or benches under a straw shelter. They seat themselves as small circles of friends around a demijohn of sorghum beer, shared in turn with a calabash cup. '*Argi* (sorghum liquor) was also consumed in tiny clear jars as shots. Needless to say, in a wave of alcohol consumption, the *ŋgel-yii* is often raucous; the stresses of urban life and work are assuaged in banter and *yii*. In this environment, learning the *gurna* song is difficult.

Furthermore, in the city, there are few opportunities to dance. Urban death celebrations involve much less dancing, in part because there is no system of *gurna* camps to draw upon. In an effort to fill this vacuum, composers produce songs for Tupuri cultural associations and *gurna* clubs in schools. Performance of the song is limited to national holidays that have been "Tupurized." For example, in Maroua, the New Year's holiday is celebrated by refashioning the indigenous Tupuri new year celebration practiced in rural areas, called the Maaserew (part of the Dore clan's *few kage,* Festival of the Cock). One urban composer, Ringwa, a student in a teacher-training college, complained to me that the *gurna* dancers in Maroua failed to learn his song well, even after he cut its verses from seventy to thirty-five. They did not have the time to put into memorizing it. To his chagrin, the dancers reverted in the end to a song that everyone knew from last year.

In the countryside, the *gurna* arose in concert with the seasonality of farming. It is hardly surprising that in urban areas, where social organization and value revolve around salaried work (or the lack of it), the practice of the *gurna* would be replaced by other forms of leisure and collectivity. In the city, men gather for drinking and conversation, usually after church on Sunday. Groups of friends are guided by signs (*drapeau,* French), plastic sacks affixed to stakes in the ground to indicate the beer parlors that dot Tupuri quarters. Drinkers and nondrinkers alike complained frequently to me about the corrosive influence of alcohol consumption in the city. The forms of collectivity and sociability supported by the *gurna* in rural areas have been replaced in Maroua by less formal ties among men and the primacy of convivial intoxication. In this environment, the *gurna* and its song system are of little importance.

Additionally, lack of competency in the Tupuri language is occasionally another problem for urban song learners. In the rural *gurna* camp, competence in the song is highly valued; it is considered vital for individual prestige as well as the prestige of entire *jak-kaw*. In the city, although the song might serve to unite the Tupuri dispersed in a multiethnic environment, mastery of the song is not a widely held value, in part because the *gurna* identity overall is marginalized.

The experience of sharing the song—adopting, mastering, and performing it publicly—was a fundamental aspect of *gurna* collectivity. To be a *gurna* was by definition to be a dancer, and in order to dance one must know the annual song. The song occasions a sociability and display of competence that provides a bonding among members within a camp and across camps in a large region that spans many villages. As a public sphere, the *gurna* song system allows for the participation of individuals who in effect "post" their views: whether they promote themselves, greet their friends, or "burn" their enemies. The song has become an annual collective commentary on the state of Tupuriland, seen through the eyes of the *gurna* members. However, not everyone can comprehend the song lyrics during the dances, and even to understand their literal meanings does not mean that interlocutors are necessarily privy to the microlevel circumstances in villages that motivate the lyrics. They don't necessarily know the stories behind the story. For these reasons, the wider community gains access to selective parts of the song through *radio trottoir* (gossip) when the song is first launched by the composer. The ability to interpret the song's meanings is generally contingent on one's proximity to the *gurna* practice in the village. However, levels of "insiderness" to the *gurna* society are relative, and knowledge of the song's content is graduated.

If, as Barber suggests, "social knowledge is distributed unevenly and piecemeal among participants, and . . . the 'meaning' of a text is variably construed,"[12] it seems ironic that the song acts as the glue that binds *gurna* to *gurna* and village to village in wide swathes of Tupuriland. Even though meaning is contingent and variable, the creation of a shared public sphere in which this meaning is construed tends to unify widely dispersed populations. Obscurity and variability in the meanings of the song lyrics are not pressing problems for either the *gurna* or their spectators at the dance. No matter what the stories are behind the song, how vitriolic the lyrics are, or how fierce the composers' competition are, the song-and-dance performance at death celebrations constructs an imaginary of unity and strength that affirms the community.

SIX

"Rise Up, Gather Like Storm Clouds"

Poetics of Gurna *Song* (Siŋ Gurna)

In the preceding chapter, I suggested that there is not simply one *gurna* song; rather, there are, in a manner of speaking, three. Each guise of the song is vested with certain priorities and meanings. First, the *gurna* song takes on an appearance of unity and *communitas* when dancers perform it publicly. In this guise, the song "holds up" the dance, providing coherence to hundreds of dancers moving en masse and the spectators who take in the scene. In its second guise, the song is launched as a textual object by specialized composers. In the *gurna* network, the song acts as a symbolic marker of the composer's popularity and the politics of affiliation as camps select their song for the year. As an object of learning for individual *gurna* members in their camps, the song text provides a basis for shared knowledge and the building of group competence. However, outside of the *gurna* society, the song takes on a third guise as it seeps into the surrounding community. The non-*gurna* majority can never know the song in its entirety—it is too long and complex; however, they absorb the important news within it. In this broad view, the song disintegrates into morsels of scandal as clever verses from the songs circulate through the neighborhood. Understanding the song in this fashion—as having three guises, depending on audience and context—affects how one might understand the poetics of the song.

When I first attended *gurna* dances, I was barely aware that the deep groaning of the dancers was, in fact, a performance of oral poetry. Only much later, after having transcribed and translated *gurna* song for many months, did I became fascinated by the multifaceted nature of the text. I was struck by the many functions of the song, even if its lyrics were mostly incomprehensible during the dance performance. It contained phrases to win dancers, rouse enthusiasm for the *gurna*, elicit laughter, embarrass fools, wreak revenge, confer honor and appreciation, moralize, and socialize. This chapter describes the rhetorical building blocks of *gurna* song based on textual analysis as well as conversations with song composers. Five rhetorical forms seemed to me to be most salient: a) praise and greeting; b) metacommentary on the dance; c) insult (*ɖarge*); d) recounting of shameful acts (*sōore*); and e) social commentary.

The juxtaposition of diverse units in a single *gurna* song, its layered (or cobbled-together) quality, is striking. Samuel Kléda and Suzanne Ruelland (1998) have approached the analysis of *gurna* song by cataloguing the many themes of a single song. Taking a different tack, I aim to give the reader a deeper sense of how each of the five rhetorical types operate across *many* songs. This tactic enables me to explore some of the typical conventions that mark each form. At the end of the chapter, I consider how the structure of *gurna* song shapes the values of spontaneity, constancy, and polyvocality in the genre. Throughout, I emphasize the "handprint" of the processes of song production visible in the rhetorical conventions.

If the song has multiple guises in the public sphere of the *gurna*, how does its poetics reflect this polyvalence? How might a composer deploy these various rhetorical forms for different intentions? Or how might the song be fashioned so that it said different things to different people? Different parts of the song have different audiences, even if composers are wont to say that every Tupuri-speaker understands the entire song. Far from being transparent texts, *gurna* song lyrics are crafted for both insider and outsider audiences. On the one hand, composers and their informants insert insult (*darge*) and stories about shameful behavior (*sōore*) into the song to bring maximum embarrassment to their targets, knowing that these nuggets would be widely circulated *au quartier*. On the other hand, composers also insert strings of names into the song as a form of praise and encouragement to their most loyal dancers. Only the *gurna* themselves can possibly keep track of the thicket of names in each annual song, tracking shifts in fame of individuals and camps. Deploying a variety of rhetorical forms, the composer creates a work of oral poetry that speaks to multiple constituencies simultaneously.

"MOTIVATION OF NAMES": PRAISE AND GREETING

Gurna song enacts and makes public—and therefore "real"—the social networks among men created by the *gurna* society. The key modality for this process is praise-naming. Much of the text of *gurna* song is taken up with praises and greetings to individual dancers. They represent the composer's effort to drum up enthusiasm for the dance and garner dancers to his side.

> *Demangue wii Garsoumo ndao Djaolane deban*
> *Ndi de ndum mon pasɔ Lemasse.*
> *Tchanwalé nday de Waisso fɛr wɛ nen Bisreo da.*
> *Legaigue her jak ne Djoday Ndandewa Gaossoumo Ndersale Baiguili*
> *Numra un lay sɔ Yembe,*
> *Wangba Koubouli Namsala Gaona Salmaï*
> *Naa manyaabaa na.* (T., 97/98, v. 32)

Demangue asks after Garsoumo to give strong support to Djaolane.
I bellow out the song again, Lemasse.
Tchanwalé, you along with Waisso, return to Bisreo.
Legaigue, greet Djoday Ndandewa Gaossoumo Ndersale Baiguili
You're number one also, Yembe.
Wanga Koubouli Namsala Gaona Salmaï
Gather together like storm clouds.

Many different forms of African praise song have been explored, as have the sociological problems they evoke (Barber 1991; Gunner 1995; de Moraes Farias 1995). At the risk of oversimplifying a rich and complex ethnographic record, I have found that praise and greetings in *gurna* song are unique. They do not resemble the Mande griot (*jeli*) tradition, in which the praise singer addresses a patron in the context of a public performance. De Moraes Farias describes the crux of these forms of praise: "their capacity to seize upon the 'truth' of the praisee's being, and to activate it and generate acknowledgment of it by the praisee's private self and by the public at large" (1995, 225). Barber describes Yoruba *oriki* similarly: Whether flattering or not, "[t]heir point is . . . to go to the heart of a subject's identity by evoking whatever is distinctive in it" (1991, 13). These forms of praise-singing put the praisee on the spot, because to be praised publicly is to place "unavoidable demands on him/her" (de Moreas Farias 1995, 225). In their examinations of Hausa praise song, Smith (1957) and Pellow (1997) emphasize its role in maintaining hierarchical patron-client relations that permeate Hausa society.

In contrast, praise and greeting in Tupuri *gurna* song neither emphasize the distinctiveness of individuals nor maintain the existing social hierarchy. Rather, they emphasize the values of friendship, popularity, and "political" mobilization symbolized by getting people to come out for the dance. In my view, *gurna* praise more closely resembles visual and oral forms of appreciation popular in hip-hop culture in the United States. As an extension of "sampling" or "cutting and mixing" (Perkins 1996), rap performers call out names of those who have supported them (giving them their "props"). Hip-hop radio announcers invite listeners to call in to the station to thank their friends on the air. Graffiti artists have translated this oral form into a visual format by listing friends and supporters ("shout-outs") in a corner of their graffiti pieces (Ignatowski 1997). This naming of names, recognizing and greeting one's supporters, is a form of aesthetic politics that resembles *gurna* composers' calling out of names in their annual songs.

These panegyrics involve a string or accretion of names—names of certain dancers and villages the composer has strategically selected to insert into the song in an effort to cultivate their favor. He may have chosen them based on his own judgment of their enthusiasm for the dance or as a recognition of their support or the likelihood that they will support him in the future. The appearance of names in the song might be the result of a meeting earlier in the season between the dancers and the composer. Like African panegyric in other contexts, praise can never be taken at face value but must be considered as strategic and situational. Behind each name are efforts on the part of the composer and the dancers to position themselves optimally in the eyes of the broader community.

The basic principle of praise (*tugodge*) in *siŋ gurna* is to gain fame by amplifying one's name throughout the region: this is *raage ɗu* (to announce a name, in the sense of making a noise). When an individual's name appears in the song, he is publicly identified as an enthusiast for the dance, a supporter of the *gurna*. In his song, the composer calls out the names of specific dancers "to get up to dance" as a way of encouraging them to promote his song and the *gurna* institution in general. Here the vital energy of dancers is celebrated, a foundational value in most African dance (what Thompson calls "vital aliveness" [1974, 9]). Frequently the composer foments competition in the dance, bragging that he will beat out all others this year. However, even when individual names are announced, they are understood as elements in a constellation of fictively affined men. To single out one individual's name is to name his *jak-kaw* and the entire village represented by the camp. The individual, the camp, and the village are then understood to be strong in the dance, dynamic, vital. Even though praise operates through the naming of atomic individuals, the effect of the praise has a ripple effect.

Composers count on this ripple effect when they use praise to activate their networks of supporters. Composers do not randomly name dancers and villagers; they strategically select those whom they judge to be pivotal nodes in the web of dancers. That is, one *gurna* member may motivate others to join and may be able to influence which composer the *jak-kaw* chooses to affiliate with. Composers recognize that over the years it is important to rotate among the many villages who support them through their affiliation. Dancers need to be recognized and cultivated or they are likely to defect to another composer. Some *gurna* visit the composer, offering gifts in exchange (they hope) for the pleasure of seeing their names in the song that year. All of these factors, favors, and strategic considerations shape the decisions composers make about who is praised in the song.

Praise in *siŋ gurna* is signaled through certain stylistic conventions. The logic of *raage ɗu* (to announce a name) means that greetings of dancers in the song operate as praise, even though distinctive qualities of individuals are not emphasized. The composer greets individual dancers and groups of dancers in a practice called *heege jage* (lit. "put-mouth," glossed as hello). This greeting is not, however, one-dimensional; it takes on three dimensions when the composer through his authorial voice asks specific dancers to accompany him to greet other dancers, whose names he also lists.

> *Tchanwal ndɔ wɔ liŋ.*
> *Nday hee jak ne Djelombe.*
> *Ndi fɛr gɔ wɛr ndalge Baissa wɛr gebɛɛ po bay caw wa sɔ lay.*
> *Poudarna Karmaï wɔ de nda ɗu kan me hee jag ne Hadale.*
> *Dulnya ciŋ jak ɓi ma ndalge.*
> *Ndi no hay wɛ lɛ liŋ yo bay lay ne.*
> *Ndi hay laa ɗu naa Golonkare.*
> *Sonlao Daram Sogole ɓɛ wãayn biŋ bale.* (T., 97/87, v. 12)

> Tchanwal, you're going home.
> Greet Djelombe.
> I'll come back to chat with Baissa, that there is no more slavery.
> Poudarna from Karmai, shout out my name
> and accompany me to greet Hadale.
> I've many things to express in my song.
> If I were in the village too,
> I would hear our name come to Golonkare.
> Sonlao from Daram, Sogole's mother gave birth to an elephant.

These greetings can take on a variety of possible combinations: The composer greets dancer A, the composer asks dancer A to greet dancer B, the composer tells dancer A that dancer B greets him or "asks for" (*wiige*) him, the composer asks dancer A to accompany him to greet dancer B, or dancer A greets dancer B directly (without the rhetorical insertion of the composer's persona). The possibilities are dizzying. A common metaphor in *gurna* discourse for such a relay communication system is the "telephone." The voice of the composer, and thus the song itself, acts as a "telephone" between two friends.

When the composer "asks for" (*wiige*) one through another, he underlines the public nature of friendship: the avenues through which one is linked to another.

Fonkomdi Golbode wii Ndikna Sogsouma
Nen daa ga no baa mo men naa ɓɔ' jak dulnya gɔ. (T., 97/98, v. 20)

Fonkomdi Golbode asks after Ndikna Sogsouma.
Let's hope that God grants us a long life.

In this way, the *siŋ gurna* becomes a textual representation of the linkages of friendship. The overall effect is of accretion of multitudinous individuals, *jak-kawre,* and villages, bonded in solidarity. Praise-greeting in *gurna* song does not lionize solitary leaders; it charts networks of contacts and promotes loyalty to the group. The song enacts the underlying ideology of the *gurna* institution; it is a vehicle for the formation and solidification of male friendship.

As I collected and translated *siŋ gurna,* I noticed that the names in the verses are framed by the movement of the composer as he travels from village to village. The sounding of names in *siŋ gurna* operates through metaphors of motion, like the movement of a journey. A composer would journey—both in life and in the text—to greet specific dancers. Commenting on his own activities, he might "spend the day laughing" or "chatting" in a particular village. The song mirrors the social processes involved in its production. It illustrates—in an idealized fashion—friendship, networking, visitation, and affiliation of *jak-kawre* to composers, all of which are social processes that undergird the *gurna* society.

However, not until later did I understand the songs to be not merely denotative but also performative in an Austinian sense. That is, the performance of the song in the dance context actually enacts the "work" of the words themselves. A dancer greets his friend through the song, a greeting that is, in effect, reproduced each time that song is performed at death celebrations (*yii-huuli*). When the song is sung by the dancers, friendship is enacted, made public, when the greetings that riddle the song are actually performed. The song *contains* greetings but is also itself the performance of greetings.

My understanding of the metaphor of journey as an index for the composer's power to greet was deepened through discussions with Dangmoworé, an 18-year-old composer at the Lycée de Doukoula. He explained praise in these terms: At the beginning of the *gurna* season, the composer travels from village to village to recruit dancers to his side. In the song lyrics, he "travels" from village to village to praise exemplary dancers, to curry their favor. Dangmo likened the song's power to travel in an airplane; from high in the sky, the composer circles over the villages in his song. He chooses to land in particular villages in order to visit and greet his supporters there. Through the song, he calls out their names, then he climbs back in and flies away to another village to sing their praises. In this way, the song is a vehicle and through it, the composer has a superior power in Tupuri society. Dangmo likened this power to the omniscience of God. Although most composers would probably refrain from such a direct comparison to God—in fact, they tend to emphasize that composition is a gift *from* God—they do insist on the panoptical powers of the song in society.

The reverberation of names in song is couched in another trope of motion: "*ti faage,*" or meeting friends on the road and en route.

> *'Anco jɔŋ wɛ ndi yaŋ wii ma jōore Aska*
> *'Ur ciŋ sam hum*
> *Wogaï 'ē-la?*
> *Wur nduu wii Djegaïna Nanga fɛr sen ne haara.*
> *Ndɔ laymaa gaw mbirna¹ nday a hun-la*
> *Djoklong <u>faage caa wɛ hee jaak ne Lemassé.</u>*
> *Tchougoulna nday hee ti Lamtoing Lefene.*
> *Naa wɔ ɓɔ' ti tiŋ mbaŋ hun-la?* (T., 97/98, v. 3)

It's harvest season and I'm looking for the dancers of Aska,
that they get up energetically to dance.
Wogai, how's it going?
We came to ask for Djegaina Nanga to tell them,
The youth who drink milk, when are you going to come?
Djoklong, <u>meet me on the road to go greet Lemassé.</u>
Tchougoulna, you head over to Lamtoing Lefene's.
When will be the next death celebration?[2]

The metaphor of *ti faage* operates at multiple levels. During the afternoon of a death celebration (*yii-huuli*), dancers stream to the dance site from all directions, dressed in their costumes, carrying their dancing sticks (*garaw*) and accoutrements. They travel in groups with the other dancers from their *jak-kaw*. While dancers would certainly meet one another on the road as they converged on the village sponsoring the *yii-huuli,* there is another meaning to *ti faage*. Dancers often walk all morning to reach the dance site by the afternoon, and they often stop at a *jak-kaw* with which they are friendly to rest and rekindle their friendships. If it has the resources, the hosting *jak-kaw* slaughters a chicken to celebrate. Hosting, visiting, forging links in the network of *gurna* are the terms in which the praise names are cast.

Ti faage also has a figurative meaning, connoting moral righteousness. In the verse below, a dancer (perhaps a *gurna* chief) is praised because his dancers "*see ti faage,*" walk the straight and narrow; that is, are morally disciplined.

> *Sereona kaŋ me ciŋ ndalge se Sokdandi.*
> *Sa' moday centre Lokro Biyam*
> *Her jak wɔ ne Kafao Waïso*
> *Ma jōore mo <u>see ti faage</u> ɓɛ.* (T., 97/89, v. 19)

Sereona, accompany me over there to chat with Sokdandi. (1)
Pin a medal on Biyam at Lokro. (2)
Greet Kafao Waiso, (3)
That your dancers <u>walk the road.</u> (4)

Like much other praise-singing, the *siŋ gurna* contains formulaic praise conventions. Many composers enliven their verse by borrowing and Tupurizing French terms. For example, a composer recognizes a wonderful dancer using an expression that literally means "to pin a medal" (*sa' moday*; line 2).[3] Or the composer might say "You're number one also, Yembe." ("*Numra un lay sɔ Yembei.*")[4] Or a dancer might "win the trophy of the dance" (*maŋ kup ma jōo,* drawing from the French term "*coupe*").[5] Although the village composers I knew were not Francophone, they had no trouble inserting terms and phrases from French, a prestige language, to lend style and zest to their songs.

The names evoked in the song as praise are often the sobriquets that *gurna* take on when they enter the *gurna* society.[6] These are usually in Massa and describe the *gurna*'s personality or physical appearance, such as Tchagalna (giraffe). Dancers are conventionally praised through the names of their fathers, either using Massa (*gorna*) or Turpuri (*je*), both of which denote "son of." This locution reveals a belief among the *gurna* that talent in dancing, including enthusiasm for the dance, is passed from father to son. It is not unusual to see fathers and sons participating in the same *gurna* camp. Mothers are recognized generically (not by name) for giving birth (*wāay biŋ*) to wonderful dancers and drummers. Thus, praise does not always center on the individual but refers also to transgenerational transmission of the dance.

Although young women (*mayre*) dance the *gurna,* they are not praised in village *siŋ gurna.* Many women's names resound throughout the region in the context of courtship by suitors and rebuke (see chapter 2 on Maïtené); however, praise is reserved for men. While the dance is a public display of women's suitability for marriage, the circulation of names in the song is a form of prestige reserved for men. Nonetheless, a recent exception to this gendering of prestige appeared in a Gurna Club song in the lycée—Dangmoworé, the student-composer mentioned earlier, praised girls too.

Wur hay lɛ ko Maïwalé
Ndi da' tergal gɔ dik wāare jōo ma cawn na
Nen baa sɔ lay na, . . .
Maïtchin diŋ lon ma jōo . . . (L., 98/99, v. 4)

We're coming to visit Maïwalé. (1)
I found *tergal* already thinking about the dance. (2)
It's God who recognizes the truth, . . . (3)
Maïtchin is strong like nylon for the dance . . . (4)

Maïwale, a female lycée student, is compared to *tergal* (French), a strong, synthetic cloth popular in the region a generation ago (lines 1–2). Maïtchin is strong like nylon (*lon,* French borrow for *nylone*), widely used in the past to make *sukway,* a pubic apron of thick dangling nylon string (line 4). Dangmoworé cleverly invented forms of praise for female dancers that connoted their strength and stamina but did not resemble typical male praises. From this, we see that song convention can change when its institutional contexts have shifted. It is significant that these praises of female dancers did not occur in the village context but in the lycée, where notions of female equality have a foothold.

In summary, *gurna* song praise takes the form of performative greeting. Rather than lionizing extraordinary "big men" who are obligated through the praise to become patrons (as in the Mande griot tradition), *gurna* praise ranges widely over all the *gurna* participants, emphasizing mass mobilization and loyalty of members. The vitality of individuals, camps, and villages are lauded, expressed as "enthusiasm for dance," a trope for the power of male solidarity.

SINGING THE DANCE: METACOMMENTARY ON DANCE

Siŋ gurna contain a wealth of commentary on the dance itself. In its performance context, the song along with the drumming paces the dance. However, at the semantic level, the song contains information *about* the dance, in effect "advertises" for it. This metacommentary about the dance in the dance itself is comparable to many other musical genres. Reggae lyrics refer to the "rock-steady beat" of the music. Soca lyrics from Trinidad give explicit instructions about when and how to "whine" ("get down"), as do many rock songs. Rather than providing instructions on the dance movements themselves, *siŋ gurna* emphasize the action of getting up to dance and the sensory experience of the dance.

> *Mon lɛ wɛ ndumgi pa sɔ ma jōore no.*
> *A 'ur ciŋ sam hum 'anco la.*
> *Wel po guwa' yaw-la?* (T., 97/98, v. 1)

> The song is starting to resound again, dancers.
> During this harvest season, you'll hear the sound of many <u>getting up to dance</u>.
> Will anyone stay at home?

The frequently occurring phrase "*'ur gɔ ciŋ*" ("getting up") represents the mass mobilization of dancers for the *yii-huuli* dance as well as the *gurna* society in general. "*Wel po guwa' yaw-la?*" ("Will anyone stay at home?") The emphasis was on mobilizing as many dancers and spectators as possible. This phrase is particularly graphic, because on the afternoon of a *yii-huuli*, the nearby villages are entirely emptied. The social pressure to attend the dance is considerable, making the decision of certain Protestant sects (especially Pentecostals and Lutherans) to eschew all "traditional" dance striking.

This insistence on full attendance at the dances was illustrated in the *siŋ gurna* with images of numerousness, such as storm clouds, fog, and swarming bees.

> *Wangba Koubouli Namsala Gaona Salmaï*
> *naa manyaabaa na.* (T., 97/98, v. 32)

> Wanga Koubouli Namsala Gaona Salmaï
> gather together like storm clouds.[7]

> *Mon lɛ sāyn wɛ pa lay Mboudga Tchanwalé.* (Z., 97/98, v. 29)

> The dance appears like fog, Mboudga Tchanwalé.

Fog (*sāyn*) represents the huge billows of dust that rise up from the dance site as hundreds of feet shuffle on the bare earth (see figure 6). The poetry evokes the multitude of dancers, *gurna* members and spectators, for it was on this basis that the dance would be judged as successful or not.

Verses that evoke swarming bees to describe the *gurna* were composed by a 16-year-old composer, Houyang, who composed for the *gurna-fiiri*, the children's *gurna* society in the village of Konkoron.

> *Ndi wii Nguinra nday mo no kay jag may yaw-la?*
> *Ndɔ hay raw liŋ jɔŋ may la.*
> *Sɛŋ la gurna hag na takla bay ma jɔŋ fɔɔ wa.*
> <u>*Ndɔ da' ra wɛ wɛr sew ka'a na de bɔlge do nyoore no lay na,*</u>
> *Ndi kɔl yɔŋge gɔ dɔɔ mbarra.*
> *Ndi hay riŋ ga ndi men nday mbi gɔ takla da sɔ.* (K., 98/99, v. 7)

I ask for Nguinra. You there, what do you say?
You went back home to do what?
This year's *gurna* is not to mess around with.
<u>If you find them under the *sew* tree, like a swarm of bees.</u>
I hid myself because of them,
I said I will leave you this year.

He explained to me the isolation that a *gurna-fiiri* member experiences when he drops out of the society.

> A boy from Nguinra was in the *gurna-fiiri*, but he dropped out and stayed at home. Then he saw how well the *gurna* were doing; people gave them money and congratulated them. The *gurna* bought meat and took it to their camp to eat. When the boy from Nguinra saw the many *gurna* in their camp, under the shade of the *sew* tree, he felt afraid. He asked himself why he had dropped out?

These images of the dance both create and mirror the strong social pressure in rural Tupuriland to participate in the dance, if not as a dancer than as a spectator. To eschew the dance is to risk social isolation.

In informal conversation as well, I noticed that many Tupuri people have internalized an ethnic self-conception of numerousness; they tend to believe that the Tupuri are a very large ethnic group in Cameroon, even though they make up only roughly 1 percent of the population.[8] The ultimate evaluation of the success of the dance is in the massiveness of the turnout of spectators and dancers. The large scale and public nature of Tupuri dance are ways that the society "shows itself off" to itself. Insular and agrarian, Tupuriland is further cut off during the rainy season (July through November) when there is widespread flooding across roads and fields. Dance in the Tupuri homeland is intended for local consumption. For these reasons, the image of numerousness valued in and through the dance and represented through word images in *siŋ gurna* can be understood as a projection of Tupuri power for Tupuri people.

In images of *gurna* members "getting up for the dance," the image of seasonality is recurrent.

Ma jōore no kɔl wɛ gɔ ciŋ dɔ <u>few</u> no Saïmane. (T., 97/98, v. 2)

The dancers appear like the rising <u>moon</u>, Saïmane.

Few (above) denotes "moon," "month," and "festival"—all interrelated concepts.

'Anco jɔŋ wɛ ndi yaŋ wii ma jōore Aska
'Ur ciŋ sam hum. (T., 97/98, v. 3)

It's harvest season and I'm looking for the dancers of Aska
That they get up energetically to dance.

Each song has a lifetime of a single *gurna* season. Within this season, there are generally two songs composed: the dry season (*'anco*) and the early wet season (*jak-tɔbɛ*) songs. These images of seasonality, along with the annual "gearing up" for the dance, suggest an intimate connection between the song, dance, nature, and agriculture. Yoking the dance to these larger forces gives it a substantiality that is common to many folk songs.

Sound, movement, and organization of the dance space constitute another cluster of images that make up the metacommentary on the dance in the *siŋ gurna*.

Souaressam raw we gɔ liŋ 'uwēe fen jōo 6ɛ. (1)
Haolana nday 'ē-la Djaogal Debane Douwoing (2)
Naa wɔ 6ɔ' fɔg day 6aa la. (3)
Guirling num wɛ lɛ caa po nday dee goga, (4)
faŋdi suwaa mbiiri gɔ mo naa. (5)
Mboudandi Kanso ndɔ wii Tchalna wɛ lay-bala'. (6)
Siŋ biŋ kal wɛ gɔ. (7)
Ndousala Blaona nduu 6il suwaa wɛr siŋ (8)
gibikri cuwaa weere jōore gɔ. (9)
Nen 6i 6il gas sɛ dɛŋ dɛŋ. (10)
Guirling man-kɔm ma jōo de kaŋge. (11) (T., 97/98, v. 33)

Souaressam went home to get dressed for the dance. (1)
Haolana, how are you, Djaogal Debane Douwoing? (2)
Before, we are also going to challenge with our dance. (3)
When Guirling resounds loudly, if the spectators don't flee, (4)
they'll be crushed to death. (5)
Mboudandi, maybe you will have informed Tchalna. (6)
The song has come out. (7)
Ndousala Blaona enters the center to sound the refrain (8)
until sweat was flowing from the dancers. (9)
I see in the center the dancers shaking one against another. (10)
Guirling resounds with a booming sound; the pivot of the dance is in place.[9]
(11)

These words aptly capture the great sweating mass of dancers as they circle the ring and the thunderous din of drummers, dancers and spectators. Stock verbs are used onomatopoetically to evoke this bellowing sound of the dance, such as *"ndum,"* to wail or howl, and *"raa,"* to resound. *"Sam hum"* connotes a low continuous grumbling sound, like thunder.

Some images capture the nested arrangement of the dance (see diagram 1). From the *6il*, the belly, or center, of the dance circle, the song leader directs the rhythm and pitch of the song. He is surrounded by a small ring of ten or so dancers who transmit his timing to the larger circle of dancers moving around them. This inner ring is called the *man-kɔm*, which literally means "senior wife," denoting one who directs the household, or, in this context, directs the dance. The spectators form the final ring around the mass of dances. This organization of the dance space is referred to in the song lyrics (lines 8–11 above): "Ndousala Blaona enters the center to sound the refrain. . . . I see in the center the dancers shaking one against another. . . . [T]he pivot of the dance [*man-kɔm ma jōo*] is in place."

Seen as awesome, the dance is frequently compared to thunder:

Ndi wii weere Tifeo
Mon mbud gēegē de law la.
Faŋdi maa dɛɛrɛ yɔŋge na ga diŋ poo baa,
Nen bay ga bay baa wa la,
We-jōore hoo mayngari dɔɔ kɔɗ na. (Z., 97/98, v. 25)

I ask after the dancers, Tifeo,
The song reverses its tone this afternoon.
The spectators flee and hide, thinking that it's thunder from God your Father,

> You know that it's not God,
> It's the dancers taking up their drums in hand.

These descriptive phrases are meant to enhance the drama of the dance and to ensure its efficacy in clearing away the specter of death. They call attention to the experience of the event as spectacle: the large crowds of dancers, the competence of the bandleader directing from within the bowels of the dance, the throbbing of the drums, and so on. This death celebration dance is the keystone of an event marking the exodus of the deceased's soul from the place of the living to the place of the ancestors. The soul of the deceased leave the family compound (*tiŋ*) for the sacred wood (*jak-siri*), where the earth-priest will care for its needs. Such a celebration requires a show of numerousness and thunderous noise in order to chase away these dead souls that might otherwise harass the living.[10]

INSULT

Calluses on a monkey's ass, a face shaped like a fish, a person born with a lizard tail—*siŋ gurna* are rife with insults (*d̃arge*). In fact, it is the biting insult and the scandals they evoke that make a *gurna* song *de cōore* (tasty); a "delicious" song is one with plenty of insults. However, since there is danger in insult, the composer does not include it in a half-hearted fashion. Insult, a form of verbal art extensively studied in African and African-diasporic performance[11] and beyond,[12] appears in the *gurna* song according to some key conventions and involving forms of protection for the composer. (The social work and effects of insult will be covered in more detail in the following chapter.)

Some insult in *gurna* song is initiated by the composer himself in his ongoing battle to maintain his supremacy in the cultural politics of song popularity. To this end, he defends his "people" (*courriers*), attacking their enemies and other rival composers in the region. Other insults are brought to the composer by villagers with a grudge or unresolved conflict they want aired in public. These plaintiffs seek revenge against their enemies by asking the composer to insult them in the song. In these cases, the composer attempts to avoid possible negative consequences of the insult by following certain poetic conventions of disclosure.

Djingue, a famous junior composer, found himself in the midst of jealousy between two of his friends: Lok Danwe and Bouwa Sougoulna. Bouwa was his *courrier*. Suspecting that the composer Djingue was closer to Bouwa, Danwe became jealous of him. So one day Danwe decided to pick a quarrel with Bouwa. In response to Danwe's belligerent behavior, Bouwa went to the composer and asked him to insult Danwe in the song. This insult was "published":

> *Attention Lok Danwe ndɔ kiŋ tum wii Bouwa de jōo* (1)
> *Ndɔ da' ne yaŋ sɛn ɓɛ de man-tɔŋtɔŋ nday wud ga,* (2)
> *Sougoulna wii me jak wɔ ga ndi mo d̃ar man Lok Danwe.* (3)
> *Bindir wɛr waale dɔɔ gefɛd̃gew,* (4)
> *Maïkinpa hay ko de way baa na.* (5) (Z., 97/87, v. 10)

> Beware, Lok Danwe, each year you ask for Bouwa with the dance, (1)
> You find yourself resembling a large bat, you say nothing, (2)
> Sougoulna asked me to insult Lok Danwe's mother. (3)

Bidir, people with lizard tails, (4)
Maïkinpa was seen with a dog. (5)

Manfel Gaossoumo kay naa lẽ lay la we-jōore (6)
Bil ɓi su ga,(7)
Wel de man-gɔngoron ndɔ da' de man-tɛntɛn raa ti faage. (8) (Z., 97/87, v. 11)

Manfel Gaossoumo, how is it going, dancers? (6)
I'm not satisfied, (7)
Someone who's like a beetle, you find him like a cricket screeching on the road. (8)

This insult conforms to certain conventions in *gurna* song. Compared to a bat, Lok Danwe is said to hail from a village (Bidir) where people are born with tails. His mother, Maïkinpa, is also insulted; she was "seen [had sexual relations] with a dog." The composer goes further, comparing Danwe to annoying insects (*man-gɔngoron* and *man-tɛntɛn*) that make irritating noise. This insult is typical of many in Tupuriland and elsewhere in its creative reference to grotesque, animal-like body features, abnormalities, and sexual impropriety, especially with the mother (Abrahams 1983).[13] In other verse by a different composer, a man was said to have a "fish-face" ("*pel ne jerɛm*"), "a strange mouth, a strange head, no bodily form at all" ("*Jak ɓɛ sara*[14] *ti ɓɛ sara*"), such that "God put [him] on the earth to be mocked by people" ("*Baa biŋ mo wɔ yo jar tabay maa fɛk mbɛ ti caw pa sɔ*"). Insults are constructed as accretions of images of grotesquery and impurity, each layer more deeply maligning the targeted individual.

As Irvine shows in Wolof insult (*xaxaar* poetry), the way in which an insult is worded—in terms of "speech forms, participant roles and discourse frames"—has a great deal to do with whether a speaker can "get away with it, i.e., vilify others without exposing themselves to retribution" (1993, 105–106). Tupuri *gurna* composers are highly aware of the possibility of dangerous retribution, either mystical or judicial, that can ensue from the addressee's wrath. Therefore, a composer protects himself through the ways he inserts names. Although actual names are used, the names of both the one being insulted and the one making the accusation are included. In this way, the composer makes a play for his own marginality to the conflict, even though, as in the case cited above, he is implicated as the friend of the insulter (Bouwa Sougoulna). In fact, the insulter is his own *courrier*. Regardless of the composer's relation to the persons named in the song, he almost always includes the name of the person who brought the accusation or desire for revenge to him. This lends the persona of the composer an illusion of impartiality and unassailability.

The above example illustrates several other features of *ɗarge*. First, the actual conditions or underlying reasons for the conflict are rarely, if ever, described in the song; the conflict is rhetorically taken for granted and left unresolved. Instead, the composer focuses on a creative use of insult. In this rhetoric, there is no expectation that the composer's insults are "real" in terms of actually describing a person's repugnant characteristics or behavior. David Parkin makes a similar point: "Serious abuse attacks social categories unambiguously. But abuse transacted in a jocular manner takes on the capacity of the joke to suspend consideration of whether the proposition . . . is true or false" (Parkin 1980, 61). He goes on to suggest that one implication of this suspension of truth validity is that the speaker is "relieved . . . of personal, direct responsibility for the attack on cherished social categories [e.g. the sanctity of motherhood] carried by the abuse" (ibid.). In Tupuri song, as long as the composer stays within the norms of poetic convention, insult provides an opportunity for him to display his creativity and verbal power without any expectation of truth validity on the part of the audience.

Insult in *gurna* song is not limited to dueling individuals. Insult, like praise, may be ostensibly directed at the individual, but it inevitably pulls in the entire village of the maligned: "Bidir, people with lizard tails" (verse 10, line 4, above). The entire village of Bidir, putatively because of their association with such a person as Danwe, is born with "tail[s] that can't be washed off." Just as praise of a single *gurna* will swell the entire camp with pride, insult of an individual will malign his family and village as well.

Insults could be ambiguous, open to interpretation in multiple ways. For example,

Weere Maga wɔ bay day.
Kaŋ man ɓɔ wɛr day ga yaw-la. (T., 97/98, v. 24)

The dancers of Maga don't have any cattle.
Can you exchange your mother for a cow?

Sogole, the composer, explained that the people of the village of Maga were so poor, they had to use their mothers to obtain cattle in order to participate in the *gurna* that year. But what is meant by this? This image works on several levels, all of which point to unthinkable, shameful acts. Breaking social norms, one might exchange one's mother in marriage in order to obtain her brideprice of cows. Or, fantastically, one might bring her to the *gurna* camp in place of a lactating cow for her milk. Or, as the insult implies, if you are too poor to have cows, then you are childlike—you might as well suckle at your mother's breast instead of joining the *gurna*. All of these possibilities work because invocation of the mother (*manbe*) signals either praise or insult. In praise, the mother gives birth (*wãay biŋ*) to a great drummer or dancer, while in insult, the normal function of the mother is subverted and corrupted. Here, she is exchanged for a cow in abhorrent ways. The polysemy of the insult strengthens it, makes it more evocative.

While the sociological effects of insult are beyond the immediate poetics of the song, there are nonetheless differences in the seriousness of invective images. The insults mentioned so far publicly shame the target. While public honor is vitally important in Tupuriland, these insults do not necessarily result in a material change in the life of an insulted individual. However, this does not hold true for accusations of witchcraft. Witchcraft (*sã'ã*) is a very serious concern in Tupuriland. If a person has been accused of witchcraft, he is likely to be exiled from the village. Ostracized, he and his family will have no choice but to inhabit one of the neighborhoods on the outskirts of towns (such as Kalfou, Guidiguis, and Tchatibali) where witches are ghettoized.

Numerous witchcraft accusations occur in the course of *siŋ gurna* insult:

Fansa baa mayn ɓɛn nyaa sã'ã dɔɔ Goyo, (1)
Fen sōore po yaŋ kigi la caw ga (2)
Fansa ko mayn ma nii ɓɛ, (3)
Ga nday jɔŋ ree sōore, (4)
Paw wɛ cii waay ne Maïgoro. (5) (Z., 97/98, v. 35)

> Fansa captured his daughter to obtain witchcraft in Goyo, (1)
> Something shameful happened again, (2)
> Fansa knows his niece, (3)
> You commit shameful acts, (4)
> Sacrifice dog blood for Maïgoro. (5)

Fansa is accused of the most shameful acts (*ree sōore*): witchcraft (*sā'ā*) and incest (*yɔɔ*). "Fansa captured his daughter to obtain witchcraft" (line 1). This line refers to the requirement that aspiring witches offer the life of an immediate family member to pay for the magical herbs that "open the eyes," that is, confer witchcraft powers. Here, Fansa is accused of offering his daughter. After he allegedly engaged in witchcraft, he is accused of committing incest with his niece, Maïgoro (line 3). He will have to "sacrifice dog blood for Maïgoro" (line 5), the ritual requirement for the purification of incest.

Because of the danger of inciting the anger of a witch, the composer is never the first to insult through a witchcraft accusation. He will include such an insult in his song only after there is widespread suspicion among the villagers that the individual is indeed a witch. The circulation of gossip in the neighborhood must precede the publication of the insult in the song. However, once an insult concerning witchcraft appears in song, the accusation contained within it will take on greater weight and the way will be cleared for adjudication of the witch.

Insult is one of the most compelling aspects in *gurna* song because composers are able to display their bravado in defending their "side" with stinging barbs directed at enemies or enemies of their friends. However, insult is treated carefully through the broadcasting of the names of the insulters along with those of the insult target. Although most insult is received as funny or entertaining, it can also result in the undoing of a person in more serious ways.

SHAMEFUL ACTS: HUMOR, RIDICULE, AND MORALITY

In Tupuri society, song is often used to morally regulate the community through the vehicle of ridicule or derision. Like praise and insult, derision is another rhetorical form widely found in African oral performance (Finnegan 1970; Furniss and Gunner 1995; Messenger 1962; Ojaide 2001; Piersen 1993/1999). In effect, the entire Tupuri community participates in public mockery when stories of foolish and embarrassing behavior on the part of villagers (*sōore*) are broadcast in song. This is intended to correct wrongdoers and mitigate against future transgressions as well as to entertain. Piersen describes this process in functionalist terms: "[S]ongs were especially useful in fostering social harmony because they permitted socially approved criticism without fostering unpleasant and dangerous personal, face-to-face confrontations. Since these satiric songs carried the propriety of custom and good manners, private slights were not allowed to fester . . . instead, grievances and frustrations could be aired before the bar of public opinion where they could be controlled and dealt with by social pressure and communal wisdom" (1993/1999, 349–350). While Piersen's analysis tends to overestimate the painlessness and impartiality of public ridicule in song, he correctly identifies how the process of song can bring "communal wisdom" to bear on interpersonal conflict or individual transgression. This wisdom appears to carry the sanctioned perspectives of the society at large, which is not to say that is unbiased or even fair.

The Tupuri performance genre most recognized for the "publication" of shameful action is the *waywa*, the "dance of the youth" which does not carry the moral authority of *gurna* song. Where derision occurs in *siŋ gurna*, it carries a stronger flavor of pedantry or moralizing than that in *waywa* song. Verses recounting *sōore* (stories of shameful behavior) typically tell about situations in families or neighborhoods: theft, discontent of wives over their husbands' behavior (and vice versa), and unfortunate incidents in courtship, such as a male suitor left shortchanged by a girl's father. While it is easy to recognize *sōore* in *siŋ gurna*, it is more difficult to interpret how they function allegorically. *Sōore* may act as insult, entertainment, pedantry, and/or satire—or any combination thereof. One person's shame is another person's entertainment. The way the composer exposes an embarrassment can be insulting to the individual shamed though instructive to the larger public. After looking across many examples of *sōore* in *gurna* song, I have thought it best to think in terms of a continuum of rhetorical functions. On the one hand, embarrassing behavior is sometimes included in the song merely for its entertainment value. It is amusing to hear how people transgress basic social etiquette, find themselves implicated in messy situations, or react to hardship in unpredictable ways. At other times, after recounting an amusing *sōore*, the composer will use it as an opportunity to moralize, to caution the audience to avoid such a problem. Composers told me that their most important role was to discipline and instruct the broader society.

In the examples of tales of *sōore* that follow, the first ones were employed by the composer as entertainment, while the later ones were employed to a greater degree as springboards for moralizing.

Ngolbodna Woursam wāa lɛ me da wur daŋ wii jak Kandandi,
Maïbil ɓay mo caw la re way yaw-la?
'A maŋ ti'n ne hen naa sɛ kɔl taw fɛg ti wāare nay no.
Mooda ma' ne sɛ kɔl cofɛr mooda bagde.
Barbi Weldi gɔr tɔp naa yiŋ mbɛ pel da pa. (D., 98/99, v. 15)

Ngolbodna Woursam, tell me something, we came to find out from Kandandi,
Your Maïmbil, did she eat the dog?
They offered her the head and she was thrown into a fit of laughter over the problem of the meat.
The car hit it—maybe she became the driver of the car.
My friend Weldi, wait until the first rains when we'll meet again.

According to the composer, Teodandi, a dog was stolen and killed in a village. A woman named Maïmbil happened to see who committed this act, and she told her neighbors. Realizing that they were apprehended, the thieves turned the story around and said that they were working in concert with Maïmbil to steal and slaughter the dog. When Maïmbil saw herself being implicated, she changed her story and said that the dog was killed when it was hit by a car. In response, the owner of the dog asks Maïmbil if now she is transformed into the driver of the car that killed the dog ("*sɛkɔl cofɛr mooda*")! Maïmbil is offered the dog meat, but she bursts out laughing. Many *waywa* and *gurna* songs refer to dogs or dog meat, suggesting that they occupy an ambiguous position in Tupuri society.[15] Since women are not supposed to eat dog meat, the song implies that women should not get involved in the affairs of men and their dog meat. However, the tone is light and the primary function of the story is to entertain.

The line between *sõore* (shameful acts) and *ɗarge* (insults) is at times blurry because the revelation of an individual's embarrassing or compromised position can be so nasty that it becomes an insult rather than a joke. The intention of the person contributing the information to the composer and the effect the song makes when the information becomes public may not be exactly aligned. Furthermore, the line between entertaining gossip and vindictive insult can be indistinct because the audience usually does not know the interpersonal situation that triggered the placement of the story (*sõore*) into the song. However, when I interviewed composers, I noticed that they did not seem to be particularly interested in controlling the effects songs might have on individuals. Like a hard-nosed news reporter who seeks to print "the truth" without regard to who is hurt in the process, the composer of *siŋ gurna* is not concerned about the sensitivities of those maligned in the song. His purpose is to produce a song compelling enough to attract crowds of dancers and spectators.

Sometimes the story of an embarrassing situation is qualified by the addition of a commentary or a moral on the problem. Here is another dog-meat story:

Darebal gar fadonne yaŋ wɔ ti fee dɛŋ no
Ndi da' caa kiida nay waay nday,
Maïyouaye wãayn yaw fɛr wãa gɔnga
Sansi Kelaïna fen sõore bay ti mbɛ. (T., 98/99, v. 32)

Darebal, judgments are being passed.
I found them in the process of judging the problem of the dog meat.
But Maïyouaye was there to tell the truth.
Sansi Kelaïna, there is no shame to her.

In this verse, a group complained to the village chief about a case involving dog meat. A man bought a dog, cooked it, and commissioned a boy to sell the meat at the market. The boy must have eaten some along the way because when he returned, the man saw that the pieces sold did not match the money that the boy gave him. When the man complained, the boy was called to the chief's compound, though he didn't show up. Angry, the plaintiff sent a message to the boy's mother, Maïyouaye, to attend the trial because it concerned her son. Maïyouaye responded, No, it was none of her business; the problem was between the man and her son. At the end of the verse, Sansi Kelaïna, the chief's envoy, says to the mother in the song lyrics: "There is no shame to her," meaning that she was right to refuse responsibility.

It is not entirely clear whether it was the composer himself who added the commentary supporting Maïyouaye's decision or whether another individual commissioned it, perhaps to get Maïyouaye out of trouble with the chief. Others considering this verse, including Balandi, Sogole's advisor, felt that the mother had a right to be angry at the man for giving dog meat to her son to sell. Although informants had a difficult time pinpointing what was wrong with dog meat, they felt that since it was shameful or inappropriate to sell dog meat in the market, the man should apologize to the mother for exploiting her son. Clearly there was some ambiguity to these moralizing stories, and interlocutors would need to know the story behind the lyrics to make full sense of them.

Individual composers have varying tastes for moralizing in the *siŋ gurna*. One composer, who was a student in the teacher-training school in the city of Maroua, composed for the school's gurna club and the neighborhood Tupuri association in the predominately Fulbe city. An earnest man in his twenties, Ringwa's songs tended to contain more moralizing and social commentary than the contemporary *siŋ gurna* in the villages. In the three verses below from his 1998/1999 song, he sang stories of theft during the famine and misjudgments made during courtship.

There was a tradition of showing in song how famine pushes people to do foolish things. In this case, an old man, named Maïtcharé, is cold at night, so he sleeps in an old burlap sack for warmth. Along comes Maïhorlong, hungry from famine. She sees the heavy sack in the compound and, thinking it is sorghum grain, steals the slumbering Maïtcharé.

Djigaïna nduu me se bay su la ga Tchanwalé,
Maa yaale baa jar Makabay.
Maïhorlong ndɔ ko tãabe Maïtchare ga mona.
Maïtchare ndɔ kɔl bugu yaw-la? (M., 98/99, v. 16)

Djigaïna came to me yesterday, Tchanwalé,
Saying that the famine threatened the people of Makabay.
Maïhorlong, you never saw the agedness of Maïtcharé.
Maïtcharé, you have become a sack?

Another story is a classic: Wives misbehave when the husband fails to provide properly for the family.

Tchoue riŋ me ga Maïsoun maŋ nay Maïdarwa. (1)
Ndikwe bay yee nay wa lay la. (2)
Domga wãayn ɓɛ kɔl pũy gɔ ti faage Charles. (3) (M., 98/99, v. 17)

Tchoué told me that Maïsoun stole meat from Maïdarwa. (1)
Ndikwe didn't buy meat either. (2)
Domga, his wife is transformed into a hyena on the road, Charles. (3)

In this case, Ndikwe, the husband, does not buy meat (line 2), so Maïsoun steals some from her neighbor, Maïdarwa (line 1). In this way, the wife is reduced to behaving like a "hyena on the road" (line 3)—that is, scavenging—because of her husband's failure to *rationner* (to provide). The verse also contains the names of the husbands, Ndikwe, Maïsoun's husband, and Domga, Maïdarwa's husband, as well as the name of another neighbor, Charles, who witnessed the entire incident. The verse mirrors the gossip that circulates in a small neighborhood when incidents such as theft are witnessed and talked and speculated about.

The following verse chides a suitor for not being more aware of the politics—and economics—of courtship:

Kandandi nduu me de mbɛrbe nen, (1)
Maïgourya re mo nen day yaw-la? (2)
Golbode kaŋ may ɓɛn wer tassa wa. (3)
Baïwang kiida bay ni wa Wouliigue. (4) (M., 98/99, v. 24)

Kandandi came to me with tears in his eyes, (1)
Did Maïgourya "eat" from you the equivalent of a cow? (2)

Golbode didn't give his daughter away for small piles. (3)
Baïwang, there is no justice, Wouliigue. (4)

Kandandi is courting a girl in Palar, a Tupuri neighborhood in Maroua, with the intention of marrying her soon. Suddenly, the girl, Maïgourya, is given to another wealthier suitor. Kandandi bemoans the fact that he gave many small gifts during his courtship of Maïgourya, such as cloth and beer, whose value equaled that of a cow (line 2). However, since he never paid the bridewealth itself, which would be in the currency of cattle, another suitor was able to steal Maïgourya away. The last line, "There is no justice" contains the names of advisors of the chief: Baïwang and Wouliigue. In an interview, Ringwa was critical not only of the naiveté of Kandandi, the poor suitor, but also of the father, Golbode, who was motivated by greed to give his daughter in marriage to the highest bidder (line 3).

The recounting of shameful behavior in the *gurna* song serves primarily to instruct and entertain, though they might also be taken as insulting to those who are embarrassed. *Gurna* song composers primarily see themselves as social disciplinarians, and the tool they wield for this purpose is the license to reveal the embarrassing actions of individuals for public mockery. However, in an effort to avoid abuse of this license and to deflect responsibility from himself, the composer includes the names of many actors implicated in observing, evaluating, and broadcasting an act of shameful behavior.

SATIRE AND SOCIAL COMMENTARY

African orature is well known for its capacity to check the political power of rulers; to rein in abuse of sovereign power and remind those on top of the subordinated histories of the marginalized (Agovi 1995; Apter 1998; Vail and White 1991). In the section above, I discussed how ordinary people are kept in line through ridicule in song. This public scrutiny is extended to public authority figures in the form of satire designed to hold them accountable for their actions while still upholding the integrity of the political office. Discussing such satire as "vilification," the "co-wife of praise," Furniss points out that in Hausa *maroki* (praise song), "vilification tends to concentrate upon the negative qualities of the individual while maintaining the positive view of the structure within which the individual is expected to operate. The poet does not vilify chieftainship or the values associated with the role of the patron but the individual's failure to live up to the expectations of the role" (1995, 134–135).

At different historical times, the *siŋ gurna* has become a more or less powerful arena for satire and social commentary. Nearly every adult Tupuri knew the name of the renowned composer Dang Biina (1934–1969), born in the village of Zouaye, a village still famous for song composition. When he composed during the 1960s, Dang Biina sang out against the tyranny of the traditional chiefs (*lambe*) in his *siŋ gurna,* lambasting them for their severe punishment of villagers and their greed and corruption. Tupuri priest and seminarian Samuel Kléda (1983) has conducted research on Dang Biina's *gurna* song. During his time, Temwa, the *lamido* of Doukoula from 1955 to 1965, was an authoritarian chief who required forced labor from villagers. He enforced this policy through the threat of *razzia* (raiding). In response, Dang Biina vilified him in his annual *gurna* song:

Pūy raa Temwa takla sɔ gebɛɛ Jamba.
Baa de mbuk ti tiŋ Temwan gɔ,

Temwa kɔl buy kakre wɛ sɔ
Wāay de piŋ jak, waŋ Temwa de piŋ jak dɔɔ yɔɔ,
Temwa huu ti waŋ ga.
Semtway Sayman Wanso sali Ayjo.
Baa de vrum tiŋ Temwan gɔ.
A le' baa gɔ, Temwa d'ar baa.

Hyena announced this year the death of Temwa, slave of Jamba.
God is destroying Temwa's compound,
He is reduced to slavery to care for his chickens.
A woman never had a beard, but, because of this impurity, Temwa's mother has a beard,
This is why Temwa will die on the throne of the chieftaincy.
Semtway Sayman and Wanso, greet Ahidjo.
God is about to destroy Temwa's compound.
One should never offend God, but Temwa has offended him.[16]

In revenge and in effort to silence Biina, Lamido Temwa sent his men to arrest him at the site of a death celebration dance. Biina fled for his life to Chad, where he died in exile.

No composer since Dang Biina has approached his stature. Older Tupuris lionize him for his courage in standing up to the power of the traditional chieftaincy, which represented the administrative power of the state. His songs are still remembered and sung *au quartier* by admirers. One Tupuri intellectual with whom I often discussed Tupuri culture believed that *siŋ gurna* today was a "degraded" form because it contained little of the satire and social commentary present in Dang Biina's day. He viewed contemporary composers' posturing and insults of their rivals as demeaning to the art form and the copious praise and greeting in the song as a waste of time.

However, even though composers no longer satirize political leaders, there is some social commentary in contemporary *siŋ gurna*. It occurs when the composer makes an explicit reference to society at large (*Kamrun*/Cameroon), pointing out its deficits and calling for improvement. Such critique is less common in the *gurna* song I collected in villages than those produced in school's *gurna* clubs and in urban cultural associations. In recent years, there has not been an immediate public target of satire, as there was in Biina's lambasting of the *lamido* of Doukoula. Rather, the critique was more diffuse and nostalgic; "*dulnya*" (life or modern life) is the culprit of social disorder. For example, Sogole sang:

Fala dulnya maa padraa weere gɔ mo naa Yaksala Koïne. (T., 97/98, v. 23)

Fala, modern life has estranged the youth, Yaksala Koïne.

The implication of these lines is that young people are no longer joining the *gurna*, that they are detached from village-level traditions and all that represents. The metaphor used to convey this estrangement is intriguing. "*Maa padraa*" refers to a children's game: If a person is holding something precious in their hand, another person comes up and tries to knock it out with a quick slap. If the object falls on the ground, it belongs to the attacker. In the verse, children (*weere*) are, metaphorically, the precious object in the hands of the elders. It is "modern life" (*dulnya*) that has knocked them to the ground—that is, out of the grasp of the village community. Although it is not stated directly in the song, most Tupuri people would say that it is young people's migration to cities, attendance in school, and overriding concern with employment that is taking them away from the *gurna* and the lifeworld of the village it represents.

I found that *siŋ gurna* produced by students in school contexts contain more strands of social critique than song from village *gurna* composers. Dangmoworé of the lycée of Doukoula uses his songs to criticize corruption among school administrators, sexual relations between female students and male teachers, and the inaccessibility of college for the poor. For example, he sang about a southern teacher, Sabikanda, a French teacher at the Lycée de Doukoula who was the faculty advisor for the Theater Club and, under it, the Gurna Club. One year the students did not receive their small funds allocated by the school, and they believed Sabikanda was responsible. In response, Dangmo accused him in the song of 1997/1998:

Sabikanda coo raw jɔŋ weeren lay tɛm mo dɛŋ ga,
Nday re sulay,
Takla ndi wii nday gɔ. (L., 97/98, v. 10)

Sabikanda, because the children are poor,
You steal money,
This year, I'm warning you.

Making a class-based critique, the composer points out that Doukoula students are from impoverished, farming families, so a wealthy teacher from the south may think he can get away with "eating" their funds.

In the *gurna* song composed by Ringwa, the upset in the balance of power between the genders in contemporary Cameroon is an important theme. He sang of Maïyelé (also called Graobé), who was the president of the dance but who fled his own home for several days after he fought with his wife.

Maïyelé daŋ la da' Dourga faage, (1)
Ga wãayn raw sɛ ti bɔn ga. (2)
Je tuwar men tiŋ gɔ ne wãayn yaw na. (3)
Naare kɔl wo wɛrpeere, (4)
Graobé day de la men Merling gɔ. (5) (M., 98/99, v. 27)

Maïyelé fled, finding Dourga on the road, (1)
That a woman can never overwhelm me. (2)
There are certain men who leave the house to the wife. (3)
Women become men, (4)
Graobé almost left behind Merling. (5)

In line 5, he almost abandons his son, Merling. According to the composer, to overturn the patrilocality of Tupuri marriage is to invert the roles of women and men, a danger that he saw in *dulnya* (modern life).

Although there is a history of satire of corrupt, abusive political leaders in the *gurna* song, most social commentary in the song in the late 1990s was aimed at the general condition of "modern life": women taking over the power of men and youth neglecting cultural tradition, tricked by the unfulfilled promises of Western schooling. It is striking that although Cameroon has been ruled in an authoritarian fashion since Independence and the country was by the late 1990s and early 2000s wracked by extreme corruption, *gurna* song composers had yet to take on the national leadership as a subject for satire. Although they might address social concerns in general terms, they reserved their most invective insult for those close to home. Whether composed in rural or urban settings, *gurna* song was staunchly parochial, even insular.

STRUCTURE: LOCATING SPONTANEITY AND STABILITY

Maybe what makes the *gurna* dance so compelling is that it is at once hypnotic and exciting to watch. There is a creative tension between the predictable and the unpredictable, the expected and the spontaneous. Dancers are expected to present themselves as stoic and masterful performers, able to withstand famine, heat, and hovering crowds. At the same time, dancers can erupt spontaneously from the dance circle with a *bɔ'ge fɔgɛ* challenge that insults the audience with a humor laced with attitude.

The structure of the song also reflects this dynamic tension. On the one hand, the song as an oral text is highly stable and constant. During the late 1990s, *siŋ gurna* had a fixed form—usually seventy verses separated by a midpoint break, called the *baoge*. At the *baoge*, the song leader (*entonneur*) raises the pitch and continues with the second half of the song. Each verse is four to nine lines, for a total of approximately 350 lines per song. *Gurna* dancers memorize the song and it is sung from beginning to end as a verbatim recitation. It is repeated numerous times during the dance. Because the dancers sing in unison, there is virtually no room for improvisation in the song performance. Rather, it provides a steady background against which dancers improvise their *bɔ'ge fɔgɛ* challenges and dance steps. Although much has been written about improvisation in African verbal arts, it is interesting to note that *gurna* performers seek to provide an effect of stability, unison, and constancy in their presentation of the *gurna* song.

On the other hand, freshness and shock effect in *gurna* performance is highly valued. Dancers are lauded for individual creativity in their dance moves and costuming. For composers, the domain of creativity is of course in the lyrics. The appeal of *gurna* song lies in the surprising juxtapositions of what I have called rhetorical forms. Biting insult is sandwiched between ordinary greetings and praise, followed by reference to an embarrassing scandal. These shifts are rapid and unannounced. Other elements add interest and showcase the composer's verbal virtuosity: clever turns of phrase; use of the prestige languages of French, Massa, and Fulfulde; and use of the first-person indexical through which the composer persona boasts and postures. In these ways, the song appears fresh and spontaneous and, most important, it has bite.

The multidimensionality of the song—its ability to be deployed for multiple tasks and audiences within Tupuri communities—has other advantages in addition to enhancing its aesthetic appeal. *Gurna* song is called upon to perform many social functions simultaneously: to permit individuals to vent and duel, to correct and instruct the community, and to flatter supporters of the *gurna*. In its polyvocality, the song permits speech—be it insult or praise—between individuals under the witnessing gaze of the larger community. It contains insider messages about conflict and micromaneuverings for power that only *gurna* members might pick up. And it contains messages to the larger society about the state of Tupuri civilization in the contemporary world. The simultaneous occurrence of these multiple levels of speech within the same song make it impossible to interpret a single meaning projected by the song. Rather, there are multiple meanings for multiple purposes and for various subaudiences within the public at large. The image of a public sphere that emerges is one that is fragmented: one with multiple agendas pursued within a single performance.

FIGURE 17. *Gurna* dancers in costume waiting for the death celebration dances to begin. Bouzar, 1998.

FIGURE 18. *Gurna* drummers in the center of the dance, 1998.

FIGURE 19. Tupuri girls in dance costume, ca. 1957.
Photo: Joanny Guillard.

FIGURE 20. *Gurna* dancers, ca. 1957. Photo: Joanny Guillard.

FIGURE 21. Gurna preparing to perform at state ceremony for the installation of a new *sous-préfet*. Doukoula, 1998. The jeep was used to shuttle local dignitaries to the whitewashed covered dais. The town *fou* (insane person) mimics the *gurna* dancers (center).

FIGURE 22. Club Kwoïssa practicing the *gurna* at their compound in Biyemassi, Yaoundé. June 1999.

FIGURE 23. As spectators watch, two *gurna* dancers (left) perform a *ɓɔ'ge fɔgɛ* (gesture of challenge) at a death celebration in Doukoula. December 1998.

FIGURE 24. *Gurna* dancers in their costumes of white shorts, hip decoration, and long socks. Their backs are smeared with white dust (*puuli*) to increase the appearance of their size. 1998.

FIGURE 25. Selling home-brewed sorghum beer (*yii*) in small beer markets. Customers are seated in the background. Doukoula, July 1996.

FIGURE 26. Selling sorghum in the Doukoula market. Widely fluctuating seasonal prices make trading in grain profitable for those with capital. July 1996.

FIGURE 27. Grand finale of the *gurna* dance at Baolang. February 1998.

FIGURE 28. Dangmoworé, *lycée* student/*gurna* song composer, relaxes with a calabash of sorghum beer at his brother's compound. Zouaye, November 1998.

FIGURE 29. A class of sixty-seven students at the Lycée de Doukoula. March 1998.

FIGURE 30. The anthropologist translates *gurna* song with members of *gurna* camp of Mogom and research assistant Awé Jean-Pierre. January 1998.

FIGURE 31. Research assistant Awé Jean-Pierre transcribing interviews. Doukoula, November 1998.

FIGURE 32. Teodandi, *gurna* song composer from Dawa, Chad (in white hat, center), with his retinue of *courriers*. Warsaï, February 1998.

FIGURE 33. Sogole, *gurna* song composer. Tuksu, February 1998.

FIGURE 34. Mbulna, a Tupuri diviner, uses eggs, cowries, and sticks to prophesy and heal clients. Pont Vert Quarter, Maroua, September 1998.

FIGURE 35. RDPC supporters of President Paul Biya, "Le Meilleur Choix," with signs and Biya-printed cloth shirts, at ceremony for the installation of the new *préfet*. Maroua, September 1998.

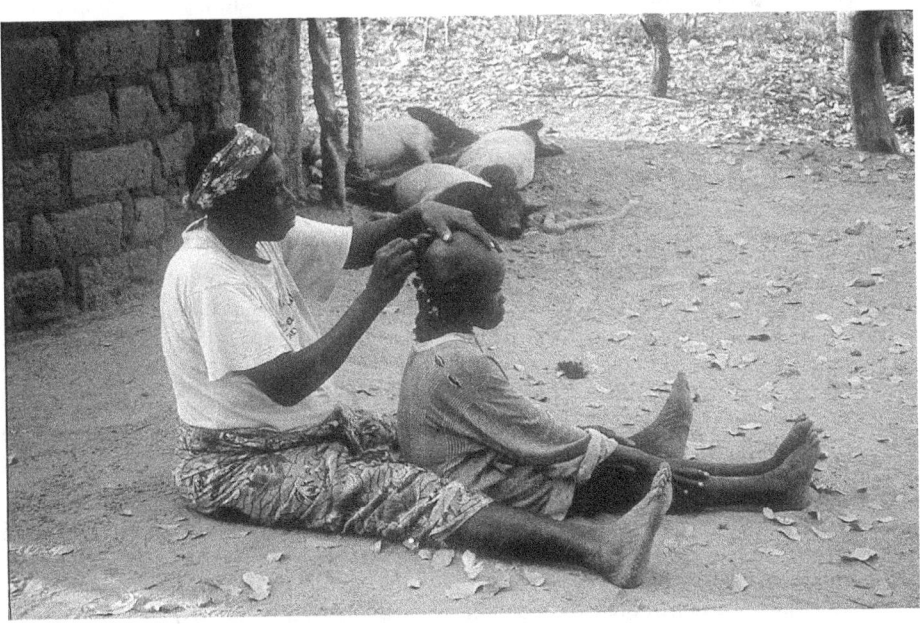

FIGURE 36. Maïcomshuki, the third wife of Domsou, shaves the head of her grandson. She wears her headscarf in a fashion to indicate that she is mourning the death of a family member. Doukoula, November 1997.

SEVEN

"I Become Your Boy"

Power, Legitimacy, and Magic in Song Composition

Modern forms of power associated with the Cameroonian state have made many inroads into Tupuri society. The authority of the security forces, civil service, schooling, and the chieftaincy have left their traces in even the smallest villages. However, Tupuri song is still considered to be powerful in certain realms of life, where it takes on institutional powers. These realms have to do with building up and tearing down personal reputation and with fracturing and knitting together networks of individuals. Earlier chapters have discussed how power is wielded in Tupuri society through song, dance, and village associations. This chapter discusses the ways that power is lodged in the role of the *gurna* song composer (*je kaŋ siŋ gurna*). In village-level politics, the composer is an important figure because of his capacity to publicly humiliate, laud, and capture the attention of the populace. For these reasons, the processes of song composition are not merely aesthetic; they involve the use of power, some of which is mystical.

This chapter discusses how the *gurna* song composer enhances his ritual power and legitimacy as a composer. Much research on African oral literature refers to the authority of poetic license in African societies (e.g., Vail and White 1991) and in some cases attempts to trace the roots of this power. In this chapter, I consider three areas vital to the power associated with *gurna* song composition: a) the transmission of the social role of the composer through localized "dynasties"; b) the use of magical herbs in the composition process; and c) strategic construction and erasure of the composer persona in the song text itself. These are best viewed as fields on which contests for legitimacy are waged. I also explore key elements of the composition process: collaboration and apprenticeship and the checks and balances on the role of the composer.

In my discussions with composers, I found that the vulnerability and danger inherent in the composer role is a constant concern for them. This was especially evident when the subject of magical herbs (*saŋgu*) was raised. It also came into play when we considered the competing or overlapping authority of the state to determine legitimate speech.

Power associated with song composition cannot be entirely explained in terms of authority and legitimacy; it must include the notion of responsibility. As the chapter title suggests, composers like to call attention to their social role as a servant to the community. "I Become Your Boy" comes from a *gurna* song in which the composer borrows the French term "boy" for domestic servant, suggesting that in his composer role he serves the wider good of society. How do composers carry out this role they aspire to as righteous moralizers of society? What rules must they adhere to when exposing foolish actions (*sõore*) or delivering insults in the song? In constructing a persona through the song, what does the composer want his audience to believe about his integrity as composer? The chapter concludes with an exploration of aspects of the composer role embedded in the song text. Through these self-referential pragmatics, composers call attention to their own trials as they attempt to shape the behavior of *gurna* dancers, the purported moral leaders of Tupuri society.

TRANSMISSION OF *SIŊ GURNA* COMPOSITION

Composers in Cameroonian Tupuriland recognize a dynasty of composers in two locations, one in the village of Zouaye in Cameroon and the other in Dawa, Chad (see map 2). This dynasty was more like a guild or association of composers than a caste in the sense that the term has been used in Mande studies (Irvine 1993, 112). The lineages of transmission involve transmission through agnatic descent, but not strictly or uniformly. The composer role in Tupuri society is exclusively male; it is specialized and high status, though it is not seen as a social category determined by birth. Any man with a gift for song composition can, through apprenticeship, become a recognized composer.[1]

I found the process of mapping out the historical transmission of song composition to be complex and confusing for several reasons (see diagram 2). First, there was no formulaic recitation of names as is seen in oral genres organized around "faithful" transmission of a clan or nation's history. The *gurna* genre is not concerned with authoritative speech from a putative ancestral past. The composer is the sole authority of his annual song, which, though formulaic in some respects, is nevertheless unique. Second, composers work collaboratively in partnerships of a junior and senior composer. Usually one identity is more obscure, though the more obscure partner is not necessarily the junior. During my sojourn, Djingue at age 23 was more widely known than his senior partner, Noumnamo. Their song was known as "the song from Zouaye" or "Djingue's song," though Noumnamo did most of the composition. Third, at any given time, there are several competing composers, although Dang Biina was remembered as a single composer who unified all of Tupuri Cameroon. Although composers have long runs of composition—ten or more years—a view of the region over longer periods of time revealed that the composition scene was fluid and shifting. The popularity of composers is continually waxing and waning. A composer is not a composer without an audience—a mass mobilization of *gurna* camps which gravitate toward his song and choose to adopt it. Behind every popular composer is a staff of advisors, memorizers, and arrangers who assist him.

These complexities aside, there are important patterns to be discerned in the historical transmission of the *gurna* composer role. The diagram below presents the relationships among the major composers after *siŋ gurna* composition was brought to *ɓaŋ-gɔ*, the northern region of Tupuriland.[2]

Diagram 2 shows two major lineages of song composers (designated 1 and 2), divided by moiety (Dore and Gwa). *Gurna* practices entered Tupuriland from

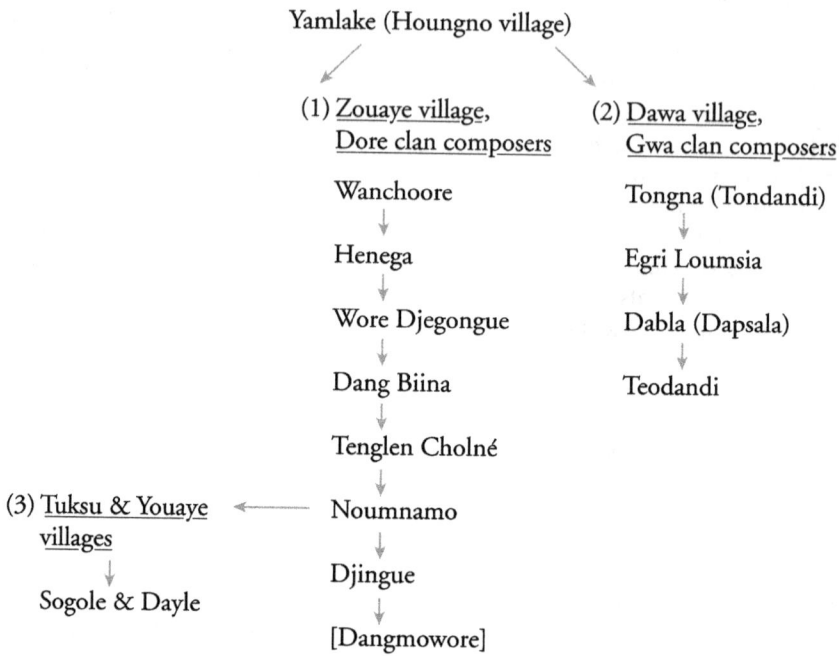

Diagram 2. Transmission of the art of composition

the northeast, from the Massa ethnic group. At that time, since there were no Tupuri composers, the Tupuri *gurna* members danced to the song produced by a Massa composer, Yamlake, in the village of Houngno. Houngno is located on the floodplain around Véré, a transitional region between the Massa and Tupuri ethnic groups. Tupuri from the south and west called residents from this area Barre, or Massa, as their language was a hybrid of Massa and Tupuri.[3] The Massa composer Yamlake apprenticed Wanchoore and Tondandi, who each carried the song composition to Tupuriland proper. Gradually the language of the song shifted to Tupuri rather than Massa, though many vestigial Massa phrases remain. Wanchoore brought the song to Zouaye, while Tondandi brought it to Dawa, several miles away, just over the Chadian border. Wore, an elder who learned the art of composition from Wanchoore and his younger brother Henega, said that Wanchoore brought the song composition to Zouaye in approximately 1928.

During the 1950s, Wore taught the famous composer Dang Biina. However, in the 1960s, when Dang Biina was composing his politically insurgent songs against the traditional chieftaincy of Doukoula, Wore, fearful of the power of the chiefs, stepped back and acted as his assistant. "In those days, the chiefs whipped people often," explained Wore, an elderly patriarch who was retired from composing at the time of my research. Dang Biina was succeeded by Tenglen, who died in approximately 1995.[4] Upon his death, his composer-partner, Noumnomo, took on young Djingue to be his successor. This lineage of composers is said to compose for the Dore, one of the two Tupuri moieties.

The second lineage of composers, founded by Tondandi and located in Chad, was said to compose for the Gwa, the other moiety. Tondandi was succeeded by Egri Loumsia, who was succeeded by Teodandi (see figure 32). During the time of my research, Teodandi partnered with Dabla (Dampsala), who remained in

Chad, while Teodandi visited Cameroon regularly. Each composer composed half of the annual song, one catering to Chadian villages and the other to Cameroonian.

Noumnamo and Teodandi, composers from both of these lineages, identified a third composer active in ɓaŋ-gɔ, Sogole (see [3] on diagram 2). To them, Sogole was a threatening rival, even though Sogole had apprenticed in Zouaye under Noumnamo. After learning the art of composition, Sogole broke off and started "his own party" (song), as Noumnamo described it. Competing with the composition centers of Zouaye and Dawa since the early 1990s, Sogole (see figure 33) operated from his own village of Tuksu, several miles from Zouaye (collaborating with Dayle of Youaye). Although the root of the animosity between Sogole and the other two composers is unknown, it is clear that he was operating outside the two recognized nexuses of song composition, incurring the disdain of both.

In contrast to their enmity with Sogole, the composers of Zouaye and Dawa saw themselves in a relationship of invigorating rivalry, as between two brothers. I was told that the composition was divided between Zouaye and Dawa because the region was large and the dancers numerous. The split between Dore and Gwa does not appear to be politically significant today; members and composers of either group can participate together in the *gurna*. These moieties were defined by the intricacies of the ritual sacrifice required by their ancestors during the annual harvest festival. The division of the song composition between Dore and Gwa referred to a rough geographical division of the *gurna* camps rather than a clan affiliation—which is not surprising because *gurna* membership intentionally cuts across clans.

The historical transmission of *siŋ gurna* composition through individual composers was strongly marked by consanguinity, but not uniformly. Even though the tradition of song composition is recent in Tupuriland, Noumnamo described it as already deeply rooted: "It has become hereditary. It's in the blood. It couldn't just stop with me only. This *gurna* will persist until the end of the world, especially here with us, in this branch of our family." In Zouaye village (see diagram 2), the composers Wanchoore, Henega, and Wore were brothers. Three of Wore's sons (Noumnamo, Djingue, and Dangmoworé) were also composers. The only one to have attended lycée, Dangmoworé, did not figure into this dynasty of village-level composers because his compositions to date had been for the Gurna Club in the Lycée de Doukoula. During an interview with Noumnamo, I was surprised to learn that he was unaware that his younger brother Dangmo was continuing the family tradition by composing *gurna* songs for the lycée in Doukoula. (Clearly there was a vast social gulf between the lycée and the surrounding community.) In 2000, Dangmo passed away at age 25 after a lengthy illness.

Lest it appear that all parentage in the composition occurred along the patriline, Teodandi, who composed out of Dawa, apprenticed under his maternal uncle. Furthermore, there are plenty of cases (such as for Dang Biina and his successor Tenglen) in which kinship was not a factor in the transmission of song composition. In their discourse about the composition tradition, composers focused less on the influence of parentage and more on the importance of individual talent and apprenticeship.

BECOMING A COMPOSER

In addition to transmission of song composition through actual and fictive kin lineages among composers, informants described to me three other concurrent factors involved in the creation of a composer: apprenticeship, transmission of *saŋgu,* and inborn talent (*"un don,"* French). A composer usually began his career as a *courrier*; that is, an assistant to the composer, one who masters the song alongside the composer and then teaches it to the *gurna* members. As the *courrier* works with the composer, he might occasionally ask to include some of his own lines. The composer tries to keep his *courriers* loyal by leaving room in the song for their contributions. Noumnamo, the senior composer, described his collaboration with his apprentice Djingue:

> I composed the song entirely. Then I turned to Djingue to see if there were certain friends in the villages, so he could insert their names into the song. Or, if he had particular problems with someone . . . he could insert them. I left a few couplets, so that he could complete it afterwards, for him to feel satisfied.

The composer also depends on the collaborative effort of his *courriers* for the musical arrangement of the song. He works with them to synchronize the rhythm of the song with the lyrics, especially during the first performances of the season. The revision process occurs after the composer has heard the song performed several times.

In addition to apprenticeship in the craft of composition, there is also a process of public acceptance of the candidate as a recognized song composer. Upon the death or retirement of a composer, his successor must be voted in not only by the mass of *gurna* but also by the entire village of Zouaye. Noumnamo described this election process as a solidifying force in the village: "It was the entire village of Zouaye. It is something in common for us all. It doesn't just depend on the composer; it depends on everyone here at Zouaye."

He singled out the composer's toughness as a major factor in this choice. Song composition is a difficult career: "You must be strong . . . to be able to tolerate it all." As author of insults and attacks, the composer must be able to survive counterattacks, some of which may occur through occult powers and others through the formal judicial system.

However, the politics of representation is at play here as well. The transmission of song composition in the lineage and through the election is not the only way composers establish themselves. The current composers at Zouaye and at Dawa regard the composer Sogole as an illegitimate composer, an upstart who began to compose only three or four years ago. They suggest that he began composing simply to acquire money and had no real claim to the song. Although Sogole operates from his home village of Tuksu, he was nonetheless trained in Zouaye. If he gains enough followers through the power of his song and his campaign to publicize his song, then he will be publicly recognized as a composer. The composers are answerable not only to their follow composers but to the mass of *gurna* members in the region.

On the Day in 1997 when I made my first contact with the composers of Zouaye (Noumnamo and Djingue), the village seemed to be unusually busy. The booming weekly market of Zouaye was coinciding with a death celebration where dancers were to perform. When I saw crowds of men at Djingue's compound, I was simply told that the *gurna* had come to learn the new song for the year. I didn't realize that they were also there to chastise the composers for being late in releasing the new song for the season. I was granted a short interview with Djingue in one corner of the compound while crowds of men waited in other areas, talking energetically among themselves. My interpreter was a close friend but probably an inappropriate person for the task. A young woman and community organizer from a Christian family, she knew next to nothing about the *gurna*. The interview was confusing to both of us as we discovered that Djingue answered all my questions in riddles. Unable to even translate them, my friend-interpreter could do nothing but laugh. At the same time, Djingue himself seemed very nervous, shaking hands with the steady stream of visitors entering his compound. One of his couriers tried to explain the bustling situation—"Djingue is like a president to us"—though on this day "the president" was being pressured by his people.

The role of composer is pivotal in the broader Tupuri society as well. Although the position is stressful and at times dangerous, being a composer also involves fame. Teodandi reflected: "I notice that I am very honored. Many people come [from far away] to see me with their own eyes." As much as they enjoy ritual status within the society, composers are not oblivious to the impingement of the modern economy. Noumnamo advised his younger brother, Dangmoworé, to continue his studies at the lycée, because "with school, you can have some way to raise your children. But with the song, you have only enough to eat for yourself. It doesn't work to support the entire family."

In all my interviews with composers, they were surrounded by an entourage of their *courriers*. In addition to assisting the composer with the arrangement of the song and ferrying the song to the villages and information from the villages to the composers, the *courriers* also had the responsibility of acting as advisors to the composers. In the production of the song, there are many micropolitical decisions to make, consequences to foresee and weigh. The *courriers* are responsible for ensuring the moral standards of composer's behavior. I also noticed that the *courriers*, who are extraordinary for their powers of memory, act as repositories for the past songs. Although literacy has recently been added to the repertoire of song-learning techniques in the *gurna* camps, the tradition is still overwhelmingly oral and aural. Therefore, when I would query a composer for examples of various subjects from past *gurna* songs, he would always turn to his *courriers* and ask a particularly able one to retrieve a verse from memory and sing it for me.

Once when he was reviewing a tape of an interview with a composer, my research assistant pointed out to me hushing sounds in the background. The *courriers* seated behind the composer were excitedly coaching him. My questions at that point were sensitive, regarding the implication of the composer in national party politics. Behind cupped hands, the *courriers* whispered, "Be careful! Be careful! Speak properly here!" Clearly, the composer was at the center of a network of specialists who saw themselves as as much accountable for the integrity of the song and the "party" as the composer himself. Even though the composer was a renowned artist who was courageous enough to stand up to the social pressures of the role, he needed to be supported by a ring of assistants who ensured that he made wise decisions in his handling of the song content and in negotiating with those who sought audiences with him.

COMPOSITION AND THE FACTOR OF MAGIC

Composers often recount mysteries in their composition process. Ringwa, a well-educated urban composer, described how a song appeared to him: "The song is . . . a gift. If I am ready to compose . . . the song just comes to me while I am sleeping. When it comes, it comes as twenty or forty verses. In the morning, I sing the song entirely, while the day before I could not." Although most composers described their talent as a gift from God (*baa*) and thus not entirely in their conscious control, the question remains about whether the song is tied to types of magic subject to human manipulation.

Many, both inside and outside *gurna* society, insist that the composition of *siŋ gurna* is intimately tied to the power of magical herbs (*saŋgu*, Tupuri; *gri-gri*, French). The use of *saŋgu* (also translated as "medicine") is not limited to *gurna* song composition. They are widely used—or a discourse of their use is widely circulating in Tupuri society. There are *saŋgu* for practically every imaginable need: to keep thieves out of farms and cow corrals, to keep women faithful to their husbands, to attract a lover, to thwart an enemy, to help students perform well in school, even to protect against highway banditry while traveling. During *gurna* dance performances, drummers, their hands bloodied from beating their instruments though feeling no pain, are said to use *saŋgu* to drum like virtuosos.

As other analysts have found (Geschiere 1997), it is notoriously difficult to research the occult, precisely because its very potency is connected to the fact that it is hidden from view. Furthermore, in cases of witchcraft and poisoning, occult powers are frequently utilized by those with nefarious purposes who would obviously want their activities kept secret. Fortunately, the use of *saŋgu* in the *siŋ gurna* is not related to "eating people," as is witchcraft (*sā'ā*). However, prophetic injury is involved in song composition. In my own research, I suspected that my informants—*siŋ gurna* composers and their advisors—might tend to assume that I was associated with the Christian missionaries and that I would disapprove of such magical practices. It was therefore some time before I even became aware that *saŋgu* was a factor in song composition, and then more time before I developed the level of trust with the composers to discuss the intimate mechanics of the song composition process. Even after I had leapt these hurdles, the question of *saŋgu* continued to perplex me. Each of the composers with whom I worked had a different stance toward his own use of these powers. It was not clear to me whether each individual made different uses of *saŋgu* or whether they had different levels of comfort with me about revealing their secrets.

In my interviews with song composers, I was concerned about the possibility of reducing the power of the *saŋgu* merely by discussing it (as perhaps they were, too). I remembered well my efforts to interview a diviner (*je halge*) who is famous for providing his divination services to Tupuri people living in Maroua (see figure 34). After a divining session with my research assistant and me, we had just begun an interview when he was forced to quit. We were politely encouraged to end our visit. During our next visit a week later, the diviner reported that during the night he had been tormented terribly by the spirits who possessed him and powered his visions. The spirits had clearly rejected interviews for their medium. While the use of *saŋgu* and possession by spirits are not identical, Tupuri cosmology holds that unseen, spiritual entities (*sõore*) are at the root of any extraordinary power, including the power to compose song. These powers required sacrifices (*co' sõore*) and could balk at human efforts to manipulate them without their consent.

In interviews with the composer Teodandi through an energetic interpreter, Farsia, a local politician, farmer, and community development agent, I learned how critical *saŋgu* is for the composers of *siŋ gurna*. Farsia explained: "*Saŋgu* is a weapon of defense; the composer must defend himself. If I sing and injure you [in the song], these insults are going to hurt you. There! You are obligated to go look for *saŋgu* to kill me. So I have to go get *saŋgu* to defend myself." For this reason, the public role of the composer is considered to be dangerous. It is he who was responsible for perpetuating injury through the song, so it is he who is vulnerable to possible revenge and retaliation by those who are maligned. The role of the composer demands the use of extraordinary technologies such as *saŋgu*.

Farsia went on to explain that composers also use *saŋgu* to attract their audiences. Certain *saŋgu* have the power to bring popularity to the composer, to draw people to his song. A third type of *saŋgu* goes one step beyond; it lends performative efficacy to the composer's words. Although one could translate this power as the power to curse (in French, *porte-malheur*), the meaning is broader. In addition to cursing (willing misfortune on another), it can also mean the power of prophecy (seeing into the future) and the power to persuade. I was told about cases in which individuals put *saŋgu* into their mouths before going in front of a judge in a court hearing. Because of the magical powers of *saŋgu*, everything they said was believed and interpreted in their best interests. *Saŋgu* is thought to be at the root of all highly efficacious speech.

These three types of *saŋgu* used by composers each require their own annual sacrifices, most often of a chick without feathers. These periodic sacrifices strengthen the *saŋgu* as one might recharge a battery. Furthermore, sometimes the transmission of the power to compose involves the passing of the *saŋgu* from senior to junior composer. The composer Teodandi said that he received the *saŋgu* he uses to attract his audience from his maternal uncle, Wore, who apprenticed him in song composition. Dangmo, the high school student-composer, reported that he knew that this same Wore, who was not only the famous retired composer but also his father, possessed *saŋgu* for composition but that he hadn't discussed passing them on to Dangmo yet. Given the primal power of this magic, I was not at all surprised when, in my interview with Wore, he entirely denied using *saŋgu* in his composition.

The most well-known case of the use of *saŋgu* in song composition was the prophecy of Dang Biina. This renowned composer of the 1960s sang against the *lamido* of Doukoula, in part out of the rivalry between Doukoula and the composer's village of Zouaye. Zouaye chafed under the administrative rule of Doukoula, the *chef-lieu de canton*. In his *gurna* song, Dang Biina charged the *lamido* with disrespecting God and prophesied that as a result his chieftaincy would be destroyed. Several months later, when the winds kicked up at the onset of the rainy season, a massive gust came down and ripped the roof from the *lamido*'s palace. No other compound in the neighborhood was touched. This event was quickly attributed to the power of Dang Biina's *saŋgu*. Of course, in listening to these kinds of stories, one might wonder about the distinction between public discourse about the exercise of power—which usually occurs when the effects are made visible—and the actual practices of the magic. However, this distinction is nearly impossible to make; the public discourse *about* the exercise of power was a critical component of the power itself.

Although the logic of *saŋgu* in the composition of *siŋ gurna* was fascinating to me, it was even more interesting to learn of the very different ways the composers articulated their particular relationships to *saŋgu*. The composers with whom I worked ran the gamut in their use and avoidance of magic. On the one hand, Sogole, the most tough-talking of the composers, insisted numerous times that he completely eschewed *saŋgu*. He said that his father, who was not a composer, forbad his son from using *saŋgu,* warning him: "You should never take it, because if you do, you will die before me. I warn you, you will die immediately." Sogole explained that this "became something hereditary. My grandfather, too, forbad *saŋgu.*" Later when Sogole quit being the *courrier* to the composer of Zouaye at the time, Tenglen, in the hope of composing for himself, he was potentially vulnerable:

> "When I left Tenglen, he was so angry. On the day that I went off to compose, I had a dream about Tenglen. He had gone to buy 'those things' and was attacking me. We fought fiercely in the dream. I had this dream over and over again.[5] If my father hadn't warned me to stay away from *saŋgu,* I would have gone to get some for myself in order to fight back . . . if my father hadn't warned me."

"But how do you protect yourself?" I asked

"It's God [*baa*] who protects me."

Often composers identified *baa* as their protector and the source of their talent for song composition.

On the other hand, Teodandi was less straightforward about his use of *saŋgu.* In March 1998, I asked him if he used *saŋgu* to compose his songs. He and all his advisors, who were surrounding him, laughed. Then, when the laughter subsided, it came out that perhaps he had *saŋgu* to protect himself from the jealousy of others. Seven months later, I asked him again if he used *saŋgu,* likening it to "a stick to defend oneself" from those angered by insults in the song. He repeated that he did not use it to protect himself but conceded that he did use *saŋgu* to "motivate" people; that is, to make his song irresistible to the public. A bit defensive, he added that his father did not have *saŋgu* designed to protect himself, only to attract an audience. If he were to go out looking for such powerful herbs, this could bring even greater problems. I assumed he was referring to *sa'a,* nefarious witchcraft for which accused users could be exiled for life. But this begged the question of how Teodandi defended himself from counterattacks. A sociable man, he said that he protected himself with amicability. When he visited people in their villages, flattered hosts would offer him sorghum beer, which he in turn would promptly share with all around him. Once he was pleasantly drunk, anyone who had intended to harm him would no longer be interested.

The third composer, Noumnamo, at first denied flat out that *saŋgu* had any part in his song composition. At that moment, my research assistant, who had been watching the interview, intervened. Ever provocative, he threw in from the sidelines a piquantly worded question. Noumnamo reacted immediately: there were many types of *saŋgu,* and these secrets should not be revealed because some *saŋgu* could cause death. Gradually, Noumnamo admitted that *saŋgu* was the primary force in motivating the dancers to select a composer's song. He explained, "For example, if certain people were on the side of Sogole, and then today, they come to listen to my song, it was first of all the *saŋgu* that brought them." He needed to perform sacrifices to maintain the *saŋgu.* But if people stopped listening to his song, he would consult a diviner (*je halge*), who would require sacrifices to reconstitute the *saŋgu* to make them efficacious again.

Noumnamo said that there were also *saŋgu* to assist in the process of composing the song and that Tenglen, the composer under whom he apprenticed, gave these to him at the moment of his death. Noumnamo said that at his own death, he might pass them on to Djingue, his junior partner and brother. At this moment,

Dangmo, who was also a brother, could not help but emphasize that it was not a forgone conclusion that Djingue would be the successor. Dangmo nurtured hopes of becoming a Zouaye composer himself.

Noumnamo seemed to embrace the centrality of *saŋgu* in the composition of *siŋ gurna* and its proper transmission between composers. Later, he recounted that when his ancestor, Wanchoore, received the song composition from the originator in Houngno, the passing on of the *saŋgu* was included.

Given such variability in discourse about *saŋgu* and a healthy skepticism that anyone would tell me the truth in a transparent manner, I nonetheless drew two conclusions. First, in discussing his capacity to use *saŋgu*, each composer referred to his father or ancestors as an anchor to justify his stance. Sogole was forbidden by his father to use *saŋgu*, and the prohibition seemed to be a familial taboo. Teodandi described how he used some types of *saŋgu* but not others because these were the ones he had inherited from his father. Noumnamo reported receiving *saŋgu* as part of the transmission process from his mentor and emphasized the role of *saŋgu* in the establishment of the Zouaye dynasty of composition. Regardless of the stance of each composer vis-à-vis magic, each recognized that particular practices were inherited from one's elders.

Second, if we understand the *gurna* song as a vehicle for influencing the public, certain factors are operative in that sphere that composers must master in order to be successful. They must have power to attract people to their side and maintain that attraction year after year. Composers must also have power to repel the evil intentions of those who are jealous or angry because of what they must do—insult, embarrass, and selectively choose recipients of their praise. Since these are challenges all composers face, we can understand the discourse of *saŋgu* to be a metaphor for the power of a composer to attract supporters and defend himself in the highly volatile public arena of the song, regardless of whether or not he actually uses the magic.

PICADOR OF THE HUMAN CONSCIENCE: THE SOCIAL ROLE OF COMPOSER

Composers are blunt about describing themselves as moralizers or disciplinarians of the society. They are fond of making statements such as: "If someone does something wrong in the village, I put him in the song so that others won't do the same shameful thing." They see themselves as involved in cleaning up society, as muckrakers. One composer described his role as "to interrogate the human conscience." They also saw themselves as *animateurs* (organizers, leaders) of the dance; their song enlivened people to dance. In their view, it was self-evident that the dance reflected the peace and prosperity (*jam*) of society—so self-evident that one composer snapped at me, "What? Don't you have this in your society?" It is no surprise that composers prefer to focus on this aspect of their work and avoid talking about their less savory use of the song to insult other composers and perpetuate personal vendettas among villagers.

But what are the responsibilities of the composer as the producer of the song, particularly when sensitive material might destroy an individual's reputation? Who checks the composer? All the composers expressed caution about inserting insult into the song. Ringwa warned, "I don't put in insults *just like that*," he emphasized. "Someone must come to me with a problem. And then, if I put the insult in, I also put in *his* name [the originator of the insult] as well."

As discussed in chapter 6, the composer's inclusion of both the names of the insulted and the insulter in the song is understood as creating a paper trail, so to speak. The composer demonstrates that he is not the instigator of the insult; rather, he is merely allowing another individual to speak through him, through the song, in order to get his word out. This convention creates a rhetorical illusion of impartiality on the part of the composer. However, this impartiality was not that invoked by a judge in the context of a judicial hearing; the composer does not arbitrate the conflict in the song, he just reports it. The composer is impartial in the sense that he makes himself available to the public as a "bullhorn" for their conflicts. The role is comparable to that of a newspaper that solicits advertisers. The newspaper is open to any and all advertisers, but the relationship between the newspaper and the advertiser involves an agreement, financial and otherwise. (Also, advertisers must submit advertisements in accordance with the newspaper's guidelines.) Similarly, the composer would have had an interview (*ndalge*) with the solicitor of the insult and would likely have received a gift as well. The composer represents in the song the perspectives of those who come to him with their problems, though he is potentially open to all. In this sense, the composition of the song is collaborative and the song is porous with the broader society, although the composer always retains his gatekeeper position.

How then do composers and their staff describe the characteristics of a good composer? An advisor to the composer Teodandi said,

> "A good composer must be proud, receive everyone, have the spirit of the group, be attentive. . . . He must attend to everything. There are cases with ones whom we don't know. That he must welcome them and consider them like his brothers."

"But are there problems that the composer will not agree to put into the song?" I asked Teodandi.

> "I don't admit little problems, problems like everyday conflicts. Like if there was a plate of food with meat and I ate it all, and my brother complained. . . . I don't accept that kind of thing. I want it to be a public affair, that everyone has seen it and that it is important."

According to Teodandi, when a villager comes with a submission for the song, he must first "look in his heart"; that is, consider whether it seems plausible and worthy. Then, he said, he sends his secret agents back to the villager where the event took place to see if others corroborate it. If he finds that the event did not take place, he refuses to include it in the song. Teodandi reported that in addition to cross-checking by his secret agents, he also likes to include events that he has personally witnessed. For example, the time that two women fought in the marketplace until they stripped each other nude. Or the time a young man arrived at his in-laws and was given '*argi* (grain alcohol) to drink. He drank until he had diarrhea. Teodandi laughed heartily as he recounted these shameful acts.

Gregarious and jolly, Teodandi never took himself too seriously. Leading his entourage of *courriers* in laughter, he recounted how one year he was faced with a dilemma: he had to include a shameful story (*sõore*) in the song that involved a member of his own family. Someone broke down the door of his father's compound and stole sorghum, cow beans, and Bambara groundnuts from his wives. It turned out that the thief was a family member, and his father agreed that Teodandi could sing about the incident as long as he did not include the thief's name. As he told this story, Teodandi laughed uproariously at himself as the near-perpetrator of a *sōore*. The famine of 1998 was so severe that he thought he would die of hunger. He barely restrained himself from "climbing the granary," a metaphor for stealing food, a favorite transgression reported in *gurna* song.

> *Ndi lɛ laɓge sōore ba me wer waŋ jōo-day no.*
> *Ndi hay ɗii boole ɓi gɔ lay.* (D., 98/99, v. 17)

> I was starving to death, but I was gripped by shame as chief of the *gurna* dance.
> I was about to climb a granary.

He only held back because as a composer, "chief of the *gurna*," he was obligated to set a moral example.

Composers see themselves as impartial interrogators of public morality. In their role as gatekeepers of the song, they are beholden to standards of accuracy. Like scientific researchers, they are required to document names publicly—who is insulting whom and who is the informant of shameful stories.

POETIC CONSTRUCTION OF THE COMPOSER PERSONA

The *siŋ gurna* text itself is another site where the social role of the composer role is constructed. In the song lyrics, the composer develops his persona as narrator and public figure. He embellishes the song with commentary on the processes of production and reception that in the real (nontextual) world supports—or sometimes threatens—the song. Because composers seek dominance vis-à-vis other composers, they claim to be uninterested in politics. They complain about how the dancers sometimes disappoint them, how members of the larger society, especially the youth who are potential *gurna* members, don't support them as they should. The composer's authorial voice, his critical commentary, runs alongside the "business as usual" praises, greetings, and insults in the song. A range of voices make up the composer persona: disciplinarian, overworked servant of the song, and successful political operator influencing dancers to stay on his side. In the opening verses of a song, composers often seek to establish their own authority as composers and impart warnings to their followers.

Teodandi cautioned his dancers in the first verse of his 1998/1999 song:

> *Bɛl baa mo we jak yuwaale ndɔ nyoo wɛ naa,* (1)
> *Burgui ndar la jobo kon yaŋge?* (2)
> *Maïlao Sarba Dabsoumo Lamra ndi nduu wɛ.* (3)
> *Mbaramga jōo wɔ ra nday mbuɗ jak jiili debaŋ.* (4)
> *Nday mbɛ dɔɔ jar no lay sɛ bay hɔr wɛ ni sɛn ga mo pa.* (5) (D., 98/99,
>   v. 1)

> When the leopard catches you at the back door, you'll be surprised, (1)
> Can anyone see anything but the dust rising? (2)
> Maïlao Sarba Dabsoumo, I have come. (3)
> Lethargic dance, you dancers really bother me. (4)
> You are like all the others, you don't care about what you do. (5)

In this case, the leopard (*bɛl*) represents Dayle, the competing composer from Youaye (line 1). The leopard stealthily enters the family compound through the small hole in the straw fence (*yuwaale*) created by the livestock. In the blink of an eye, the leopard captures a goat, leaving nothing but a cloud of dust in his wake. Similarly, Teodandi warns, the dancers affiliated with him will be snatched away by his competitor, Dayle, if they are not vigilant.

Teodandi complains that some of the dancers are lazy: "They want their names announced in the song, but they don't spend time in the *gurna* camp or attend the dances as they should." These slothful dancers annoyed him, and by calling attention to this problem in the song, he hoped to shame the dancers into more enthusiastic performance. In this narrative voice, the composer was a disciplinarian.

Sogole sang along similar lines:

Wur hay de Gasiso wɔ su ndalge.
Nday lɔɗ gɔ 'a sii ti fɛk ne Walia.
Tongna, jōo ɓay turda nde ler yaw-la?
Weere Walia sayn ndi wɔ liŋ ɗa.
Jam jɔŋ wɛ na wɔ raa ɗuu pa sɔ Selda.
Fona je Kenso ndɔ 'ē-la Haoge? (T., 97/98, v. 6)

We were with Gasiso yesterday to chat.
You were confused and that made everyone laugh all day at Walia.
Tongna, does your dance have fixed hours?[6]
Dancers from Walia, I must return home now.
If my health permits, we will be famous, Selda included.
Fona, the son of Kenso, how are you, Haoge?

Sogole explained that this verse reprimanded dancers who, confused and disloyal, did not seem to know their own minds when it came to affiliating with a composer. The particular incident referred to a composer in the village of Walia who attempted to compose. But his song was unsuccessful, so after the first year, his dancers switched a camp that was singing Sogole's song, where they spent two years. Then one part of these dancers went off to affiliate with the composer from Zouaye; later, a few wanted to return to Sogole. Discouraged, some have left the *gurna* society altogether. Sogole decried this lack of loyalty on the part of the dancers.

He continues several verses later:

Gorna Manhou Fanbadna ndi laa we nday jam Manwore ɓil bii. (1)
Su we sɔ Kelna. (2)
Gorna Foudoumgue ndalge baa mo mo waŋ weere jōore. (3)
Djemagna Ngaimo kamliri nday wii ra de sɛn sɛn ga, (4)
'A nduu we ti few bāaare wel wɔ 'o yaŋ pel ɓaara ni lay? (5) (T., 97/98, v. 13)

Manhou's son, Fanbadna, I heard that you are in good health near Manwore pond. (1)
So finally I am happy, Kelna. (2)
Foudoumgue's son, you like to chat, chief of the dancers. (3)
Djemagna and Ngaimo, children, since you don't counsel them, (4)
When the dance starts up in December, who will have the nerve to stand up in front of them? (5)

After complimenting the *gurna* camp at Guissia village ("near Manwore pond") for their strength and enthusiasm (line 1), he returns to the troublesome *gurna* from Walia (line 4). He refers to them as children (*kamliri*) who wander erratically back and forth between *gurna* camps. He calls for his two advisors, Djemagna and Ngaimo, to counsel the confused members, flattering them by praising their awesome power as dancers: "Who will have the nerve to stand up in front of them?" (line 5).

The following year the Tuksu song continued to admonish stray dancers: "*Mababo yeed wɔ gɔ raw wɔ gɔ yoo wa Gidsoumma.*" ("Some are lost in the bush, Gidsoumma"; T., 98/99, v. 1). Although his partner Dayle composed this section, Sogole explained, "At Tuksu most dancers are with me, but there are a few who don't want to take to the song, so they are 'lost in the bush.' " Dayle opened the song with a similar admonishment against disloyalty:

> *Sangfaï Dayle maŋ komanda we-jōore maa mbi kamrun taw ga.*
> *Attention gay we se ɓay wa.* (T., 98/99, v. 1)

> Sangaï Dayle takes command of the never-ending dancers of Cameroon.
> Careful, don't sway left and right.

Part of the composer's role as leader of the song is to chastise *gurna* who appear to undermine the cohesiveness of the society and the dance and to encourage those who support him.

Through the song, the composer also projects a public image of himself as competent to produce the song and powerful enough to vanquish his enemies. Bowing to his father (Kawbik), the composer Djingue opened the 1997/1998 song by portraying himself as morally at ease, pure:

> *Bɔn ɓay se ɓi wa.*
> *ɗu ɓi ga Djingue Djonyang, je Kawbik,*
> *'Ur ciŋ pa lay yaw-la?*
> *Ndɔ hay tɛm mo dɛŋ maa po cɛrge se ɓɔ.* (Z., 97/98, v. 1)

> I don't suffer as you do.
> My name is Djingue Djonyang, son of Kawbik,
> Must you flee so quickly?
> You were in such a hurry because you feel guilty about something.

Dayle opened his song by establishing his authority through God (*baa*):

> *Baa biŋ me gɔ yoo jar tabay ma ndalge ɓi kamrun dɔɔ jōo na.*
> *Ndi yaŋ mbi prêt 'a siŋ de'ɛlɛ.* (T., 98/99, v. 1)

> God put me among my people in Cameroon to converse with the dance.
> I'm ready with a fine song.

The composer also projected himself as the nexus of countless relationships. Sogole expressed this as a continual stewardship to his audience of *gurna*: "*Djambe ndi le' buy Gaosoumo Saigue.*" ("Djambe, I put myself in service to others, Gaosoumo Saigue"; T., 97/98, v. 30).[7] The composer Djingue implores the dancers to forgive him for not having the time to visit their camp. Working hard to disseminate the song, the dawn surprises him while he is still visiting *gurna* camps:

> *We-jōore nday cɛr me wa,* (1)
> *Naw taw gɔ, wur kon me ti faage de siŋ no.* (2)
> *Ndi maŋ sir dɔɔ ga, ndi men liŋ lam la.* (3) (Z., 97/98, v. 26)

> Dancers, don't reproach me, (1)
> I haven't had the time, dawn surprised me on the road with the song. (2)
> I did not take my village with me, I left it anyway. (3)

Djingue is so sought after by dancers begging for a meeting (*ndalge*) with him and to have their names appear in the song that eventually he gets tired of this. With so many *ndalge* and different demands, how is the composer to please everyone?

> *Wāare maa jak jar Tupur na da' faage gɔ me ga mo na.* (Z., 98/99, v. 44)
>
> Stories from the mouths of Tupuri people overwhelm me.

As the last phrase of the song, Djingue simply concludes, "*Ndi sõo siŋ de pere.*" ("I have composed an insufficient song"; Z., 98/99, v. 55). There are so many dancers in the camps who deserve to be praised that there isn't enough room in the song to mention them all.

Composers also called attention to their own activities through the use of first-person indexicals. This syntax allows for a textual construction of the composer's social role as public leader.

> *Gastoing Fougale jaksu la see gēege 6ɔ.* (1)
> *Bar <u>6i</u> Derguelna ni salu 6ay Gomray.* (2)
> *Dargal <u>kaŋ me</u> ni je Boufon.* (3)
> *Wanba Legaigue sir le' yaŋ nday mo ti la.* (4)
> *<u>Ndi 'a ndal</u> nday Sansi.* (5)
> *Jōo day mo kay la taw cooren ga.* (6) (T., 97/98, v. 8)
>
> Gastoing Fougale, the first here put forward your voice.[8] (1)
> <u>My</u> friend, Derguelna, greetings to you at Gomray. (2)
> Dargal <u>accompanies me</u> to the house of Boufon's son. (3)
> Wanba Legaigue, your dance zone will get along well. (4)
> <u>I'm coming to chat</u> with you, Sansi. (5)
> The *gurna* won't finish the grain.[9] (6)

The composer indexed his own activities within the song in an attempt to galvanize dancers behind him. In formulas of greeting by name, sometimes the composer greeted individuals directly and other times the composer was merely a mouthpiece for one party to greet another. Composers' visits to *gurna* camps involved conversation—*ndalge,* a general term for verbal interaction—ranging from chatting and joking to interviewing and informing. It can also connote courtship (*ndalge may* means chatting with a girl in order to gain her interest and consent). This sense of courtship through skillful talk is an appropriate way to describe the composer's relationship to the dancers. As line 1 (above) suggests, proper talk is perceived to be at the root of peaceful relations among people.

Although the composer may chastise and discipline dancers in the course of his song, when he is campaigning in the villages, he woos the dancers as politicians woo their electorates. In fact, the French word "*campagne,*" expressed as "*jɔŋ kampain*" in Tupuri (*jɔŋ;* "to do"), is explicitly employed in the song to describe the composer's wooing of potential dancers to his side. And as they wooed dancers, composers commented on the politics of popularity in the dance:

> *Man may hay hadˇ gɔ de nay bay da' nay wa.*
> *Sɛ kaŋ waŋ-jak na ti may la Saolo.* (T., 97/98, v. 24)

The girl's mother is used to getting meat, but now she doesn't find any.
Why does she complain, Saolo?

Circumlocutiously, Sogole from Tuksu refers here to the people of the competing composers of Zouaye as "the girl's mother." He explained to me, "Before, they would come and visit in Tuksu and be well received 'with meat.' But now [due to the competition among composers], they receive nothing, and they are complaining."

Sogole sang further about a dancer named Mongale from Bouzar, a village where there were two *gurna* camps. One camp was affiliated with Sogole and the other with his competitor, Djingue. In Sogole's view, Mongale was his dancer. The people of Bouzar would continuously mock him and try to convince him to switch camps (line 3).

Je sɛn lɛd́ me la caa bɔg-bɔg baa? (1)
Siguidna Tchalna Kolandi ndi hay bay ti poltik wa weere dulnya. (2)
'A jãa ne jak ti waare Mongale gorna Walna wel maa ndalge. (3) (T., 97/98, v. 26)

If someone attacks me, can he flee all the way to God to escape me? (1)
Siguidna Tchalna Kolandi, I wasn't involved in politics, *gurna* dancers. (2)
They are trying to convince you to speak, Mongale, Walna's son, a guy who
    loves to talk. (3)

With these lines, Sogole praises Mongale to encourage him to stay with his song from Tuksu.

However, not all efforts to lure dancers to the composer's side and keep them there were so indirect and coy. Sometimes a composer might state simply: "*Nday daw dulnya me Jean-Richard Dourandi.*" ("You [pl.] support my song, Jean-Richard Dourandi"; T., 97/98, v. 22). And composers were not shy about situating themselves as power brokers, men with the power to confer reputation. Teodandi sings: "*Ndi hã du konkur yaŋ gɔ.*" ("I will 'post' the names of the competition"; D., 98/99, v. 23). He uses the metaphor of state-sponsored exams (*concours*) to represent the praise-names that come out in his *gurna* song. As the composer, he is at the top of the system; it is he who selects the names to be announced in the annual song.

Although much of *gurna* song is directed out toward the public—it is not a solipsistic genre—the composer nonetheless takes every opportunity to promote himself as both servant and disciplinarian of the populace. The persona he endeavors to project through the song lyrics is one of a powerful survivor, one who is above the fray of the politics of the dance (*poltik weere*). And, finally, he attempts to project an aura of impartiality in his reportage of bad behavior and vengefulness.

How do composers have the right to compose? Previous analysis of the construction of authority in African orature has focused on the power of the ancestors (Agovi 1995, 54), the wrath of the grandmothers (Apter 1998, 70), or the hoariness of the lineage at the root of artists' poetic license. *Gurna* song composers claim none of these. Rather, they acquire their right to compose directly from their ability to attract *gurna* dancers and the wider public. The power of this attraction is so vital that it is conceived in mystical terms, tied to magic herbs and gifts from God (*baa*). Tupuri people conceive of their society as one of relentless gossip, backbiting, and vengeance. Those who can prevail over this adversity and rise above it are widely admired. It is this ability to prevail above envy and political machinations that a composer strives to embody in his public role as composer and to project in his lyrics. Ultimately, it is this stamina which gives him the right to compose song—to assail, discipline, and laud others.

> His eyes are like a bush toad's, and he has epilepsy.
> (Z., 97/98, v. 12)
>
> He came down with cattle disease. (T., 98/99, v. 12)
>
> Her prolapsed hemorrhoid came out red in front of everyone.
> (T., 97/98, v. 18)
>
> You are half a man, like a motorboy. (Z., ca. 1997)

EIGHT

Staging Conflict through Insult

Competing Systems of Justice

In insult (*d̃arge*), *gurna* song composers have a special chance to display their creativity and verbal virtuosity. In addition to the ridicule of shameful acts (*sõore*), insult makes *gurna* song entertaining to the public. However, entertainment value is not the only function of insult; it also operates as a sanctioned mode for playing out interpersonal rivalries and for meting out justice in Tupuri society.

The analysis of insult in *gurna* song begun in chapter 6 described three ways that insult is put to use in the annual song. In the first, composers use insult to "destroy" their rival composers, to enhance their fame among *gurna* dancers and the wider public. Here, insult is part and parcel of the familiar politics of the dance (*poltik-jõo*). In the second, villagers commission composers to insult their enemies as a way of publicly staging their grievances and strengthening their reputations in the gossip mill of the community. Here insult broadcasts the existence of conflict, even if it does not necessarily resolve it. And third, insult can be used satirically to rein in those who are abusing their power to the detriment of the larger community. All of these rhetorical functions are protected by the composer's poetic license, and all have been reported in the verbal arts of many other African societies.

There are, however, aspects of insult in Tupuriland that have not been considered in research on African song; they are the subject of this chapter. If song is to be understood as a mechanism for maintaining a regime of social norms and equilibrium among villagers, then it is vital to examine its relationship to another major form of justice-making in African societies: witchcraft. Witchcraft accusation has been interpreted by analysts as an intimate way for communities to explain tragedy (Evans-Pritchard 1937) or to maintain a level political-economic playing field among members (Geschiere 1997). Rumor and gossip are almost always implicated in witchcraft accusation (White 2000). If Tupuri song, as another form of communal discourse, is deeply imbricated with gossip, how does song contribute to the process of identifying and trying witches? I address this question in an effort to answer the larger question of how song acted as a resource for justice-making in Tupuri society.

Although they are far from the Cameroonian capital in the south, Tupuri communities in the Far North make active use of state-sponsored judicial institutions to resolve conflict—the court system, the police and gendarmes, the government administration, and the *lamidat* (the traditional chieftaincy empowered by the state to try many types of crimes). This interwoven system of modern justice was progressively created through the colonial periods (under Germany and then the United Nations mandate) and the post-Independence regimes. But what of the power of indigenous Tupuri song to "try" individuals before the court of public opinion? Song-making predates these modern institutions and in many ways may still be the preferred way to air and manage conflict in the society. In this chapter, I am concerned with how modern state-sponsored institutions compete with the institution of song to maintain social justice. The increasing hegemony of the national court system, and its attendant threat of lawsuits for libel, has had a dampening effect on the use of verbal abuse in Tupuri song to "keep score." The interface of national and local forms of justice is important, because it is here that we begin to understand whether institutions intended to be "modern" and "ameliorative" in Africa are in fact so, and if so, for whom.

The first two sections of this chapter examine in some detail the use of insult as a form of song duel. They show how insult is a strategic tool rival song composers and feuding villagers use to attempt to consolidate their own power. The next sections take on the problem of modernization and the song, including how Tupuri people in an urban milieu have shifted their understanding of insult in song in accordance with their new context; in the city, they were more likely to find the song intrusive and dangerous. Then I consider the effect of the threat of libel on composers' freedom to insult one another in song. Finally, I will explore the relationship of song to witchcraft accusation and trials in Tupuriland as a way of examining the relationship between informal and indirect versus formal and direct methods of justice. I am also concerned with the effects of modernization on the poetic license of verbal abuse.

TRADING ABUSE IN NDOURNDOUR: CONFLICTS AMONG VILLAGERS

First let us summarize aspects of insult (*d'arge*) in *gurna* song discussed in earlier chapters. Villagers seek revenge against their enemies by bringing stories of conflict to the composer and requesting that he compose an insult for inclusion in the next year's *gurna* song. These insults are understood to be both damaging to the individual being insulted as well as entertaining to the public; there is no conflict between these two aspects. The composer protects himself from retaliation that might result from the abusive lyrics in three ways. First, the composer's *courriers* cross-check the story in the village to be sure that it has indeed occurred and is publicly recognized. Ideally, the insult caps or crystallizes already-circulating gossip in the village. Second, he usually includes in the lyrics both the name of the accused or insulted and the name of the accuser. This textual strategy enables the composer to buffer himself from the conflict at hand, to temper his accountability for any volatile results that might ensue. And third, some composers use magical herbs (*saŋgu*) to protect themselves from retribution by angry persons who have been "burned" by the song. At the very least, composers benefit from the circulation of discourse about the power of *saŋgu*, because that, in and of itself, affords some degree of protection against attack. When they do not admit to using *saŋgu,* composers call on more socially acceptable forms of "magic"; that is, the protection of the Christian God or the animist *baa.*[1]

Except for witchcraft accusation, most insult in Tupuri song lyrics does not describe the actual incident or conflict that occurred between the two parties. Rather, it focuses on accusations of moral impurity and physical deformities. *Darge* cannot be said to resolve conflict as much as stage it. And it is open to interpretation whether this public performance of insult is cathartic and ameliorative or whether it exacerbates conflict. Furthermore, as Irvine (1993) has pointed out, the boundaries of insult are blurry. The recounting of *sõore* (shameful acts) by individuals in *gurna* song is understood to be both moralizing and funny, but it can also shade into insult, depending on the context. On the other hand, some veteran *gurna* brag about times they were insulted in the song, saying that since they had become famous, it was a kind of "praise."

In the following case, a conflict in the village of Ndourndour was played out in song. Two individuals from the village attacked one another in *gurna* songs over successive years, commissioning competing composers. The case illustrates how the *siŋgurna* system works dialogically and diachronically to produce an arena for individuals who wage contests for dominance.

Ndourndour, a small village adjacent to the town of Doukoula, is close enough that villagers can attend the large Wednesday market and still farm their fields and guard their cattle outside town. There was a single *gurna* camp in Ndourndour, aligned with the composer of Zouaye, Djingue. However, several years ago, the camp suddenly split into two, and the splinter group aligned with the rival composer. The root of the conflict was between two feuding *gurna* members: Yambarré, a butcher, and Foudam, a tobacco merchant. It happened that Yambarré had an affair with the wife of Foudam's brother. Foudam reacted angrily. He separated from Yambarré and the *gurna* camp, creating his own camp aligned with the rival composer from Tuksu, Sogole.

Before the fissure, a well-known *courrier* of the composer of Zouaye used to visit the village, and in those days the Zouaye camp was large. Over time, however, the camp for Tuksu at Ndourndour had become larger. Ndourndour was a small village where Christian churches had dissuaded many from joining the *gurna.* Even so, when the envoy of the Sogole visited the camp, a goat was slaughtered and *yii* was served in his honor. As a result, many men in the village wanted to join the Tuksu camp. By contrast, the composer from Zouaye was not as regular in visiting his camp in Ndourndour.

Apparently the dominance of his Tuksu-affiliated camp was not enough for Foudam, or perhaps he felt that with this upper hand, he could afford to go on the offense against his enemy, Yambarré. Yambarré had no children after many years of marriage. So Foudam went to Sogole, the composer from Tuksu, and asked him to sing that Yambarré "had no testicles," was impotent. The song for that year included this verse:

Yambarré mo caw se ɓɔ bay bay.
Yɔɔ ɓɛ 'uwar Cholné takla mo na.
Nday tɛm mo dɛŋ si bay so no,
Ga yiŋ wɔɔ de kaara wur few paqué. (T., ca. 1996)

Yambarré doesn't have testicles.
His impurity murdered Cholné this year.
You hurry now,
They ran into us on Easter.

When the song circulated in Doukoula, everyone knew about the conflict. They were shocked by the attack because the butcher was a successful entrepreneur. Perhaps they thought that such a successful person could not be so maligned. The effect of the song on Yambarré was devastating. He was so embarrassed he stayed in his house, hiding, for a whole year. He lost weight. Then he took his wives to the traditional healer for *saŋgu* (traditional medicine) so they would get pregnant. After they were treated, the *saŋgu* overacted. It made the women so sexually excited that they went around sleeping with many of the young men of the village and, of course, they got pregnant. Yambarré then said he had children, but everyone knew he was not the father. Nevertheless, feeling strong, he went to his composer at Zouaye to counterattack Foudam in the song. This is the verse that came out:

Foudam pel ne jerɛm ndi ga baa tɔp sɛŋ gɔ.
Kaŋ haage Werbe.
Je de bay cōore caa me ti faage.
Ndi da' wɛ ti ŋgel lumo dɛŋ na.
Jak 6ɛ sara ti 6ɛ sara.
Ŋgar 6ɛ ga lay.
Baa biŋ mo wɔ yo jar tabay maa fɛk mbe ti caw pa sɔ Foudam.
Ndɔ mo de ndusi dɔɔ kare lay sɔ Foudam.
Ndɔ mo de ndusi sɔ lay ndɔ fɛr ga ndɔ wɔ leg je Jakra.
Foudam ka ma leg baa ga.
Foudam 'ur ciŋ dɔɔ maŋ 6ɛ kelee. (Z., ca. 1997)

Foudam, fish-face, I say that God has abandoned him.
Take up a throwing knife, Werbe.
A bad guy has come and found me on the road.
I found him in the marketplace.
His mouth is strange; his head is strange.
He has no form either.
God put you on the earth among people so that you would be mocked by
    them, Foudam.
You are half a man, like a motorboy, Foudam.
You are half a man as well, and you say that you have come to look for prob-
    lems with Jakra's son.
Foudam cannot cause problems with God.
Foudam got up to walk when he was small.

Foudam was viciously insulted in the song, called a "fish-face,"[2] "half a man," physically deformed, a "motorboy,"[3] and so forth. In the last line, an insult—"Foudam got up to walk when he was small"—refers to the concept of *yɔɔ*, which, loosely defined, is a fundamental transgression against social norms, an impurity. It could come about through human action; for example, the act of incest. Or, a *yɔɔ* could appear spontaneously as a sign of bad luck: a bizarre unnatural act, such as animals speaking or a baby talking or standing up to walk precociously. (Such a baby is usually abandoned for fear that he will bring misfortune.)

When I left Doukoula, the duel between Foudam and Yambarré was at this stage. There may have been further actions after my departure. But even thus far, this case illustrates the dynamic nature of insult in *gurna* song. First, it was publicly witnessed by practically the entire community. Even though most people may not have comprehended the exact verses in the song during its performance at the death celebrations, the most scandalous phrases would have circulated through everyday gossip. Second, the seasonal cycle of the song allowed the insults to unfold over several years and to proceed dialogically. With each new *gurna* season, there was an opportunity to "publish" anew one party's revenge against an enemy. Third, the competitive organization of the composers and the camps provided the possibility that individuals from the same community could call on rival composers to act as their mouthpieces. Feuds among individual *gurna* members played out through fissures in *gurna* camps and their affiliation with competing composers—which was mirrored in the verbal abuse that appeared in the songs. In this way, interpersonal conflict was publicly enacted as individuals attempted to sway communal opinion in their own favor.

INSULT IN COMPOSER RIVALRY

Insult is not limited to individuals in communities who have an axe to grind with one another. A composer of *siŋ gurna* also initiates insult against his own personal enemies and rival composers. Through insult, he seeks to reduce his rivals' popularity and promote his own cleverness as a composer, thereby attracting more *gurna* dancers to his song. Here, power vis-à-vis other composers is measured in the sharpness of a composers' verse. As one composer sings, "I am a spiny fish in a pond whose sting will never leave you!" (T., 97/98, v. 11). *Gurna* song competition is less immediate than face-to-face poetic dueling (Abrahams 1962; Caton 1990; Mathias 1976). Since *gurna* song unfolds over the years and does not assume a single unique performance, the composer competition is less direct, even if the lyrics are caustic.

As described in chapter 7, the composers in Zouaye consider the partnership between the composers Sogole of Tuksu and Dayle of Youaye to be a challenge to their "dynasty." In order to knock them down to size, Djingue from Zouaye composed the following insults against Dayle. The insults drew on grotesque imagery of animals, deformed bodies, and medical conditions. Dayle was accused of having bulging eyes like a toad's and of suffering from epilepsy (line 3), considered to be a shameful, polluting disease.

Ndi nduu Youaye Pesna Guidwa, (1)
Wel lɛ'd ndi ga lɛ? (2)
Nen de man-nyaa bas ga dɛŋ mbulur lɛ'd ne ndi laa mbi wɛ. (3)
Nday de hay gad ne gɔ ga lɛ? (4)
Ndi hay laa baa naa ga pan ɓɛn hay tɔp hɔɔlɛ maa ni man ɓɛn gɔ dɔɔ mbulur, (5)
Jɔŋ fen sōore, (6)
Baa pɔr sir hān ne naare wɔɔ ra. (7) (Z., 97/98, v. 12)

I came to Youaye, Pesna Guidwa, (1)
Why do you always attack me? (2)
With his eyes like a bush toad's, he has epilepsy, I know. (3)
Why haven't you slaughtered him? (4)
I heard that ever since his father had rejected his mother's meals, because of
    the epilepsy, (5)

> He did shameful things. (6)
> Take him and purify your village, give him to the women. (7)

Trying to determine the veracity of insults, I asked Noumnamo (Djingue's partner) whether Dayle really did have epilepsy or whether this was just a conventional insult. He claimed that Dayle actually did have epilepsy but noted that the insult lay in the fact that the song called attention to this.

The composer continued this verbal abuse, claiming that Dayle's father rejected his mother by rejecting her meals (line 5, above). The offering of meals by wives and their consumption by the husband is the central symbol of marriage (and consensual sexual relations) in Africa. The abuse continues with the composer suggesting that the village should be purified of the epileptic Dayle by handing him over to the women for ritual sacrifice!

The following year, the composers at Zouaye continued their insult of Dayle. Not all insult is located in images of the body; it frequently recounts an alleged rupture of Tupuri social convention. In the verses below, Dayle was said to have transgressed the norms of correct behavior associated with funerals. Normally, when there is a death, the family leaves the house and possessions of the deceased intact until after the death celebration (*yii-huuli*). The *yii-huuli* ceremonies include the ritual destruction of the house where the deceased slept. But in this case, Dayle was accused of having sold his deceased mother's bed before the death celebration (line 2):

> *Ndɔ na jõo ɓaa se ɓɔ jɔŋ fen mbon na ndɔ kan gɔ ne wel po gale?* (1)
> *Ndɔ yee lit man ɓɔ gɔ,* (2)
> *Ndɔ Beswé armoir bɔɔŋ pee Bokga,* (3)
> *Nday but tiŋ gɔ sɔ bakla Bogao.* (4) (Z., 98/99, v. 35)

> You pass your youth doing shameful things; why do you impute them to another? (1)
> You sold your mother's bed, (2)
> One "famine" cupboard remains, Bokga, (3)
> You split up the house even so, Bogao.[4] (4)

These lyrics are clever: in line 3, only one cupboard (French borrow term, *armoir*) remains from the illicit sale, and this piece of furniture is so decrepit that it couldn't even feed a family if sold during a famine! This entire concept is encoded in the word "*Beswé*" (line 3), the name of a severe famine that took place in Tupuriland during the early twentieth century. This alleged travesty against the memory of his mother shamed Dayle and his family for having disrespected tradition.

For their part, Dayle and Sogole did not neglect to insult their rivals in return. Dayle heard that a man named Bouwa was planning to go to the composer at another center of song composition in Dawa to insult him, so he insulted Bouwa preemptively. Bouwa is said to have come down with a bovine disease that produces large sores on the back: "ganglion" (line 3). He is also alleged to have acquired witchcraft (*kereŋ*)[5] from his mother (line 5), which was inherited from her mother (line 8):

> *Dulnya coo wɛ pa wãare maa de fãy yaŋ pa.* (1)
> *Ndi hay mbi ne boga kangilyon kan ga,* (2)
> *'A day ga Bouwa kangilyon gɔ se ɓay bo la jar Mbiya* (3)

Docteur wɔ mbɛ Bouwa lay na. (4)
Nday de kereŋ de man 6ɔ. (5)
Nday ga wāa wāa lay na. (6)
Nday taw Holing gɔ mo na. (7)
Kereŋ maa 6il kaa Bouwa mo na. (8) (T., 98/99, v. 12)

Life has changed—there are troubling stories. (1)
I thought that people couldn't get ganglion, (2)
But you say that Bouwa came down with ganglion, people from Mbiya. (3)
The doctor will have to cure Bouwa. (4)
You took witchcraft with your mother. (5)
You prevent people from talking. (6)
You killed Holing. (7)
There is witchcraft in Bouwa's grandmother. (8)

Often insults are gendered, likening men to women—that is, demasculating them. Sogole sang phallocentrically that only "a few men" (dancers on his side) were potent and that his opposition was like women frightened by the loud noise of guns:

Jar ma po baa caa 6ĩini ne sɛn dɔ hāa.
Bay ga je tuwar wa 6aa.
Djebongue man-naare jāa wɔ ga wuu no. (T., 97/98, v. 25)

God gave penises only to a few men.
These are not real men.
Djebongue, they are frightened like women in front of guns.

The same year, the competing composers at Zouaye were insulting Sogole's dancers, calling them "weak, not numerous" and like "large women" (*man-naare*) (line 1) who did foolish things:

Man-naare po jɔŋ wɔ fen sōore . . . (1)
Manquant jɔŋ raa debaŋ tu sɛn. (2) (Z., 97/98, v. 41)

The large women do shameful things . . . (1)
Losers complain a lot like that. (2)

In summary, some insult in *siŋ gurna* is unrelated to the management of conflict in villages; rather, it represents an agonistic posturing between composers every year in their songs. This injury is comparable to insults, taunting, and booing by sports fans at a game, although in *gurna* song, this agonistic insult is not spontaneous; rather, it is regulated by the formalities of the song composition and performance.

SECRETS IN THE CITY: REINTERPRETING THE POWER OF INSULT

The repartee of insult among competing individuals I have described is common and entirely acceptable in rural Tupuriland. This form of highly public, discursive battle is seen to contribute to the management of conflict in the villages. When it occurs among song composers, it is understood to drum up excitement for the dance. However, many Tupuri people who have migrated to urban areas, such as Maroua (the capital of the Far North Province), find that such use of song no longer held sway. In fact, in the city, insult in song is seen as dangerous and undesirable rather than playful.

Kaoga Rigobert, a deejay for the Tupuri-language radio program in Maroua, described the perils of song composition in Maroua and the effect it has had on Tupuri culture among urban émigrés. Kaoga's friend Dourwe asked him why the *gurna* and Tupuri culture in Maroua seemed to be weakening. Kaoga responded:

> "People don't seek to renew [Tupuri culture]—for example, the *gurna* songs. When the songs are sung, it's an announcement of events. Maybe you have stolen your mother-in-law's goats. That must automatically be put into the song. And it gives moral lessons, because tomorrow, you won't dare to steal again.... Here in town, they don't manage to formulate these songs. There is no one who is dynamic to compose or to arrange the songs. But there are also events that happen here in town, like petty theft."

"But what limits the song here?" I asked Kaoga.

"It has to do with our contemporary situation.... In Tupuriland, for example, you come across two children who are involved in fighting. You can take a whip and beat them—in the village. There is perhaps your own child there and a neighbor's child; you whip them both. The other child returns home. At eight or nine p.m., he says that he has a headache. Suddenly, the father of the child comes to your house to talk to you. He says, 'You whipped my child at noon, and now the child has a headache.' When actually, the child could have some other illness. Maybe the child had been sick for two or three days before, but now the father says that you whipped his child.

When you compose a song, a person is going to say that you composed a song concerning him. He takes you to court. Like insults—you know, in the song, you must put insult in them. In all songs, there are insults."

"So, if you do that here in the city, they put you in jail?" I asked.

"Yes!" Lowering his voice for contrast, he went on, "In the village, there is the chief of the village. He is there; he smoothes things over. He says, 'No, according to the past custom here, we do this. If you commit an act, then a song must be composed. How can you come and complain about that now?' The chief fixes that. But here [in Maroua], if you compose a song against someone, they take you to the police station and they arrest you. They're going to say that there are insults in there.

Could you have sexual relations with your mother-in-law? That can't be done! So, it's cases like that when a song will be composed. If the person who did that did it discreetly, in secret, another person could hear about it. The person who composes—people come and bring him news. It's not that he hears about it because the event happened in front of him. No, it could be far away. If an event happens far away, a person leaves there with the news, and he carries it and reports it. Then everyone sees that a week later the song has come out already. And he is going to put his name in there, like in the village, that it was he who composed the song. His name is there. And that's how things are fixed.

But here [in Maroua], an event that happens in secret like that, it's like you *divulged* that, the secret of the family of someone. So, that's why people don't like to enter into this."

"So families keep their secrets better here in the city?" I asked.

"Yes, the families keep their secrets. They keep them because they are afraid. When it has already come to the level of the courts, that is going to fall on your back. Are you going to get out of that? You're going to find yourself in jail the next day.

"But," he added, laughing, "there is gossip [*un leger congossa*]!⁶ People recount it. There is lots of *congossa* there in the city. But you can't hear who said it. You just hear. One talks and the other leaves with it, one talks and the other leaves with it.... Finally, you notice that it's 'sung' in the entire neighborhood. But, in the end, you cannot know who was at the origin, who let the secret out. You're not going to find out the person. No one is going to tell."

"So people who could be composers here in the city are too afraid to be composers?"

Kaoga concludes, "Yes, they are too afraid. There is this problem of the courts. And it's that that makes people keep to themselves."

I have quoted Kaoga at length because his explanation gets at some complex interrelations in the song tradition, as well as the subtlety of shifts in it brought on by the urban milieu. First, through the example of the parent who whips both his own child and his neighbor's child, Kaoga shows how it is normative in the village that misbehavior is punished though the performance of song. There is free license to discipline where discipline is needed (as long as it is from superior to inferior). Any appeals in the village will be smoothed over by the village chief, who in effect explains the ritual frame of the song to plaintiffs—that the song is something "of our ancestors." However, in the city, there have been significant shifts in the relations between families, in the social fabric at the most fundamental level. Insults or shameful acts proclaimed in the song in the village become grounds for charging either the composer or the commissioner of the insult for libel in the court of law in the city.

According to Kaoga, the reason the song is seen as intolerable in the city is that it reveals "family secrets" in a context where people felt less secure. The fear that urban Tupuri have of the police, the gendarmes, and the justice system has a dampening effect on their song composition tradition. Not only are people afraid to bring news to a composer for song production, those who can compose do not dare. Still, the need to regulate and punish misbehavior through public oral discourse is not diminished, as Kaoga noticed. He snickered mischievously, describing how even *without* the formal song, misdeed is "sung" throughout the neighborhood through gossip (*congossa*). Who can track down the originator of gossip?

This discussion illustrates two points of fluidity or ambiguity in Tupuri verbal abuse. First, there is a porousness between song and gossip. As composers have told me, sounding out the vigor of the gossip surrounding a scandal is a vital part of the composition process. But the composers do not investigate a lead as a court of law investigates a case—that is, for its truth validity. Rather, the song is a crystallization of already-circulating gossip. It takes the problem to the next level of publicity or notoriety. This heightened publicity is thought to have a corrective effect on the wrongdoer and a cathartic effect on the community. Therefore, there is a mutually supporting relationship between gossip and song; gossip makes up the bedrock of public opinion underlying the scandal recounted in song. Embarrassing or insulting stories in song lyrics in turn generate more gossip and, it is to be hoped, correct the behavior of individuals. This dynamic relationship between song and gossip is evident in both rural and urban contexts. However, in the city, the song tradition is greatly curtailed by fear that the police will not understand this quintessentially Tupuri code of conflict resolution and will permit libel charges to go forward. Many Cameroonian ethnic groups perform some form of injurious song, so intolerance or misunderstanding of them might have been less a question of cross-cultural misunderstanding than of differences in codes of conduct in rural versus urban contexts. Social relations in urban areas are generally less intimate than in villages and thus are more likely to be mediated by modern institutions (such as the courts and police). These institutions are in turn more present and stronger in the city than the village. In the village, such charges are dismissed as ridiculous, and chiefs and elders work to assuage bruised egos. As a result, in the city, gossip continues to carry the weight of public opinion, weight that elsewhere would have culminated in song.

The second area of fluidity in Kaoga's description is that between insult (darge) and the recounting of shameful acts (sõore). Irvine has pointed to the difficulties of identifying insult as insult and identifying it dichotomously as either direct or indirect (1993, 106–107). She points out the importance of examining "the relationship between the wording of the abusive message, its meta-communicative frame, and the structure of the social occasion in which it takes place" (107). In Kaoga's metacultural discussion of injurious song, he explained that at times in a song there is a fusion, or "melting together," of sõore that is intended to moralize and insult that is intended to injure. In specific contexts and situations—here, the city—sõore are interpreted as not only insulting but as intolerably threatening. He noted that the feeling of outrage that a Tupuri person might feel to be "sung" in this manner in the city might be so great that he would reach outside the enclave of his "brothers" to press charges in the formal Cameroonian justice system. Such a process would begin with filing a complaint with the gendarme brigade, which would issue a convocation. Further legal action might proceed in the courts. Given the corruption and rigidity of the judicial system, few song composers or informants to the composer would risk this danger.

Even though insult in rural Tupuri song may appear to be vituperative or even shocking, it is, in a broad view, a highly flexible way of airing and ameliorating conflicts among individuals. However, some Tupuri émigrés felt that the urban context does not provide the consensual openness and trust necessary for these song traditions to continue unhindered. They are intimidated by the threat of libel charges and the pay-as-you-go "justice" of the formal court system. Insult in song in rural areas performs a specific type of social work—that is, it mediates relations between feuding parties. However, in order for it to work in this fashion, there must be a shared belief in the cathartic effect of the song and a willingness to refrain from going beyond the system to state-sponsored forms of justice. Such consensus seems to be much more difficult to maintain in the dynamic and unpredictable context of the city, where suspicion runs high even among Tupuri "brothers."

SOGOLE'S LEGAL PROBLEMS: THE THREAT OF LIBEL

Although the intervention of the formal justice system in the dynamics of Tupuri song has been presented as a conflict between urban and rural codes of conduct and security, that dichotomy is too facile. In fact, the threat of libel is not limited to cities. The composer Sogole was dragged to court several times from his village home of Tuksu. Although Sogole's song became a liability for him—he was charged or threatened with a charge of libel—he also used his song composition as a strategic resource with which to seek revenge against individuals who brought legal charges against him. In the following case involving Sogole, we see how he used insult to retaliate against his enemies and how he attempted to frame conflict in terms of the politics of popularity among composers. The threat of being taken to court was a constant concern for him, and he resisted the notion that composers could be held accountable for libel.

When I first arrived at the village of Tuksu to meet the composer Sogole, I was well received, even if it was unclear to *gurna* members why a *je-wuu* (European) would be visiting. In the course of my interview with Sogole, I began to realize that he was in the midst of a serious problem, even though his behavior was nonchalant. We were interrupted when he gave a boy money to rent a bicycle. The boy was to pedal twenty miles to the Department capital, Yagoua, in order to respond to a legal summons on his behalf. At the same time, Sogole, with his *courriers'* aid, was patiently explicating his 1997/1998 *gurna* song for me. This explication included verses of his song where Sogole sought to wreak vengeance on his enemies and reestablish his reputation. Later, I understood that Sogole's legal problems were tied to his song.

Puzzled by the song lyrics, I asked Sogole how it was that he was "transformed into a wild cat" (line 1):

> *Sela gɔŋga ndi kɔl timiini pel baara sɛŋ.* (1)
> *Je Lefenne ga hay kɔl ciŋ few jõo.* (2)
> *Ndi yaŋ 6ɔ' man-jaw 6i.* (3)
> *Bay bay raa naa ti naa weere Tinnin.* (4) (T., 97/98, v. 4)

> Sela, it's true, I transformed myself suddenly into a wild cat in front of them. (1)
> Lefenne's son said to prepare for the dance season. (2)
> I'm among you, thrusting my large spear. (3)
> The chief's drums announce the presence of the people of Tinnin. (4)

Although he was not immediately forthcoming about explaining the legal summons weighing on him that morning, Sogole was willing to explain his predicament through the mediation of his song lyrics: "Those people who threw me into prison are like dogs, so I transformed myself into a wild cat (*timiini*) to combat them." When I expressed incredulity, he went on:

> I was thrown in jail for eight days. The people of Tinnin are of my own clan [line 4]. They had been discouraged when I was imprisoned. So, when I say I thrust my large spear [*man-jaw*], it means that I returned to the dance with my dancing stick [line 3]. In spite of hardship, I survived and others are jealous to see me back.

As we went through the song verse by verse, the conflict leading up to Sogole's imprisonment kept reappearing in the form of elaborate insult against the perpetuators. Eventually this is what Sogole told me about the underlying conflict motivating his insult:

> Last year, there was a composer from Chad [Dawa] whose *gurna* camps are here in Cameroon. Some of these dancers came to my camps. The Chadian composer came and confronted me, saying that I had stolen his dancers. Some of the composer's dancers [from Youaye] came and threatened me at my house, so I hit them. The dancers went then and lodged a complaint in Yagoua [the District capital].

In Sogole's view, the root of the problem stemmed from the jealousy of another composer because he had lured away his dancers. So he sought revenge through his lyrics.

Sogole explained to me that Dabsoumo (line 4 below), Djogdougue (line 6), and Damsala (line 9) were relatives of the thugs who attacked him at his compound (the Dawa-affiliated dancers from Youaye). He accused them of being witches of the *kereŋ* type, mocking them about the ineffectiveness of their witchcraft: "Have you caught me yet?" (line 7). His enemies "have opened their mouths in hopes of eating meat" (line 5), referring to their hope of "eating" Sogole. ("*Rege nay*," "to eat meat" is a conventional expression for the spiritual cannibalism of witches.)

Mindif Selda ndɔ wii Kolomso. (1)
Wanga ndi yaŋ wɔ seege her jak wɛ. (2)
Youaye rod sir ɓaŋ sɛn gɔ. (3)
Mon nday wɔ sɔ jar ni Dabsoumo. (4)
Nday ciŋ saŋ gɔ maa re nay yaw-la? (5)
Ndɔ raa maa ga na Djogdougue wɔ mbay ko way de kereŋ. (6)
Ndi ga nday baa me sɔ yaw-la? (7)
Tchanwalna, ndi bay mbi lɛd jar tabay wa. (8)
Nday lɛd me lay na Damsala ndi wii mo da la. (9) (T., 97/98, v. 10)

Selda from Mindif, you ask after Kolomso. (1)
Wanga, I'm coming to greet you. (2)
Youaye invaded the villages of this region. (3)
This song has come down to you, people of Dabsoumo. (4)
You opened your mouth to eat meat, didn't you? (5)
Now you cry, Djogdougue, go complain to the witch. (6)
I say, have you caught me yet? (7)
Tchanwalna, I'm not attacking the others. (8)
You provoke me also, Damsala, I'm telling it to you. (9)

Later in the song, the composer continues his insult. Again he accuses his enemies of witchcraft and valorizes his own power. Boasting, he likens himself to the *haw* fish, a variety of mud fish with long spines that can easily injure an unsuspecting fisher (line 2 below). Djerou (line 4) is the man who filed suit against Sogole in Yagoua, so the composer asks, in effect: "Are you trying to prevent me from composing?" In lines 5 and 6, he accuses his enemies of using witchcraft to try to control the influence of the song, expressed as "hold Cameroon in your hands" ("*sir Kamru dɔɔ ɓɔ*").

Graobe Sangue ndɔ wii jar ɓay de kereŋ ga (1)
Ndi diŋ haw nen bii ɓe' mo la nen no ga. (2)
Manla jōo re Kaosir gɔ takla. (3)
Djerou ndɔ baa me ga daw sir Kamru wa. (4)
Ndi laa wɛ diŋ je malum hay wɔ re jar tabay de kereŋ na. (5)
Sir Kamru ndɔ ɓɔ yaw-la? (6) (T., 97/98, v. 11)

Graobe Sangue, tell your people who are witches (1)
That I am a spiny fish in a pond whose sting will never leave you. (2)
Manla, the dance is to beat out Kaosir this year. (3)
Djerou, you call on me to not support Cameroon. (4)

I heard that it was a witch who went there to eat people with witchcraft. (5)
But do you still hold Cameroon in your hands? (6)

Several verses later, Sogole's insult continues just as trenchantly, although some insults are less obvious to a non-Tupuri audience. "You got up from your mother's hands" (line 3 below) refers to the impurity (yɔɔ) explained earlier; extreme precocity in babies, walking too early, is a harbinger of bad luck.

Djagna nday wii je Djagsoumo Taiwe Fankomdi naa fɛr wɛ raa jōo day no.
(1)
Sint yaŋ wɔ seege Fidsela Walne. (2)
Ndɔ hay 'ur ciŋ ba lɛ dɔɔ man 6ɔ na. (3)
Ndɔ fɛr 'ii je Mana mo no fen de bay cōore man 6il hɔrge. (4)
Ndɔ wɔ da'ge mbɛ ti 6ɛ dɔ haw maa nen bii, (5)
Bil hɔrge ne man 6ɔ, (6)
Bagde gɔlɔg de tɔŋrɔŋ ne wel-mbaydaŋ. (7) (T., 97/98, v. 16)

Djagna, ask Djagsoumo Taiwe's son, Fankomdi, to come back to the dance.
(1)
The song's about to come down on you, Fidsela Walne. (2)
You got up from your mother's hands. (3)
You return to kill Mana's son over jealousy, like a swollen stomach. (4)
You are going to find his head like a mud fish in water, (5)
Belly swollen like your mother's, (6)
Like the calluses on a young monkey's ass. (7)

Sogole explained the personalities in the following verse who are implicated in the fight at his house and the ensuing court case. Fidsela Walne (line 5 below), the man who filed the legal suit against Sogole, is insulted, as well as his mother, father, and daughter. Walne's mother (line 1–2) has an embarrassing "disease of the colon" (*baahuuli*). His daughter, Maïdanso (line 4), went crazy because, according to Sogole's explanation, Fidsela "gave birth to his own daughter"; to have been birthed by a man accounts for her insanity (*lɔdge*). And then, this Fidsela Walne is said to have killed his brother, for which he had to provide animal sacrifices. Unfortunately, this Fidsela was so dim that he attempted to complete the sacrifice with an entirely inappropriate animal: a giraffe (line 7–8)!

Baahuul nduu gɔ desēe wer nen jar ka'a. (1)
Nday ga nduu na wer man Walne. (2)
Ka'a se 6ɔ diŋ baahuul maa lɔd je Fayno. (3)
Walne fɛr kod Maydanso lɔdge pa. (4)
Je Mana Fidsela Walne ndi laa mbi wɛ. (5)
Fek jɔŋ me ti maa ga ndɔ hay 'uwar hen 6ɔ. (6)
Bala ga kɔl sōo lɛ. (7)
Mo no co' 6ɛ de manpirbaa yaw-la? (8) (T., 97/98, v. 18)

Her prolapsed hemorrhoid came out red in front of everyone.[7] (1)
You say it came from Walne's mother. (2)
It's the disease of the colon that drove Fayno's son insane. (3)
And then Walne went to Maïdanso and drove her insane again. (4)
Mana Fidsela's son, Walne, I heard about you (5)
and I laughed because before, you had killed your brother. (6)

This affected your mind. (7)
Did he really make a sacrifice with a giraffe? (8)

Up to this point, I have recounted this case from the point of view of Sogole, showing how he crafted revenge through creative insult in his annual *gurna* song. However, other interlocutors hold different perspectives. An official at the *sous-préfecture* of Doukoula familiar with the conflict explained it quite differently:

> The dancers from Dawa came to Sogole's house. He had two wives there, as well as a girl. Sogole's wife had made sorghum beer, so it was served. The people from Dawa drank and flirted with the girl. When it got dark and the *yii* was finished, the visitors still did not go home. So, Sogole, "What's going on? What's keeping you?" Still they refused to leave, so Sogole tried to force them out of the compound and a fight ensued. As a result, one man from the group from Dawa brought a legal suit to Yagoua.

As this official explained the case, he insisted that it was *un problème de femme* (a fight over a woman), not one of competition for popularity in the *gurna* song, as Sogole saw it. What Sogole had told me earlier in his village, was, of course, the version he wanted me to hear. He chose to use the trope of the competition of the dance as the explanation for events that were outside that arena. During my research I gradually came to realize that the rhetoric of *gurna* competition was often used as an idiom to discuss—and even explain—all kinds of conflicts and struggles for dominance that had no immediate connection to the *gurna*.

This dominant trope of *gurna* competition emerged humorously after my first interview with Sogole. I had been assisted by Dourwé, who was pleased to accompany me to Sogole's village because he was courting his fiancé in Tuksu and conducting outreach health education there for the regional hospital. A few days after our visit to Sogole, which I had seen as successful and not at all rushed, a rumor circulated that Dourwé and I had been "chased" from Tuksu. I was told this by a man who was working for a well maintenance company in Oulargo, near Tuksu, as he passed by my house to deliver a letter. The logic behind the rumor that we had been "chased" was that Dourwé was from the "enemy camp." Dourwé's natal village was Madalam, which happened to be affiliated with the composer from Zouaye. Of course Dourwé, who is thoroughly *évolué*, had no affiliation with a *gurna* camp or composer. But I couldn't help smiling over the fact that Sogole (or his people) would not let an opportunity slip by to promote themselves in the *gurna* politics of fame, especially when he could claim to have "chased" a *je-wuu* (European). Later, I realized that the rumor could as easily have been launched by dancers affiliated with the competing Zouaye composer to undermine any prestige that Sogole acquired by receiving a visit from a *je-wuu*. In any event, the trope of *gurna* competition was rampant. Sogole explained his encounter with the justice system as yet another extension of this cultural politics: a rival composer was jealous of his power to attract dancers, and this necessitated a response of lyrical insult.

A year later, Sogole revealed to me the results of the legal suit. He said when he and the plaintiffs from Youaye went to court in Yagoua, the court threw out the case and told them to go home. When Sogole was summoned to court during my visit, it was the second time, and this time it was for libel. The plaintiff said that Sogole had called him a witch (*kereŋ*) in the 1997/1998 song lyrics just explicated. ("This song has come down to you, people of Dabsoumo. / You opened your mouth to eat meat, didn't you? / Now you cry, Djogdougue, go complain to the witch" [T., 97/98, v. 10]). But again the case was thrown out. Although my research did not extend to the Yagoua court system, I imagine that the case may have been handled like one described to me by the composer from Zouaye. He told of a man from Tchatibali who, angry about an insult in the song, pressed charges against the commissioner of the insult. The composer, Noumnamo, was called upon to account for the song. The case was eventually dismissed in part because the insult was considered "the judgment of the *gurna*"—the right to such speech was retained by the *gurna*.

Sogole consistently insisted that a composer cannot be arrested for his song composition. So imagine my surprise when Sogole's rival, Noumnamo, told me that Sogole himself had already pressed charges with the police for insults in the 1998/1999 song—before it even came out. Apparently, Noumnamo's "people" (*courriers*) whispered to Sogole that he was to be slandered. I was unable to confirm this with Sogole himself, but what is important is the discourse of "spying" and the threat of the insertion of the formal security forces into the domain of the song.

But should the composer be protected from libel charges? Is the poetic license of the song sacrosanct? Sogole's assistant, Balandi, who is in part responsible for protecting the composer, reflected on the taken-for-granted immunity of the composer:

> Before, people couldn't complain about the song. They would ask you if you like to dance. If you do (and everyone does), then you have to admit that the songs you have been dancing contain insults that you yourself sang. So no one can complain.

But Balandi reflected further on changes in the past years. "Before, if you insult someone in the song, they didn't do anything. Now they can take you to court and take money from you." He went on to invoke the powers of the legendary composer Dang Biina.

> Dang Biina sang that the wind would take everything from Temwa [the *lamido* of Doukoula at the time], and it did. With *sangu*, if the composer sings that you will lose an eye, you must lose it. That's obligatory.... But, now with modern life [*dulnya*], someone could come and take you to court.

But what Balandi did not consider was that even in the past composers suffered terrible consequences as a result of their compositions. Dang Biina fled capture by the forces of the *lamido* and died in exile from the country. Composers and their defenders (usually *courriers*) may be engaging in some strategic nostalgia for the past when they speak of past freedom of expression. Although the legal activity in which composers are implicated today may differ from the persecution faced by composers in the past, it is likely that insult in song has been dangerous for the composer for quite some time.

In the past, verbal abuse in *siŋ gurna* was seen as part of a consensual ritual performance that spared no one, not even the powerful. Even if a composer faced the revenge of injured parties, there was no question that the composer had a right to sing out against corrupt rulers and to handle commissions of insults from ordinary people. Today, it appears that the modern judicial system may be extending its hegemony to the judgment of indigenous discursive genres such as the *gurna* song, though this extension is controversial or incomplete, since cases like these are likely to be thrown out. Furthermore, Christian churches in Tupuriland promote the notion that local song foments conflict among villagers in the place of what should ideally be unified "Christian fellowship." The court system and Christian churches pose a threat by questioning the right of composers to compose according to the current conventions of the song. Joel Kuipers reported a similar situation in Indonesia, where the government banned certain ritual speech events among the Weyewa ethnic group, whom it sought to "modernize," calling the rituals "wasteful" and "backward" (1992, 103). Although the Cameroonian government has not, to my knowledge, attempted to ban ritual speech, the effect of being able to successfully prosecute composers for libel might be similar. However as Kuipers reported for the Weyewa in 1992, I believe it is too early to tell the effect of the penetration of the formal judicial system on the Tupuri song tradition.

LOCAL JUSTICE: INSULT AND WITCHCRAFT ACCUSATION

Those who use the court system to retaliate against insult in *gurna* song are attempting to trump one system of justice with another. Like the court, the song is itself a system with the power to establish justice. The song is a form of trial and punishment in that crimes and follies were exposed and punished through public shame. However, embarrassment and ruined reputations are not the only modes of punishment it can bring. In cases of witchcraft, insult in song articulated to other forms of publicly performed ritual justice. In Tupuriland, cases of witchcraft can be resolved by either the gendarmerie or a traditional witchcraft trial called *dāa*. Gurna song is implicated in this process as an avenue of accusation, resulting in an individual's submission to investigation at the gendarmerie or the *dāa* trial.

Throughout my time in Tupuriland, Tupuri people from all walks of life brought up their concerns about witchcraft. It seemed to be a consensus that one of the most serious problems facing the society is the corrosive power of witchcraft, sometimes termed "jealousy" ("*hun*," Tupuri, or "*jalousie*," French). Witchcraft represents the power to sabotage others, even to kill them, out of jealousy over their good fortune or in the greedy desire to get ahead of others.

Two forms of witchcraft were present in Tupuri society at the time of my research: *kereŋ* and *sā'ā*. (Although magic herbs, *saŋgu*, are involved in transmitting and detecting witchcraft, the forms of *saŋgu* discussed in Chapter 7 are not witchcraft per se.) *Kereŋ* is an older, hereditary form of witchcraft associated with old women and, to a lesser degree, old men. They are said to transform themselves into a *buuya*, a "vampire," which resembles a lizard or a winged toad with sparks flying from its mouth. They fly around at night looking for "food," that is, innocent people walking around. If they fly over you, I was told, they "eat you," consume your soul. Eventually the victim will fall ill and die. Having inherited *kereŋ* from their mothers—who would have had to have "eaten" a person while pregnant—witches are well known in village communities, but they are not exiled. Their presence is tolerated because *kereŋ* is considered involuntary and naturally occurring; that is, not the fault of the individual.

In contrast, *sā'ā* is a recent form of witchcraft that is considered more nefarious than *kereŋ*. The Tupuri believe that *sā'ā* came to them from the Moundang, the neighboring ethnic group to the west. The Moundang in turn had brought *sā'ā* from southern Cameroon within the past forty years or so. Known throughout the south by various names (*famla,* Bamiléké; *djambe,* Maka; and *evu,* Beti), this "modern" form of witchcraft is what is known in the New World as "zombiism."[8] The witch acquires *sā'ā* from another witch by ransoming the life of a family member, then proceeds to enslave people by stealing their souls. The enslaved souls labor at night in the fields of their master, enriching him. Meanwhile the physical bodies of the victims atrophy until eventually they die what is termed "an unnatural death," in contrast to a death "willed by God."

Individuals who possess *sā'ā* are widely feared and hated. They can be detected when members of their family and their neighbors start to die off around them. They also reveal their powers through their inexplicable increase in wealth, which neighbors understand to have been acquired through the nocturnal labors of their victims. Accusation of witchcraft is not comparable to a legal suit brought by one individual against another or the arrest of a criminal by the police for a particular act. Instead, a gradual accumulation of malicious, accusatory discourse about the suspected individual begins to circulate in the community. The community gradually develops its case through the circulation of gossip. As community consensus builds, song, especially the *gurna* song, enters in. When there is enough gossip in circulation and a triggering incident, an insult accusing the individual of witchcraft (*sā'ā*) can be inserted into the song. When a person is publicly maligned as a witch, he is more likely to be brought before one of the systems of justice—the traditional chief, the gendarmes, or the ritual *dāa* trial. At this point there will be a communal consensus that the accused individual is indeed a witch. This accusation tends to be so airtight that usually the accused person will not be exonerated. If taken to the gendarmerie, he will likely be beaten. In the end, he will be exiled from the village to one of the quarters reserved for witches in the larger Tupuri towns.

There are, however, ways that an accused witch in Doukoula can exonerate himself; one is by undergoing the *dāa* trial at Mankargou pond.[9] Every year a ritual specialist from Chadian Tupuriland announces his arrival in Doukoula. All those who have been accused of having *sā'ā* are made to undergo the trial to prove their innocence or guilt. The specialist takes them into the bush for two days, where they fast. Then at a public ceremony at Mankargou pond, in front of scores of spectators, each accused person drinks two calabashes of a solution containing a magical herb, called *dāa.* Those who are innocent immediately vomit, but those who are guilty keep asking for more and more water. They display an insatiable thirst such that they will drink until they burst. This is the proof of guilt. From this point on, the condemned witches are exiled from the village, either upon the request of the chief or by the continuous harassment of their neighbors.

Insults involving both *kereŋ* and *sā'ā* appear in *gurna* song. To accuse someone of *kereŋ* is to attempt to isolate them in the community and call attention to their disgusting state. In one instance, the composer from Dawa said that his insult of *kereŋ* was a metaphor for one composer "eating" the reputation of another.

Ndɔ 'o nen desēe guum dɛŋ baa me wa.
Maa kereŋ ɓɔn, ndi luwa' suŋ la ga ndɔ de baa ndi mo na,
Bil ɓi laa ga—ndɔ fɛr re nay ɓɔ ni kawre ɓɔ. (D., 98/99, v. 2)

> You stand there with bright red eyes—don't catch me.
> With your witchcraft, I dreamed last night that you were chasing me,
> I refuse—go back and eat your meat among your brothers.

However, accusing someone of *sā'ā* has greater consequences. Someone who has obtained *sā'ā* is not merely pitiful but is morally reprehensible, having gone to great lengths to kill others out of greed. This accusation can result in eventual exile from the village. Furthermore, I was told that many accused witches are among the thousands of Tupuri people who migrated out of Tupuriland through government-sponsored resettlement programs in the North Province in the 1980s and 1990s. Whether or not this is true, such discourse lends weight to the interpretation of witchcraft accusation as a mediator of material wealth (Geschiere 1997). That is, these who had gained more wealth than others were dispossessed or displaced from the community through the power of witchcraft accusation.

In this view, when insult in the *gurna* song pertains to witchcraft, it is not merely for entertainment or to display aesthetic virtuosity or to galvanize dancers to the composer's side. Rather, it is connected to the larger moral system in Tupuriland. It is one step in local judicial processes that could culminate in a public trial, albeit not a Western-style court trial. Clearly, the modern judicial and security systems that Cameroon inherited from colonialism are not the only forms of formal investigation present in Cameroon. Tupuri song should not be seen as an informal vehicle of justice whose formal counterparts are necessarily Western-style courts. Rather, the song is one link in an indigenous system of justice that involves the movement of a complaint from gossip to song to ritual trials such as the *dāa* trial (or trial at the local gendarmerie). In a practical sense, individuals in Tupuriland, like all Cameroonians, made free use of both "modern" and "traditional" forms of justice, depending on their financial means and their perceptions of the strategic advantages of each.

Insult in the domain of song entertained, as well as provided a resource for managing conflict and seeking justice. That these words could have serious effects is clear from some of the consequences faced by composers and *"chasonnés"* (those who are "songed," or made the butt of a song): formal charges of libel in the court system or, in the case of witchcraft accusation, exile to the witches' ghetto. While the public sphere of Tupuri song is autonomous from the Cameroon state and from traditional authorities, actors who call upon song knew that in certain circumstances it can be as powerful as those formal institutions.

NINE

Multipartyism and Nostalgia for the Unified Past

Discourses of Democracy in Gurna *Politics*

CULTURAL POLITICS AND MULTIPLE CONFIGURATIONS OF THE "POLITICAL"

If the *gurna* is "a society within society," it reaches institutional status by nature of its power to stage and manage conflict, mete out justice, and sway public opinion that can be called upon when a ritual authority or individual plaintiff seeks to enforce customary law. This realm of power in the arena of aesthetic performance creates a "multilevelness" typical of many African postcolonial societies, where secret societies, hunter's societies, dance associations, masquerade, and healing rituals of all kinds continue to thrive alongside government administration and politics. Often ethnically particular associations such as the *gurna* tend to hold themselves apart from the state and gain their meaningfulness from local (or regional) understandings of value and power, framed in such terms as prestige, beauty, popularity, or vitality. Just as Abner Cohen (1993) saw culture to be deeply imbricated with politics in his study of Caribbean carnival in London, *gurna* practitioners create a culturally specific form of politics: a *gurna* politics (*poltik weere*). I argue that such a notion of cultural politics is most useful when the very manner of conceiving of politics is seen itself to be a polysemous symbol. The politics of the *gurna* are deployed in many ways to comment upon and, at times, to affect power relationships within the Tupuri homeland and in the larger Cameroonian nation.

Furthermore, given the multilevel quality of postcolonial societies, it is not unusual to observe the movement of symbols and discourse across social levels, from one kind of public domain to another. A lexicon circulating at the national level can seep into local discourse and vice versa. The challenge is to interpret the significance of this borrowing or "poaching" and to gauge its potential to generate sociocultural change. At times change is barely perceptible, involving minute shifts in local discursive patterns, in shared values, and in frameworks of what constitutes the local and the extralocal. It is ironic that the power to strategically cultivate distinctions between the local (or the parochial) and the national may have the effect of further knitting together diasporic communities.

This chapter explores the creative ways that Tupuri *gurna* capitalize on the popularity of "democracy" as a symbol to conceptualize and reinvigorate their local institutions and poetic forms, how they found correspondences between national-level multiparty politics—a key element of democracy—and their own local societies of dancers. Of interest is how an apparently transparent discourse such as democracy could be put to use in a rural setting far from the metropolis where such a lexicon was created. This borrowing of a lexicon involves more than a simple homology between a national political ideology and a local one. In appropriating the discourse and symbols of democracy, *gurna* practitioners reshape and resignify its meanings to speak to the cultural politics of their *gurna*.

Regardless of—or perhaps because of—the reworking of meanings, outside observers might wonder whether such an adoption of extralocal symbols means that *gurna* members are disseminating an empty notion of democracy and multiparty politics, especially given the troubled history of democracy in West and Central Africa (for example, Apter 1999; Ferme 1999). Was it merely a stylish way to signify privilege and modernity, regardless of whether the corresponding political practice of democracy was put into place? Because of possible discrepancies between symbol and practice, this analysis must include elements of irony, play, and skepticism as well as the larger sociopolitical context of a struggling (some would insist failed) democracy in Cameroon. My consideration of humor in cultural-political discourse is inspired by Achille Mbembe's oft-cited 1992 Bakhtinian analysis of parody and satire in Cameroonian political culture (Mbembe 2001). I seek to add to this discussion by considering discourse that, far from the nation's capital, is deeply embedded in a local ritual complex.

I first came across metaphors of democracy in the *gurna* quite unexpectedly when I returned to Tupuriland after having been away for nine years. It was the midst of the rainy season and *gurna* society members had broken up their camps and returned to their family farms for the agricultural season. Eager to learn the news of the *gurna*, I asked a friend how the dance association was faring. After reflecting for a moment, he responded mischievously, with a grin: "*Oui, le multipartisme est venu!*" Seeing my confusion, he added to clarify, "Each one dances for himself!" I was mystified until I learned that by "multipartyism," he was referring to a change in the presentation of the *gurna* dance at village death celebrations. Instead of one large ring of dancers, there were now several rings, each at its own site on the field (*laale*) at the village sponsoring the death celebration. To have multiple rings of dances at the death celebration meant that there were multiple song composers with whom the *gurna* camps could chose to affiliate. Putatively, in the past there was only one unified ring of dancers moving en masse in an expression of solidarity, or *communitas*.

At first brush this "multipartyism" might appear to be a small shift in cultural practice, but I later learned that the competitive postures of the *gurna* song composers—and the entire network of *gurna* societies—was a domain in which Tupuri people articulate their concerns about changing political mores in Cameroonian society. In particular, there is a marked anxiety about growing divisiveness associated with democratization and modernity (*dulnya*) writ large. So in addition to the stylish association of modernity with claims of "democracy," there is also a genuine concern about the harmony and cohesiveness of society. For this reason, this chapter tacks back and forth between wordplay in *gurna* song and the larger political climate created by the hegemony of the presidency of Paul Biya in Cameroon. I suggest that *gurna* members' engagement with national discourses through symbolic reappropriation is one way that ritual practitioners, although they appeared to be marginalized outsiders, maintain their connection to the political life of the nation, albeit on their own terms.

ANXIETIES AND SHIFTS IN THE FRAMING OF POLITICS

After a colonial period when multiple political parties existed and a bloody guerilla war was fought by the Union des Populations du Cameroun (UPC),[1] Cameroon's first president, Amadou Ahidjo, managed to establish a single-party state. In the early 1990s, the regime of Cameroon's second president, Paul Biya, who had already been in office for nearly a decade, was forced by popular demand and international pressure to accept political liberalization, including the establishment of opposition political parties. With the legalization of opposition parties in 1990, over seventy new parties emerged overnight (Gros 1996, 119). One party, the Mouvement pour la Défense de la République (MDR), had its popular base in the Mayo Danay Department where the Tupuri homeland is located. The national political discourse of democracy was picked up in Tupuriland and applied to the local realm of village associations. The phenomenon of multiple *gurna* song composers who competed with one another for dancers was likened, with glee, to the opposition party politics that embroiled the nation. This plurality of composers was thought of as new, a deviation from the ancestral tradition. Through it, Tupuri people expressed anxiety about new forms of factionalism, albeit playfully.

In the social formation of the *gurna* society, members promote a local politics that is strikingly different from the "politics of the belly" said to characterize the Biya regime and, more broadly, the state in Africa (Bayart 1993). According to Bayart, the politics of the belly is a politics of patronage that is widespread in Africa and involves the accumulation of economic and political power by leaders who "eat" resources nominally held in common (such as international development aid and state funds). Nepotism, corruption, and the mystique of sorcery (Geschiere 1997) enable the elite to amass wealth at the expense of the masses. As these political-economic formations extend along ethnic lines, Cameroon's growing sectarianism has become the subject of much recent scholarship: Burnham (1996) on interethnic violence in the Adamawa; Nyamnjoh and Rowlands (1998) on the rise of "ethnicised elite associations"; and Monga (2000) on political discourse designed to exploit ethnic division. All have noted that the rise of multiparty politics in Sub-Saharan Africa beginning in the early 1990s has given rise to new regionalism or, as Geschiere and Gugler put it, "an obsession with 'autochthony' " (1998, 319). While interethnic conflict was not the primary reason Cameroon's transition to democracy failed, some analysts suggest that after losing its single-party status, the Cameroonian national government fostered ethnic factionalism in order to consolidate its own power (Gros 1996, 117; Mehler 1998).[2] Others have suggested that regional elite associations are arising as an alternative to multipartyism (Geschiere and Gugler 1998). Such developments occurred when citizens realized that multipartyism in Cameroon was fraught with government manipulation. With their "control over economic rents . . . [authoritarian regimes such as Cameroon's] have bought off dissident politicians and financed the creation of a multitude of small parties which have fractured the opposition" (Bayart 1993, xi). During the period of my study, the difference between fair competition and insidious factionalism was ambiguous and a constant concern in Cameroon as well as a source of much cynicism. Many Tupuri with whom I spoke expressed a similar anxiety about the dangers of "modern" divisiveness in society. When these concerns appeared within the *gurna*, they served as metonyms for the threat of interethnic sectarianism in the nation as a whole.

The specialized discourse of the *gurna* enables Tupuri dancers to refer to an alternative *poltik* of their own characterized by fluid shifts in popularity and individual status. Although they use the metaphor of multipartyism, *gurna* composers eschew participation in actual party politics. Instead, the terms of democratization, already emptied of their meaning by the near-dictatorship of the Biya regime, are used playfully by the *gurna* as metacultural commentary (Urban 2001) on their indigenous cultural-political system. In order to understand how the *gurna* came to be an arena for metacultural debate about the nature of politics, it is necessary first to understand how this association operates as a cultural-political system.

THE DYNAMICS OF COMPETITION IN THE *GURNA*

Competition and micropolitical maneuvering—among individuals and entire villages—are played out in the *gurna* through the elaborate discourse of song (*siŋ*). At the level of social practice, politics is played out through affiliation by *gurna* camps to rival composers. Competition and friendship staged through the song are mirrored in the underlying social organization of the *jak kaw* the *gurna* members joined. I referred earlier to the tendency of the politics of composer affiliation to channel existing rivalries among men in Tupuri villages. The following case from Touloum village illustrates how far these microlevel cultural politics can go when they became enmeshed in local struggles for dominance among kin and neighbors.

Gurna song composer Sogole and his secretary Balandi went on a campaign visit to villages far from the heart of their region (that is, where dancers knew the composer and chose his song). When they arrived, they were surprised to learn of local struggles that had been transpiring in these villages. The secretary recounted the story to me:

> "One day we went to the village of Touloum. Before, the camp there sang another composer's song. Then there was a quarrel between one part of the camp that wanted to join Sogole and the other part that wanted to stay with the other composer. This side [that wanted to stay] used 'spiritual' [*saŋgu*, magical herbs] to kill people on the other side. Deaths started to occur in a village nearby, Sarmaï. There were three deaths in four days. When they [the *gurna*] came to tape-record Sogole's song at Tuksu, one person died when they brought the song back to the village. At Dandaywa, two people died after having taped the song. At Dorega two more died. Seven people total died."
>
> Ever skeptical, I asked, "How do you know it was *saŋgu* that caused the deaths?"

Patient in the face of the obvious, Balandi replied, "Because during the quarrel, they threaten you. They say, 'Just wait; you'll see.' Then a few days later, people start to die. They warn you first.

At Gernigue, someone put *saŋgu* in the compound of the *gurna* chief (*waŋ-gurna*), but he's not dead; he's fine! The *waŋ-gurna* wanted to join Sogole. But his brother wanted the song from Dawa. So the brother planted *saŋgu* in the *waŋ-gurna*'s compound, but he himself fell sick. The *saŋgu* came back on him because the *waŋ-gurna* was stronger.

Later, people came to the *waŋ-gurna* and told him that his brother was sick. He said, 'That's not a problem,' and went to pasture his cows. The next day, he went to see his brother.

'What's wrong?' he said.

'I have a sore throat and soreness in my chest,' said the brother.

The *waŋ-gurna* massaged his brother's throat and chest and then he felt better. That evening, the *waŋ* came back to visit the brother, massaged his throat and chest, and asked him how he was. He felt better.

The *waŋ* then said, 'You wanted to do me harm, but God didn't want this. So now you know that I am stronger than you. You know it was I who paid the brideprice for your wife. I am your blood and still you wanted to kill me. You shouldn't do it again.'"

Sogole's advisor continued, "It turned out that the person from whom the brother got the *saŋgu* is a man from Saochaï. This man wanted to sing Sogole's song. So he put a *saŋgu* in the house of an army veteran at Gernigue who wanted to sing the song from Dawa. He said that the day of the *few kage* (Festival of the Cock), the veteran will fall ill. But the festival passed and the veteran was still alive, not even sick. He said to the man from Saochaï, 'You were trying to kill me, but I beat you. So from now on, you must recognize that I'm stronger than you.'"

"So how is this conflict resolved?" I asked.

"It's not resolved. There could be more deaths. The *saŋgu* are still there."

At this point, I noticed that Sogole had been silent throughout our conversation in French, so I asked him, incredulously, "What do you think of all this? These deaths are all happening because people are fighting over a song?"

The composer responded in his characteristically stoic fashion, appealing as he often did the authority of dancers. "There is nothing I can do. If the dancers ask me to stop composing, I'll stop. Otherwise, I'll continue."

Unwilling to let it go, I queried, "Isn't it too much to kill a person for a song?"

At this point, Balandi jumped in, "When someone brings a song into his village, he will be famous. The composer will put his name in the song. If another person in the village brings a song from another composer, that threatens people's pride and stirs up jealousy. Each one wants the honor. Each one says that he is better than the other. It gets to this."

Balandi's comments point to how the adoption of the *gurna* song was a public act that had become an arena where interpersonal power dynamics were played out. A *gurna* member gains power vis-à-vis other *gurna* by being the one to introduce a composer's song to the village and to convince his fellow *gurna* to adopt it for the year. Some would even use covert, mystical means (*saŋgu*) to bring others under their influence. In the two cases described by Balandi, neither man who used *saŋgu* to attack his rival was successful. In both cases, the point of the argument was to prove which man was stronger and to have that be recognized by the other ("You know it was I who paid the brideprice," "You must recognize that I'm stronger than you."). And in both cases, it was the desire to affiliate with one or the other composer (here, composers from Tuksu or Dawa) which acted as the catalyst for the use of *saŋgu* to attack the enemy. From this, it is clear that the *gurna*'s affiliation with particular composers works as a grammar or a rubric within which interpersonal rivalries in villages are played out—with or without the knowledge of the composers themselves. This *poltik* flies in the face of the front-stage ideology of *gurna* solidarity.

In addition to factionalism, peace and solidarity were equally values of the *gurna*. A farmer friend who had returned to the village after a stint working in the southern city of Douala in a cigarette factory used to tell me proudly that he was in a small cooperative of men who pooled their cattle and took turns herding them for the day. From this friendship, the men decided to form a *gurna* camp in their village. Generally, men join the *gurna* in order to develop friendships with other men and participate in a network that might help them with future needs. There is a great deal of talk about the solidarity of this association and its role in promoting peace (*jam*) in society at large. However, much like sports teams, the solidarities of such imagined communities are created through the dynamic power of competition. Competition is not so much antithetical to solidarity as constitutive of it.

Competition in the *gurna* is multitiered and is played out among dancers, drummers, *gurna* camps, and their affiliations with the song composers. Dominance is judged through the exhibition of the most enthusiastic, competent participation in the *gurna* (both the dance and society). The *gurna* song itself has come to be an arena for judging the prestige of individuals, in the same way that school students scramble for higher exam scores. This comparison was made by the *gurna* song composer who borrowed the French term *concours* (the all-important exams that make up the lycée system) to designate the "posting" of the names of prestigious dancers in the annual song. This metaphor draws on the familiar routines of individual competition in modern Cameroon: students hover around lists of exam grades posted in school walls and the ears of civil servants are cocked to the radio to hear the newest listing of state transfers. In the realm of the *gurna*, names of skilled and avid dancers are publicly announced with each performance of the song at village death celebrations.

Ultimately, competition involves villages to the degree that they are represented by their *gurna* camps. Competition among the multiple *gurna* composers—the putatively *new* "multipartyism" of the *gurna*—is played out over sizable geographical swathes as each village-based *gurna* camp selects a composer with whom to affiliate that year. Camps select composers for a variety of reasons: the vagaries of public taste for the song, perceptions of the popularity of composers, the efforts of composers to "campaign" among and "woo" dancers, and the machinations of village-level politics. For an individual to lead his camp to a particular composer is to demonstrate his power to influence. However, affiliation with composers is not entirely ruled by the dynamics of village-level politics. More-neutral factors, such as geographic proximity to a composer's home base, also come into play. Villages that are geographically close to one another tend to affiliate with the same composer unless they wanted to signal their difference by affiliating with a competing composer.

Gurna competition is gauged in terms of the value of numbers. Composers compete with one another to garner the greatest number of dancers and camps to sing their song that year. There are many images of numerousness in the song lyrics: Dancers are compared to flocks of birds, villages are emptied because all have gone to the dance, and so forth. It is easy to discern which composer was dominating in this competition in the way the dance is organized at the dance site (*laale*). At the death celebration (*yii-huuli*), camps divide according to their affiliation with composers; they divide into separate dance rings on the field near the compound of the deceased who was commemorated. I attended death celebrations in which there were up to three separate groups of dancers, representing each of the three current composers. In this context, it was easy to see which composer had attracted the most dancers to his song. Because the dance represents collective strength, the ability to present one's group as numerous and dynamic is what is most important. Merely to see other rings of dancers at the site is enough to foment competition.

On the other hand, an assumption of unity is built into the system: Each camp is required to affiliate as a unit with only one composer. When a camp performs at the death celebration dance, it joins with all the other *gurna* camps that have affiliated with the same composer and mastered his song. At a practical level, the song is too long for members to learn more than one each year. One elder told me that *gurna* song evolved to its current length because the longer songs enabled dancers to be "on stage" longer and thus to dominate the other dancers. Stamina and the display of unity are the primary values of the performance. Valuing solidarity within the camp, *gurna* members are obligated to come to a consensus about their selection of the song for the year. Where such consensus could not be reached, camps splinter, each camp taking a new location. Often less than a kilometer apart, these camps then choose rival composers, creating a situation in which they can express their antagonism.

However, the question remains: Why are these microcultural politics important? I suggest that in addition to the real effects they have on the lives of individuals, the cultural politics of composer affiliation tie into a wider discourse of competition, solidarity, and factionalism in Tupuri and Cameroonian society. Often *gurna* (and others who reflect on the tradition) debate about whether composer "multipartyism" represents "healthy" competition in the *gurna* society or whether it points ominously to a "degradation" of the system, mirroring sectarianism in the broader Cameroonian society.

I found Tupuri people to be concerned with problems of economic development in terms of values of solidarity and egalitarianism in the face of divisiveness. In discussions, they often wondered aloud why their region was among the poorest in Cameroon. They tended to blame neither the low prices farmers received for their cotton cash crop nor erratic rainfall nor even the debilitating effects of pandemic malaria. Rather, they were more likely to point to factionalism (*poltik*) in Tupuri society. They pointed to the detrimental effects of jealousy (*hun*) and witchcraft (*sā'ā*), the ultimate example of social divisiveness and personal greed. They cited the neglect of elites who had migrated from the village but gave neither material support nor a hand up to their "*petits frères*" left languishing on the farm. In these conversations, Tupuri made a point of contrasting their elder brothers with the Bamiléké,[3] who were—as the discourse went—expert at helping their kin.

Other salient forms of Tupuri sociability were seen as marked by this putatively new and growing "individualism" or "selfishness." Conventionally in Tupuriland, a place well-known for enthusiastic beer drinking, male friends would gather in a circle around a jug of sorghum beer (*yii*) to share drink and conversation. Whoever had means to buy *yii* did so and it would be shared equally among friends, even newcomers. In contrast, in the 1990s, a practice called *gew-gew* had developed in which friends contributed 100 francs CFA to purchase a jug of *yii*. When additional friends came by without the requisite 100 francs to contribute, they would not be offered drink. This may appear to be a small change in social practice, but for the Tupuri, for whom sharing of *yii* has important ritual and social functions, the shift was significant. It indicated deeper changes of value in society, a shift in the structure of feeling (after Raymond Williams 1977, 132) toward greater individualism or an every-man-for-himself ethos which was associated with *les blancs* (Europeans). Tupuri people tend to interpret individualism as dangerous because in their view, it seeds selfishness, jealousy, and divisiveness in society. When "brothers" would not help "brothers," *la misère* was exacerbated.

Competition is inherent in the structure and practice of the *gurna* and its specialized discourse. For this reason, it provides a useful idiom with which Tupuri people can discuss factionalism of all kinds. The next section looks more closely at the cultural construction of "politics" among the *gurna*.

POLTIK WEERE: POLITICS OF THE DANCERS

The political potential involved in the affiliation of *gurna* camps with song composers became evident to me only gradually. At first, *gurna* members assured me that the selection of the annual song was purely an aesthetic matter. They would say that they chose particular composers because their songs were best (*de cõore*; lit. "tasty"). *De cõore,* as opposed to *de ɓalakge* ("broken" or "spoiled"), meant that the song "sounded good" and insulted often and cleverly. Indeed, in many cases this aesthetic evaluation may have been the primary reason for choosing a composer and his song. Upon closer examination, however, it became clear that there were also other factors at play, such as the current popularity of the composer, the vitality of his outreach to the camps, and interpersonal rivalry.

In his analysis of modern inflections of witchcraft in southern Cameroon, Peter Geschiere (1997, 70–71) discerns two registers of politics: one based in the state politics of the urban elite and one in the villages that features councils controlled by the traditional chiefs. This dual-level approach to power requires that we examine closely how various realms of "politics" may operate independently of one another. How is the *gurna* complex (dance, song, camp organization, and composer affiliation) conceived of as "political"? How is *gurna* politics reminiscent of other politics? I answer this question through two interwoven threads. First, I consider how composers describe their "campaigns" among *gurna* members, how they understand the nature of their relationships with the dancers. Second, I examine how politics is conceived of in the lyrics of *gurna* song through metaphors such as *poltik* and "campaigning." What is significant is that these terms were borrowed from the French-language national discourse on democratization and then mapped onto the local, insular cultural politics in the *gurna* context.

While some Tupuri intellectuals were fond of telling me that the *gurna* was "just a folkloric dance," there was, in fact, continuous reference to the "political" aspects of the *gurna* and a running analogy with the practice of "politics." My conundrum was to discern the extent of this analogy: How far could one go in calling the *gurna* "political"? The metaphor of politics applies to the *gurna* in many ways. Generally speaking, in democratic party politics, politicians gain and hold political influence by knowing where they have strong support in individuals or groups who can turn out the vote. These individuals are scattered across geographical space and expect to be recognized for their local power in return for the politician's attention. *Gurna* song politics are quite similar. The composer knows which dancers are leaders in their villages—that is, those who have a strong enthusiasm for the dance and will motivate others to join the *gurna*. Local dance enthusiasts can be counted on to bring out the dancers, usually expressed as "*daw sir*" ("support the region"). In turn, they are publicly lauded in the song by name. "Wanba Legaigue, your dance zone will get along well." ("*Wanba Legaigue sir lɛ' yaŋ nday mo ti la.*")

References to *gurna* politics are expressed through a specialized metaphorical language. Building on Comi Toulabor's (1981) work on derisive political lexicon in Togo, Mbembe describes how Cameroonians purged the conventional meanings of words to "buil[d] a whole vocabulary, equivocal and ambiguous, parallel to the official discourse" (2001, 105). Certain highly charged words, such as government slogans, were inflected with scatological or ribald meanings in order to deconstruct and satirize the dominant political authority. Such a parallel lexicon existed in *gurna* song, though devoid of the satire that Mbembe describes. Instead, *gurna* discourse co-opted quotidian meanings for its own purposes. For example, "*sir*" generally means "land" or "village," but in the *gurna* world, "*sir*" takes on the meaning of the composer's "zone of influence" or "region of control." The term for "youth" (*weere*) is used to mean "dancers" or "*gurna* members," reflecting the belief that to dance is to be youthful, regardless of age. In everyday usage, "*mo*" (or "*mon*") means "thing," but in *gurna* song lyrics, it denotes the song or dance.

The term "*poltik*," from the French "*politique*," appears frequently in *gurna* songs and in everyday discourse about the *gurna*. However, its meaning is unstable, shifting according to context. In the examples below, *poltik* refers alternately to *gurna* politics, community politics (here, gossip), and national party politics. In short, *gurna* politics (*poltik weere*) means the use of song to assert dominance. This politics is not limited to poetics or the content of lyrics but includes the politics of the dissemination and adoption of the song. In the domain of *gurna* politics, the cultural politics of taste and popularity of the artist can involve a subterranean enactment of village-level tensions and conflicts through the song.

In their lyrics, composers used the term "*poltik*" to various effects. When they refer to the *gurna* politics, composers obscure their own involvement from the public, even if it is widely known that composers incite rivalry among themselves and cater to it among villagers. With humorous disingenuousness, composers bemoan the strenuousness of competition and one-upmanship central to the *gurna* practice and boast about their own stamina. The composer from Tuksu village sang:

Ndi hay bay de gayre dɔ role poltik weere Kamrun wa. (T., 97/98, v. 29)

I'm not too tired to defend myself from the politics of the *gurna* in Cameroon.

Frequently *poltik* was juxtaposed with the polysemous term *dulnya*, which in its most general usage denotes "life" or "generation" (and, more narrowly, "modern life"). However, *dulnya* also denotes all aspects of the *gurna*: the society, the dancers, the song, and the putatively wonderful lifestyle that emanates from these (line 1). The tawdry side of politics is highlighted by the opposing imaginary of *dulnya*: well-being specifically associated with the *gurna* (line 1).

Nday weere maa mbi dulnya mo na, Mando salut! (1)
Courrier day nday ge yaŋ mo po. (2) (L., 95/96, v. 5)

You who live the good life, Mando—greetings! (1)
The envoy of the song will come to you. (2)

Composers define *gurna* politics as the politics of popularity and public taste, manifested in dancers scurrying back and forth between composers. Sogole points to his distaste for these politics in the following lyrics. He refers to the rivalry in Bouzar village, where there were two camps: one for Tuksu (Sogole, designated by his home village) and one for Zouaye (designating the composer Djingue). People in Bouzar were trying to convince the *gurna* Mongale in the Sogole camp to switch to the Djingue camp (line 2).

Siguidna Tchalna Kolandi ndi hay bay ti poltik wa weere dulnya. (1)
'A jãa ne jak ti wāare Mongale gorna Walna wel maa ndalge. (2) (T., 97/98, v. 26)

Siguidna Tchalna Kolandi, I wasn't involved in politics, *gurna* dancers. (1)
They are trying to convince you to speak, Mongale, Walna's son, a talkative guy. (2)

In his song, Sogole encourages Mongale to remain loyal while at the same time arguing disingenuously that he is uninterested in politics (line 1). It is an irony that through these lyrics he contributed to the *poltik*.

The term *poltik* was also used by composers to refer more directly to conventional political authority. Ringwa, a composer for the émigré Tupuri in the city of Maroua, used "*poltik*" to mean "to undermine a leader." In the case below, Djakdjing Semangué, an assistant chief to the leader of the Tupuris in the neighborhood of Pitoaré in Maroua, was considered an "old lush." He was known to frequent beer parlors (*ŋgel-yii*) and then insult people when intoxicated.

Djakdjing Semangué poltik ɓe no,
Jak kaw rɛm lɛ jak wɛ,
Semangue ko hay waŋ ga.
Ndɔ da' waŋ wɛ ndɔ dar jar yaw-la? (M., 98/99, v. 26)

Djakdjing Semangué, *politics* is here,
All the brothers are in agreement,
Semangue doesn't know how to remain chief.
When you become chief, do you insult people?

Here *poltik* took on the meaning of the communal gossip circulating within a group, a discourse that was the precursor to the removal of the leader from power.

A third use of the term *poltik* was national party politics. Explicating the line below to me, the composer explained that Tchigaï had asked him to join a political party but he had responded, "No, I'm just a composer."

Tchigaï wii me ga poltik jɔŋ may-la? (T., 97/98, v. 7)

Tchigaï wants to know what difference do politics make?

During my study, I did not observe composers who were affiliated with the national political parties in the area. Even though composers had no qualms about "publishing" interpersonal insult and championing their own dancers, they were very wary about becoming mouthpieces for political party recruitment. Although composers were deeply implicated in these politics of the *gurna*, they publicly presented a stoic nonchalant posture, as if they were above such plebian rivalries.

Poltik is not the only French loan word co-opted by *gurna* discourse—that is, whose meaning has been reshaped to apply to *gurna* practices. The term "*kamrun*" also appears often in the song. Rather than denoting the nation-state of Cameroon or even the Cameroonian versus the Chadian side of Tupuriland, *kamrun* means "zone of dancers," connoting the largeness of a nation. When a composer boasts that he controlled *kamrun,* he meant that a wide region of *gurna* camps had adopted his song. The term "*kapital*" was used to denote "the capital of the dance"—that is, the composer's village or a village that had many enthusiastic dancers.

A significant aspect of *gurna* politics is campaigning. Each composer (or at least one composer of a collaborating pair) makes frequent visits (*ndalge*) to the camps to recruit dancers to his song. When he arrives at a *gurna* camp, he is received as a celebrity and treated to meat and *yii*. This visiting is likened to political party campaigning: "*Ndi kay wɔge jɔŋ kampain jõo go ɓaŋ Touloum.*" ("I'm going to do the campaign for the dance near Touloum"; T., 98/99, v. 11) When I asked Dangmoworé, a lycée student-composer and the son of a famous composer, how composers keep dancers on "their side," he said: "Because he is a composer, he has a certain rhetoric. He knows how to talk to 'his people.' . . . He puts words forward to them better than Sogole [his rival composer]."

The composer of Zouaye, Noumnamo, explained some of his campaigning tactics. In order to visit all his dancers, he strategically rotated among numerous camps: "I go towards the east. The next year towards the west. I pass the night telling them certain words, to maintain them on my side. Then I go to another camp."

As the composer conducts his "campaign" for his song, he inevitably becomes embroiled in microlevel village politics based on interpersonal rivalry, jealousy, and pride among the *gurna*. These rivalries are sometimes played out through insult and praise in the song. On the other hand, composers also described these networks of friendship as "people who come to be tied to [each other] through the song," as Noumnamo put it. The discourse of "friendship" (*barge*) is used to describe this support: these dancers back him rather than his rival composers.

Part of this campaigning involves the extension of the composer's "ears" into villages through his loyal contacts there. These contacts, the *courriers,* also known as "*agents secrets,*" carry news from the village to the composer to include in the next song. And when the composer launches his annual song, they bring it back to the village to teach the *gurna* dancers. Although these agents do not have formal titles in the camp, they are prestigious by virtue of their direct connection to the composer. These campaign networks in villages often fall along existing lines of friendship and enmity. A composer can also subtly exploit such microlevel village politics to generate more support for his side.

Let us return to the question of how and why language from national-level democracy discourse was mapped onto the cultural politics of the *gurna*. What is the effect of this semantic "poaching" (Mbembe 2001, 106)? I suggest that it produced a special poetic lexicon that called attention to the insider/outsider structure of knowledge of the *gurna* in Tupuri society. That is, only *gurna* (or former *gurna*) can truly grasp the more subtle political machinations in the song—for example, why one dancer's name appeared over another or why one camp was praised and another reprimanded. Lending French terms to these local cultural-political processes enhanced their prestige. In contrast to the popular notion of an inviolable binary of "tradition" versus "modernity," the *gurna*—operating in the register of the "traditional"—borrowed from the modern, national realm where terms such as "campaign" and "Cameroon" originated. This poaching or borrowing of French rejuvenated *gurna* discourse, made it appear fresh and "modern," even though, ironically, the dance was metonymic of the ancestors.

INTERVILLAGE STRUGGLE: MOGOM, MADALAM, AND THE HORSE'S HEAD

The alleged poisoning in Touloum described above and the song dueling through insult described in earlier chapters are rooted in interpersonal struggles for dominance. However, larger political relations among villages also come into play in *gurna poltik*. At times, alliances and fissures among villages are reflected in and played out through song lyrics. Sometimes the song lyrics about tensions between villages are indirect and jocular, as in a recent rivalry between the villages of Mogom and Madalam. At other times, such as in the 1960s, there was armed conflict, as there was between Doukoula, the *chef-lieu* of the district, and Zouaye, a large village under its jurisdiction. In this volatile context, song lyrics produced by the renowned *gurna* song composer, Dang Biina, involved a high-stakes provocation of political authorities.

In contemporary Cameroon, all territory is under the *commandement* structure, the centralized administration inherited from French colonialism. There is a cascading top-down administration from the capital to the ten provinces within which there are *départements,* which are broken into *sous-départements* and then *cantons*. However, during my stay in Tupuriland, elders spoke of precolonial forms of political organization which assumed much more fluid relationships between villages. The acephalous segmentary lineage structure of precolonial Tupuri society put a greater emphasis on cultural forms such as song, dance, funeral celebrations, and ritual festivals to mediate political relations between villages. In my discussions with elders they frequently described eruptions of intervillage conflict in the context of funeral dances and the insecurity individuals felt when they attempted to move between villages. In fact, the reunion of villages in the *gurna* dance itself was understood as an opportunity to create solidarity across the region, though the event required careful coordination to prevent conflict. One elder described the danger of conflict during funerals in these terms:

> If a village is dancing the *kombar* [*kombarre* or *kombarra,* a funereal dance involving circumambulation around the house of the deceased] and the people from another village start dancing the *kombar,* this creates a disorder. If in this case the first village turns again [around the house], the second village might attack them. . . . So when there is a funeral [*huuli*] and people are dancing the *kombar,* two or three climb up on a horse and monitor the area to make sure that no other village starts another *kombar.* If they see another village start, they intervene and tell them to stop. If men on horses don't intervene, then there will certainly be a fight. If at that point, you don't have a fighting/dancing stick [*garaw*], then you will die on the spot. There is no judgment, so the *garaw* is to defend yourself. . . . When a Tupuri dances, he dances with force [*maa 'ekre*]. When he doesn't have a *garaw* in hand, he feels weak.

Another elder who was an octogenarian and only months from his death described how difficult it was in the past to move freely around the region.

> I've heard today that an individual can hear that there is a dance in Tchatibali and set off for there by himself. Before, you couldn't do that; you would have to go with a group.[4] If not, they could attack you. . . . There wasn't a reason for these fights. You couldn't just walk into a village; you would have to enter only through the assistance of someone of the village who knew you. If not, they would strike you and this is what caused a lot of hate that would explode erratically into fights. There weren't real reasons for the warfare.
> There was a lot of theft. If someone from Mogom had their sheep stolen, they thought it was someone from Doukoula. So they announced that no one from Doukoula could come to their village. That's how there were fights.

Intervillage rivalry that played out in song and was encoded in the collective discourse of the *gurna* society was rooted in real experiences of danger and conflict among villages—though these dangers were likely to have been greater prior to Independence.

The political underside of *gurna* poetics is revealed also in its usage of pronominals. When one dancer's name was proclaimed in the song, it was interpreted not just as praise for that single individual but also as representing the entire camp, even the entire village. In the example "*Ndogno nday hee jaak ne Tchigaï*" ("Ndogno, you should greet Tchigaï"; T., 97/98, v. 20), "*nday,*" the second-person plural, implies that there are other supporters behind Ndogno. So even though *gurna* lyrics are filled with the names of individuals, the effect was not to trumpet individualism but rather to position camps vis-à-vis one another and elevate the composer's status. Most of the dancers and the audience know who is affiliated with whom, so it is sufficient to note just one individual to either praise or slander an entire group. The following case shows how a village chief was slandered in the song and the entire *gurna* camp responded as a unit by shifting its composer affiliation. This *gurna* "*poltik*" involved the entire fluid process of positioning dancers, camps, and composers in a web of reputation.

Mogom was an important village because during the colonial era it was selected by the French administrators to be the *chef-lieu* for the new *canton* of Kar Hay. However, through political maneuvering, Doukoula, the village two kilometers south on the same road, muscled out Mogom for the honor. Today Doukoula hosts a bustling weekly market and is dotted with administrative, police, and military posts. In contrast, Mogom is a sleepy village. Nevertheless, important local personalities hail from Mogom, including its chief, Belandi, a manager in the cotton company SODECOTON. Madalam, which borders Mogom, is an even smaller village.

Mogom appeared in chapter 2 as the spot where a horse was hit by a truck next to the culvert and Maïtené was reprimanded in song for allegedly having acquired the horse's carcass for her meatball business. Maïtené is not the only person insulted in song by an imputed association with the horse meat, a taboo food for the Tupuri. Belandi was similarly maligned in a 1997/1998 *gurna* song:

> Madalam Mogom de ndar manyaabaa naa. (1)
> Kembe tag lɛ wāare pir no. (2)
> Tchaklama kay jak mayn yaw-la? (3)
> Djiguaina nday ne bay ba 'ē-la? (4)
> Mbogom no tii wɛ pa nday caa sɔ nday maŋ tiin gɔ ne waŋ. (5)
> Belandi ndi day re nayn pir ga. (6)
> Balda Laksouma Biyame Koswe day Guirle wɔ 'ē-la Saolo. (7) (Z., 97/98, v. 37)

> Madalam Mogom presents a rainbow. (1)
> Kembe, tell me the story about the horse. (2)
> Tchaklama, what is it? (3)
> Djegaina, how are you? (4)
> Mbogom, them there, you cut and give the head to the chief. (5)
> Belandi, I don't eat horse meat. (6)
> Balda Laksouma Biyame Koswe, *gurna* of Guirle, go well Saolo. (7)

Composed by Djingue of Zouaye village, the main competitor to Sogole, the composer from Tuksu village, these lyrics insult Chief Belandi by suggesting that he eats horse meat (lines 5–6). In November 1997, when the song came out, the *gurna* camp at Mogom felt compelled to defend their chief by eschewing Djingue's song and affiliating with Sogole. Furthermore, Sogole was known to be a friend of the former legislative representative, Wambarra Jacques, who was Belandi's brother. In this way, the *gurna* camp represented the interests of its village.

However, the political effect of the song radiated out further. Geographically, the village of Madalam was adjacent to Mogom. Perhaps to enact its independence from the powerful chief of Mogom, the *gurna* camp of Madalam chose to affiliate that year with the composer of the insulting song, Djingue. The result was two neighboring villages, each affiliating with a rival composer. These intervillage tensions seemed to be prognosticated in the song.

Madalam and Mogom appeared together in the song, along with the image of a rainbow (*manyaabaa*, line 1). *Gurna* poetry operates through metaphor and ellipsis, so it is difficult to decode all the possible meanings, although in other contexts "rainbow" connotes an impediment. Because rainbows appear in the sky when the sun begins to clear the rain, there is a popular belief that the rainbow inhibits the rain. This is encoded in the word for rainbow, *manyaabaa*, which means literally "mother-in-law." There are many mother-in-law taboos in Tupuri society, such as the prohibition on eating and washing in front of one's mother-in-law. Just as the son-in-law must hide from the mother-in-law, so the rain must hide from its "mother-in-law" when the rainbow appears. In the song, Mogom presents itself as a rainbow, an inhibiter to the village of Madalam. An inhibiter of what? Perhaps to the chiefly regime of Belandi of Mogom, the putative eater of horse-meat, that dominated Madalam.

One day when I met Belandi at a death celebration dance, I wanted to emphasize my adopted kinship with his region, so I explained that my research assistant was a native of Madalam. At the time, I was ignorant of the details of these intervillage rivalries, but I certainly caught his annoyance when he said in a pointed way that ended the conversation: "Madalam is a *quarter* of Mogom." Emphasizing "quarter," he seemed to be anxious about the uppity attitude of the people of Madalam. Furthermore, he may have been reminding me that I was conducting my research in his jurisdiction.

There was likely a thicket of micropolitics between the villages of Mogom and Madalam that I could hardly grasp. But what was evident to me was how *gurna* song was rife with barbs that resulted in hundreds of microlevel shifts and repositionings each time it was recited to the public. One way these shifts in power were expressed was through the selection of composer affiliation. It was also evident that *gurna poltik* was often village politics—efforts to garner and extend authority and influence. Such efforts do not allow a so-called cultural realm to be separate from a so-called political realm, as Cohen (1993) points out. The *gurna* song is a key arena of cultural politics.

This cultural politics is covert, however: one that will not necessarily be explained in so many words. When I returned to the *gurna* camp of Mogom the next year (1998/1999), I was surprised to learn that it had adopted the song of Djingue, even though the previous year it was staunchly behind the rival Sogole. Why had the camp decided to change sides? As I should have expected, I was told that Djingue is so popular in this region—there were many dancers with him—that really it was best to follow along with the others. Perhaps the camp had made its point the previous year and could now go back to their preferred composer. But whether or not there was some underlying strategic reason for their selection of Djingue, the *gurna* thought it appropriate to keep discussion of such decisions in the safer terms of aesthetics and popularity.

To investigate the role of song in more significant intervillage rivalry, it is best to look to the past. Earlier I described how Dang Biina used verbal abuse to critique the tyranny of the traditional chief of Doukoula.[5] Although Dang Biina's songs served as the flashpoint of conflict between his village of Zouaye and the ruling chieftaincy in Doukoula, there were more deeply rooted political struggles between these regions. This conflict, which is remembered in Tupuriland as "tribal warfare," involved clan identities and the revenues from cotton sales and ended in Lamido Temoa's arrest and exile of the chief of Zouaye (Kléda 1983). Temoa, who was *lamido* of Doukoula from 1955 to 1965, held the population in a stranglehold, requiring forced labor from villagers and punishing rebels with *razzia* (raiding) of their cows. According to composer Teodandi, Dang Biina used the *gurna* song in Zouaye to provoke Temoa to battle. After this conflict, the cultural politics of the *gurna* continued to be an arena where the enmity between the two regions was expressed. The *gurna* of Doukoula refused to take the song of Zouaye and instead took up songs that began to be newly composed from the village of Lara, only a few kilometers from Zouaye.

Until at least the recent past, insults in the *gurna* song carried significant weight in political struggles between regions in Tupuriland because of the insurgency they tapped into. This role for aesthetic forms in Africa has been noted in anthropological literature (Apter 1992; Comaroff 1985; Glassman 1995; Lan

1985). It is not unusual for African musicians to use popular music to consolidate insurgent identities and collective movements against political oppression in Africa. (Consider, for example, Thomas Mufomo's *chimurenga* music in Zimbabwe and Feli Kuti's Afropop in Nigeria.) However, in Tupuriland, after the era of Dang Biina (the 1970s), the power of traditional chiefs diminished with the rise of the Cameroon nation-state, administrated centrally from Yaoundé. With this shift in political power, the politics addressed by the *gurna* song became more local. Tupuri composers, by their own admission, seemed *not* to have found new political targets for their satire. "We no longer sing against the big names of the *canton*, against the big people," noted Teodandi. Even though Tupuri citizens are as disgusted as other Cameroonians over corruption and incompetence in the Cameroonian government, during my sojourn composers rarely, if ever, attacked political leaders in their songs.

Dang Biina's song was intended to defend the rights of the people of Zouaye against the rule of the more powerful representative of the *canton*. By the 1990s, however, Zouaye was under the rule of a different *canton* (Datcheka) and was no longer administered by the *lamido*; today it is administered by the national *préfecture* system. *Razzia* (raiding of wealth) has become more subtle and bureaucratic, mediated by taxation and official corruption. Contemporary song composers have yet to react to these newer forms of state oppression in *gurna* song.

MULTIPARTYISM AND NOSTALGIA FOR THE UNIFIED PAST

What are the political reaches of the *gurna* song? Was *gurna* politics implicated in contemporary national party politics? These proved to be complex questions that eventually sorted themselves into several levels. First is the question of whether composers align themselves with political parties by using insult or praise to raise or lower the status of political party leaders and their organizations. Second is the question of whether *gurna* members organize their camps with an eye to party affiliation. And third is the more subtle question how multipartyism is used as a metaphor to describe local cultural practices unrelated to party politics.

Due to its popular egalitarianism, the *gurna* was quite dissimilar from the prevailing national "politics of the belly," in which the elite "eat" with impunity. However, not unlike the nation's history of single-party rule, the *gurna* tended to emphasize the value of unity. They expressed nostalgia for an imagined past when all the *gurna* were united under a single composer. Not surprisingly, this nostalgia for solidarity occurred without regard to actual past practices. These metacultural commentaries on politics are of interest because they reveal a creative interpenetration of discourse from the national public sphere into the local scene. Tupuri people have hijacked the discourse of multipartyism from national and international discourse about democracy and strategically selected and reworked it to explain changes in local cultural practice and shifting ethics in the use of political power.

The movement from single-party rule to democratic multiparty systems began in Sub-Saharan Africa in the late 1980s and early 1990s. Gros (1996) and Mehler (1998) have described the case of Cameroon. Since Independence in 1960, Cameroon had been ruled under a single-party system, first the Union Camerounaise (UC) under President Amadou Ahidjo and then, after 1982, the Rassemblement Démocratique du Peuple Camerounais (RDPC) under his successor, President Paul Biya. From the 1950s to the 1970s, the ruling government violently crushed the armed insurgent movement and opposition political party, the UPC, based in the southern Bassa and Bamiléké regions. Multipartyism did not reappear until 1989, when Yondo Black, a prominent attorney, tried to set up a new political party and was arrested. National and international outcry ensued. President Mitterand of France declared that in the future, allocation of aid would be tied to progress toward democratization. There was internal pressure on the Biya government as well. John Fru Ndi, from the Anglophone region, created the Social Democratic Front (SDF), which became a mouthpiece for Anglophones calling for a federalist government to replace authoritarian centralism.

In 1990, a law was written that permitted the creation of political parties, although technically this had not been illegal before. In a very short period of time, dozens of parties were created. Emerging from this turbulent situation were the largest parties: the SDF, the Fulbe-dominated Union Nationale pour la Démocracie et le Progress (UNPC), and the Mouvement pour la Défense de la République (MDR). Founded by Dakolé Daïsala, the MDR had a strong base in the Mayo Danay Département in Far North Province among the Tupuri, Massa, and Moundang. A reconstituted version of the old insurgent UPC reemerged. When the government did not respond to calls for a national conference on democratization, as had been convened in many francophone African countries, the opposition coalition called for national strikes (Opération Villes Mortes/Operation Ghost Town). These strikes crippled the country, depressed the economy, and were ineffective against the government's military power. France continued to back the Cameroon government economically throughout this period. In 1992, Biya won the national election through voting fraud within the Ministry of Territorial Administration, which was responsible for administering the elections (Dicklitch 2002; Gros 1996; Mehler 1998).

When I visited Cameroon during the Christmas break in the chaotic Ghost Town operations of 1991, I was amazed by both the depths of the resulting economic crisis and the headiness of Cameroonians as they experienced the freedom of expression and association that had been so restricted in the 1980s. Anything seemed possible. But by the time I returned in 1996 and 1997, the Cameroon populace had been sobered by the failure of the popular movement. Firmly entrenched through its RDPC party, the government seemed invincible, thanks to the support of France and its own military. Although the major opposition parties—the UNDP, the MDR, and the SDF—were still active, they had been effectively co-opted by the government though diplomatic incorporation that resembled Mobutu's approach to political opposition in Zaire. Unable to launch a unified front against the ruling party, this "fractured opposition," according to Gros, "was hobbled by narrow goals and leaders who were too vainglorious to band together (1996, 117).

In the small town of Doukoula, civil servants overwhelmingly supported the RDPC, not wanting to appear to bite the hand that feeds. The power of the traditional chiefs was also firmly in the hand of the RDPC. Many were disappointed in the opposition MDR party when its Tupuri leader, Dakolé Daïsala, took a government post, as did the leader of the UNDP. The radical SDF party, which had exuberantly campaigned in the north in the early 1990s, had withdrawn. So by the late 1990s, there was no question about the power of Biya's government and party, even though a multiparty system was in place. The hollow symbolism of multipartyism was performed during state functions in Doukoula. Each party's militants paraded in colorful uniforms, even if a deeper democracy was still elusive. (See figure 35 of Biya supporters in Maroua. Biya's slogan "Le Meilleur Choix" [The Best Choice] was deformed into "Le Seul Choix" [The Only Choice] by those who doubted the transparency of the elections.)

How did this national political scene affect the local cultural politics of the *gurna*? In an attempt to answer this, I asked each composer whether he was affiliated with one of the political parties. When asked directly, they denied any such involvement. Noumnamo said: "I am approached by all the political parties, so I have a wide range of choices. At this time, I plant myself in the center of them, and each pulls me to his side. . . . But I am neutral, because all the parties are fine to me."

Although composers were resistant to becoming embroiled in party politics, *gurna* members occasionally were affected by party politics in their formation of camps, but this mixing of party politics and *gurna* practice was frowned upon. At least until my departure from the region in 1999, Tupuri *gurna* in rural areas were largely uninterested in aligning their camps along national party lines. However, this did not stop them from occasionally performing for party events in Doukoula—for remuneration. *Gurna* practice remained solidly oriented toward the local and regional, though *gurna* members and observers alike freely called upon national political discourse to describe competitiveness and factionalism.

One composer exclaimed in his song "*Kosir, multipartisme 'a gɔ*" (Kosir, multipartyism has arrived"; T., 98/99, v. 47). Here a term from the national scene was mobilized to explain local cultural politics—that is, the competition among song composers. This analogy also appeared in discussions I had with composers and *gurna* members about the most recent composer on the scene, Sogole of Tuksu. When asked to comment on his rise to fame, many people remembered it not only as coinciding with the era of the national democratization movement (the early 1990s) but also in the same terms as "multipartyism." One high functionary in Doukoula said to me, "Sogole has a tendency toward the MDR, and Zouaye to the RDPC." He used the metaphor of Cameroon's political parties to characterize Sogole as the upstart gadfly in the song competition (the underdog MDR), opposing the "establishment" party of Zouaye (the RDPC). (Zouaye is considered the epicenter of song composition because of its long lineage of famous composers.) This local power configuration mirrors the national—though of course in an entirely different domain. The Tupuri-dominated opposition party, MDR, created in the 1990s, was a fly in the ointment for the state-sponsored party of the president, the RDPC.

However, as playfully as these metaphors are used by informants, when pressed, they will admit that there is no tangible relationship between changes in Cameroonian electoral politics and the rise of new "opposition" composers in Tupuriland. That is, everyone knows that national multipartyism did not create competition or factionalism in the *gurna*, but they still revel in a putative synchrony of these two changes: one local, one national. The discourse of multipartyism was ambiguous: on one hand it connoted what was new, exciting, and contemporary, while on the other hand, it was as vaguely threatening, dangerous, and unpredictable as the factionalism of the national political scene.

This discourse of multipartyism was also meaningful because it facilitated a particular nostalgia for the Tupuri past. The existence of multiple song composers was widely thought to be a new phenomenon in Tupuriland; people are fond of remembering the renowned Dang Biina as the sole composer for all of Cameroonian Tupuriland. While it is undeniable that Dang Biina was extremely popular in the 1960s for his attack on the *lamido* of Doukoula in injurious song, investigation into the history of *gurna* song composition reveals that multiple composers operated throughout Tupuriland. Kléda and Ruelland found five composers operating in Cameroon and Chad in 1974 (1998, 6). This plurality of composers was created by numerous overlapping factors: the vicissitudes of public taste for the song, geographical distance necessitating more composers,[6] intervillage one-upmanship, and political, sometimes violent, conflict among regions (such as between Doukoula and Zouaye). Retired composer Wore Djegongue explained the fact of multiple overlapping composers as merely a product of the geographical distance between villages. He remembered seeing as many as six rings of dancers at death celebrations decades ago, which he explained as a product of the importance of dance in the past. He contrasted this with contemporary life: "People didn't like school much in the past. Zouaye had a huge group [of dancers], and so did Baïga. Then, when people started to like school, the mass [of dancers] was reduced. For this reason, they had to bunch up in order to have enough." School and, Wore insisted, "the love of money" prevented youth from dancing and joining the *gurna* society. School was a competing form of socialization and social affiliation that was largely incompatible with the practice of the village-level *gurna* society. In this context, the notion of unity in the dance—bringing all the dancers together under a single triumphant composer in one dance ring—took on greater significance in contemporary Tupuriland. In spite of this nostalgia for a past of unified dancers under a single composer, there were probably always multiple composers and affiliations of dancers. Yearning for such unity was projected onto the past as a nostalgia for something that in fact never existed. Nonetheless, through this nostalgia, *gurna* and their supporters express solidarity for local value systems and practices that are challenged by social change associated with modernization.

Marilyn Ivy provides fascinating insights into the workings of nostalgia in Japan. She speaks of "an ambivalent longing to erase the temporal difference between subject and object of desire, shot through with not only the impossibility but the ultimate unwillingness to reinstate what was lost. . . . Despite its labors to recover the past and deny the losses of 'tradition,' modernist nostalgia must preserve, in many cases, the sense of absence that motivates its desires" (1995, 10). This perspective helps us to understand why Tupuri people continue to embrace aspects of modern life that obviate the need for the *gurna,* such as schooling and urban migration, at the same time that they revel in the continuation of the practice. The contemporary *gurna* is a communal practice of a pastoral nostalgia. *Gurna* members explicitly speak of their practice as "of their ancestors" at the same time that they enjoy modernizing elements that fit the *gurna*'s underlying aesthetic principles (such as replacing goatskins with white shorts in the dance costume). To call the *gurna* nostalgic does not mean that it was in any way "unreal"; it only suggests that it strategically borrows its imagery from the past and asserts its value as a viable social form in the present.

In spite of Cameroon's heterogeneity, regional, ethnic, and religious factionalism continues to be a source of anxiety; Cameroon's neighbors—Nigeria, Chad, and the Democratic Republic of Congo—provide vivid negative models.[7] A lurking fear of regional balkanization and ethnic conflict in Cameroon has only served to entrench the Biya regime more firmly in power. However, the introduction of multipartyism in the 1990s created a new set of possibilities for political organization in Cameroon that many believed would challenge the authoritarianism of the presidency. While many of the promised benefits of democracy (regime change, meaningful popular participation, etc.) have yet to materialize in Cameroon, a new discourse, a new set of symbols has been introduced. In Tupuriland, it is clear that national multiparty politics do not *create* factionalism in the *gurna* (at least they had not done so in the late 1990s), but they provide a metaphorical language or model for describing existing indigenous cultural practice. The playful metaphor of multipartyism in *gurna* discourse reflects a particular Tupuri reflection on larger debates in Cameroon concerning the risks of opposition politics. At the pragmatic level, the *gurna* avoid the actual politics of party identification in their association even while occasionally accepting a commission to dance, folklorically, for a state-sponsored celebration. *Gurna* consistently resist efforts to explain the ins and outs of *poltik weere* and the influence it represents in terms of national political party affiliation. Instead, they preserve the *gurna* arena as a kind of public sphere insulated from the eyes of outsiders and subject to its own rules. There, in poetic terms, they "discuss" the politics of the nation, bringing into the open anxieties about corrosive forms of competition that might masquerade under the rubric of democracy. Tupuri people intentionally guard the parochialism of their *gurna* sphere. Even while *gurna* song is a highly public expression, members preserve it as a cushion against the machinations of political parties and the state, which they view as potentially dangerous to their regional form of social solidarity.

TEN

Conclusion

DRESSING AND UNDRESSING: REVEALING MULTIPLE VALUE SYSTEMS

"*Le Kirdi: Habillez la vérité, l'Histoire la déshabillera.*" The homespun cultural journal *Le Kirdi*, which sought to socially rehabilitate the animist peoples of Cameroon's Far North Province, asserts in its subtitle "Dress Up the Truth, History Will Undress It." This jab at "clothedness" and nudity refers to what were marked as "traditional" differences between Muslim and animist northerners in Cameroon. Prior to the Independence era (1960s), animists—the so-called Kirdi[1]—wore noncloth body coverings composed of plant leaves, animal skins, or loose strings. In contrast, the invading Muslim Fulbe, who sought to subdue, enslave, and convert the "Kirdi" wore long robes. Amadou Hampaté Bâ encapsulates Fulbe conceptions of nudity: "In Fulbe symbolism 'to appear naked' does in fact mean to divest oneself of one's personality and of all human dignity, and to sell one's soul to evil powers" (1973/1999, 19). The journal's slogan asserts that "the truth" about the animist peoples will be revealed by a symbolic "disrobing"—that is, a revelation of the underlying cultural heritage of people whose value has been obscured by Muslim "clothing"—read, dominance.

Self-consciously modeled after the Negritude movement of Leonard Senghor and Aimé Cesaire, Kirditude was a cultural-political movement created by elite northern politicians in the 1990s under the organization Dynamique Culturelle Kirdi (DCK). Its romantic vision of cultural revisioning, nostalgia, and revitalization was inspired by a poem by Jean-Baptiste Baskouda, *Kirdi est Mon Nom* (1993), published by the Catholic Church in Yaoundé.[2] As a cultural-political movement, DCK sought to revalorize the integrity of the cultures of northern animist peoples, which include the Tupuri—and organize these disenfranchised peoples into a more potent political force. Although in its literature DCK was careful to point out its commitment to national integration, its project presupposed a divergence between the political-economic interests of the "Kirdi" from both their former Muslim rivals and the substantial southern Cameroonian bloc (primarily Béti and Bamiléké). However, in Tupuriland, I found very little recognition of this Kirditude movement, even though it sought to speak for the mass of animist peoples. Farmers understandably had little knowledge of these formulations in Yaoundé and at the universities, and intellectuals tended to distrust what other intellectuals were doing cloaked in the mantle of their own "cultural tradition."

I have briefly noted the existence of DCK—and, throughout this study, Tupuri-based cultural-political organizations modeled after the *gurna* society—in order to point up some of the implications of the initial question that opened the study. I asked: How are alternative moral orders and value systems negotiated in society, both individually and collectively? How does change emerge from the familiar, especially in the realm of dance and oral performance, and its underlying social organizations? For DCK and other cultural-political projects of a modernist neotraditional type, the ostensible project was to negotiate between competing social groups and their respective value systems, which are inevitably marked as either subordinate or hegemonic and are identified by visible cultural traditions (such as clothing, dance, rites, etc.). For example, animist nudity was reformulated from its colonial status as "savage" to that which was "truthful" and "historical," while Muslim clothedness "dressed up" or obscured the truth. However, as this study has endeavored to show with the *gurna,* the practice of cultural traditions on the ground is more complex than a dichotomy of hegemony and subordination would allow.

I have taken continuity of tradition as inherently problematic; that is, I have not assumed continuity but have asked the data to demonstrate it. Why would the *gurna* be perpetuated in the village context? Why would it be perpetuated in the city, albeit in a modified form? Approaching the problem in this fashion—as a negotiation of competing value systems on the terrain of tradition—revealed a number of complexities. First, I found that institutions such as the *gurna* provide opportunities for Tupuri men and women to participate in collectivities that differ radically from forms of social organization sponsored by the nation-state (such as schools, civil service employment, the military, and so on). However, in limited ways, these collectivities can be modified to fit into modern institutional settings. Dance and song perpetuated by *gurna* members (and other song-genre practitioners) maintain a discursive space whereby "governing" and "judicial" activities are carried out but in fashions radically different from the state government and court system. That this lifeworld of song, dance, and association should continue to thrive has implications for both the Tupuri people and the Cameroonian state.

The *gurna* provides a safety net for the Tupuri people to which they often return as a point of reference for centering social values and forms of collectivity and solidarity. This safety net is more important when the modern sector administered by the state breaks down, such as during the "troubles" of the 1990–1992 democracy movement and the extended economic depression of the 1990s. Institutions such as the *gurna* are important not just in the village, where disillusioned youth return, unable to make their way during the economic crisis, but also in the elite settings of universities and the nation's capital, where Tupuri people find themselves faced with the challenges of living in multiethnic settings.

The second area important to an understanding of why traditions such as the *gurna* have been perpetuated is the struggle to maintain the power of poetic license and authority. In this study I have understood *gurna* song as a complex of social activities: from information gathering to song production, dissemination, socialization, performance, and community reception and commentary. In order for this song complex to continue to be meaningful for the Tupuri people, it has been critical that the song composer's power be protected. We have seen how the composer's status is enhanced through discourse about the practice of magic, through the activities of his entourage (*courriers*), and by the song lyrics themselves. If power is buttressed by respect for power, then the poetic license of the song is not independently held by the ritual specialist but is a social relationship, a sacred trust, created through practices of the entire community. Poetic license associated with Tupuri song is important because it is the mechanism by which announcements are made and are *permitted* to be made to the larger community. This involves decisions about which information or commentary is broadcast and how, when, where, and by whom. For example, women can make trenchant commentary on the behavior of their husbands as long as it is contained within the performance of the *lɛɛlɛ* song genre. Similarly, *gurna* members can insult other men in the *gurna* song. The song system itself contains within it a repertoire of expected consequences for information broadcast through the song. Individuals maligned by insult may themselves call on composers to make counterinsults. Counterarguments about community controversies (for example, descriptions of Maïtené's modern behavior) can be asserted in different song genres. Finally, information put forward in song may provide the impetus for individuals to pursue formal judicial means to resolve their conflicts (such as through a witchcraft trial or the gendarmerie). The license to speak publicly is critical to the health of Tupuri song as a mechanism to do social work: the song provides a resource for building prestige and networks and the power to damage personal reputations in ways that can lead to social ostracism. As long as this license continues to be conferred, Tupuri song and dance will continue to be produced.

A third set of conclusions responds to the popular assumption that tradition is unitary, that it somehow represents the consensus value of that particular society. While it is true that general principles underlying performance may be widely held in the society—for example, among the Tupuri, that dance is public and communitarian or that song is a social space that permits insult and revenge—this does not mean that cultural practice requires social uniformity. From my study of Tupuri song, it is clear that within the register of "traditional" song, multiple constituencies are assumed, even though performers may project images of communitarian solidarity. As we saw in chapter 2, the subject of young men's song (*waywa*) could be responded to in women's song (*lɛɛlɛ*). In chapter 3, Christians differentiated themselves from "pagan" dancers, interpreting a "satanic" intention to the well-known power of the dance to attract viewers. And throughout this study we have seen how competition among individuals, villages, and composers through the medium of the song/dance is at the very root of the *gurna*. One implication of this multiplicity of performers, audiences, and interpretations is that cultural performance has become a resource for social governance rather than the law itself and that those other than members of the dominant class have access to its power. The men of the *gurna* society have their song complex through which to amplify their perspectives and desire, but it was just one of many song discourses such as the youth's *waywa*, women's *lɛɛlɛ*, children's *gurna-fiiri*, and others that may be invented in the future.

If "tradition" within Tupuri society is no longer viewed as unitary, then it is also important to recognize how sociocultural forms operating at the national level—schooling, literacy, electronic technology, citizenship, or state bureaucratic administration—have penetrated aspects of Tupuri culture. My study has been concerned with how national forms of socialization, communication, and justice have interacted with the *gurna* institution. At times, this interaction must be seen as competitive or antagonistic. Modern education has thinned the ranks of the *gurna* and *gurna-fiiri*; school has largely replaced the *jak-kaw* as the site for the socialization of children. *Gurna* song composers complain that the administrative court system, where individuals may be tried for libel, threatens the conventional poetic license of the song. On the other hand, discourse and symbolic forms from the national level (such as the language of democratization or the competitive exam system) are pulled in by *gurna* practitioners to point up synchronies between the local and the national, thereby drawing symbolic power to the local network.

At other times, modern bureaucratic contexts—such as schools, universities, and state ceremony—have offered new avenues for the practice of Tupuri custom, as have new Tupuri émigré communities in urban neighborhoods hundreds of miles from the homeland. In these contexts outside the villages where the Tupuri *gurna* was first developed, newly fashioned elite *gurna* have modified the forms of the practice by creating clubs that do not rely on the ownership and collective herding of cattle. *Gurna* clubs in these new settings are inflected with nostalgia and a self-consciousness about reproducing the tradition. Equally important, these club members position themselves for economic development—both for their own personal accumulation and for the benefit of those remaining in the villages—under the rubric of community development. At this point, neither Tupuri elites nor villages have attempted to employ the *gurna* social organization or symbol as a political force, but that may come in the future; cultural movements such as the DCK seem to point in that direction.

TUPURI CULTURE IN THE NATIONAL VIEW

As Geschiere (1997) has noted in reference to witchcraft, White (2000) in reference to rumor, and Barnes (1996) in reference to chiefly ritual, so-called traditional beliefs and practices have not withered away but instead have become part of the fabric of African modernities. Still, not enough is known about how African peoples are employing indigenous performance and associational forms in the context of modern state-sponsored institutions. My study focuses primarily on the *gurna* in the village setting and how value and micropolitics are negotiated within Tupuri communities, but nonetheless it points to pressure points where local Tupuri forms challenge the dominant national forms. Future research might look more closely at how students in lycées and universities throughout Cameroon use their *gurna* clubs to mediate between their home culture and the set of challenges they face as young citizens in the Cameroon nation. How does their *gurna* challenge the poverty they face as sons and daughters of farmers? Does their *gurna* seek to rehabilitate the status of Tupuri as "backward northern pagans" in the eye of the multiethnic nation? Or, do they—in dance—primarily speak among themselves of their connectedness?

In addition to schools, the justice system may also be an important site in which to discover how particular cultural forms are faring within state institutions. In Cameroon, even though witchcraft has as many variations as there are ethnic groups, it is treated as a criminal offense that can be tried in the court system. Similarly, slanderous or libelous speech is treated as a criminal offense of critical importance to the Biya government.[3] Fearful of losing its grip on power, the regime, now widely viewed as a dictatorship,[4] tries opposition newspaper editors for libel, damping freedom of expression. Although Tupuri song discourse has not reached the level of being viewed as a threat to the national regime, it is nonetheless considered threatening to individuals with the power to take song composers to court. Future study might examine how libel works in the court system for an indigenous genre such as the *gurna* that thrives on the power of public insult and the disclosure of scandal. What will happen when a system such as the *gurna,* which has its logic for containing conflicts that emerge from injurious speech, meets a system that uses harsher methods such as censorship and imprisonment? Answers to questions such as these help us understand how indigenous means of communication and governance shape contemporary institutions in Africa. It is likely that the economic and political challenges facing Africa will not result in the withering away of local cultural traditions but will instead precipitate new ways of looking back to the past—new nostalgias, strategic parochialisms, and re-creations of tradition.

NOTES

1. Introduction

1. See Gubry (1996) for a study of reruralization as a function of Cameroon's economic crisis.

2. Often in Western parlance the term "ancestral" connotes hoary roots going back thousands of years. I have at times placed this term in quotation marks to signal the Tupuri use of this word which can simply mean "of our fathers and grandfathers," either with or without the hoary connotations. In any case, after Hobsbawm and Ranger (1983), the ancientness of any tradition is understood to be historically constructed and strategically remembered.

3. African performance is generally multimodal: that is, it may involve music, verbal art, dance, and visual imagery simultaneously (Thompson 1974; Finnegan 1970). However, for the sake of brevity, I will use the term "song" at times to designate all aspects of its performance.

4. Others might use the term "moral economy."

5. In her examination of discursive practices in Xavante (Amazonian) men's council meetings, Laura Graham shows how specialized speech performances "effectively detach individuals from the content of their speech" (1993, 717). She asserts that this "collective production of multiple voices" such that the individual identity of speakers is obscured differs fundamentally from the Habermasian notion of public consensus emerging from "individually ratiocinating speakers" (718). She shows that collective political discourse in a public sphere can take forms other than the rational-critical debate that Habermas valorized.

6. Work focusing on verbal arts includes Abu-Lughod 1986; Barber 1991; Coplan 1994; Feld 1990; Furniss and Gunner 1995; Hofmeyr 1993; White 2000. Analyses of dance and ritual performance have been equally influential for me, including Cohen 1993; Cowan 1990; Drewal 1992; Glassman 1995; Heath 1994; Kratz 1993; Mendoza 2000; and Ranger 1975.

7. Repercussions were felt later in the 1990s when many bilateral and international nongovernmental organizations (including USAID and Save the Children) pulled out of Cameroon because of lack of confidence in the state's management ability and its handling of the 1992 presidential elections.

8. Before his election to a fifth term in October 2004, Biya had held the presidency for twenty-two years. The new term was for seven years. Political abuses attributed to the regime are documented in reports by the U.S. Department of State, Transparency International, and Amnesty International. Cameroon has been described as a "partial democracy."

9. So named for its shape on the map of Cameroon, which is said to resemble a chicken or duck.

10. Such as Moundang, Massa, Kéra, and Pévé. When they are asked where the Tupuri came from, educated elites often say they are from the Sara in southern Chad and even from southern Sudan. Although there is no firm evidence for this, a cursory glance at Northern-Central African dance and cattle-centered associations suggests that there may well be affinities.

11. The other Tupuri moiety, the Gwa, inhabit the southern Chadian region (Ganhou and Mindaoré) and have ritual practices that distinguish them from the Dore. Igor de Garine finds evidence in their exogamous taboos with the Viri (of Wina) that they may be of

Massa or Moussey origin (Garine 1981, 180). In my study, the categories of Dore and Gwa were sometimes used to describe different locations of *gurna* song composition (Zouaye versus Dawa) and different tempos in drumming. After much questioning, I concluded that the distinction between Dore and Gwa was not particularly significant in *gurna* practice.

12. Cameroon was annexed in 1884 by Germany. After World War I, when Germany lost its colonies, Cameroon was placed under the League of Nations (and later the UN) mandate and divided into West and East Cameroons, administered by the British and French, respectively. (Tupuriland lies in the Francophone region.) Practically speaking, France administered East Cameroon as part of its Central African colonies, but because of the UN mandate, Cameroonian men could not be drafted; they could only be recruited into the military.

13. Amadou Ahidjo, the first president of Cameroon after Independence in 1960, was closely aligned with the French.

14. Famines are given proper names in a way similar to the naming of hurricanes in the Atlantic. Beswe and Nõore (honey) were two colonial era famines. (I was told that the Honey Famine was so named for a sticky substance secreted by insects that attacked sorghum weakened by drought.)

15. The song material for this study was collected in Cameroon from 1997 to 1999 and is noted in the bibliography.

16. Strictly speaking, there is no Tupuri word for clan. *Kaw* (sing.) is a relational term for family or kin. Depending on the context, it can refer to family, clan, civic association, or ethnic group.

17. The term *"lamido"* was borrowed from the Fulbe/Hausa chieftaincy system of West Africa, which, ironically, the Tupuri had successfully resisted during the nineteenth-century jihad. Even today Tupuri chiefs legitimize their office by borrowing liberally from Fulbe courtly symbols: flowing robes, court praise singers, and festooned cavalry performance (*fantasie*).

18. In the late nineteenth century, Djonga, who came originally from Chad to occupy the Doukoula region, negotiated with the Fulbe *lamidat* of Mindif for the use of a cavalry to subdue the region as a vassal. The *lamido* of Mindif was an outpost of Fulbe expansion that emerged from Yola, Nigeria. In a surprise move, Djonga turned against the *lamido*, seizing his cavalry and selling the soldiers to slave traders. He then established himself as a *"lamido"* equal to that of Mindif even though no such title and authority existed in Tupuri political culture (Fendjongue 1991, 7–8).

19. According to colonial *tournée* reports of the 1920s, French officers were particularly concerned about cattle theft in Fulani villages by Tupuri raiders (Yagoua, Rapports de Tournées, APA 11893/B). Informants recalled this raiding by their grandfathers as the way the Tupuri first acquired the cattle that today constitute the basis of personal wealth through brideprice exchange.

20. *Waaŋ-wuu* translates as "administrative chief." *Wuu*, literally "fire," refers to firearms Europeans used to conquer the region. By extension, *"wuu"* refers to the modern world, including administrative authority.

21. Under pressure from the first president of Cameroon, who was a Fulbe Muslim, some Tupuri chiefs, such as that of Tchatibali, underwent highly visible conversions to Islam. This consolidation of power continues today: some traditional chieftaincies, such as Rey-Bouba in the North Province, hold absolute control over their region and flaunt national laws with impunity, permitting slavery and torture.

22. It is unclear how and why this ban was carried out; many informants offered different explanations. Most often the ban was thought to be motivated by the Fulbe hegemony of the Ahidjo regime, which sought to crush any Tupuri (non-Muslim) display of power. It may also have been an effort to preempt cultural-political activity that resembled the 1970s *authenticité* movement in Chad, through which a Sara president forced all civil servants to undergo Sara initiation. Others suggested that the Catholic Church played a role. In any event, families who sent their sons to Chad for the initiation of 1975 had their fields burned.

2. Maïtené's Modern Life

1. Because this book is about the dynamics and ethics of publicity and fame, the anthropological convention of pseudonyms presented dilemmas to me. The compromise I have reached is to use the real names of composers and persons (perhaps already-known personae) who appear in Tupuri song, since they have already circulated publicly. I have used the real names of informants, research assistants, and friends who contributed to this project's success. However, where I suspected that the individuals might feel embarrassed by what is revealed, I used a pseudonym.

2. The label of "traditional" has been extensively overhauled in African studies. The "mainstream" Africanist view, which Barber defines as a foil to understanding popular arts more generatively, characterizes traditional arts as "transmitted more or less intact, though changing slowly, from a pre-colonial past" (1987, 9). Drawing on Ulli Beier (1962), she adds that, in this paradigm, traditional art was thought to be "communal, consensual, embedded in social and ritual practice, and produced according to rigid codes by highly trained, skilled craftsmen" (Barber 1987, 9). While some aspects of this definition might hold in some cases, there are probably more exceptions than not.

Although "traditional" Tupuri dance and song assume a large degree of social consensus for their enactment, they are nonetheless a site of intense competition and contestation. Also, for all of its collaborative aspects, Tupuri song highlights the individual—in fact, even fetishizes it—by stringing together names of individuals and glorifying particular composers in the *gurna* genre. Furthermore, the traditional becomes visible as such—some have said it is "invented" (Hobsbawm and Ranger 1983)—when other forms, constructed as "modern," enter the scene. In Tupuriland, the *waywa* was "traditional" against the "modernity" of *makossa,* an electronically synthesized popular music style from Southern Cameroon that is often heard in Doukoula blaring from stereo systems in bars.

3. Sometimes adults recall their experiences with the poetic license afforded to children. Reveling in nostalgia, Kidmo, who holds a doctorate and a high administrative position, frequently recounted to me his exploits as a child composer of *waywa:*

> Once there was a man who used to take girls out into the bush and rape them, so I sang about his crimes, but he ignored it. Then I sang about one of the man's wives who was a thief. Again the man tolerated it. Then, finally, I sang that he had taken *sā'ā*, witchcraft powers. This was something that he wouldn't take sitting down. He got his gun and came out to the *laale* [arid patch of land] when we youth were dancing. Phew! I took off, nude, running all the way to Yagoua [40 kilometers away]. Later, when the man saw me again, he hit me on the top of the head. You see, I have a place now where hair won't grow!

Children use song to taunt and exerted their will over adults, while normally they have no right to contradict or discipline their elders. Although the case of Maïtené is not cross-generational, the same poetic license of youthful song was at its root.

4. As a lynchpin of Cameroon's bilingualism policy, the national curriculum required lycée students to study both French and English and even a third language (German or Spanish).

5. Expressed as the Tupuri verb "*boo,*" to build, combined with the French loan word for sheet iron, "*tôle.*"

6. Expressed as the Cameroonian-French borrowed term "*bordelle.*"

3. "Better than Family, Better than Girls"

1. Ethnic relations between the Tupuri and the Massa in the Mayo Danay have been peaceful, with much cultural borrowing and intermarriage. The Massa adopted Tupuri agricultural practices, such as transplanting of dry-season sorghum (Haman 1996, 88), while the Tupuri adopted Massa forms of socialization and solidarity, such as the *gurna* (Ruelland 1988, 16) and the initiation ritual, *gɔɔni*. However, the Tupuri and Massa languages stem from different families—Adamawa-Ubangi, Niger-Kordofan, and Chadic, respectively (Boutrais et al. 1994).

2. I have chosen the term "analyst" to indicate any observer and critical commentator of the *gurna,* regardless of whether they were academics. Although many Tupuri students have written theses and dissertations about various aspects of Tupuri society, only two scholarly monographs have been published: an anthropological study of nutrition conducted in the 1950s (Guillard 1965), and Ruelland's invaluable Tupuri dictionary (1988). Priests, students, community development workers, and local intellectuals have produced photocopied monographs on a myriad of topics, such as a cultural journal called *Ka'arang* produced by émigré Tupuri in Bremen, Germany. These informal monographs circulate widely, so it was not unusual to hear Tupuri educated functionaries theorize about the *gurna* in terms such as a "state within a state" or a "folkloric dance."

3. T., 97/98, v. 31.

4. In Tupuri society, distinctions between clans and their principle moiety (Dore and Gwa) are delineated through their celebration of the new year. Defining features include when the celebration is held, the particular animals that are sacrificed, and which vegetables are regarded as taboo before the celebration. Clans in the Dore moiety, whose leadership emanated from the high priest (*waaŋ-kuluu*) of Doré, Chad, celebrated the *few kage* (Festival of the Cock). After village meetings of atonement and the signals of the *waaŋ-kuluu* and the village priest (*waŋ-siri*), each family head sacrificed a chicken to their deceased parents. For the Gwa moiety, the celebration occurs after the *few kage* with the sacrifice of a ram and before the celebration of the Barre in December (*few barre*). (Barre is the Tupuri ethnonym for the Massa ethnic group.) The *gurna* session begins only after the Dore *few kage*; in fact, it is the celebratory *waywa* dance that provides the context for the organization of the *gurna* camps.

5. Because Tupuri society is exogamous and patrilocal, women are continually being incorporated into families and villages. The term of address for newly married women, *may-waare,* means "girl-stranger." (In Tupuriland, I was frequently addressed as *may-waare,* a term that captured both my apparent youth and foreignness.)

6. Other names praised the cows: Dankarra ("better than all the others"), Maïdané ("looked everywhere for her"), and Manboloro ("*man,*" "large" + "boloro" is Tupurized "Mbororo," pastoral Fulbe whose cows are known to have much milk).

7. The practice of the *guru-walla* among the Massa involves an even greater emphasis on body fattening. Garine and Koppert's (1991) detailed nutritional study found that *guru* practitioners gorged themselves for two and a half months for weight gains of 29–34 kilograms, or 45 percent of their initial body weights. Massa informants explained that in addition to the prestige of the fattened body, the *guru-walla* had durable effects: that after one had gained weight, he would gain it back more quickly in the future. The hypothesis that the development of fat cells facilitated future weight gain was borne out in *guru-walla* cases studied by Garine and Koppert (1991, 12). This research moves toward assessing whether such body-fattening practices provide greater biological fitness to the population overall or whether it serves to nutritionally deprive those who are excluded—women and children.

8. In Francophone sub-Saharan Africa, couscous is a boiled ball of starch that can be made from a variety of grains or tubers: rice, cassava, millet, sorghum, corn, etc. In Anglophone regions this is called *foufou.* Francophone Cameroonians call the semolina-style North African couscous *couscous algerien* to distinguish it from their own.

9. Robert Farris Thompson has written of "ephebism," or youthfulness, in African aesthetic sensibility. "People in Africa, regardless of their actual age, return to strong, youthful patterning whenever they move within the streams of energy which flow from drums or other sources of percussion. They obey the implications of vitality within the music" (Thompson 1974, 6–7).

10. James Ferguson provides a useful survey of this "puzzle of cultural dualism" in *Expectations of Modernity* (1999, 86–93).

11. This approach to the movement and reconfiguration of cultural forms over space is inspired by Barnes's *Africa's Ogun* (1989).

12. Rather than celebrating an independence day (from the French and British administration under UN mandate on January 1, 1960), Cameroon instead celebrates May 20, 1972, when the East and West Cameroons were unified as a single republic.

13. This lack of self-consciousness came out humorously when I asked some *gurna* members whether they had ever attracted tourists with their spectacular dance. They misinterpreted me in a significant manner. Not accustomed to being viewed by outsiders, they claimed: "Oh, yes! Last year, we rented a truck and went up to Waza [the game park in the north] to 'do tourism'!" In this way, they deftly skirted my suggestion that they might be objectified for tourists' consumption.

4. Defying the Modern

1. Spectators or dancers would occasionally confront me when I was filming, concerned that I might be with a TV station and would make a lot of money from the video footage. Although these confrontations were uncomfortable for me, I considered them salubrious, because it meant that local people were questioning how they are situated, both economically and symbolically in the global and national orders. It also forced me to articulate my intentions: my video was destined for use in educational settings and was unlikely to generate revenue. Cameroonian TV and radio stations that film the *gurna* dance for use in national programming generally offer an "envelope" to the dancers, a modest cash gift. I offered support for the *gurna* society by giving cash gifts to the song composers and camps when I visited them in situ.

2. With their characteristic humor, Cameroonians explained that they weren't awarded the dubious honor in 2000 because by then the government had succeeded in corrupting Transparency International (TI)! (According to TI's Corruption Perceptions Index, Cameroon was the seventh most corrupt of the countries surveyed in 2000; in 2001, it was the sixth most corrupt.)

3. Here I refer specifically to the *gurna* and *waywa* genres. Other Tupuri music/dance genres, such as the *didilna* and the *lɛɛlɛ*, do not involve such play between dancers and audience, even though their song lyrics are often just as provocative.

4. "Ya' wɛ gɔ 'ane. Ti bay de hɔpge mo dɛŋ no." (19) Unlike the songs in this study, I have chosen to provide the Tupuri versions of the ɓɔ'ge fɔgɛ in endnotes rather than alongside the English in the text. This is to preserve the improvisational, dialogic quality of this discourse, avoiding the rigid entextualization that is more fitting for composed songs. The number following each Tupuri version refers to its sequence in my corpus.

5. Suzanne Ruelland (personal communication) pointed out this homology between head-shaving among *gurna* and the more general mourning practice.

6. "Naa wɔ ɓɔ'ge fɔg day ɓaala. Guirling num wɛ lɛ caa po nday dee go ga faŋdi suwaa mbiiri gɔ mo naa." (T., 97–98, v. 33)

7. At one time, wrestling played important roles in certain Tupuri rituals, such as in the reintegration of the young man after his *nage may*, sexual initiation, and after the collective work for parents-in-law (*tɔrla*) required of marriage suitors. However, today wrestling seems to have diminished in importance in Tupuriland. Although soccer is a more popular sport for boys and men, occasional wrestling matches draw large and enthusiastic crowds. Wrestling has been modernized by the addition of Greco-Roman rules and its sponsorship by the government administration.

8. "Hay yo man-day ɓi no! Nday laa ti gurna ga mbay de ŋgokre dɛŋ dɔɔ day maa de lik leda n kɔd. Leege-baa daŋ de jobo 'ansɔ." (4)

9. The battle between the Fulbe of Mindif (at the northern reaches of Tupuriland) and Tupuri war chief Djonga in the late nineteenth century is frequently remembered. After luring the *lamido* of Mindif into a pacifist pact, Djonga turned on him, stealing his cavalry horses and kidnapping his bodyguards. Then he won a decisive triumph over the Fulbe of Mindif, which prevented further incursions into Tupuriland and enabled him to establish a chieftaincy at Doukoula (Fendjongue 1991, 10). It is ironic that the dynasty of Tupuri chiefs modeled themselves after the Fulbe *lamidat* system, taking on their trappings of power in costume and courtly organization.

10. Union des Populations du Cameroun. See chapter 9 for further explanation of this colonial-era insurgency movement.

11. "Hay yo, man-day yaŋ dɔɔ ɓi de pāa. Nday wɔ wɛ wɔ ndi hā wɛ. Nday ko de coo nen ɓi debaŋ." (6)

12. *"Ndi de gɔɓre mo dɛŋ diŋ wɛr man-day ɓi ma ga dɛŋ Tchabroud mo no."* (26)
13. *"Bufda ɓi no! Bufda ɓi no! Man-day maa rege jak saŋne. Man-day maa rege jak saŋne."* (23)
14. *"Nyaa wɛ 'argi, nen cii ɓay patala diŋ se. Maa mbi n pāa ɓi yaŋ la."* (14)
15. *"Nygɔk mo mo dɛŋ diŋ 'argin ga yaw la?"* (9)
16. *"Fɛr liŋ de crise ɓɔno, pāa kay no. Ndɔ yaŋ joge no sulay bay mo po wa."* (30)
17. *"Nday jar maaga ti bay mo jel gesiŋ wa mo no, nyaa wɛ suwɛɛ mo kay no."* (2)
18. *"Gɔɓ wɛ mo dɛŋ diŋ usa, maa wur, gɔɓ wur diŋ pāa."* (8)
19. *"Nday jɔŋ kare bɔɔŋ bɔɔŋ. Nen jeege je sɛ.n jee sɛ ɓa la ga. Ndi yee day ɓi mo kay no ndi yee day suwa'a. Koŋnɛ lɛ me wɛ no, ndi yee gɔ ɓɔgɛ. Ti mbay de bakge dɔɔ jak-sir wɔ mo dɛŋ dɛŋ kɔdɛ. Kay dɔɔ ɓi no."* (16)
20. *"Nen jeege je ɓɛ n jee ga, kal wiigi ga 'a yaŋ ɓɛs coore. Nday laɓ gɔ na takla mo pa."* (17)
21. *"Ndi yee d sɔŋre na ɓɔg ɓɔg mo pa. Kay no sɛŋ taw gɔ. Ndi yee ma tikriŋ wɛ ni."* (18)
22. *"Baa mo kiŋ gɔ ciŋ! Baa mo kiŋ gɔ ciŋ! Weere-jõore mo ndar nen gɔ. Weere-jõore mo ndar nen gɔ."* (24)
23. Due to the Cameroon government's concerns about the volatility of ethnic competition and conflict, reliable statistics of school attendance by ethnic groups are difficult or impossible to obtain. I base my assertions about Tupuri school attendance on perceptions of both Tupuri and non-Tupuri informants I questioned during fieldwork. The proportion of Tupuri students at the teacher-training institution (ENIEG) in Maroua, the capital of the Far North Province, was large.
24. *"Nday bay da' wuu de dɛrɛwal bay wɔ wa lay, nen maa-ga nday kal gurna nday kal ga lay, nday bay ko de coo de bɛ dɛŋ dɛŋ da sɔ."* (1)
25. The term *"wuu,"* which literally means "fire," has come to mean "Europeans"—and now, by extension, all elites, foreign or not. The term was said to refer originally to firearms brought by the German colonialists.
26. *"Nday mbay gɔ de yeege dɛŋ dɛŋ kɔdɛ. Ya' wɔ me de 'i' mɓay no."* (7)
27. *"Hay yo! Nday weere lakɔl no ya' wɛ ɓil mbay wɔ gɔ me. Mooɓi bay de ko sɛn wa."* (5)
28. Makossa is Cameroon's best-known pop music genre. Reaching its height of popularity in the 1980s, Makossa was created by modernizing and electrifying indigenous rhythms of the Beti of south-central Cameroon.
29. *"Fen po de cõore diŋ jõo, na jar po ga lakɔl po? Proviseur, ndi da lakɔl mbay ga sɔ."* (15)
30. *"Nday weere lakɔl no, suŋgu ɓay da' ge dɔɔ mbay maa bic wa. Ya' mo kay no. Maa wur no, wur jo mbɛ pāa da sɔ. Ya! Yo!"* (22)
31. *"Sous-prefet, ndi re mo dɛŋ diŋ cee maa de heg, jo la diŋ pāa de hɔɔlɛ gara ɓi, ndi de gɔbre mo riŋ dɛŋ no, maa bɔɔŋ ndɔ re wɛr nay wɔ gɔ buy ndɔ mbɔ de 'ngokre, 'a lɛ me jo pāa lam."* (12)
32. *"Day mbay bay wa lay, 'a wɛ lɛ daa'd pāa de ŋgar mbay. Sir maa nen mbɛ n jɔŋ mo-po sɛ mbay ga, Monsieur le Proviseur."* (13)
33. *"Nday ga ni tuwee pel ɓɔg ga. Ko me da sɔ: ndi wejõo, diŋ wel lakɔl pa. Nday de cuwāage na!"* (11)

5. "Telephone of the Dance"

1. Often expressed as *"téléphone-jõo"* (telephone-dance) or *"téléphone-day"* (telephone-cow). *"Day"* (cow) is a metaphor for the *gurna* because of its essential role in *gurna* society.
2. In studies of dance and music clubs of the African diaspora, such as the Nottingham Carnival (Cohen 1993) and Trinidadian steel bands (Stuempfle 1995), scholars have emphasized that competition and political contestation are vital elements of institutions and festivals that also serve to unite the populace. Also, see literature on competitive jousting and aesthetic virtuosity in African and African diasporic verbal performance (Abrahams 1983; Caponi 1999; Malone 1996).

3. Commenting on African precedents of dance among New World slave populations, Jacqui Malone notes their "tendency 'to dance the song' " (1996, 28).

4. More precisely, there are partnerships of song composition in three locations—Zouaye, Tuksu, and Dawa; each song is composed by two composers working in collaboration. The number of composers shifted over time. (See chapter 7 on song composition.)

5. Creative collaboration in African performance has not been widely studied as such, though Agovi reports that in Ghanaian *avudwere,* there is "a healthy spirit of cooperation and respect among poet, cantor and singer" and significant community input into the content of songs composed by specialized "poet-intellectuals" (Agovi 1995, 49–50).

6. "*Agents secrets*" (French); "*jar ma wāare*" (Tupuri; "people with stories").

7. Barber 1991; Gunner 1995; de Moraes Farias 1995; Furniss 1995; Irvine 1989; Pellow 1997; Smith 1957; Vail and White 1991.

8. Patrons were often elites returning from the city to their natal villages, candidates for public political offices, traditional chiefs, and the highest-ranking males of a family on the occasion of funerals, marriages, birthing parties, and so forth.

9. I did not find a Tupuri term for this important role (other than *man-kɔm,* which denotes the entire configuration of the song leader surrounded by the lead chorus).

10. Tupuri society was also stratified by age-sets instituted by ritual youth initiation, *gɔɔni,* banned since 1975.

11. Literally, "place-sorghum beer."

12. Personal communication, November 10, 2001.

6. "Rise Up, Gather Like Storm Clouds"

1. "*Ndɔ laymaa gaw mbirna*" is a Massa phrase. The songs are peppered throughout with Massa terms and phrases, a carryover from the fact that the Tupuri borrowed the *gurna* practice from the Massa. Before the introduction of French, Massa functioned as a prestige language among the Tupuri, and it still does in the context of the *gurna* song. Many Tupuri understand these phrases formulaically.

2. "*ɓɔ' ti tiŋ*" translates literally as "taking a turn around the house." During a funeral (*huuli*), mourners dance a special funerary dance (*kombarre*) around the house of the deceased, where his or her body lays in wake. During death celebrations (*yii-huuli*), the *gurna* dance in a circumambulatory fashion around the deceased's house to conclude the dance.

3. *Sa',* Tupuri, "attach"; *moday,* French borrow *médaille.*

4. *Numra un,* French borrow "*numero un*" (T., 97/98, v. 32).

5. Z., 97/98, v. 49.

6. Contrary to the now-outdated assumption that individuals in "traditional societies" (i.e., small-scale, face-to-face societies) have a single, fixed identity, the system of naming in contemporary Tupuri society suggests that each individual has multiple identities. Most men and women had two names given to them by their parents at birth: one Tupuri name and one French name (for example, Laaga Robert or Maïdaï Josephine). There are special classes of names for twins. When a boy was initiated (*gɔɔni*), his Tupuri name is transformed with the addition of one of the initiation suffixes: "-kreo," "-andi," "-sala," and so forth. When girls marry, they are called by the name of their natal village with the prefix "Maï-."

7. *Manyaaba* is usually translated as "rainbow," but the composer Sogole explicated that with the term, he meant to evoke the great volume of storm clouds often found near a rainbow.

8. The Cameroonian Tupuri population can be estimated as 200,000, based on Ruelland's estimate of 300,000–400,000 for Tupuri in both Cameroon and Chad (1999, 1). (These figures are extrapolated from population density rates in a 1976 census.) The national population of Cameroon is 15,422,000 (Ramsay 2001, 16); it has 250 ethnic/linguistic groups. As a result of this cultural pluralism, even as less than 5 percent of the total population, the Tupuri are in fact a prominent group among northerners.

9. This poetic language is difficult to translate. A more literal translation would be: "The leaders of the dance from Guirling have taken their place."

10. Clearing away dead souls by making noise is also practiced during the Tupuri new year in a dawn ritual called *du'gi*.

11. Abrahams 1962; Apter 1998; Avorgebor 2001; Brenneis 1980; Irvine 1993, 1996; Labov 1972; Parkin 1980.

12. Eckert and Newmark 1980; Mathias 1976.

13. Obscene sexual references to the other's mother as a form of ritual insult has been termed "mother-rhyming" (Abrahams 1983, 56).

14. *Sara* literally means "a neighbor who takes advantage of the meal offered in a collective work group (*tɔrla*) without doing any work" (Ruelland 1988, 236).

15. A dog (*waay*), or more precisely a puppy (*wel-waay*), is used to purify acts of incest in sacrifice ceremonies. The dog is symbolically associated with the patrilineage because it protects the family by guarding the compound (Ruelland 1999).

16. Kléda 1983. The English translation is mine from Kléda's French translation of the Tupuri. I have altered Kléda's Tupuri transcription to conform to Ruelland 1988.

7. "I Become Your Boy"

1. Women composed song outside the *gurna* in the *lɛɛlɛ* genre.

2. Ruelland typologizes regions of Tupuriland in order to note dialectical variation and linguistic admixture (1988, 19–20). *Baŋ-liŋ* ("near home") refers to the Tupuri heartland in Mayo Kebbi, Chad. *Baŋ-gɔ* ("near the other side") refers to the northern Tupuri territory in Cameroon.

3. The term "*ɓaŋ-wɛrɛ*" was also used. Ruelland (1988, 20) describes *ɓaŋ-wɛrɛ* as the eastern region of Tupuriland, near Fianga, Chad, where the influence of the Kéra language is strong. I found that farther north in Cameroon, the term "*ɓaŋ-wɛrɛ*" was used to refer to the east near Golonpoui, where Massa is the major admixture.

4. Although it is extremely difficult to provide accurate dates for the composers' periods of activity, Kléda and Ruelland (1998) report that in 1974, Dabla, Loumsiya, and Tenglen were well known.

5. Magic, whether it is witchcraft or through other kinds of mysterious herbs (*saŋgu*), is often associated with dreams. Usually a witchcraft victim has dreams about struggling with the person who has bewitched him or her. Part of the cure for the victim is to reveal the witch's identity as revealed in these dreams.

6. Part of the art of composition is the clever insertion of other languages into the Tupuri lyrics: Massa, Fulfulde, and French. These loan words are Tupurized. For example, "*ler*" is the French "*l'heure*" ("on time").

7. The term "*buy*" is an English borrow word into French ("*boy*"), referring to the colonial-era term for "domestic servant." Sogole explained that he meant to connote the sense of being in service to all.

8. Figuratively, according to the composer, "If there is peace among people, it's because of the way they speak to one another."

9. The symbolic and literal connection between the abundance of sorghum and *gurna* practice is powerful. Figuratively, the line suggests that the *gurna* will never end.

8. Staging Conflict through Insult

1. In spite of over fifty years of Christian missionary activity, perhaps only about 15 percent of Tupuris were Christian in the late 1990s. However, Christian discourse was so widespread that talking about spirituality in French involved some degree of syncretism. The indigenous Tupuri spirit that most resembles the supreme creator deity that Christians call God, *baa*, was always translated in French as "Dieu." Therefore, in order to understand whether an individual was referring specifically to the Christian God, it was necessary to probe whether he or she meant "*jak-baa*," literally, the "word of God," or the Bible. Tupuri Christians tend to subsume the animist *baa* under the Christian God, thereby neutralizing the power of its difference.

2. *Pel ne jerɛm*, literally "short forehead" which in interviews, the composer likened to a fish.

3. "*Kare*," after "*car*" (French for public bus), denotes a "motorboy," the youth who

is responsible for loading luggage onto buses. Due to the trials of his occupation, he usually appears to be filthy and dim-witted.

4. Bogao was the name of the "secret agent" who ferried this information to the composer. By including his name, the composer conferred fame on the agent.

5. Two major forms of witchcraft will be described later. What is essential here is that the accusation of *kereŋ* is insulting, but it is not the type of insult that could result in grave consequences.

6. "*Congossa*" is a term from Southern Cameroon meaning "*radio trottoir*," or gossip. This term circulates widely in urban areas of the north, though monolingual Tupuri use the Tupuri term "*wāare*" to mean stories or gossip.

7. Prolapsed hemorrhoid. Ruelland (1988, 29) defines "*baa-huuli*" as "a mythic animal that lives in a woman's womb." This "mythic animal" could be understood to be manifested by a prolapsed hemorrhoid.

8. Geschiere provides a detailed description of these witchcraft forms (1997, 61–68).

9. Another witchcraft trial, *co'ge jak-siri*, involved the summons of the entire village to the *jak-siri* (sacred forest) by the earth priest of the village (*waaŋ-siri*). A cow was sacrificed and wood from the sacred forest was used to cook it. Everyone ate the meat. If someone was a witch, the spirits of the sacred forest would trap his soul and keep it. When this person returned home, he would die soon after, since his soul had been retained by the ancestral spirits of the sacred forest.

9. Multipartyism and Nostalgia for the Unified Past

1. A left-wing nationalist movement that had emerged by 1948 from the Southern Cameroon Bamiléké and Bassa regions.

2. The ruling party, the RDPC, sought to split the northern opposition party, the UNDP, by capitalizing on the long-standing resentment of Christian and animist ethnic groups, such as the Tupuri, against the Fulbe.

3. The Bamiléké from the West Province own many of the businesses in Southern Cameroon and are known for their entrepreneurial networks.

4. Even today *gurna* move in groups (as camps) with dancing stick in hand to the dance site.

5. See the song lyrics in chapter 6.

6. This was the putative reason for the creation of the Zouaye-Dawa rivalry, which ran along the clan moiety divisions of Dore and Gwa, respectively.

7. The increased risk of armed conflict due to proximity to other countries in conflict is bluntly termed "bad neighborhood" in the literature on conflict.

10. Conclusion

1. In common parlance, "Kirdi" refers to the non-Muslim peoples of Northern Cameroon. Today the term has pejorative connotations, especially along elite Fulbe—that is, it is used to connote enslaved, backward people of the mountains. However, "Kirdi" is an Arab word etymologically connected to the Kurds of Iran, Iraq, and Turkey. It was used by the Arab warrior Rabah to designate the mosaic of peoples of the Mandara mountains (near the Western Nigeria–Cameroon border), who, under the Mandara (Wandala) Empire, were pivotal to his quest to conquer the Hausa-Fulani empire of Nigeria (Mashing 1997).

The Tupuri, as inhabitants of the alluvial plains of the Kebbi River, are distinctly different from the Mandara peoples. However, cultural-political movements such as the DCK (which published *Le Kirdi*) sought to consolidate as many ethnic groups as possible under the animist rubric in order to strengthen their position. It is ironic that although the so-called Kirdi were united by their paganism, many have converted to Islam and Christianity.

2. Baskouda was an advisor to the journal and a high-level civil servant in the Cameroon government. In *Kirdi est Mon Nom*, he draws on the work of anthropologists to weave together poetic cultural portraits of twenty-five northern ethnic groups.

3. The 1999 Country Report on Human Rights Practices for Cameroon by the U.S.

Department of State notes that Cameroon's "Penal Code libel laws specify that defamation, abuse, contempt, and dissemination of false news are offenses punishable by prison terms and heavy fines. These statutes are invoked by the Government to silence criticism of the Government" (2000, 14). Amnesty International (2001) and the U.S. State Department (1998, 1999) have documented scores of cases of harassment and imprisonment of journalists.

4. The 1999 U.S. State Department Report diplomatically notes that the ruling RDPC/CPDM party has "remained in power and limited political choice," and that "[n]o President has ever left office in consequence of an election" (2000, 1). Biya was elected in 1984 and 1988 in a single-party system with "99 percent" of the vote. His reelection in 1992 in a multiparty race was widely considered fraudulent and sparked demonstrations that were harshly put down. In both 1997 and 2004, he won after the opposition split; meanwhile, Biya had become expert in co-opting his opponents.

BIBLIOGRAPHY

Archival Documents

Yagoua, Rapports de Tournées, APA 11893/B, 1924–1959, National Archives, Yaoundé.
Yagoua, Cameroun Affaires Politique, 11854/F, November 18, 1932, National Archives, Yaoundé.

Song Corpus

Gurna song (*siŋ gurna*), 1997/1998, Tuksu village, Sogole.
Gurna song, 1998/1999, Tuksu village, Sogole and Dayle (of Youaye).
Gurna song, 1997/1998 and 1998/1999, Zouaye village, Noumnano and Djingue.
Gurna song, 1998/1999, Dawa village (Chad), Dabla and Teodandi.
Children's *gurna* song (*siŋ gurna-fiiri*), 1998/1999, Konkoron village, Houyang Jean.
Gurna song for Gurna Club, Lycée de Doukoula, Doukoula, 1995/1996, 1996/1997, 1997/1998, 1998/1999, Dangmoworé.
Gurna song for Tupuri Cultural Association, Marouac Pitoaréc, 1998/1999, Ringwa.
Gurna song for Club Kwoïssa, Yaoundé, 1998 and 1999, Fouroum Mangale.
Lɛɛlɛ (women's song), #1–27, collected in Doukoula 1997–1999.
Waywa (youth's song), #1–18, collected in Doukoula 1997–1999.

Books, Dissertations, Reports, and Articles

Abrahams, Roger D. 1962. "Playing the Dozens." *Journal of American Folklore* 75: 209–220.
———. 1983. *The Man-of-Words in the West Indies: Performance and the Emergence of Creole Culture*. Baltimore: Johns Hopkins University Press.
Abu-Lughod, Lila. 1986. *Veiled Sentiments: Honor and Poetry in a Bedouin Society*. Berkeley: University of California Press.
———. 1998. *Remaking Women: Feminism and Modernity in the Middle East*. Princeton, N.J.: Princeton University Press.
Agovi, Kofi. 1995. "The King Is Not above Insult: The Politics of Good Governance in Nzema *Avudwene* Festival Songs." In *Power, Marginality and Oral Literature*, ed. Graham Furniss and Liz Gunner. Cambridge: Cambridge University Press.
Allison, Anne. 1994. *Nightwork: Sexuality, Pleasure, and Corporate Masculinity in a Tokyo Hostess Club*. Chicago: University of Chicago Press.
Amnesty International. 2001. "A. I. Report 2001: Cameroon." A. I. Publications. Available online at http://web.amnesty.org/web/ar2002.nsf/afr/cameroon?Open.
Appadurai, Arjun. 1996. *Modernity at Large: Cultural Dimensions of Globalization*. Minneapolis: University of Minnesota Press.
Apter, Andrew. 1992. *Black Critics and Kings: The Hermeneutics of Power in Yoruba Society*. Chicago: University of Chicago Press.
———. 1998. "Discourse and Its Disclosures: Yoruba Women and the Sanctity of Abuse." *Africa* 68 (1): 68–97.
———. 1999. "IBB 19: Nigerian Democracy and the Politics of Illusion." In *Civil Society and the Political Imagination in Africa*, ed. John L. Comaroff and Jean Comaroff. Chicago: University of Chicago Press.

Avorgbedor, David K. 2001. " 'It's a Great Song!' *Halǒ* Performance as Literary Production." *Research in African Literatures* 32 (2): 17–43.
Bâ, Amadou Hampaté. 1973/1999. *The Fortunes of Wangrin.* Trans. Aina Pavolini Taylor. Bloomington: Indiana University Press.
Barber, Karin. 1987. "Popular Arts in Africa." *African Studies Review* 30 (3): 1–78.
———. 1991. *I Could Speak Until Tomorrow: Oriki, Women, and the Past in a Yoruba Town.* Washington, D.C.: Smithsonian Institution Press.
———. 1997. "Introduction." In *Readings in African Popular Culture,* ed. Karin Barber. Bloomington: Indiana University Press.
———. 1999. "Obscurity and Exegesis in African Oral Poetry." In *Oral Literature and Performance in Southern Africa.* Oxford: James Currey.
Barber, Karin, and P. F. de Moraes Farias. 1989. "Introduction." In *Discourse and Its Disguises: The Interpretation of African Oral Texts,* ed. Karin Barber and P. F. de Moraes Farias. Birmingham University African Studies Series no. 1. Birmingham, UK: Birmingham University, Center of West African Studies.
Barnes, Sandra T. 1989. *Africa's Ogun: Old World and New.* Bloomington: Indiana University Press.
———. 1996. "Political Ritual and the Public Sphere in Contemporary West Africa." In *The Politics of Cultural Performance,* ed. D. Parkin, L. Caplan, and H. Fisher. Providence, R.I.: Berghahn Books.
Barthes, Roland. 1972. *Mythologies.* New York: The Noonday Press.
Baskouda, J. B. Shelley. 1993. *Kirdi Est Mon Nom.* Yaoundé, Cameroon: Imprimerie Saint-Paul.
Bauman, Richard, and Charles L. Briggs. 1990. "Poetics and Performance as Critical Perspectives on Language and Social Life." *Annual Review of Anthropology* 19: 59–88.
Bayart, Jean-François. 1993. *The State in Africa: The Politics of the Belly.* New York: Longman.
Beier, Ulli. 1962. "Nigerian Folk Art." *Nigeria Magazine* 75.
Binet, Jacques. 1974. "Dance et Éducation dans la Vie Sociale: Les Fangs du Gabon." In *Dossiers Pédagogique: L'Enfant en Afrique, Education et Socialisation II* (10): 21–26.
Bourdieu, Pierre. 1972/1989. *Outline of a Theory of Practice.* Trans. Richard Rice. Cambridge: Cambridge University Press.
———. 1984. *Distinction: A Social Critique of the Judgment of Taste.* Cambridge, Mass.: Harvard University Press.
Bourdieu, Pierre, and J.-C. Passeron. 1977. *Reproduction in Education, Society and Culture.* Beverly Hills, Calif.: Sage Press.
Boutrais, Jean et al. 1994. *Le Nord du Cameroun: Des Hommes, Une Région.* Paris: ORSTOM.
Brenneis, Donald. 1980. "Fighting Words." In *Not Work Alone: A Cross-Cultural View of Activities Superfluous to Survival,* ed. Jeremy Cherfas and Roger Lewin. London: Temple Smith.
Briggs, Charles, and Richard Bauman. 1992. "Genre, Intertextuality, and Social Power." *Journal of Linguistic Anthropology* 2 (2): 131–172.
Burnham, Philip. 1996. *The Politics of Cultural Difference in Northern Cameroon.* Washington, D.C.: Smithsonian Press.
Butler, Judith. 1990. *Gender Trouble: Feminism and the Subversion of Identity.* New York: Routledge.
Caponi, Gena Dagel, ed. 1999. *Signifyin(g), Sanctifyin', and Slam Dunking: A Reader in African American Expressive Culture.* Amherst: University of Massachusetts Press.
Caton, Steven C. 1990. *"Peaks of Yemen I Summon": Poetry as Cultural Practice in a North Yemeni Tribe.* Berkeley: University of California Press.
Chernoff, John M. 1979. *African Rhythm and African Sensibility: Aesthetics and Social Action in African Musical Idioms.* Chicago: University of Chicago Press.
Clifford, James, and George E. Marcus, eds. 1986. *Writing Culture: The Poetics and Politics of Ethnography.* Berkeley: University of California Press.

Cohen, Abner. 1993. *Masquerade Politics: Explorations in the Structure of Urban Cultural Movements.* Berkeley: University of California Press.
Comaroff, Jean. 1985. *Body of Power, Spirit of Resistance.* Chicago: University of Chicago Press.
Comaroff, Jean, and John Comaroff, eds. 1993. *Modernity and Its Malcontents: Ritual and Power in Postcolonial Africa.* Chicago: University of Chicago Press.
Coplan, David B. 1994. *In the Time of the Cannibals: The Word Music of South Africa's Basotho Migrants.* Chicago: University of Chicago Press.
Cowan, Jane K. 1990. *Dance and the Body Politic in Northern Greece.* Princeton, N.J.: Princeton University Press.
Diawara, Mamadou. 1997. "Mande Oral Popular Culture Revisited by the Electronic Media." In *Readings in African Popular Culture,* ed. Karin Barber. Bloomington: Indiana University Press.
Dicklitch, Susan. 2002. "Failed Democratic Transition in Cameroon: A Human Rights Explanation." *Human Rights Quarterly* 24: 152–176.
Dominguez, Virginia R. 1992. "Invoking Culture: The Messy Side of 'Cultural Politics.'" *Southern Atlantic Quarterly* 91: 19–42.
Drewal, Margaret Thompson. 1991. "The State of Research on Performance in Africa." *African Studies Review* 34 (3): 1–64.
———. 1992. *Yoruba Ritual: Performers, Play, Agency.* Bloomington: Indiana University Press.
Dumas-Champion, Françoise. 1983. *Les Masa du Tchad: Bétail et Societé.* Cambridge: Cambridge University Press.
Eckert, Penelope, and Russell Newmark. 1980. "Central Eskimo Song Duels: A Contextual Analysis of Ritual Ambiguity." *Ethnology* 19 (2): 191–211.
Erlmann, Veit. 1996. *Nightsong: Performance, Power, and Practice in South Africa.* Chicago: University of Chicago Press.
Evans-Pritchard, E. E. 1937. *Witchcraft, Oracles and Magic among the Azande.* Oxford: Clarendon.
———. 1940. *The Nuer.* New York: Oxford University Press.
———. 1956. *Nuer Religion.* Oxford: Clarendon.
Eyoh, Dickson. 1998. "Through the Prism of a Local Tragedy: Political Liberalisation, Regionalism and Elite Struggles for Power in Cameroon." *Africa* 1: 338–359.
Feckoua, Laurent Laoukissam. 1977. "Les Hommes et Leurs Activités en Pays Toupouri du Tchad." Doctoral dissertation (Geography), Université de Paris VIII, Vincennes, Faculté des Lettres et Sciences Humaines.
Feld, Steven. 1990. *Sound and Sentiment: Birds, Weeping, Poetics, and Song in Kaluli Expression.* Philadelphia: University of Pennsylvania Press.
Fendjongue, Houli. 1991. "La Dialectique de la Tradition et la Modernité dans un Systeme Politique Toupouri: L'Exemple de la Chefferie de Doukoula." Mémoire, Faculté de Droit et des Sciences Economiques, Université de Yaoundé, Cameroun.
Ferguson, James. 1999. *Expectations of Modernity: Myths and Meanings of Urban Life on the Zambian Copperbelt.* Berkeley: University of Chicago Press.
Ferme, Mariane. 1999. "Staging *Politisi*: The Dialogics of Publicity and Secrecy in Sierra Leone." In *Civil Society and the Political Imagination in Africa,* ed. John L. Comaroff and Jean Comaroff. Chicago: University of Chicago Press.
Finnegan, Ruth. 1970. *Oral Literature in Africa.* Oxford: Oxford University Press.
Foucault, Michel. 1975. [1977 trans.] *Discipline and Punish: The Birth of the Prison.* New York: Random House/Vintage.
———. 1976/1994. "Two Lectures." Reprinted in *Culture/Power/History: A Reader in Contemporary Social Theory,* ed. Nicholas B. Dirks, Geoff Eley, and Sherry B. Ortner. Princeton, N.J.: Princeton University Press.
Fraser, Nancy. 1992. "Rethinking the Public Sphere." In *Habermas and the Public Sphere,* ed. Craig Calhoun. Cambridge, Mass.: MIT Press.
———. 1997. *Justice Interruptus: Critical Reflections on the "Postsocialist" Condition.* New York: Routledge.
Furniss, Graham. 1995. "The Power of Words and the Relation between Hausa Genres."

In *Power, Marginality and Oral Literature,* ed. Graham Furniss and Liz Gunner. Cambridge: Cambridge University Press.
Furniss, Graham, and Liz Gunner, eds. 1995. *Power, Marginality and Oral Literature.* Cambridge: Cambridge University Press.
Gable, Eric. 1995. "The Decolonization of Consciousness: Local Skeptics and the 'Will to be Modern' in a West African Village." *American Ethnologist* 22 (2): 242–257.
———. 2000. "The Culture Development Club: Youth, Neo-Tradition, and the Construction of Society in Guinea-Bissau." *Anthropological Quarterly* 73 (4): 195–203.
Garine, Igor de. 1981. "Contribution B l'Histoire du Mayo Danaye (Massa, Toupouri, Moussey et Mousgoum)." In *Contribution de la Recherche Ethnologique à l'Histoire des Civilisations du Cameroun,* ed. Claude Tardits. Paris: Éditions du CNRS.
Garine, Igor de, and Georgius J. A. Koppert. 1991. "*Guru*-Fattening Sessions among the Massa." *Ecology of Food and Nutrition* 25: 1–28.
Geertz, Clifford. 1973. *Interpretation of Cultures.* New York: Basic Books.
Geschiere, Peter. 1997. *The Modernity of Witchcraft: Politics and the Occult in Postcolonial Africa.* Charlottesville: University Press of Virginia.
Geschiere, Peter, and Josef Gugler. 1998. "The Urban-Rural Connection: Changing Issues of Belonging and Identification." *Africa* 68 (3): 309–319.
Glassman, Jonathon. 1995. *Feasts and Riot: Revelry, Rebellion, and Popular Consciousness on the Swahili Coast, 1856–1888.* Portsmouth, N.H.: Heinemann.
Gluckman, Max. 1963. *Order and Rebellion in Tribal Africa.* New York: The Free Press.
Goody, Jack. 1977. *The Domestication of the Savage Mind.* Cambridge: Cambridge University Press.
Gourlay, Kenneth. 1999. "The Making of Karimojong' Cattle Songs." In *Composing the Music of Africa: Composition, Interpretation and Realisation,* ed. Malcolm Floyd. Aldershot: Ashgate.
Graham, Laura. 1993. "A Public Sphere in Amazonia? The Depersonalized Collaborative Construction of Discourse in Xavante." *American Ethnologist* 20 (4): 717–741.
Gros, Jean-Germain. 1996. "The Hard Lessons of Cameroon." *Journal of Democracy* 6 (3): 112–127.
Gubry, Patrick, Samson B. Lamlenn, Emmanuel Ngwé, Jean-Marie Tchégho, Joseph-Pierre Timnou, and Jacques Véron. 1996. *Le Retour au Village: Une Solution à la Crise Economique au Cameroun?* Paris: Harmattan.
Guillard, Joanny. 1965. *Golonpoui: Analyse des Conditions de Modernisation d'un Village du Nord-Cameroun.* Paris: Mouton.
Gunner, Liz. 1995. "Clashes of Interest: Gender, Status and Power in Zulu Praise Poetry." In *Power, Marginality and Oral Literature,* ed. Graham Furniss and Liz Gunner. Cambridge: Cambridge University Press.
Gupta, Akhil, and James Ferguson. 1992. "Beyond 'Culture': Space, Identity, and the Politics of Difference." *Cultural Anthropology* 7 (1): 6–23.
Habermas, Jürgen. 1962/1989. *The Structural Transformation of the Public Sphere: An Inquiry into a Category of Bourgeois Society.* Trans. Thomas Burger. Cambridge, Mass.: MIT Press.
Hall, Kathleen. 1995. " 'There's a Time to Act English and a Time to Act Indian': The Politics of Identity among British-Sikh Teenagers." In *Children and the Politics of Culture,* ed. S. Stephens. Princeton, N.J.: Princeton University Press.
Hall, Stuart. 1981. "Notes on Deconstructing the Popular." In *People's History and Socialist Theory,* ed. R. Samuel. London: Routledge.
Haman, Amadou. 1996. "Les Massa de la Rive Gauche du Logone (Nord-Cameroun): Origin, Migrations et Processus d'Implantation." Memoire dans le Département d'Histoire, Université de Yaoundé I.
Handler, Richard. 1988. *Nationalism and the Politics of Culture in Quebec.* Madison: University of Wisconsin Press.
Hannerz, Ulf. 1992. *Cultural Complexity: Studies in the Social Organization of Meaning.* New York: Columbia University Press.
Haraway, Donna. 1991. *Simians, Cyborgs, and Women: The Reinvention of Nature.* New York: Routledge.
Harvey, David. 1989. *The Condition of Postmodernity.* Cambridge, Mass.: Blackwell.

Heath, Deborah. 1994. "The Politics of Appropriateness and Appropriation: Recontextualizing Women's Dance in Urban Senegal." *American Ethnologist* 21 (1): 88–103.
Hill, Jane H., and Judith T. Irvine, eds. 1992. *Responsibility and Evidence in Oral Discourse.* Cambridge: University of Cambridge Press.
Hobsbawm, Eric, and Terence Ranger, eds. 1983. *The Invention of Tradition.* Cambridge: Cambridge University Press.
Hofmeyr, Isabel. 1993. *"We Spend our Years as a Tale That Is Told": Oral Historical Narrative in a Southern African Chiefdom.* Portsmouth, N.H.: Heinemann.
Hutchinson, Sharon E. 1996. *Nuer Dilemmas: Coping with Money, War, and the State.* Berkeley: University of California Press.
Ignatowski, Clare A. 1997. "Marking Presence, Taking Space: Graffiti and Murals in Philadelphia." Unpublished manuscript.
———. 2004a. "Multipartyism and Nostalgia for the Unified Past: Discourses of Democracy in a Dance Association in Cameroon." *Cultural Anthropology* 19 (2): 276–298.
———. 2004b. "Making Ethnic Elites: Ritual Poetics in a Cameroonian Lycée." *Africa* 74 (3): 411–432.
Irvine, Judith T. 1989. "When Talk Isn't Cheap: Language and Political Economy." *American Ethnologist* 16 (2): 248–267.
———. 1993. "Insult and Responsibility: Verbal Abuse in a Wolof Village." In *Responsibility and Evidence in Oral Discourse,* ed. Jane H. Hill and Judith T. Irvine. Cambridge: Cambridge University Press.
———. 1996. "Shadow Conversations: The Indeterminacy of Participant Roles." In *Natural Histories of Discourse,* ed. Michael Silverstein and Greg Urban. Chicago: University of Chicago Press.
Ivy, Marilyn. 1995. *Discourses of the Vanishing: Modernity, Phantasm, Japan.* Chicago: University of Chicago Press.
James, Deborah. 1999. "Sister, Spouse, Lazy Woman: Commentaries on Domestic Predicaments by Kiba Performers from the Northern Province." In *Oral Literature and Performance in Southern Africa,* ed. Duncan Brown. Oxford: James Currey.
Ka'arang: Organe d'Information du Cercle de Réflexion sur la Culture Tpuri (CRCT). Bremen, Germany: Ka'arang.
Kaspin, Deborah. 1993. "Chewa Visions and Revision of Power: Transformations of the Nyau Dance in Central Malawi." In *Modernity and Its Malcontents: Ritual and Power in South Africa,* ed. Jean Comaroff and John Comaroff. Chicago: University of Chicago Press.
Kléda, Samuel. 1983. "Analyse d'un Chant Gurna de Dan Biina." Unpublished manuscript. Guidiguis, Cameroon.
Kléda, Samuel, and Suzanne Ruelland. 1998. "Tradition and Creativité dans un Genre Oral Chanté." *Ka'arang* 19: 5–10.
Kofele-Kale, Ndiva. 1986. "Ethnicity, Regionalism, and Political Power: A Post-Mortem of Ahidjo's Cameroon." In *The Political Economy of Cameroon,* ed. Michael G. Schatzberg and I. William Zartman. New York: Praeger.
Kondo, Dorinne K. 1990. *Crafting Selves: Power, Gender, and Discourses of Identity in a Japanese Workplace.* Chicago: University of Chicago Press.
Koulandi, Jean. 1999. "Le Bili-Bili et la 'Liberation' de la Femme Tupuri." Unpublished manuscript. Cameroon.
Kratz, A. 1993. *Affecting Performance: Meaning, Movement, and Experience in Okiek Women's Initiation.* Washington, D.C.: Smithsonian Institution Press.
Kuipers, Joel C. 1992. "Obligations to the Word: Ritual Speech, Performance, and Responsibility among the Weyewa." In *Responsibility and Evidence in Oral Discourse,* ed. Jane H. Hill and Judith T. Irvine. Cambridge: Cambridge University Press.
Labov, William. 1972. "Rules for Ritual Insults." In *Studies in Social Interaction,* ed. David Sudnow. New York: The Free Press.
Lan, David. 1985. *Guns and Rain: Guerillas and Spirit Mediums in Zimbabwe.* Berkeley: University of California Press.
Lavie, Smadar. 1990. *The Poetics of Military Occupation: Mzeina Allegories of Bedouin Identity under Israeli and Egyptian Rule.* Berkeley: University of California Press.

Levinson, Bradley A., Douglas E. Foley, and Dorothy C. Holland, eds. 1996. *The Cultural Production of the Educated Person*. Albany: State University of New York Press.
Lock, Margaret. 1993. "Cultivating the Body: Anthropology and Epistemologies of Bodily Practice and Knowledge." *Annual Review of Anthropology* 22: 133–155.
Lutz, Catherine A., and Lila Abu-Lughod, eds. 1990. *Language and the Politics of Emotion*. Cambridge: Cambridge University Press.
Malone, Jacqui. 1996. *Steppin' on the Blues: The Visible Rhythms of African American Dance*. Urbana: University of Illinois Press.
Marcus, George E., and Michael M. J. Fischer. 1986. *Anthropology as Cultural Critique: An Experimental Moment in the Human Sciences*. Chicago: University of Chicago Press.
Mashing, Abaga Martin. 1997. "A Propos du Mot Kirdi." *Le Kirdi* 3: 11–12.
Mathias, Elizabeth. 1976. "*La Gara Poetica*: Sardinian Shepherds' Verbal Dueling and the Expression of Male Values in Agro-Pastoral Society." Unpublished manuscript.
Mbembe, Achille. 2001. *On the Postcolony*. Berkeley: University of California Press.
Mehler, Andreas. 1998. "Cameroun and the Politics of Patronage." In *History of Central Africa*, ed. David Birmingham and Phyllis Martin. New York: Longman Press.
Mendoza, Zoila S. 2000. *Shaping Society through Dance: Mestizo Ritual Performance in the Peruvian Andes*. Chicago: University of Chicago Press.
Messenger, John C. 1962. "Anang Art, Drama, and Social Control." *African Studies Bulletin* 5 (2): 29–35.
Miller, Daniel. 1994. *Modernity, an Ethnographic Approach: Dualism and Mass Consumption in Trinidad*. Oxford: Berg Press.
Miller, Laura. 1998. "Bad Girls: Representations of Unsuitable, Unfit, and Unsatisfactory Women in Magazines." *U.S./Japan Women's Journal* 15: 31–51.
Mitchell, J. Clyde. 1956. *The Kalela Dance: Aspects of Social Relationships among Urban Africans in Northern Rhodesia*. Rhodes-Livingstone Paper no. 27. Manchester: Manchester University Press.
Monga, Yvette. 2000. "'*Au village!*': Space, Culture, and Politics in Cameroon." *Cahiers d'Études Africaines* 160 (40): 723–749.
Moraes Farias, P. F. de. 1995. "Praise Splits the Subject of Speech: Constructions of Kingship in the Manden and Borgu." In *Power, Marginality and Oral Literature*, ed. Graham Furniss and Liz Gunner. Cambridge: Cambridge University Press.
Nyamnjoh, Francis, and Michael Rowlands. 1998. "Elite Associations and the Politics of Belonging in Cameroon." *Africa* 68 (3): 320–337.
Ojaide, Tanure. 2001. "Poetry, Performance, and Art: Udje Dance Songs of Nigeria's Urhobo People." *Research in African Literatures* 32 (2): 44–75.
Ong, Aihwa. 1999. *Flexible Citizenship: The Cultural Logics of Transnationality*. Durham, N.C.: Duke University Press.
Ong, Walter J. 1982. *Orality and Literacy: The Technologies of the Word*. London: Routledge.
Parkin, David. 1980. "The Creativity of Abuse." *Man*, n.s. 15: 45–64
Pellow, Deborah. 1997. "Male Praise-Singers in Accra: In the Company of Women." *Africa* 67 (4): 582–601.
Perkins, William Eric. 1996. "The Rap Attack: An Introduction." In *Droppin' Science: Critical Essays on Rap Music and Hip Hop Culture*, ed. William Eric Perkins. Philadelphia: Temple University Press.
Piersen, William D. 1993/1999. "A Resistance Too Civilized to Notice." Reprinted in *Signifyin(g), Sanctifyin', and Slam Dunking*, ed. Gena Dagel Caponi. Amherst: University of Massachusetts Press.
Pontie, Guy. 1972/1984. "Les Sociétés PaVennes." In *Le Nord du Cameroun*, ed. Jean Boutrais et al. Paris: ORSTOM.
Pred, Allan, and Michael J. Watts. 1992. *Reworking Modernity: Capitalisms and Symbolic Discontent*. New Brunswick, N.J.: Rutgers University Press.
Public Culture. 1994. *Public Culture* 7 (1) (special issue on *The Black Public Sphere*).
Ramsey, F. Jeffress. 2001. *Africa*. 9th ed. Guilford, Conn.: McGraw-Hill/Duskin.
Ranger, Terence O. 1975. *Dance and Society in Eastern Africa, 1890–1970: The Beni Ngoma*. Berkeley: University of California.

Reed, Susan A. 1998. "The Politics and Poetics of Dance." *Annual Review of Anthropology* 27: 503–532.
Rich, Frank. 2000. "The Age of the Mediathon." *New York Times Magazine,* October 29: 58–94.
Rofel, Lisa. 1999. *Other Modernities: Gendered Yearnings in China After Socialism.* Berkeley: University of California Press.
Ruelland, Suzanne. 1988. *Dictionnaire Tupuri-Français-Anglais.* Paris: PEETERS/SELAF.
———. 1999. "L'Homme et l'Animal en Pays Tupuri: Réalités et Représentations." In *L'Homme et l'Animal dans le Bassin du Lac Tchad,* ed. Catherine Baroin and Jean Boutrais. Paris: IRD.
———. Forthcoming. "La Créativité dans l'Art Chanté Tupuri: L'Exemple d'un Compositeur de Chants Waywa." In *Oralité Africaine et Création (African Orality and Creativity).* Paris: Karthala.
Sanday, Peggy R. 1996. *A Woman Scorned: Acquaintance Rape on Trial.* New York: Doubleday.
Schilder, Kees. 1994. *Quest for Self-Esteem: State, Islam, and Mundang Ethnicity in Northern Cameroon.* Aldershot: Avebury.
Schultz, Emily. 1984. "From Pagan to Pullo: Ethnic Identity Change in Northern Cameroon." *Africa* 54 (1): 46–63.
Seignobos, Christian. 1995. *Terroir de Sirlawé: Saturation Foncière et Émigration Encadrée.* Yaoundé, Cameroon: MINAGRI/SODECOTON/ORSTOM.
Smith, M. G. 1957. "The Social Functions and Meaning of Hausa Praise-Singing." *Africa* 27 (1): 26–43.
Spitulnick, Debra. 1997. "The Social Circulation of Media Discourse and the Mediation of Communities." *Journal of Linguistic Anthropology* 6 (2): 161–187.
Stewart, Kathleen. 1996. *A Space on the Side of the Road: Cultural Poetics in an "Other" America.* Princeton, N.J.: Princeton University Press.
Street, Brian V., ed. 1993. *Cross-Cultural Approaches to Literacy.* Cambridge: Cambridge University Press.
Stuempfle, Stephen. 1995. *The Steelband Movement: The Forging of a National Art in Trinidad and Tobago.* Philadelphia: University of Pennsylvania Press.
Thompson, Robert Farris. 1966/1999. "An Aesthetic of the Cool: West African Dance." Reprinted in *Signifyin(g), Sanctifyin', and Slam Dunking,* ed. Gena Dagel Caponi. Amherst: University of Massachusetts Press.
———. 1974. *African Art in Motion: Icon and Art.* Washington, D.C.: National Gallery of Art.
Toulabor, Comi. 1981. "Jeu de Mots, Jeux de Vilain: Lexique de la Dérision Politique au Togo." *Politique Africaine* 3: 55–71.
Transparency International and Göttingen University. 1998, 1999, 2000, 2001. "TI Press Releases: Corruptions Perceptions Index (1998–2001)." Berlin.
Turner, Victor. 1967. *The Forest of Symbols: Aspects of Ndembu Ritual.* Ithaca, N.Y.: Cornell University Press.
———. 1987. *The Anthropology of Performance.* New York: PAJ Publications.
Urban, Greg. 1996. *Metaphysical Community: The Interplay of the Sense and the Intellect.* Austin: University of Texas Press.
———. 2001. *Metaculture: How Culture Moves through the World.* Minneapolis: University of Minnesota Press.
U.S. Department of State. 1999, and 2000. Country Reports on Human Rights Practices for Cameroon for 1998 and 1999. Released by the Bureau of Democracy, Human Rights, and Labor. Washington D.C.
Vail, Leroy, and Landeg White. 1991. *Power and the Praise Poem: Southern African Voices in History.* Charlottesville: University of Virginia Press.
Waterman, Christopher. 1988. "Asiko, Sakara and Palmwine: Popular Music and Social Identity in Inter-War Lagos, Nigeria." *Urban Anthropology* 17 (2–3): 229–258.
———. 1997. " 'Our Tradition Is a Very Modern Tradition.' " In *Readings in African Popular Culture,* ed. Karin Barber. Bloomington: Indiana University Press.

White, Luise. 2000. *Speaking with Vampires: Rumor and History in Colonial Africa.* Berkeley: University of California Press.

Williams, Raymond. 1977. *Marxism and Literature.* Oxford: Oxford University Press.

Yankah, Kwesi. 1997. "The Sung Tale as a Political Chart in Contemporary Ghana." Paper prepared for "Words and Voice: Critical Practices in Africa and in African Studies," Bellagia, Italy, February 24–28.

INDEX

Page numbers in italics refer to illustrations.

Ahidjo, Amadou (President), 13, 20, 27, 30, 55, 80, 179, 192, 204n13
alcohol, 50, 54, 82–84, 107, *136*
allegory, 25, 29

biculturalism, 91
Biya, Paul (President), 11, 20, 90, 179–180, 192, 195, 200, 203n8, 212n4
body, 51, 77–80, 84
body fattening, 3, 44, 51, 58, 81, 206n7; and Tupuri identity, 79
brideprice/bridewealth, 29, 31, 33–35, 59, 81, 102, 204n19; and respectability, 38

Cameroon, 3, 11–12, 16, 20, 33, 88, 117, 128, 143, 178–179, 183, 187–188, 192, 195, 197, 204n12; and corruption, 203n7, 207n2
Chad, 13, 19, 37, 49, 187
children, 26, 49. *See also gurna-fiiri* (children's gurna)
Christianity, 9, 13, 48, 57–58, 63, 78, 88–89, 92, 210n8:1
clans, 13, 45, 144–145, 203n11, 204n16, 211n9: 6
Club Kwoïssa, 41, 63, *134*
communitas, 8, 52, 78, 109, 178
composers: campaign for acceptance, 187; competition, 43; lineages, 143–145; and magical herbs, 147–151; and national politics, 186, 194; role of, 123, 147, 151–152, 157; status of, 143, 199
composition, 209n5. *See also under gurna* song; magical herbs
costume, 1, 3, 24, 49, 51, 54–56, *131, 132, 135*
courtship, 20, 32–34; in dance, 51–52; language of, 32–33
cultural association. *See under* Club Kwoïssa; cultural politics
cultural politics, 177, 191–192, 197–198

dance, 53–54, 208n2; as discursive space, 75–77, 209n5:3; and moral order, 7; and social commentary, 82. *See also gurna* dance
Dang Biina, 126–127, 144, 149
Dangmoworé (composer), 17, 88, 113, 115, 128, *137*, 145, 147, 151, 187
Dawa, 143–145
death (*huuli*), 52–53
death celebration (*yii-huuli*), 1, 3, 20–21, 46, 49, 52–54, *74,* 95, 104, 113–114, 119, 164, 178, 182–183, 209n2; and intervillage rivalry, 189
democracy and democratization, 42, 49, 178
didilna (harp and praise-song genre), 16–17, *66,* 97
discourse, 25, 39, 93–95, 177–178
divination, *140,* 148
Djingue (composer), 146–147
Doukoula, 14–16, 30, 45, 60–61, 98–99, 103, 144–145, 161, 175, 182, 188–189, 193
drumming, 41, 50, 54–55, 104, *131,* 204n11
Dynamique Culturelle Kirdi, 197

earth priest (*waŋ-siri*), 19–20, 119, 211n9
economic crisis, 15–16, 33, 77, 203n1; and brideprice, 102
education, 16, 87–90, 105–106, *138,* 200
egalitarianism, 20, 50
elites. *See évolué*
ethnicity, 2, 13, 60, 79–80, 208n23
évolué, 20, 47–48, 91, 105, 172

famine, 13–14, 58, 82, 85–86, 125, 153, 164, 204n14
farming, 13, 87; valorization of, 85
Festival of the Cock (*few kage*), 19–20, 34, 45, 107, 181, 206n4
folklorization, 21, 60–63, 196
Fulbe, 13, 55, 85–86, 197, 204n17
funeral (*huuli*), 44

gender, 34–37; and male solidarity, 41, 47, 59; and modernity, 25, 29–32, 102–103; and praise in song, 115; and women's voice, 28, 35–37, 58–59
German annexation, 19, 204n12
gossip, 97, 103, 108, 122, 159, 211n6; and insult, 167
gurna, 3–4, 41–46; and Christianity, 9, 57–58; competition, 180–184; as cultural association, 41–43, 62–63; and death celebrations 52–54, 56–57, 87; as expression of Tupuri identity, 3–4, 63–64, 78, 92, 108; and farming, 51, 86; and modernization, 8–9, 60–63, 92; origins of, 43–44, 143–144; as political process, 177–179, 184–188; in rural context, 42; season, 45, 117; socialization within, 49–51; solidarity associated with, 45–48, 182–183, 198; in urban society, 62–63, 97, 107, 200; women in, 46–47. *See also gurna* camp;

gurna (cont.)
  gurna dance; *gurna* society; *gurna* song; *gurna-fiiri* (children's *gurna*)
  gurna camp (*jak-kaw*), 14, 41, 46–47, 50–51, 72, 74, 154, 156–157, 178, 180, 187; and death celebration, 43; and intervillage rivalry, 190; and selection of composer, 182–184, 191
  gurna dance (*jōo*), 65, 74, 133–135, 137; and composers, 96; description of, 1, 41, 44, 54–56, 75, 77–79, 118; as discursive space, 82–83; at educational institutions, 61–62; gesture (*ɓɔ'ge fɔgɛ*), 76–79, 135; roles in society, 19–20; in urban context, 14, 41–42
  gurna society, 3, 33, 43, 46–50, 113, 177; and courtship, 51–52; individualism, 184; and inversion, 90; leadership within 50–51; male friendship in, 45, 82, 92, 113; membership in, 46–48; place of cattle in, 81; and sobriquet, 47; as social organization, 20
  gurna song (*siŋ gurna*), 22, 26, 93–130; composers, 17, 100–102, 112–113, 119, 145–158, 163; composition of, 96, 113, 146–148; insult in, 101, 119–122, 159–176; learning of, 46, 103–108; metacommentary on dance, 115–119; praise in, 8, 110–115; rhetorical forms within 109–110; ridicule in, 8, 122–126; social commentary in, 122–129; and social networks, 93, 108; and socialization, 103–108; translation of, 98–103; in village politics, 188–192; and witchcraft, 174. *See also* composers
  gurna-fiiri (children's *gurna*), 49, 63, 73, 116–117
guruna (Massa), 43–44, 206n7

individualism, 184
initiation (*gɔɔni*), 3, 20, 49, 53, 204n22
insult (*ɗarge*), 119–122, 159–176; and conflict, 159–165; fear of libel, 168–171; poetic license associated with, 173; in urban setting, 167–168; and witchcraft, 121
International Monetary Fund, 82, 86
Islam, 13, 79, 88–89, 204n21

jihad, 79
judical system, 159–160, 174, 176, 200

Kirdi, 211n10:1

lamido/lamidat, 20, 160, 204n17; at burial, 52; critique of gurna, 59; of Doukoula, 126–127, 149, 173, 191, 204n18, 207n9
lɛɛlɛ (women's song), 8, 16, 26, 33, 57, 199; 204n18; libel, 168–169, 172–173, 200–201
lip disks, 71
literacy, 104–106

magical herbs (*saŋgu*), 55, 122, 148, 175, 210n5; and drumming, 148; inheritance of, 151; and song composition, 142, 148–150
Maroua, 12, 14, 31–32, 61–62, 98, 107, 125, 148, 165–166, 186

marriage, 29–31, 34–35, 206n5
Massa, 43–44, 47, 144, 203nn10–11, 205n3:1, 209n1; and *gurna*, 43
maylay (festival), 45, 68
MDR Party (Mouvement pour Défense de la République), 27, 31, 179, 193
metacommentary, 6, 115–119, 180
milk drinking, 44, 46, 50, 83–84
modernity, 2, 6–7, 29, 178–179; antimodernity, 92; and education, 89–90; and gender, 25, 29, 103, 128; perils of, 36; and prostitution, 37–39; and tradition, 6, 106
modernization, 4, 6, 9, 15
Mogom, 24, 27, 31, 32, 189
morality, 2–4, 49, 50
multipartyism, 178, 192–195

naming, 209n6:6. *See also gurna* society, and sobriquet
nostalgia, 89, 195, 201

Operation Ghost Town (*Opération Villes Mortes*), 193

patrilineage, 19, 35–36, 81, 210n15
performance, 7–11, 203n3, 208n2
poetic license, 3, 8, 10, 26, 142, 157, 159, 199, 205n3
politics, 178–180, 192–194. *See also* cultural politics; *gurna*, as political process
poverty, 14
praise, 96–97, 106, 110–115, 209n5:8
press, 200, 211n10:3
prostitution, 35–39
public sphere, 4–6, 40, 94–96, 103, 108, 130, 176, 192, 196, 203n5

Rassemblement Démocratique du Peuple Camerounais (RDPC), *141*, 193–194, 212n4
Ringwa (composer), 62, 147
rural settings, 42, 60

sacred woods (*jak-siri*), 53, 119, 211n9
satire, 126–129
sexual initiation (*nage may*), 49–50
shameful acts (*sōore*), 46, 122–124, 152
social discipline, 8
social order, inversion of, 83
socialization, 49, 91. *See also* under *gurna* song
Sogole (composer), 100–101, 140, 145, 169–173, 209n6:7
song, 3, 9–11, 16, 39–40, 94–95; and collectivities, 7; as communication, 20, 96–97; composers, 143; as cultural identity, 11; genres of (Tupuri), 16–17; and gossip, 167; inspiration, 147; and moral order, 7–9, 123; as public censure, 26; and public debate, 5; as public justice, 5; and social control, 8, 39, 122; and socialization, 95; as sources of fame, 29; translation of, 99–100, 106. *See also gurna* song

taboo (yɔɔ), 31, 39, 190
Teodandi (composer), *139,* 144–145, 148, 152
tradition: 198–200, 205n2; and modernity, 6
Transparency International, 77, 207n2
Tupuri: clans, 19, 206n4; dialects, 210n7:3; identity, 3, 79–80, 209n6:6; livelihoods, 12–14, 45, 85–87, 91; migration, 13–14, 176; performance genres of, 16–17; population, 208n6:8; socio-political organization of, 18–21, 204n12, 206n5

Union des Populations du Cameroun (UPC), 80, 179, 192–193
Union Nationale pour la Démocracie et le Progress, 193
urban settings, 61–63, 106–108, 165–168

value(s), 2–3, 7
verbal arts, 9–11, 118–119, 203n3

waywa (dance of the youth), 16, 24, 26, *66–68,* 123, 199
witchcraft, 39, 42, 50, 121, 148, 174–176, 183, 210n5, 211n5; and gossip, 175; and justice, 159; and modernity, 6
women's song. *See* lɛɛlɛ
World Bank, 82
wrestling (*gumu*), 78–79, 207n7

Yagoua, 13
Yaoundé, 14, 60, 63, 80, 192
youth, 2, 26, 45, 48, 90, 206n9

Zoueye, 143–146, 149, 161, 188, 192, 194

Clare A. Ignatowski is a visiting scholar at the African Studies Center, University of Pennsylvania. She currently works for the United States Agency for International Development in Washington, D.C.

www.ingramcontent.com/pod-product-compliance
Lightning Source LLC
Chambersburg PA
CBHW070841160426
43192CB00012B/2267